Corpus Linguistics Beyond the Word

LANGUAGE AND COMPUTERS: STUDIES IN PRACTICAL LINGUISTICS

No 60

edited by
Christian Mair
Charles F. Meyer
Nelleke Oostdijk

Corpus Linguistics Beyond the Word

Corpus Research from Phrase to Discourse

Edited by
Eileen Fitzpatrick

Rodopi

Amsterdam - New York, NY 2007

Cover design: Pier Post

Online access is included in print subscriptions:
see www.rodopi.nl

The paper on which this book is printed meets the requirements of "ISO 9706:1994, Information and documentation - Paper for documents - Requirements for permanence".

ISBN-10: 90-420-2135-7
ISBN-13: 978-90-420-2135-8

Printed in The Netherlands

Contents

Corpus Applications: Pedagogy and Linguistic Analysis

Preface

The papers published in this volume were originally presented at the Fifth North American Symposium on Corpus Linguistics, co-sponsored by the American Association of Applied Corpus Linguistics and the Linguistics Department of Montclair State University. The symposium was held from May 21-23, 2004 at Montclair State in Montclair, New Jersey. The conference drew more than 100 participants from 14 different countries. Altogether, 41 papers were presented.

The symposium papers represented several areas of corpus studies including language development, syntactic analysis, pragmatics and discourse, language change, register variation, corpus creation and annotation, as well as practical applications of corpus work, primarily in language teaching, but also in medical training and machine translation. A common thread through most of the papers was the use of corpora to study domains longer than the word.

The 15 papers presented here capture the expansion of the discipline into the investigation of larger spans of linguistic productions from the syntactic patterns of phrases up to and including rhetorical devices and pragmatic strategies in the full discourse. Not surprisingly, fully half of the papers deal with the computational tools, linguistic techniques, and specialized annotation needed to search for and analyze these longer spans of language. Many of these papers use statistical techniques new to the area of applied corpus linguistics. Most of the remaining papers examine syntactic and rhetorical properties of one or more corpora with an applied focus. These distinct concentrations dictated the division of the volume into two sections, one on tools and strategies and the other on applications of corpus analysis.

The first paper in the tools and strategies section, by Barrett, Greenberg, and Schwarz, explores the idea of distinguishing document domains – here medicine, military, finance, and fiction – on the basis of part-of-speech tag densities alone, supporting the notion that automated document classification, for applications in machine translation and elsewhere, is possible using methods other than the commonly used lexical methods. Such methods, the paper argues, are ideal for creating syntactically as well as lexically balanced corpora.

While Barrett et al. distinguish domains on the basis of syntactic information, Grieve-Smith offers a caution in the use of grammatical information to discriminate text genre. Grieve-Smith emphasizes that certain features can be expected to co-vary based on their grammatical effects rather than on the situation of language use, or genre, and that this co-variation must not be conflated with the situational co-variation that should be distinguishing the genres. Grieve-Smith, borrowing the notion of 'envelope of variation' from sociolinguistics, maps the occurrence of third person pronouns and demonstrative adjectives, which should show a negative grammatical correlation, but no situational correlation. Grieve-Smith's success in demonstrating a significant effect of grammar in the correlation of these factors points to the difficulty inherent in teasing apart the features used to discriminate among genres.

While the Barrett and Grieve-Smith papers examine syntactic issues in text classification, the paper by Deane and Higgins uses local context to classify words into similar syntactico-semantic classes, such as terms for body parts and kinship, for applications like the TOEFL synonym test. Local context, unlike the more sematically oreinted methods like Latent Semantic Analysis (Laudauer and Dumais, 1997), is heavily influenced by syntactic parallelism. Deane and Higgins use a vector space model approach that views words and contexts as vectors in a large multidimensional space, allowing for similarity between words and/or contexts to be mathematically determined based on the closeness of the vectors. Comparison of their approach with the semantic approaches shows interesting differences in judgments of word similarities that can be exploited in language modeling, language testing, judgments of text cohesion, and automatic lexical acquisition.

In an effort to improve the output of a partial parser and its supporting part-of-speech tagger, Sebastian van Delden's paper discusses recurring tagging and parsing errors and offers simple heuristics that were implemented to improve the performance of the information retrieval system that they support and outlines further large-scale improvements.

Mark Davies' paper details the syntactic annotation of the 20 million word "1900s" portion of the Corpus del Español, which contains equivalent sizes of conversation, fiction, and non-fiction. The corpus was annotated for nearly 150 syntactic features, and feature frequencies in the 20 different registers were calculated. Davies details the types of annotation used, and gives illustrative comparisons of features across registers that demonstrate the value of the annotation for studies of the nature of syntactic variation in Spanish.

The last three papers in this section deal with the treatment of linguistic phenomena that do not readily lend themselves to computational solutions. Garretson and O'Connor describe the use of linguistic proxies – discrete tokens that give a reasonably good index of an elusive phenomenon – and a method that involves alternating passes of automated and manual coding to analyze data, with the possessive alternation in English as a case study. The paper also describes the reusable computational tools created for the project and considers the distinct advantages of using human-computer alternation to further linguistic analysis in terms of consistency and accuracy on a large scale.

Maynard and Leicher, on the other hand, concentrate on features that lack obvious linguistic proxies. Their paper details ongoing efforts to manually annotate the Michigan Corpus of Academic Spoken English (MICASE) for pragmatic information using an inventory of 25 pragmatic features, such as evaluations, introductions, narratives, and requests. Abstracts describing content and salient pragmatic features are given for each speech event (lab, seminar, office hour, etc.) and each transcript header describes the relative frequency of each feature. In addition, a representative subcorpus of fifty transcripts has been manually tagged for 12 of the features and will soon be computer searchable.

The paper by Maria Jose Garcia Vizcaino demonstrates the value of working with pragmatically tagged corpora, while noting the issues involved in dealing with annotations that do not conform to a coherent taxonomy. Garcia Vizcaino describes the use of two annotated corpora, the British National Corpus and the Corpus Oral de Referencia del Español Contemporáneo (COREC), a corpus of Peninsular Spanish, to contrast politeness strategies in Spanish and English. The paper describes the annotations in the two corpora that are needed for pragmalinguistic studies and provides step-by-step details of her adaptations of the corpora for such analysis.

The second section of the book presents applications of corpus work in education and linguistic research. While most of the papers on corpora in education deal with second language pedagogy, the first paper in this section, by Boyd Davis and Lisa Russell-Pinson, deals with corpus re-use in K-12 content area education and medical education. Using the Charlotte Narrative and Conversation Collection – with input from speakers in and around Mecklenburg County, NC, who span a range of ages, ethnicities, cultures and native languages – the authors describe the value of corpora in sensitizing K-12 teachers to their increasingly diverse student population and as a resource for content area lessons. In addition, a subset of the CNCC covering older speakers is compared to a corpus of on-going conversations with speakers diagnosed with dementia for research on disordered speech and for teaching healthcare providers to communicate effectively with the elderly.

While Davis and Russell-Pinson use corpora for content area and medical education, Margrit Zinggeler uses the online brothers Grimm fairy tales for German language teaching to intermediate and advanced learners of the language. Zinggeler exemplifies detailed exercises on parts of speech and grammatical structure created from the tales and notes that students use the newly acquired forms readily in writing their own fairy tales and in class discussions about the content and meaning of the tales.

The next two papers, by de Haan and van Esch and Neff et al., analyze the linguistic features of argumentative essays written by students of English as a Foreign Language. The data collected by de Haan and van Esch from the same group of native Dutch speakers over time allow them to do a longitudinal study of the development of writing skills at three proficiency levels. Some of the features studied by de Haan and van Esch result in ambiguous findings; for example, while mean essay length increased over time, mean word length did not increase at the same rate, and type/token ratio fell. The paper provides insight as to what features should be expected to correlate and why, as students advance in their written English skills.

The Neff et al. paper examines the Spanish data from the International Corpus of Learner English Error Tagging Project in the contrastive error analysis framework. The results show that grammar (35%) and lexis (28%) account for two-thirds of the errors, while punctuation, form, word, lexico-grammatical factors, register, and style account for successively fewer errors. The paper proposes useful areas of investigation within English-Spanish contrastive data.

The final three papers in the volume use corpora to study linguistic features of spoken and written language. Shehzad's paper, with a practical application in the teaching of expository writing, examines the structure of a portion of computer science articles, while Murzaku and Jacobson look at the more theoretical questions of pronoun distribution in Albanian and relative clause complementizers in 19th century English respectively.

Shehzad examines patterns in the endings of the introductions to 56 research articles in computer science, based on John Swales analysis of the structure of introductions (Swales, 1990) as well as on Lewin et.al. (2001), with a special focus on how articles in CS outline the structure of the text to follow, a move that, Shehzad argues, adds considerably to the length of introductions in CS as opposed to articles in other branches of engineering.

Alexander Murzaku brings a corpus approach to bear on the status of the distal demonstrative forms as personal pronouns in Albanian -- a question of linguistic analysis that has previously been treated, inconclusively, on historical and introspective grounds. Murzaku's quantitative approach provides substantial evidence for a view of Albanian as a two-person personal pronoun language with the demonstrative forms filling in for the 3rd person pronouns.

The final paper, by Christine Johansson, considers the distribution of the *wh-* and *that* relativizers in 19th century English, a period during which the forms showed considerable differences from previous and present usage.

I would like to express my thanks to several individuals who helped in the preparation for the symposium and for this volume. Rita Simpson and Ken Church gave provocative plenary talks that created a good deal of discussion. Susana Sotillo and Steve Seegmiller contributed valuable support to the symposium and to the initial choice of papers for this volume. Thomas Upton was always ready to give advice and information about what was done at the previous symposium, held at Indiana University Purdue University Indianapolis, and what went into the previous volume in this series. Charles Meyer has been the impetus and main support for the volume; Chuck has the fastest email turnaround time I know of. Finally, I would like to thank my husband, Ralph Grishman, for his help with the more arcane features of Word and PDF files, for his critiques, and most of all for his constant support.

Landauer, T. K. and S. T. Dumais (1997), A solution to Plato's problem: The latent semantic analysis theory of acquisition, induction, and representation of knowledge, *Psychological Review*, 104(2):211–240.

Lewin, A., Fine, J. and Young, L. (2001). *Expository discourse: a genre- based approach to social science research texts.* London/ New York: Continuum.

Swales, J.M. (1990). *Genre Analysis: English in Academic and Research Settings.* Cambridge: Cambridge University Press.

Montclair, New Jersey, April 2006

Eileen Fitzpatrick

A Syntactic Feature Counting Method for Selecting Machine Translation Training Corpora

Leslie Barrett

EDGAR Online, Inc.

David F. Greenberg

New York University

Marc Schwarz

Semantic Data Systems

Abstract

Recently, the idea of "domain tuning" or customizing lexicons to improve results in machine translation and summarization tasks has driven the need for better testing and training corpora. Traditional methods of automated document identification rely on word-based methods to find the genre, domain, or authorship of a document. However, the ability to select good training corpora, especially when it comes to machine translation systems, requires automated document selection methods that do not rely on the traditional lexically-based techniques. Because syntactic structures and syntactic feature densities can heavily affect machine translation quality, syntactic feature-based methods of document selection should be used in choosing training and testing corpora. This paper provides evidence that document genres can be distinguished on the basis of syntactic-tag densities alone, supporting the idea that automated document identification is possible using alternative methods. Such methods would be ideal for creating syntactically as well as lexically balanced corpora for both genre and subject matter.

1. Introduction

For a little more than a century, researchers have attempted to use statistical analyses of texts to identify their authors. These efforts were initiated by the American physicist T. C. Mendenhall (1887, 1901), who used a crew of research assistants to tally the distribution of word lengths in the writings of various authors by hand, and on this basis intervened into debates as to the authorship of the plays attributed to Shakespeare.

After a hiatus of some decades, a new generation of investigators extended Mendenhall's methods to include the use of particular words, lengths of sentences, sequences of letters, and punctuation to resolve questions of authorship

(Yule, 1944; Holmes, 1994). These methods have been applied to the Federalist Papers (Mosteller and Wallace, 1964, 1984; Bosch and Smith, 1998) the Junius Letters (Ellegard, 1962a, 1962b), the Shakespeare plays (Brainerd, 1973a, 1973b; Smith, 1991; Ledger and Merriam, 1994) Greek prose works (Morton, 1965) ancient Roman biographies (Gurney and Gurney, 1996. 1997), a Russian novel (Kjetsa, 1979), English works of fiction (Milic, 1967) , Dutch poetry (Hoorn et. al., 1999), and books of the Bible (Radday, 1973; Kenny, 1986)

In some applications, these efforts have had remarkable success. For example, Hoorn et. al. (1999) were able to assign authorship to three Dutch poets with an accuracy of 80-90% using neural network methods. Even greater accuracy has been achieved through the use of Bayesian statistical methods to identify spam in incoming e-mail messages (Graham, 2002; Johnson, 2004). In most applications, however, accuracy is uncertain, because sure knowledge as to the true authors of the Shakespeare plays, the Federalist Papers and the books of the Bible is not to be had. The methods have been used largely on texts whose authors are unknown, not on those of known authorship.

Little attention has been paid in these efforts to parts of speech. One of the few exceptions - the work of Brainerd (1973) - concluded that parts of speech could be useful in distinguishing the styles characteristic of particular genres, but not particular authors. It is noteworthy that in almost all of the studies cited above, the goal of the classification effort was to identify the author of a text by comparing it to a limited set of texts drawn from the same genre, e.g. Elizabethan plays or Federalist Papers whose authorship was known. Only recently have these methods been adapted to the task of classifying a text into a particular domain, i.e. the substantive area or topic of the text, on the basis of the style of the writing. It is these efforts that concern us. Our goal is to develop statistical methods for classifying texts into groups according to domain for the purpose of creating test and training corpora for machine translation evaluation.

A problem that can arise in this process stems from polysemy. Words can have multiple meanings, and a machine translation program may mistranslate a passage because of the ambiguity this creates. Some recent research has attempted to reduce translation ambiguities by tuning the software for application in a specific substantive domain. Translation accuracy tends to increase when texts are chosen from the domains for which the software has been tuned. This makes it desirable to have an efficient method for selecting texts that belong to specific domains to train and test the translation software. Previous textual domain-classification methodologies have not been geared towards creating test corpora for this purpose. Earlier methods have been lexically-based, similar to the methods for identifying authors, even though lexically-based methods have never been proven optimal for the purposes of creating machine translation test corpora. Our research is intended to explore the use of a syntactic-feature-based methodology for such purposes.

2. Limitations of word-based methods

The most commonly-used methods for carrying out text classification are lexical, and have a fairly long history (Maron, 1961; Borko and Bernick, 1963). Some of these efforts are based on counts of the words that appear most frequently in a text. Others require the identification of the most relevant terms for the task. Following this step, document-dependent weights for the selected terms are computed so as to generate a vectorial representation for each document[1] (Salton, 1991). Terms are weighted based on their contribution to the extensional semantics of the document. Finally, a text classifier is built from the vectorial representations of the training documents.

While lexically-based methods have proved adequate for many purposes, certain notable problems have become apparent. First, consistency in the choice of key words is relatively low. Typically, people choose the same key word for a single well-known concept less than 20% of the time (Furnas et. al., 1987). This makes the selection of relevant words for a training model unreliable, affecting the entire process. This weakness, however, would not appear in methods based on the distributions of words in the texts.

Second, it has been noted that the delimitation of domains, when defined by lexical inventory alone, varies considerably (Jørgensen et. al., 2003). There can be sizable domain-keyword overlap in some domains, leading to fuzzy domain boundaries. In a project involving the compilation of a set of domain-specific corpora in the domains of internet technology, environment, and health, Jørgensen et. al. found the largest overlaps to be between internet technology, commerce, and marketing.

Problems in defining the domains themselves, whether due to human agreement factors or lexical overlaps, present a challenge to the task of compiling test corpora for natural language processing (NLP) applications and producing reliable results in all types of text-classification tasks, so long as purely lexically-based methods are used. We propose that a grammatical-feature-based method, used either independently or in conjunction with lexically-based methods, be considered as a way to detect text-domains automatically, that is, through the use of computers to execute algorithms for assigning texts to domains.

Our hypothesis is that distinct language structures are used to discuss certain topics, and that certain parts of speech will appear in different densities consistently in different domains. This assumption of domain-specificity contrasts with the assumption of author-specificity that prevails in much of the research on author identification. We are assuming that domains have distinct stylistic conventions to which authors adapt when writing in that domain.

So far, little previous research other than Brainerd's has been conducted to connect particular syntactic structure-profiles to domains. However, there has been research linking types of textual information other than lexical to certain documents for the purposes of classification. Klavans and Kan (1998) predict the event profile of news articles based on the occurrence of certain verb types. They define "event profile" as a pairing of topic type and semantic property set. For example, they claim that a breaking news article shows a high percentage of "motion" verbs, such as "drop," "fall" and "plunge" by comparison with verbs for communication, such as "say," "add" and "claim," which are more common in interview articles. They note that verbs (in particular, the semantic classes of verbs, such as the "motion" or "communication" classes) are an important factor in determining event profile, and can be used for classifying news articles into different genres. They note, further, that properties for distinguishing genre dimensions include verb features such as tense, passive voice and infinitive mood.

Here we build on Brainerd's earlier work in order to explore the extent to which the use of syntactic categories can overcome limitations in the exclusive reliance on word-based methods for purposes of automated text classification. We do this by examining correlations between syntactic feature-sets and document domains in order to assess the existence of a characteristic syntactic "footprint" of a domain that could be used for purposes of text-categorization.

3. Data and Methods

In this exploratory study we show syntactic-feature-counting results from part-of-speech tagged domain specific corpora. Seven hand-selected documents in the medical, financial, military and narrative fiction domains were tagged, with the part-of-speech tag densities for each extracted into lists. The works of fiction (selections of Bram Stoker's *Dracula* and Robert Louis Stevenson's *Dr. Jekyl and Mr. Hyde*) were public-domain website-published documents; the financial documents were randomly selected quarterly and annual reports from the MSMoney website; the medical documents were taken from WebMD's publicly available Heath site; and the army document is a combination of law-enforcement and military training model instructions).

We used a part-of-speech tagger made by Newfound Communications both for reasons of reliability and tag-set inventory. For our purposes we needed as large a tag set as possible without sacrificing too much accuracy. The actual tag set is provided in the Appendix. The Newfound tagger uses a feature-rich tag set compared to some other commonly-used taggers, with 71 tag sets compared to average tag-sets of 30 to 40. In particular, it tags all pronominal forms, contracted verb forms, possessives and persons and numbers in both present and past verb tenses. According to the manufacturer, tagger accuracy is above 97%. Once the documents were tagged, we ran a Perl script to derive the tag-frequency counts. Descriptions of the seven texts are found in Table 1.

Table 1. Description of Texts Analyzed

Text	Domain	Tag Count
Army	Command/Control	693
Fic 1	Fiction	5879
Fic 2	Fiction	4368
Fin 1	Finance	3827
Fin 2	Finance	1234
Med 1	Medicine	1452
Med 2	Medicine	1927

We studied the counts of parts of speech in each text to compute proportions of each of the 71 part-of-speech tags for that document.[2] All subsequent analyses of differences between domains in part-of-speech densities were conducted using these empirical proportions. We did not remove tags representing traditional stopword classes such as determiner (det) or preposition (prep). Previous research has shown that such parts of speech are particularly sensitive to variation in the degree of formality of writing (Brainerd, 1973b).

The first step in our analysis consisted of computing the proportions of words in each text that belong to each of the 67 syntactic categories of our analysis. Because 17 of these categories were unrepresented in our texts, our analyses were conducted with the 50 categories actually present. Comparing the distributions of proportions among the seven texts, we found that in general they were quite similar. All seven texts have relatively high proportions of words or word phrases that are singular nouns, noun phrases, prepositional phrases or verb phrases. Yet, as is clear from Table 2, the proportions of words or word phrases in these peak categories vary from one text to another. For the 10 most common parts of speech in all seven texts combined, the table shows the proportions of each part of speech for each text. Though all texts have relatively high proportions of singular nouns, some texts have comparatively high proportions in syntactic categories that are not well-represented in other texts. For example, medical texts have more adjectives than the others. One of the financial documents has a relatively high proportion of numbers. This is not true of the other texts. Similarly, the army document has an unusually high number of imperatives.

Table 2. Proportions of Most Common Parts of Speech in Seven Texts

	Domain						
Part of Speech	**army**	**fic1**	**fic2**	**fin1**	**fin2**	**med1**	**med2**
s. noun	0.154	0.117	0.126	0.153	0.126	0.2	0.175
preposition	0.06	0.125	0.098	0.143	0.159	0.107	0.102
determiner	0.114	0.114	0.098	0.114	0.1	0.091	0.068
adjective	0.033	0.064	0.048	0.063	0.072	0.125	0.121
ycom	0.003	0.07	0.093	0.048	0.066	0.059	0.065
pl. noun	0.055	0.035	0.021	0.084	0.083	0.058	0.067
adverb	0.047	0.062	0.042	0.022	0.028	0.068	0.037
p.t. verb	0.013	0.074	0.055	0.024	0.028	0.008	0.008
pconj	0.007	0.043	0.038	0.04	0.032	0.043	0.046
pstop	0.068	0.041	0.045	0.034	0	0	0.046

Table 2 provides an over-all impression of similarities and differences, but it cannot tell us whether observed differences are larger than those that might be expected by chance alone, or how accurately the domain of a text can be predicted from its distribution of parts of speech. A more systematic investigation of these similarities and differences requires a method that assesses the magnitudes of any differences, and determines whether they are statistically significant - that is, large enough that differences are highly unlikely to be due to sampling fluctuations from a population in which there are no actual differences.

To this end, we first constructed a cross-tabulation of genre and syntactic categories. The Pearson chi-square for the 50 × 4 table is 12746.733, with 147 degrees of freedom. Phi for the table is a respectable .484, and Cramer's V is .280. The non-symmetric measures taking the part-of-speech as a dependent variable are less impressive: lambda is .000, and the Goodman and Kruskal tau is .005. When predicting domain however, these statistics improve slightly; they are, respectively, .075 and .084.

While this analysis establishes that there are differences in part-of-speech densities for the different domains, it does not establish where the differences lie. That is, it fails to specify which domains differ significantly, and which parts of speech differ in their representation among the domains. To answer that question, we specified a mathematical model representing the densities as a function of domains. We did this by positing a multinomial logistic dependence for the densities.[3] Each part of speech is indexed with the subscript i, which ranges from 1 to 50. The subscript j is an index for domain; in our work it takes on the integral values 1, 2, 3, 4. The subscript k indexes the texts within each domain. We represent the proportion of syntactic structure types identified as a particular part of speech in a given text by p_{ijk}. D_j is a dummy variable that is equal to 1 when the text belongs to domain *j*; otherwise it is equal to 0. The logistic model posits that the sources of variation in p_{ijk} contribute additively and linearly to the natural logarithm of the ratio of the probability that a given word or phrase is part-of-speech *i* to the probability that it is a reference part-of speech, p_0. The reference category can be chosen for convenience; the choice will not affect substantive conclusions. Algebraically,

$$\ln\left(p_{ijk} / p_{0jk}\right) = a_i + b_{ij} D_j \quad (1)$$

In this formula, a_i is, for each part of speech, a constant. If this were the only contribution, the proportion of words or phrases belonging to a particular part of speech would be the same for all texts in all domains. Under this circumstance, there would be no syntactic differences between domains, or between texts belonging to a particular domain, and syntactic features could not be used to identify domains. The correlation between proportions of words in different syntactic categories would be 1.0, and a chi-square statistic for the relationship between syntactic category and source would be zero.

The second term represents domain-specific syntactic differences; the strength of these domain contributions is measured by the coefficient b_{ij}. For each part of speech except the reference category there are as many of these coefficients as there are domains. If information as to the author of a text is available, and texts have been written by multiple authors, one could add to this model a term representing idiosyncratic stylistic features that might be present in all texts written by a given author.

We estimated eq. (1) with dummy variables for *fiction*, *finance* and *medicine* in SPSS version 12.0. Implicitly this makes *army* the reference category. Parts of speech not represented in any of the seven texts were dropped from the analysis automatically, leaving us with a dependent variable with 50 syntactic categories to be predicted in a data set of 19399 tags. Chi-square for the model is 10675.469 for 147 degrees of freedom. The model is highly significant ($p < .001$). The Cox and Snell pseudo-R^2 is .178; the Nagelkerke R^2 is .179. All three dummy variables contribute significantly to the model, with $p < .001$. Coefficients for the contributions the dummies make to the prediction of probabilities for the various parts of speech are statistically significant at the .05 level, but are not shown here (there are 147 of them). We caution that little attention should be given to the significance tests. Ours is not a simple random sample from a larger population, and the number of texts and domains in this exploratory analysis is very limited.

Assignment of a text to a domain on the basis of its syntactic features depends on the second term in eq. (1) making a significant contribution to the log of the odds ratio on the left-hand side of eq. (1). Reliable assignments - that is, assignments that will usually be correct - require that the second term in eq. (1) make a large contribution to the explanation of variability in tag densities. In other words, the idiosyncratic contributions specific to a particular text should be small relative to the domain-specific contributions. To the extent that there are domain-specific contributions but no idiosyncratic contributions, correlations between source proportions will be equal to 1.0 for texts taken from the same domain, but less than 1 for texts taken from different domains. Chi-square tests for differences across domains will be significant, but not significant for texts belonging to the same domain.

To consider the utility of these differences for classifying texts on the basis of their part-of-speech densities, we first computed the correlation coefficient (Pearson's *r*) between the proportions for each text, treating each syntactic category as an observation or case of the *proportion* variable for that text. This is a reversal of the usual way of computing correlations. Instead of treating the proportion of cases in each syntactic category as a variable, and using the texts as cases, we treat the text as a variable and the syntactic categories as observations. The correlation coefficient can vary between -1 and +1. If different domains are characterized by distinct syntactic patterns, correlations should be higher between sources drawn from the same domain than between sources drawn from different domains.

Correlations between the seven text variables for our sources are displayed in Table 3. Only the lower diagonal entries of the correlation matrix are shown. The highest correlation of each variable with the other variables is bold-faced. All the correlations are positive, suggesting that there are strong similarities in the density distributions of syntactic elements common to all the texts in our data set. These similarities, we suggest, are likely to reflect stylistic language usages common to a wide range of texts in different domains.

Table 3. Correlation Matrix of Parts of Speech

			Variable			
Variable	army	fic1	fic2	fin1	fin2	med1
army						
fic1	**.829**					
fic2	.827	**.962**				
fin1	.784	.894	.885			
fin2	.701	.858	.845	**.974**		
med1	.796	.885	.899	.928	.888	
med2	.816	.901	.899	.921	.883	**.980**

Above and beyond these similarities, there are differences in correlations among pairs of texts. For every domain represented by at least two texts, the correlations within each domain are higher than the correlations between any proportion variable in that domain and any proportion variable in another domain. For example, the correlation of *med1* with *med2* is .980, while the correlations of *med1* with proportion variables from other domains ranges from .796 to .928. The correlation of *fic1* with *fic2* is .962. Its correlation with other proportion variables ranges from .829 to .901.

The differences are not large, but they are consistent. The one domain for which we have a single representative, *army*, has correlations with the other proportion variables that range from .701 to .829, smaller than the within-domain correlations among the other proportion variables. This pattern suggests that there are distinct part-of speech densities associated with distinct domains of text.

To explore the relationship between domains and syntactic patterns further, we estimated factor models with various numbers of factors. The common factor model with *k* factors represents each standardized variable z_i as a linear sum of terms involving coefficients a_{ij} (factor loadings) and unmeasured factors F_j, with random error terms e_i.[4] The model can be summarized by the equation

(2) $$z_i = \sum_{j=1}^{k} a_{ij} F_j + e_i$$

The residuals are assumed to be uncorrelated with one another, and with the factors. There being no *a priori* reason to assume that the factors underlying the syntactic patterns are uncorrelated, we chose a rotation method that allows for oblique rotations (Jennrich and Sampson, 1966; Harman, 1976; Cattell and Khanna, 1977) and therefore rotated the solutions using a direct Oblimin procedure, with Kaiser normalization, and the parameter delta set at zero. To assess the sensitivity of our results to this choice, we re-estimated our models under the alternative assumptions that $\delta = -0.4$ and $\delta = -0.8$. With these choices, the correlations of the two factors were slightly smaller, and the loadings on the pattern matrix were quite similar to those found under the assumption that $\delta = 0$.

Maximum-likelihood tests applied to our data indicated that more than two factors are present, but the iterative estimation procedure was unable to converge for solutions with more than two factors. In all likelihood, this difficulty reflects the very high correlations among some of the variables, and the small number of variables being subjected to a factor analysis. Ideally, one would want to have more than one or two variables per factor.

As an alternative to the eigenvalue and scree tests for determining the number of factors to extract, we took as our stopping rule that the common factor model should provide a satisfactory fit to the observed correlations, yielding residuals that are close to zero. The one-factor solution produced residuals as high as .090 (between *fin1* and *fin2*) and .048 (between *med1* and *med2)*, suggesting that the distinctiveness of financial documents and of medical tests is not adequately captured by the one-factor model. The residual between *med1* and *med2* remains somewhat high (.054) in the two-factor solution, but no other residual exceeds .028 in magnitude.

All the domains have strong loadings on the first rotated factor (ranging from .874 to .98), suggesting that all the domains have a fairly similar pattern, but the loadings somewhat differentiate the texts according to domain. Indeed, the first factor orders the seven texts in such a way that all but one of the texts is adjacent to a text of the same domain. Only the positioning of *army* departs from this pattern.

There is less variability in the loadings on the second factor than in the loadings on the first. The correlation between the two factors is just -.158, indicating that the two factors are measuring quite distinct patterns. The factor plot (not shown), which positions each domain by using the factor loadings as coordinates, shows the seven points to be closely clustered, but with some differentiation of domains. The medical texts, the financial texts, and the fiction texts, each lie very close to one another, and a little less close to texts of other domains. This is consistent with the patterns seen in the correlation matrix. Nevertheless, this method does not strongly differentiate the domains; the points in the graph are fairly close together.

The three-factor solution could not be estimated, because a communality estimate exceeded 1 during the iteration process. As observed previously, this difficulty is very likely due to the very high correlations between same-domain proportion variables, and the small number of variables being analyzed.

Factor analysis is not always the optimal way to assess patterns of clustering in a set of variables. By relaxing the assumptions factor analysis makes about the structure of relationships among the variables being analyzed, cluster analyses are sometimes able to classify objects more effectively, in spaces of fewer dimensions (Tryon and Bailey, 1970; Anderberg, 1973; Everitt, 1974; Lorr, 1983; Aldendorf, 1984; Romesburg, 1984). For this reason, we also carried out a hierarchical cluster analysis of the variables using between-groups linkage of standardized scores, SPSS version 12.0 for the computations. This procedure has been used previously in lexically-based classification efforts (Hoover, 2001).

The hierarchical cluster analysis procedure requires the specification of a distance measure. We chose the most widely used such measure, the squared Euclidean distance

$$(3) \qquad D_{ij}^2 = \sum_{k=1}^{n} (z_{ik} - z_{jk})^2$$

This measure is proportional to 1-r_{ij} where r_{ij} is the correlation between the two variables. It is zero for two variables whose correlation is +1, and it is greatest for two variables correlated at -1. The proximity matrix is shown in Table 4.

Table 4. Proximity Matrix

Case	Matrix File Input						
	army	fic1	fic2	fin1	fin2	med1	med2
army	.000	23.872	24.195	30.302	41.821	28.608	25.757
fic1	23.872	.000	5.360	14.821	19.845	16.031	13.836
fic2	24.195	5.360	.000	16.071	21.689	14.146	14.092
fin1	30.302	14.821	16.071	.000	3.638	10.048	11.128
fin2	41.821	19.845	21.689	3.638	.000	15.659	16.328
Med1	28.608	16.031	14.146	10.048	15.659	.000	2.760
Med2	25.757	13.836	14.092	11.128	16.328	2.760	.000

We conducted the analysis agglomeratively. That is, the two variables closest together are joined into a cluster, and then further clusters are formed by joining variables. The dendrogram for the results is shown in Figure 1. It can be read from left to right.

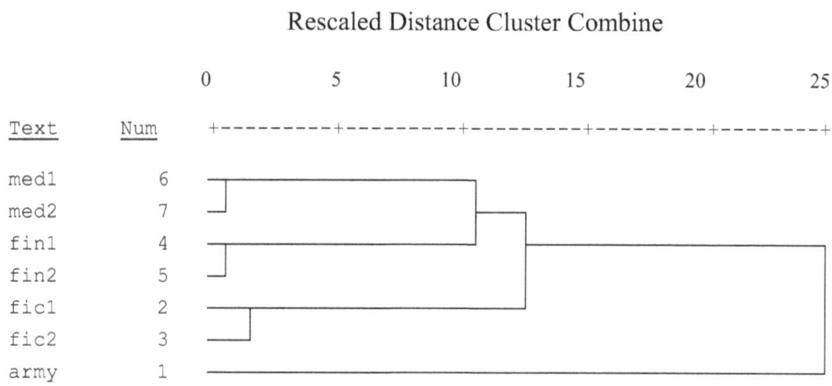

Figure 1. Dendrogram of Domains Using Average Linkage between Groups

At the first step, the dendrogram joins the two fiction documents into a cluster, the two finance documents into a cluster, the two medical documents into a cluster, while leaving *army* in a cluster of its own. Moving further to the right, the dendrogram proceeds by joining some of these clusters into super-clusters. The researcher can decide how many clusters are desirable in a solution. In our case, an *a priori* decision to seek a solution with four clusters would mean ignoring the super-clusters in favor of the assignments made at the left-most part of the dendrogram. Impressively, the dendrogram clusters each text with the other text of the same domain. No texts from two different domains were clustered together. This is perfect accuracy in classification.

In further analyses, we used the PROXSCAL procedure in SPSS version 12 to carry out a multidimensional scale analysis of the squared Euclidean distances between the texts. A similar approach has been used previously by Sigelman and Jacoby (1996). In a space of a given number of dimensions, the analysis begins by positing an initial configuration of points representing the variables. The distances between these points are computed, and compared with another set of numbers d^*_{ij} that preserves the ranks of the distances among the variables exactly, and that comes as close as possible to the distances between the variables. The coordinates are varied so as to minimize the departure from a monotonic relationship between the distances d_{ij} and the d^*_{ij}. The actual values of the original distances are never used in the computation, only their ranks.

The goodness of fit for the solution is assessed by the stress statistic. The more closely the model reproduces the rank order of the distances, the smaller the stress. Several definitions of this statistic have been proposed. For our purposes we use Young's S-stress.

This procedure can be carried out for spaces of various dimensions, and the fit calculated for each space. For the one-dimensional solution it is .050. This solution perfectly distinguishes among the four domains. A plot of the coordinates is shown in Figure 2. The plot makes obvious how distinctive the *army* text is from the others.

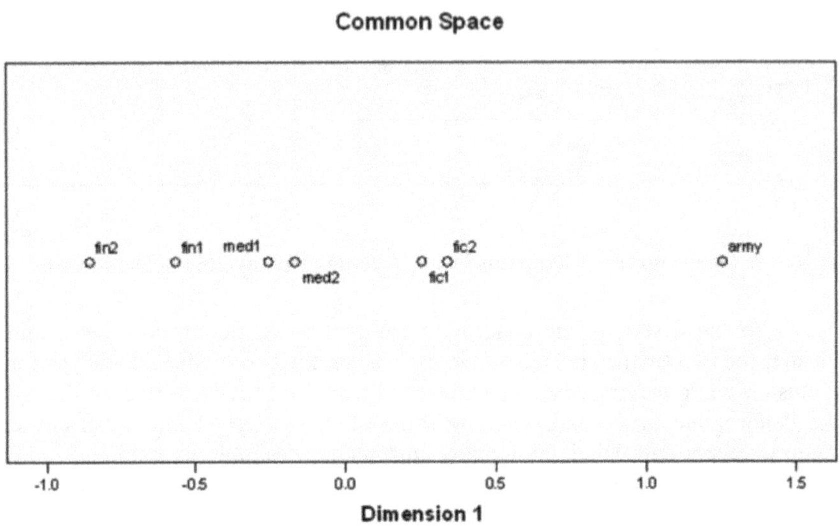

Figure 2. One-Dimensional PROXSCAL Plot

The addition of more dimensions allows for greater freedom in finding an optimum configuration. Consequently, the stress declines with the addition of more dimensions. Often it is possible to find a space of just a few dimensions that yields a small stress, and for which the introduction of further dimensions reduces the stress by a trivial amount (Kruskal, 1964; Greenberg, 1979: 186-90). Choice of the optimal number of dimensions is done on the basis of a subjective judgment as to when a fit is both satisfactory and parsimonious.

When we fit our data to a two-dimensional solution, the S-stress declined to .017, a considerable improvement. The coordinates of this solution are shown in Table 5, and are displayed graphically in the plot of Figure 3.

Table 5. Coordinates of Two-Dimensional PROXSCAL Solution

Final Coordinates

Domain	Dimension 1	Dimension 2
army	1.210	.171
fic1	.172	-.354
fic2	.097	-.469
fin1	-.502	.030
fin2	-.812	.042
med1	-.138	.313
med2	-.028	.267

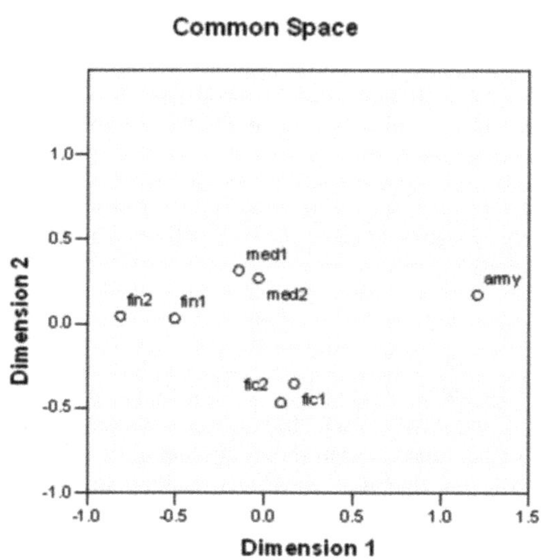

Figure 3. Two-Dimensional PROXSCAL Plot

The additional improvement obtained from a three-dimensional solution is quite limited. Given the high accuracy of classification with a two-dimensional solution, the complication introduced by the addition of a third dimension is unnecessary.

4. Conclusion

The analysis up to this point confirms our expectation that there are differences in syntactic densities for texts belonging to distinct domains. Therefore, syntactic feature counting methods should prove useful for purposes of selecting domain-specific training and testing corpora for machine translation, and may overcome problems that have plagued the use of purely lexical methods for this purpose.

Confirmation of the value of our approach in a larger sample of texts, encompassing a wider range of domains, would demonstrate that a syntactic analysis could be used to classify a text on the basis of its syntactic densities, either as a stand-alone method, or as an auxiliary to lexically-based methods.

Of course, the accuracy with which this classification could be accomplished remains to be seen. In particular, syntactically-based methods need to be compared with lexically-based methods in terms of their precision-recall performance as classification methods. Our results are certainly promising, but they are based on a small sample of texts drawn from a limited number of domains. We also have not carried out a comparison with lexically-based methods on the issue of domain-overlap.

The next stage in our research program is to repeat our analyses with a larger and more representative set of texts that include a wider range of domains and to compare the accuracy of classification achieved with our syntactically-based procedures with those achieved through word-based methods. The information from these analyses would provide us with a better picture of how well we can classify texts in practice.

Notes

1 This is often done using search-engine algorithms such as tf-idf ('term frequency/inverse document frequency'), a weighting function based on the distribution of the terms within the document and within the collection. A high value indicates that the word occurs often in the document, and does not occur in many other documents.

2 The product outputs 71 possible tags. For our purposes we do not count the tags "unknown," "verb phrase," "noun phrase" or prepositional phrase

because phrasal categories are redundant with their heads, and unknown words are removed.

3 A multinomial probit would be equally appropriate for our analysis, but would be more difficult to estimate with existing software.

4 Several authors have adopted principal component analysis (PCA) for classification purposes (Burroughs and Craig, 1994; Ledger and Main, 1994). We consider the common factor analysis to be superior for our purposes. PCA extracts a set of orthogonal components, each of which maximizes the explained variance of the variables, or the residuals that remain after the extraction of components. The common factor analysis, however, is better suited to the explanation of correlations among a set of variables. It assumes that some of the relationships arise from the common factors, but that there are also contributions to the error variance that are unique to each variable. For discussion see Greenberg (1979).

References

Aldendorf, M. S. (1984), *Cluster analysis.* Beverly Hills: Sage.

Andenberg, M. R. (1973), *Cluster analysis for applications.* New York: Academic Press.

Borko, H. and M. Bernick (1963), 'Automatic document classification', *J. ACM,* 10.2: 151-62.

_____ (1944), *The statistical study of literary vocabulary.* Cambridge: Cambridge University Press.

Bosch, R. A. and J. A. Smith (1998), 'separating hyperplanes and the authorship of disputed Federalist papers', *The American mathematical monthly* 105.7: 601-608.

Brainerd, B. (1973a), 'The computer in statistical studies of William Shakespeare', *Computer studies in the humanities and verbal behavior* 4.1: 9-15.

_____ (1973b), 'On the distinction between a novel and a romance: a discriminant analysis," *Computers and the humanities* 7: 259-70.

_____ (1987), 'Computers and the study of literature', *Computers and written texts.* Oxford: Blackwell.

_____ (1986), 'Modal verbs and moral principles: an aspect of Jane Austen's style', *Literary and linguistic computing* 21.2: 60-70.

_____ (1987), 'Word-patterns and story shapes: the statistical analysis of narrative style', *Literary and linguistic computing* 2.2: 60-70.

Burrows, J. F. (1987), 'Word patterns and story shapes: the statistical analysis of narrative style," *Literary and linguistic computing* 2: 61-70.

_____ and D. H. Craig (1994), 'Lyrical drama and the 'Turbid Mountebanks': Styles of dialogue in Romantic and Renaissance tragedy', *Computers and the humanities 28: 63-86.*

Ellegard, A. (1962a), *A statistical method for determining authorship : the Junius letters 1769-1772*. Gothenburg Studies in English No. 13. Goteborg, Sweden: Acta Universitatis Gothenburgensis, Elandes Boktryckeri Aktiebolag.

_____ (1962b), *Who was Junius?* Stockholm: Almqvist and Wiksell.

Furnas, G. W., T. K. Landauer, L. M. Gomez and S. T. Dumais (1987), 'The vocabulary problem in human-systems communication', *Communications of the ACM* 964-971.

Gorsuch, R. L. (1974), *Factor analysis*. Philadelphia: Saunders.

Graham, P. (2002), 'A plan for spam', www.paulgraham.com/spam.html.

Greenberg, D. F. (1979), *Mathematical criminology*. New Brunswick, NJ: Rutgers University Press.

Gurney, P. J. and L. W. Gurney (1996), 'Disputed authorship: 30 biographies and six reputed authors. a new analysis by full-text lemmatization of the *Historia Augusta*', Presented at ALLC/ACH '96. Bergen, Norway, June 25-29.

_____ (1997), 'Multi-Authorship of the *Scriptores Historiae Augustae*: How the use of subsets can win or lose the case.' Presented at ALLC/ACH '97. Kingston, Ontario.

Harman, H. H. (1976), *Modern factor analysis*. Chicago: University of Chicago Press.

Holmes, D. I. (1994), 'Authorship attribution,' *Computers and the humanities* 28: 87-106.

Hoover, D. L. (2001), 'Statistical stylistics and authorship attribution: An empirical investigation', *Literary and linguistic computing* 16: 421-44.

Jennrich, R. I. and P. F. Sampson (1966), 'Rotation for simple loadings,' *Psychometrika* 31: 313-323.

Johnson, G. (2004), 'Cognitive rascal in the amorous swamp: A robot battles spams,' *New York times* (April 27): F3.

Jørgensen, S. W., C. Hansen, J. Drost, D. Haltrup, A. Braasch and S. Olsen (2003), 'Domain specific corpus building and lemma selection in a computational lexicon', in: *Proceedings of the Corpus Linguistics 2003 Conference*, Lancaster University, UK, pp. 374-83.

Kaiser, H. F. (1960), 'The application of electronic computers to factor analysis,' *Pyrometrical* 23: 187-200.

Kaufman, L. and P. J. Rousseeuw (1990), Finding groups in data: an introduction to cluster analysis. New York: Wiley.

Kenny, A. (1986), *A stylometric study of the New Testament*. Oxford: Oxford University Press.

Kjetsa, G. (1979), 'And quiet flows the Don through the computer', *Association for literary and linguistic computing bulletin* 7: 248-56.

Klavans, J. and M.-Y. Kan (1998), 'Role of Verbs in Document Classification', *Proceedings of COLING-ACL* 1998, Montreal, Canada,. 680-86.

Kruskal, J. B. (1964), 'Multidimensional scaling by optimizing goodness of fit to a nonmetric hypothesis', *Psychometrika* 29: 1-29.

Ledger, G. and T. Merriam (1994), 'Shakespeare, Fletcher, and *Two Noble Kinsmen*', *Literary and linguistic computing* 9.3: 234-48.

Lorr, M. (1983), *Cluster analysis for social scientists.* San Francisco: Jossey-Bass.

Maron, M. (1961), 'Automatic indexing: An experimental inquiry', *J. ACM.* 8: 404-417.

Mendenhall, T. C. (1887), 'The characteristic curves of composition', *Science* 9.214 (supplement): 237-49.

_____ (1901), 'A mechanical solution to a literary problem'. *Popular Science Monthly* 60.7: 97-105.

Milic, Louis T. (1967), *A quantitative approach to the style of Jonathan Swift.* The Hague: Mouton.

Morton, A. Q., (1965), 'The authorship of Greek prose', *Journal of the Royal Statistical Society* (A) 128: 169-233.

Mosteller, F. and D. L. Wallace (1964), *Inference and disputed authorship:* The Federalist. Reading, MA: Addison-Wesley.

_____ (1984), *Applied Bayesian and classical inference: The case of* The Federalist Papers. New York: Springer-Verlag.

Radday, Y. T. (1973), *The unity of Isaiah in the light of statistical analysis.* Gerstenberg: Hildesheim.

Romesburg H. C. (1984), *Cluster analysis for researchers.* Belmont, CA: Lifetime Learning Associates.

Salton, G. (1991), 'Developments in automatic text retrieval', *Science* 253: 974-79.

Sigelman, L. and W. Jacoby (1996), 'The not-so-simple art of imitation: Pastiche, literary style, and Raymond Chandler', *Computers and the humanities* 30: 11-28.

Smith, M. W. A. (1991), 'The authorship of The Raigne of King Edward the Third,' *Literary and Linguistic Computing* 6: 166-74.

Tryon, R. C. and D. E. Bailey (1970), *Cluster analysis.* New York: Wiley.

Yule, George Udny (1944), *The statistical study of literary vocabulary.* Cambridge: Cambridge University Press.

Appendix

NNSN Singular Noun
NNPL Plural Noun
NOUN PHRASE
PNNS Singular Proper Noun
PNNP Plural Proper Noun
NNSP Singular Posessive Noun
NNPP Plural Posessive Noun
PNSP Proper Singular Noun

PNPP Proper Posessive Noun
PREPOSITIONAL PHRASE
ADJT Adjective
ADJS Adjective, Superlative
ADJC Adjective, Comparative
DET Determiner
ADVR Adverb
VERB PHRASE
VIXX Verb, Infinitive Form
VTO Verb To (for Infinitives)
VPT -ed verbs as ADJTs (participle)
VRT -ing verbs as ADJTs (participle)
VRXX Verb, Generic Present Tense
VR1S Verb, Present Tense, 1st Person, Singular
VR1P Verb, Present Tense, 1st Person, Plural
VR2X Verb, Present Tense, 2nd Person
VR3S Verb, Present Tense, 3rd Person, Singular
VR3P Verb, Present Tense, 3rd Person, Plural
VPXX Verb, Generic Past Tense
VP1C Contracted Verb, Past Tense, 1st person
VP2C Contracted Verb, Past Tense, 2nd person
VP3C Contracted Verb, Past Tense, 3rd person
VP4C Contracted Verb, Past Tense, 1st Person Plural
VP6C Contracted Verb, Past Tense, 3rd person Plural
VR1C Contracted Verb, Present Tense, 1st person
VR2C Contracted Verb, Present Tense, 2nd person
VR3C Contracted Verb, Present Tense, 3rd person
VR4C Contracted Verb, Present Tense, 1st person plural
VR6C Contracted Verb, Present Tense, 3rd person plural
CP3P Contracted 3rd Person Plural Pronoun with Past Tense Verb(they'd)
CP3S Contracted 3rd Person Singular Pronoun with Past Tense Verb
CP2X Contracted 2rd Person Pronoun with Past Tense Verb
CP1P Contracted 1st Person Plural Pronoun with Past Tense Verb
CP1S Contracted 1st Person Singular Pronoun with Past Tense Verb
CR3P Contracted 3rd Person Plural Pronoun with Present Tense Verb
CR3S Contracted 3rd Person Singular Pronoun with Present Tense Verb
CR2X Contracted 2nd Person Pronoun with Present Tense Verb
CR1P Contracted 1st Person Plural Pronoun with Present Tense Verb
CR1S Contracted 1st Person Singular Pronoun with Present Tense Verb
PRO Generic Pronoun
P1S 1st Person Singular Pronoun
P1P 1st Person Plural Pronoun
P2X 2nd Person Pronoun
P3S 3rd Person Singular Pronoun
P3P 3rd Person Plural Pronoun

P1SP	1st Person Singular Possessive Pronoun
P1PP	1st Person Plural Possessive Pronoun
P2XP	2nd Person Possessive Pronoun
P3SP	3rd Person Singular Possessive Pronoun
P3PP	3rd Person Plural Possessive Pronoun
PREP	Preposition
PART	Participle
INTR	Interject
YCNJ	Punctual Conjunction
YSTP	Punctual Stop
YCOM	Comma
YQUE	Question Mark
YPNC	Punctuation
YSYM	Misc Symbol
YQOT	Quotation Mark
MONY	Monetary Symbol
NUMB	Number
UNKNOWN	

The Envelope of Variation in Multidimensional Register and Genre Analyses

Angus B. Grieve-Smith

University of New Mexico

Abstract

While multidimensional analysis of register and genre variation is a very promising field, a number of problems with it have been identified. Of particular importance are the problems of eliminating grammatical sources of covariation, while still maintaining a set of variables that are faithful to earlier discussions in the literature. One potential solution to both problems is to use the notion of the envelope of variation, *as established by variationist sociolinguistics, where grammatical features are counted not as a proportion of the total number of words, but as a proportion of the opportunities for these features to be produced. This technique is also valuable because it allows variables to be targeted with more precise algorithms.*

This paper describes a pilot study that integrates the envelope of variation into multidimensional analysis. It focuses on two variables (third-person pronouns and demonstrative adjectives) that we would not expect to covary according to Biber's (1988) descriptions, but for which Biber himself found a significant correlation (-0.282). Using twelve texts from the MICASE corpus (96,000 words), the two variables were corrected based on definitions in the original literature and then restated as testable hypotheses with envelopes of variation. The correlation was -0.685 when using Biber's original methods, -0.505 when using corrected algorithms, and -.511 when using corrected algorithms with an envelope of variation. The first correlation was statistically significant, while the second and third were not. However, all three were higher than Biber's original correlation, and would be significant if they were replicated with a corpus as big as Biber's. The study emphasizes how complex the counting of any given variable is in corpus analysis, and how much work is necessary to properly identify each one.

1. Introduction

Language variation takes many forms. Even in the language of an individual there is tremendous variation according to the situation of language use. This variation, sometimes called register or genre variation, is largely independent of regional or class variation, and of change over time.

One of the most comprehensive approaches to studying situational variation is the multidimensional approach of Douglas Biber (1986, 1988, 1989 and others) and his colleagues (Biber, Conrad and Reppen, 1998; Biber, Johansson, Leech, Conrad and Finegan, 1999). Although this framework has tremendous potential to help solve problems in areas such as language teaching, historical linguistics and diglossia, it also has a number of weaknesses, the most critical being the failure to separate covariation of features due to the situation of use from covariation due to grammatical structure. Since any finding under the classic multidimensional approach could potentially be due to grammatical structure, any conclusions based on it are open to challenge. Biber's data show correlations between features that are not predicted to correlate because of the situation of use, but would be expected to correlate for grammatical reasons.

The problem of separating grammatical covariation from situational covariation has been addressed in variationist sociolinguistics by the notion of the envelope of variation, where the frequency of any variable is measured against the frequency of all opportunities for that variable to occur (Labov, 1972). This is a concept that could work for situational variation as well, and in this paper I describe a pilot study that attempts to apply the concept of the envelope of variation to Biber's multidimensional text analysis.

A lesser problem, but still significant, is that while all of the variables used by Biber are in some sense "inspired by" previous work on register and genre differences, the measurements chosen are not always in line with the conclusions of the original studies. Some of this is due to the necessity of preserving independence among the variables for the factor analysis. With the use of envelopes of variation it becomes possible to fine-tune the variables to match up with previous work.

In this paper I begin with an in-depth discussion of situational variation and its applications, and then discuss the multidimensional framework and the problem of grammatical covariation. I then present a proposal to incorporate the notion of an envelope of variation into multidimensional analysis. The pilot study focuses on two linguistic features, third-person pronouns and demonstrative adjectives, that are not expected to covary due to the situation of use, but that do show a significant correlation that can be explained as the result of grammatical covariation. It examines these features in a small test corpus of a little more than 96,000 words, using both the classic multidimensional method and a modified method incorporating the concept of envelope of variation, and if the methods are appropriate it will replicate the significant correlation found by Biber, but eliminate that correlation using the proposed method.

1.1 Situational variation

The terms genre, register and style have been used in somewhat different ways in the sociolinguistic literature, but they all have in common the fact that they describe how language varies according to the situation (Biber, 1988). Other areas of sociolinguistics investigate regional and class variation and sometimes (consciously) abstract away from situational variation by assuming that the speaker/writer has no control over variation. In contrast, situational variation abstracts away from regional and class variation and assumes that the speaker/writer has complete control over variation. These two idealizations assume that situation and dialect are never conflated, but there are sociolinguists in the subfield of standardization such as Ferguson (1959) and Joseph (1987) who go beyond that assumption to tackle the intersection of the two kinds of variation.

Biber (1988: pages 28-46) gives an overall taxonomy of ways that language can vary with its situation, with the most important distinction being between *situations* and *functions* of particular texts. Hudson (1994) also points out that the sources of situational variation can be divided into three groups: *specialized terminology*, *discourse-pragmatic* factors, and *sociocultural* factors other than specialized terminology. Specialized terminology refers to differences in vocabulary that develop as a particular register is used again and again over time. It is easily measured by simple word counts, so I will focus on the other two sources of situational variation.

Some situational variation is the result of the physical and cognitive realities of the situation. Since the effect of physical and cognitive factors on language is the focus of discourse pragmatics, Hudson grouped these factors together under the term "discourse-pragmatic." This includes whether the communication is real-time or delayed (allowing time for planning), face-to-face or remote, interactive or monumental, confined to a single channel (like speech or text) or multi-channeled. These discourse-pragmatic factors have necessary consequences, based on the needs of humans to interact and exchange information, and the constraints on humans' abilities to produce and process language. For example, conversational situations require some mechanism for turn-taking and obtaining the floor, and do not allow the participants unlimited time to plan their utterances. If we know something about the structure of a language, we can predict how it will vary based on these discourse factors. We can thus say that the discourse factors are universal, at least in the sense that each factor has the same effect wherever it is found.

There are several ways that sociocultural aspects of a particular language situation can affect the structure of the language used. The subject matter and the goals of the participants are significant, as are notions of prestige and formality. These sociocultural factors are less constrained than the discourse-pragmatic factors. We have no way of predicting what forms are preferred in one kind of poetry or another, or which features are most highly associated with prestige or formality. It may be possible to provide motivation for some of the choices, based on what we know about the structure of the language, particularly in the case of the subject matter and goals: we may be able to understand why a particular form is frequently used in storytelling or persuasion. We can thus say that sociocultural factors are culture-specific, but not entirely arbitrary.

1.2 Applications of the study of situational variation

The study of situational variation has a number of potential applications that could prove valuable. One application, which would be of use to almost anyone who studies language, is to produce a map of the variation in a particular language or variety, showing where the various genres, registers and styles are in relation to each other along some of these continua. An example is the clustering techniques used by Biber (1989, among others), but a wide variety of visualizations are possible.

New genres and registers are always being invented, and new communication media like any of those offered by the Internet can be expected to inspire more. A good model of situational variation allows linguists to situate a new genre in relation to existing genres, for comparison and contrast. For example, it is intuitively clear to many observers that the English used in online chat facilities is closer to conversational speech than to other written forms, but how close? Close enough to be considered the same for some purposes?

There are a number of pedagogical applications of situational variation studies. The main application is that with knowledge of the text types in a language and the grammatical features that differentiate them, a student of the language can learn what text types he or she can expect to encounter, and work to master them individually. This is the goal behind the Longman Grammar of English (Biber et al., 1999).

Diachronic linguistics can also benefit from the study of situational variation. The study of language change is hampered by the fact that relatively few genres have existed for more than a few hundred years, and even those have changed over time (Herring et al., 1997). The ability to map the changing relationships among genres could allow linguists to control for some of this variation, finding genres that are the most appropriate to compare across time.

The most intriguing application of this study grows out of the connection that Hudson (1994) draws between diglossia on the one hand, and register variation as studied by Biber and his colleagues (Besnier, 1988; Biber, 1988, Kim and Biber, 1994; Biber and Hared, 1994) on the other. Diglossia is "one particular kind of standardization where two varieties of a language exist side by side throughout the community, with each having a definite role to play" (Ferguson, 1959). Ferguson defined diglossia by the four paradigmatic examples of Haiti, Greece, the Arabic-speaking world and German-speaking Switzerland, but gave no contrasting example of a non-diglossic speech community, and no clear description of the boundaries of diglossia. The study of situational variation could eventually lead to a method of quantifying the separation of the H (high-prestige) and L (low-prestige) varieties used in a particular speech community, and eventually to the ability to unambiguously identify diglossic speech communities.

1.3 The multidimensional approach

The best-developed method of studying situational variation is the Multidimensional Approach developed by Biber in his 1988 study of English and further refined in subsequent studies. Biber analyzed 67 linguistic features that had been identified by other linguists and grammarians as varying according to one situational variable or another. He developed algorithms for counting each feature automatically in a large corpus, and ran these algorithms on a corpus that he created by combining the Lancaster-Oslo-Bergen corpus of written British English (Johannsen et al., 1978) and the London-Lund corpus of spoken British

English (Svartvik and Quirk, 1980) with a collection of professional and personal letters, totalling a little over one million words.

It is important to highlight here that the multidimensional approach requires that the features be automatically countable. Biber (1988:65) writes:

> In a factor analysis, the data base should include five times as many texts as linguistic features to be analyzed (Gorsuch 1983: 332). In addition, simply representing the range of situational and processing possibilities in English requires a large number of texts. To analyze this number of texts without the aid of computational tools would require several years; computerized corpora enable storage and analysis of a large number of texts in an efficient manner.

For 67 features, Gorsuch's recommendation translates into at least 335 texts; Biber uses 481. To manually count all 67 features in 481 texts would be a long and laborious process; as Ball (1994) points out, "a few days to complete each search may amount to years worth of sustained effort." It is therefore critical that the counting be done automatically to the greatest extent possible. Furthermore, manual counting can also be unreliable, since it is difficult to maintain consistency among counters, or within the work of a single counter over time.

These frequency counts were then fed into a factor analysis to determine which linguistic features varied together. From this factor analysis, Biber identified six primary dimensions (pages 101-120), as follows:

Informational vs. Involved Production
Narrative vs. Non-Narrative Concerns
Explicit vs. Situation-Dependent Reference
Overt Expression of Persuasion
Abstract vs. Non-Abstract Information
On-line Informational Elaboration

Biber was then able to plot the texts in the corpus along these dimensions, and found that texts from the same genre did tend to have similar factor scores. For example, on Dimension 1 ("Informational vs. Involved Production"), the average score for texts in the category of "Telephone Conversations" was 37.2, "Official Documents" was -18.1, and "Romantic Fiction" was in the middle at 4.3 (Biber, 1988:122-135). The exceptions to this general principle all highlighted interesting exceptions to the genre categories themselves.

1.4 The problem of grammatical covariation

There are several problems with the methodology of the classic multidimensional analysis, discussed in some depth by Lee (forthcoming). The problem of grammatical covariation was first identified by Ball (1994), who referred to it as "hidden factors."

The factor analysis used in the multidimensional framework is very effective at finding covariation in a corpus. However, it does not distinguish the covariation due to situation (which is the point of the study) from covariation due to grammar. In the terms used by Biber, Conrad and Reppen (1998), it does not separate linguistic associations from non-linguistic associations. As Ball (1994) writes: "Because the ratio of words to higher-level units is variable, no conclusions about the distribution of syntactic phenomena within a corpus can be drawn from word-based frequency studies, and such studies are non-comparable."

To illustrate this, I will examine Biber's Dimension 1, which is interpreted by him to refer to Informational vs. Involved Production. Here are the top five features that load on Dimension 1 in each direction (i.e. the features that loaded positively were interpreted by Biber as "involved" and those that loaded negatively were interpreted as "informational"):

Top 5 Features that Load Positively	Top 5 Features that Load Negatively
Private verbs (see p. 7) THAT deletion Contractions Present tense verbs 2nd person pronouns	Nouns (other than nominalizatons or gerunds) Word length Prepositions Type/token ratio Attributive adjectives

Biber spends several pages interpreting the non-linguistic associations of these features and their implications in order to build the notion of Informational vs. Involved Production. However, he does not take into account the possibility that some or all of the observed covariation could be due to grammatical structure.

In his discussion of the feature "Nouns other than nominalizatons or gerunds," Biber observes that noun frequency has been identified as a marker of situational variation at least as far back as 1960, when Rulon Wells proposed it in his article "Nominal and Verbal Style" (Wells, 1960). There are many interpretations of this observation, but the basic idea is that texts with more nouns tend to be more "static" while texts with more verbs are more "dynamic."

For the purposes of argumentation, I will suggest that the entire Dimension 1 measures nominal vs. verbal style. This interpretation provides clear motivation for all of the features that load on this dimension. Private verbs and present-tense verbs are both kinds of verbs, and their frequency would be expected to covary with verb frequency. Contractions, second-person pronouns and THAT-deletion are all characteristics of verb phrases, and would also be expected to covary with verbs. Prepositions and attributive adjectives are noun modifiers, and so would covary with nouns. For word length, when weighted for frequency it seems that the length of nouns tends to be greater. It appears that type/token ratio is similar to word length, since there tends to be a greater diversity of nouns than verbs.

In personal communication, Catherine Travis has suggested an even stronger alternative explanation for the correlation of the features that load positively: private verbs (e.g. *think, feel* that express private attitudes, thoughts and emotions; Biber 1988:105) tend to occur in the present tense (Scheibman, 2001); and tend to occur with THAT deletion (Thompson and Mulac, 1991a, 1991b); the phrase *you know* has incredibly high text counts, which may account for the correlation between private verbs and second person pronouns (Scheibman, 2001); and *don't* is most often contracted in the construction *I dunno* (Bybee and Scheibman, 1999; Scheibman, 2000).

It is important to note that neither of these interpretations of the feature loading need be true; all that is necessary is for one to be plausible, because the classic multidimensional method does not have a way of distinguishing among plausible interpretations.

1.5 The problem of variable measurement

Biber actually does take steps to eliminate unwanted covariation, along the lines recommended for every factor analysis study. It is not appropriate to include measurements of categories and their subcategories in a single factor analysis, and he modifies his algorithms accordingly. Unfortunately, many of the resulting algorithms (1988:223-245) fail to test specific hypotheses about situational variation. For every variable, Biber refers to earlier studies that discuss situational variation in particular linguistic features, but the algorithms that he creates to measure these variables are often not accurate measures of the features described in the earlier studies.

For example, Biber (1988:236) gives four categories of adverbial subordinators: *causative, concessive, conditional* and *other*. He discusses a number of studies that find situational variation in adverbial subordination in general, and then for each of the first three subcategories he describes a few studies focusing on that particular kind of subordination.

Of course, nobody has hypothesized that there is a category of "other adverbial subordinators (having multiple functions)" that varies according to situation for a principled reason. Biber wanted to measure adverbial subordination in general, but could not because that would have introduced artificial covariation into the factor analysis. He created this category to include the additional subordinators that did not fit in any other category, but there is no indication that this actually provides useful information in a factor analysis.

1.6 The proposed solution: the envelope of variation

The problem of isolating non-linguistic sources of variation, although it puts the results of the original study in doubt, does not imply that the entire multidimensional framework is useless. On the contrary, it points to a way to modify the methods of multidimensional analysis to make it a closer model of situational variation. This modified methodology will be harder to implement, but not impossible. In fact, this problem has already been identified and dealt with in variationist sociolinguistics. Labov (1972) calls it the *Principle of Accountability*; here is a recent description (Labov, forthcoming):

> reports of the occurrences of a variable must be accompanied by reports of all non-occurrences. The definition of a linguistic variable then requires establishing a closed set ["the *envelope of variation*"] to which the axioms of probability theory apply.

On a per-word basis, the frequency counts used by Biber are relatively meaningless. What does it mean to use contractions frequently? What is meaningful is actually the fact that the speaker or writer is making a *choice*, consciously or unconsciously, to contract a phrase instead of saying or writing the full phrase. It is this frequency *per choice* that grounds the data in the intuitive observations of earlier linguists, and in a theory of situational variation.

In fact, since contractions in English are usually unconscious strategies to increase the efficiency of speech, it is best to turn the question around: what is the advantage of not using contractions? Uncontracted forms are closer to the more prestigious written forms, and acquire prestige from them. They are easier to produce in edited or written forms of language, and associated with more careful, more formal situations.

We thus expect that the use of uncontracted forms will occur mostly in edited writing and formal situations, and that it will be one of the markers of these varieties of English. This is a relatively simple hypothesis to test with a corpus. If we gather enough of these hypotheses, we will be able to determine which features work as expected and which don't, and come up with explanations for the discrepancies.

This strategy also has the effect of solving the problem of variable measurement described in section 1.5. When every variable is measured in relation to an envelope of variation, all variables are independent, and it is possible to measure, for example, both *clauses with concessive adverbial subordinators* as a fraction of all clauses with adverbial subordinators, and *all clauses with adverbial subordinators* as a fraction of all clauses.

To control for grammatical variation, therefore, each feature needs to be subject to a few modifications, as follows:

1. Determine the statement about register or genre variation that underlies the selection of this feature
2. Determine whether this statement is a testable hypothesis
3. Determine the envelope of variation for this feature
4. Construct an algorithm to measure this feature

It is interesting to note that this was close to Biber's original intent. The introduction to his pioneering 1988 study (pages 3-27) focuses on the difference between speech and writing, the fact that a number of competing explanations for this difference had been suggested, and the intention to test these intuitive explanations with a rigorous quantitative approach. In the end, the pattern that emerged from the factor analysis did not clearly favour any particular explanation, and so the idea of mapping situational variation for the entire language became more important than working out the relationships among the various hypotheses.

2. Method

This pilot study aims to test the proposal that the multidimensional approach can simply be refined by modifying each feature as described above. It narrows the focus to two features identified by Biber in his 1988 study. These are a pair of features that we would not expect to covary due to situational reasons based on Biber's descriptions, but for which he reported a significant correlation. They are two features that we *would* expect to covary due to grammar, thus explaining the covariation that shows up in Biber's results. These features will be measured in a small corpus of twelve texts (96,000 words) chosen from the Lectures subset of the Michigan Corpus of Academic Spoken English (MICASE) corpus (Simpson et al. 2000).

The hypothesis is that as measured with the classic multidimensional methodology these features will be significantly correlated, but using the proposed methods the correlation will not be significant.

The two features chosen are *third person pronouns* and *demonstrative adjectives*. Based on the descriptions of Biber and his sources these features are not expected to covary situationally, but they do show a significant correlation in Biber's results. This correlation can be explained as being due to grammatical structure.

2.1 Description of corpus

MICASE is a collection of transcripts of academic speech events recorded at the University of Michigan, available for free on the Word Wide Web (Simpson et al., 2000). It aims to sample every kind of academic speech on campus, including classroom and non-class events, monologues, dialogues and group discussions, with speakers from a wide range of ages and academic ranks represented. The corpus and a more detailed description can be found at <http://www.lsa.umich.edu/eli/micase/>.

For the purposes of this study, a smaller corpus of twelve texts was sampled from the MICASE database. All of the texts were monologues, including six colloquia, one dissertation defense, two large lectures, two small lectures and one seminar. In order to ensure representation by both narrative and descriptive texts in the test corpus, I chose six lectures that gave me the subjective impression of telling stories, and six that seemed to focus more on description. This introduces the potential for a circular argument because my judgments may have been based on some of the features discussed here, but I tried to avoid this by not focusing on particular grammatical features.

The texts have varying amounts of interaction, but each one has a featured speaker who does the vast majority of talking. Sometimes the speaker is introduced by faculty or administrators, sometimes (particularly in the small lecture and the seminar) the audience feels free to interrupt with clarification questions, and there is always a question period at the end. Since there is not enough speech from the other speakers for a sample, I isolated the speech of the featured speaker and did not analyze the other speakers.

2.2 Description of variables

Biber's 1988 book is notable because he provides so much of his raw data for cross-checking and replication. As Ball (1994) writes, "The authors are to be commended for publishing their algorithms: it is more common in reports of corpus-based research for the search method to be left unspecified." Without that information, the current study would not be possible.

Here is the description that Biber gives for third person pronouns (page 225):

> *she, he, they, her, him, them, his, their, himself, herself, themselves* (plus contracted forms)
> Third person personal pronouns mark relatively inexact reference to persons outside of the immediate interaction. They have been used in register comparisons by Poole and Field (1976) and Hu (1984). Biber (1986) finds that third person pronouns co-occur frequently with past-tense and perfect aspect forms, as a marker of narrative, reported (versus immediate) styles.

We can get additional information from the original studies. Poole and Field studied differences between the oral and written language produced by Australian first-year undergraduate students from working-class and middle-class backgrounds. They used envelopes of variation in their study, but not always ones that clearly reflected a hypothesis about variation. They found that the ratio of the *total number* of personal pronouns to total words was significantly higher for oral language than written language, but that the ratio of first-person pronouns to all pronouns was only higher (and at a lower rate of statistical significance) for the middle-class students. They did not study third person pronouns as a separate category, but only as part of the total category of personal pronouns.

In a very different study, Hu compares the original published novel of *The Great Gatsby* (Fitzgerald, 1926) with transcripts of film adaptations of the story. He observes that his random selection of excerpts of the novel "has much wider use of the third person pronominals in an endophoric way" than the same excerpts from the adaptation. He ascribes this difference to the presence of narration in the novel, which is replaced by nonverbal images in the film. This supports Biber's finding that third person pronouns are more prevalent in narratives.

Here is Biber's description of demonstrative adjectives (page 241):

> *that|this|these|those*
> (This count excludes demonstrative pronouns (no. 10) and *that* as relative, complementizer and subordinator.)
> Demonstratives are used for both text-internal deixis (Kurzon 1985) and for exophoric, text-external, reference. They are an important device for marking referential cohesion in a text (Halliday and Hasan 1976). Ochs (1979) notes that demonstratives are preferred to articles in unplanned discourse.

I chose to focus on Ochs' observation, since Kurzon, and Halliday and Hasan, study the frequency of demonstrative adjectives but do not make a clear hypothesis about demonstratives being used in contrast to other forms. Ochs used a corpus of elicited parallel texts, unplanned and planned; the subjects (her students in a discourse seminar) were first asked to describe a situation orally, then to prepare and edit a short written version. She observes that in the unplanned texts "we find frequent use of demonstrative modifiers where definite articles are used in planned discourse." Mostly the demonstrative functions to introduce a new referent, for example, the unplanned "I tried to walk between the edge of this platform and this group of people" is contrasted with the planned "Squeezing through narrow spaces and finding my way between people I continued in my pursuit of an emptier spot on the train platform and a woman whose back was turned toward me as she wildly conversed with some friends."

On closer examination, Ochs' single example contains only one noun phrase with a definite article in the planned version: "the train platform." The other referents are represented with either bare noun phrases ("narrow spaces," "people") or noun phrases with indefinite articles ("an emptier spot on the train platform," "a woman," "some friends"). It is true that the unplanned "this platform" is replaced by "the train platform" in the edited version, but "this group of people" is replaced by "a woman" and "some friends." In the framework of Lambrecht (1994) these are all "unidentifiable referents," which are mentioned in order to make them accessible for future reference, since they all play key roles in the story. Lambrecht notes that unidentifiable referents are usually referred to with indefinite noun phrases, but points out (following Prince (1981) and Wald (1983)) that colloquial English has an "indefinite *this*" construction which distinguishes referents "which are meant to become topics in a discourse" from "those which play only an ancillary narrative role."

2.3 Expected to correlate grammatically but not situationally

Based on these sources, we would expect third person pronouns to be influenced by whether the text was narrative or non-narrative (sociocultural variation), while the demonstrative adjectives would be expected to be influenced by whether the text was planned or unplanned (discourse-pragmatic variation). Since both narrative and non-narrative texts can be either planned or unplanned, we would expect these features to have no correlation with each other due to situational factors.

On the other hand, the two features are grammatically linked. In fact, they have the same basic function of referring to an object, and a given referent cannot be simultaneously referred to using both a pronoun and a demonstrative adjective. Since they are mutually exclusive, we would definitely expect a negative correlation, and in fact on page 277 Biber reports a Pearson product moment (r) of -0.282 for this pair (critical $|r| = 0.115$ for $\alpha = 0.02$, $n = 481$).

2.4 Modification of the feature *third person pronouns* according to the proposed methodology

Here I will apply the steps described in section 1.5 to the feature *third person pronouns* to yield a measure that will hopefully reflect the choices of the language users independent of grammar.

2.4.1 Determine the statement about register or genre variation that underlies the selection of this feature

Biber gives two statements about register or genre variation, in the description reprinted in Section 2.1: *Third person pronouns are more frequent in narratives than in non-narrative texts* (Biber 1986), and *Third person pronouns are less frequent in two-person dialogues than in genres with explicit narration* (Hu 1984). It seems that the first statement is not really about pronouns at all, but about reference to third-person *topics*. Because of this, the ideal measurement of this feature would count all of the active third-person topic referents.

2.4.2 Determine whether this statement is a testable hypothesis

Unfortunately, identifying sentence topics is tricky and subjective, and therefore may not be testable with the currently available techniques. As Lambrecht (1994) points out, however, the more accessible a referent is the more likely it is to be referred to with an unaccented pronominal. The frequency of pronouns is thus an approximation to the frequency of active referents.

2.4.3 Determine the envelope of variation for this feature

In terms of choices, we can say that in narration people tend to *choose* to discuss third person topics rather than first or second person topics. If we allow the frequency of pronouns to substitute for the frequency of active topics, we can say that the envelope of variation is all personal pronouns.

2.4.4 Construct an algorithm to measure this feature

While investigating these variables it became clear that the algorithms that Biber used in his 1988 study did not themselves reflect the hypothesis underlying his choice. Because of this, the algorithm used for both the "classic multidimensional" and "corrected multidimensional" methods use different algorithms. In the case of third person pronouns, Biber's original algorithm counted all instances of *she, he, they, her, him, them, his, their, himself, herself,* and *themselves*. The inclusion of *his* and *their* is highly questionable, since they are not strictly pronouns but possessive adjectives, but it can be argued that what is important is the number of third person referents that are referred to with pronouns. On the other hand, Biber leaves out the possessive pronouns *hers* and *theirs*, with no justification. In my replication of Biber's counts, I will provide two figures, "Biber's algorithm replicated" including *his* and *their*, and "corrected algorithm" removing them as well as all of the instances where *her* was used as a possessive adjective.

This "all pronouns" envelope of variation included numerous generic uses of "you," including in the fixed expressions "you know," "you see" and "if you will." In these cases there is clearly no choice between using "you" or a third person pronoun, so in the final count they were removed from the envelope of variation.

2.5 Modification of the feature *demonstrative adjectives* according to the proposed methodology

Here I will apply the steps described in section 1.5 to the feature *demonstrative adjectives* to yield a measure that I hope will reflect the choices of the language users independent of grammar.

2.5.1 Determine the statement about register or genre variation that underlies the selection of this feature

Biber repeats Ochs' (1979) conclusion that *demonstratives are preferred to definite articles in unplanned discourse.* In terms of choices, we recast Biber's statement to say that in planned discourse people choose to use definite articles, but in unplanned discourse they choose demonstratives under some circumstances.

2.5.2 Determine whether this statement is a testable hypothesis

This is a testable hypothesis.

2.5.3 Determine the envelope of variation for this feature

Following Prince (1991) and Wald (1983), as summarized by Lambrecht (1994), I will modify Biber's statement to *Demonstratives are used instead of indefinite articles in unplanned discourse.* It is possible to go even further and say *Demonstratives are used instead of indefinite articles to introduce a new referent in unplanned discourse.*

2.5.4 Construct an algorithm to measure this feature

As with the variable of *third-person pronouns*, it was necessary to make a modification to Biber's algorithm for *demonstrative adjectives*. *That* and *those* cannot be used to introduce a new referent as "indefinite *this,*" as described by Lambrecht. As with the third-person pronouns, I will give two counts, one using Biber's original algorithm including *that, this, these* and *those*, and a "corrected" count including only *this* and *these*. Indefinite articles were used as the envelope of variation, including *a, an* and *some* when it modifies a plural noun, for the reasons described in section 2.2.

The proper way to count this variable is to restrict it to instances where a new referent is being introduced to the discourse. As with active topics in section 2.4.2, there is no straightforward way to separate these algorithmically, and the process of separating them by hand is subjective and time-consuming. Additionally, the lectures contain several instances where the speaker uses demonstrative adjectives to refer to objects in slides and other visual aids, and it is not always possible to determine when this is the case. The implications of this decision will be discussed in Section 4.

2.6 Implementation of the algorithms

These algorithms were tagged using Perl 5 regular expression substitution. Where hand-tagging was necessary, it was done with the Emacs text editor. The tags were then counted with Perl 5 regular expressions.

3. Results

The results of this pilot study support the corrected method of returning to the source studies and creating a testable hypothesis based on the findings of the original studies. Unfortunately, there was only indirect support for the value of an envelope of variation, because some of these testable hypotheses are incompatible with factor analysis if they are measured as per-word frequency counts.

Recall that in his study of a corpus with 481 texts, Biber found a statistically significant negative correlation between third-person pronouns and demonstrative adjectives. In the current study, using Biber's original algorithms I also found a correlation that was statistically significant. However, using Biber's algorithms corrected as described in sections 2.4.4 and 2.5.4, the correlation for these two factors was larger in absolute value, but not statistically significant. Using the proposed method where the features are counted relative to an envelope of variation, the r for the two variables was also more extreme, and also not statistically significant. All of the correlations are negative, meaning that the more frequent one feature is in a text, the less frequent the other one is. Here is a table showing the correlations.

Table 1. Correlation values for three counts of the two variables.

Method	Observed correlation (r)	Critical $\lvert r\rvert$
Biber (1988)	*-0.282*	0.115 ($n = 481$, $\alpha = 0.02$)
Biber's algorithm replicated	*-0.685*	0.658 ($n = 12$, $\alpha = 0.02$)
Corrected algorithm	-0.505	0.658 ($n = 12$, $\alpha = 0.02$)
Corrected with envelope of variation	-0.511	0.658 ($n = 12$, $\alpha = 0.02$)

The following three charts show the relationships between the variables for each of the twelve texts. There is one chart per method, and for each chart, the striped bar represents the frequency of third-person pronouns, and the dotted bar represents the frequency of demonstrative adjectives, as calculated by that method.

The strength of the correlation is visible in each chart. The texts are ordered by frequency of third-person pronouns, so you can see that the striped bars get taller as you look to the right. Note that for the first chart representing the replication of Biber's original algorithms, where the correlation is -0.685, the dotted bars get gradually smaller as you look to the right, with the exception of a few texts. By contrast, for the second and third charts, there are some tall bars on the left and some short bars on the right, but the progression is not as clear-cut as in Figure 1.

I have also provided detailed information in the Appendix, including information about the texts, the raw data and frequency counts.

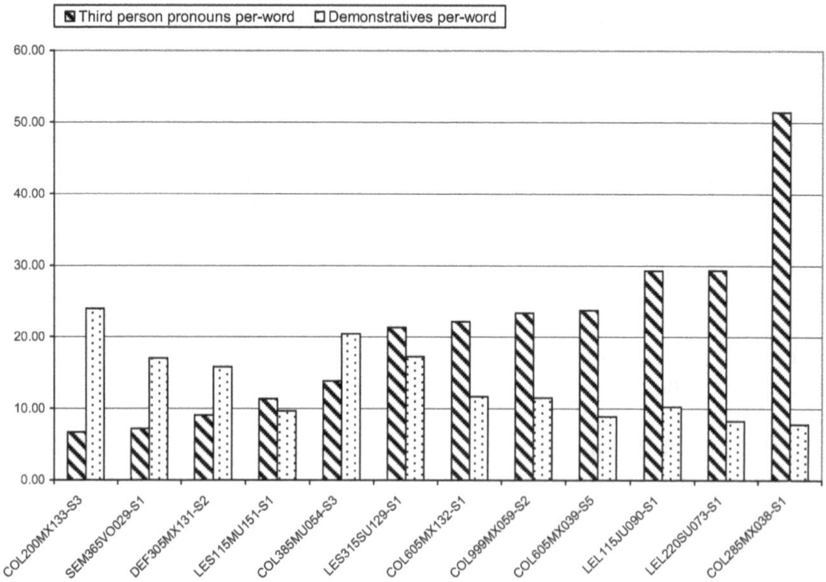

Figure 1. Frequency per thousand words using Biber's algorithm (r = -0.685, critical $|r|$ = 0.658 for α = 0.02, n = 12)

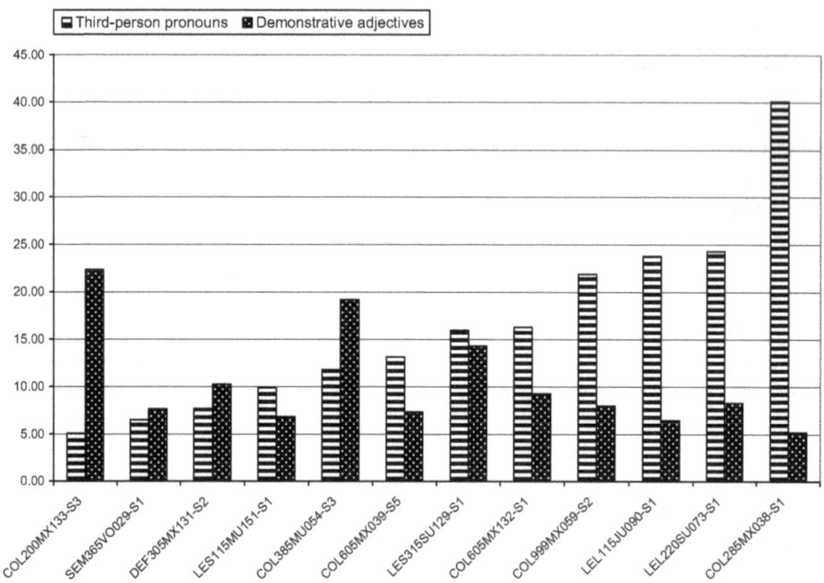

Figure 2. Frequency per thousand words using corrected algorithm (r = -0.505, critical $|r|$ = 0.658 for α = 0.02, n = 12)

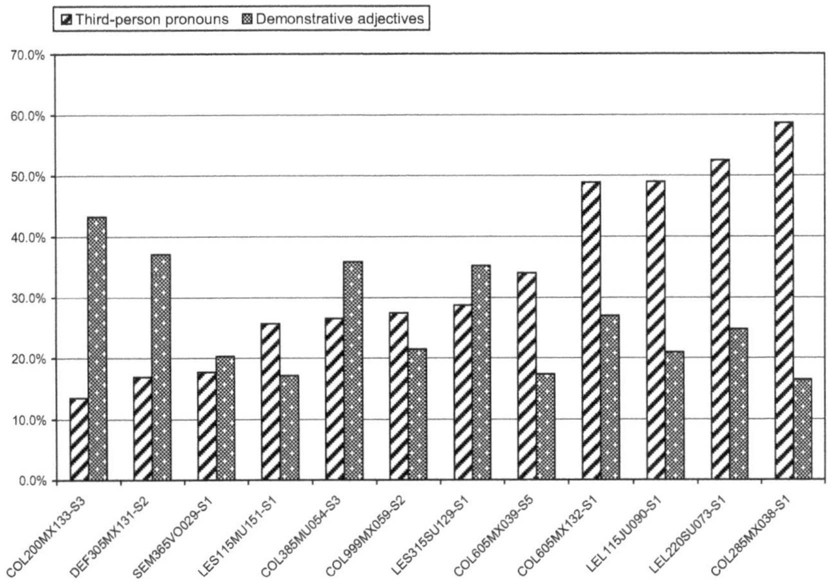

Figure 3. Frequency per choice (r = -0.511, critical $|r|$ = 0.658 for α = 0.02, n = 12)

4. Discussion

This study clearly shows the importance of having strong hypotheses based firmly in the literature about variation for each feature. There was significant but unexpected correlation between these two features that was reduced below the level of statistical significance through careful application of this principle. However, the correlation between the corrected counts is still high, in fact higher than the correlation reported by Biber, and with a larger corpus it might be statistically significant..

More importantly, the primary goal was to test a proposed improvement to the multidimensional approach, using the variationist principle of the envelope of variation. It is naturally disappointing that this test failed to show a significant improvement. One possible explanation is that the new method failed to eliminate grammatical covariation, but there is no other reason to suspect this, and there are several other potential reasons why the test failed.

The most obvious reason is that the sample is too small. In order to achieve statistical significance for Biber's original correlation of -0.282, the corpus would need at least seventy texts. For this study it was necessary to use hand reading to disambiguate the following items:

pronominal and adjectival senses of *her*
generic and specific uses of *you*
idiomatic and non-idiomatic uses of *you know, you see* and *if you will*
pronominal and adjectival uses of *this* and *these*
indefinite and quantifying uses of *some*

In addition, as mentioned in sections 2.4.4 and 2.5.4, it would have been closer to the original predictions to count all instances of third-person active topic referents and indefinite *this/these*, but this was not attempted because tagging these would have been much too time-consuming even for the twelve texts in the corpus. To work with a larger corpus, it would be necessary to find automatic ways of counting all of these features. Working with a corpus that had previously been reliably tagged for part of speech, and perhaps even parsed, might help.

It is also possible that the original predictions referenced by Biber may not have been accurate. Some of them were based on corpus analysis, but the corpora studied may not have been close enough to this corpus to show the same effect. Others were not based on corpus data at all, but on intuitive observations that may not be widely applicable.

Finally, the choice of variables may not have succeeded in eliminating covariation due to situational factors. As quoted in section 2.2, Biber points to Kurzon (1985) as showing that demonstrative adjectives are used for text-internal deixis, in phrases such as "in this section." In fact, Kurzon observes that text deixis is less common in narrative genres than in all the other genres he studied. Since we are taking third-person pronouns to be a marker of narrative, we would expect them to be negatively correlated with demonstrative adjectives. However, the demonstratives used for text deixis are not the same as the ones used for "indefinite *this*," and if we can succeed in isolating indefinite *this/these*, we can control for this problem.

5. Conclusion

The clearest theme that emerges from this study is the complexity of each of the various features used in Biber's study. In preparing this study it was not enough to draw on the information about pronouns, anaphora, information structure and demonstratives. To properly measure these features, it seems that it is necessary to be an expert in each of the relevant areas, or at least to have access to an expert consultant for each area. A complete study of situational variation would require a research paper's worth of work on each feature, its envelope of variation, the reason it has been predicted to vary according to situation, and what variation is observed in the chosen corpus, all from a consistent framework reflecting the most up-to-date understanding of that feature. Only then could those features be combined in a multidimensional analysis.

References

Ball, C. N. (1994). 'Automated text analysis: Cautionary tales', *Literary and Linguistic Computing*, 9: 295-302.

Besnier, N. (1988), 'The linguistic relationships of spoken and written Nukulaelae registers', *Language* 64: 707-36.

Biber, D. (1986), 'Spoken and written textual dimensions in English: Resolving the contradictory findings', *Language* 62: 384-414.

Biber, D. (1988), *Variation across speech and writing*. Cambridge: Cambridge University Press.

Biber, D. (1989). 'A typology of English texts', *Linguistics,* 27: 3-43.

Biber, D., and M. Hared. (1994), 'Linguistic correlates of the transition to literacy in Somali: Language adaptation in six press registers', in: D. Biber and E. Finegan (eds.) *Sociolinguistic perspectives on register.* New York: Oxford University Press. 294-314.

Biber, D., S. Conrad and R. Reppen. (1998), *Corpus linguistics: Investigating language style and use*. Cambridge: Cambridge University Press.

Biber, D., S. Johansson, G. Leech, S. Conrad and E. Finegan. (1999), *The Longman grammar of spoken and written English*. Harlow: Longman.

Bybee, J., and J. Scheibman. (1999), 'The effect of usage on degrees of constituency: The reduction of don't in English', *Linguistics,* 37: 575-596.

Ferguson, C. (1959), 'Diglossia', in: A. S. Dil (ed.) *Language structure and language use: Essays by Charles A. Ferguson*. Stanford: Stanford University Press. 1-26.

Fitzgerald, S. F. (1926) *The Great Gatsby*. Hammondsworth: Penguin.

Gorsuch, R. L. (1983), *Factor analysis*. Hillsdale, NJ: Lawrence Erlbaum.

Halliday, M. A. K., and R. Hasan. (1976), *Cohesion in English*. New York: Longman.

Herring, S. C., P. van Reenen, and L. Schøsler. (1997), 'On textual parameters and older languages', in: S. C. Herring, P. van Reenen and L. Schøsler (eds.) *Textual parameters in older languages*. Amsterdam: John Benjamins. 1-32.

Hu, Z. L. (1984), 'Differences in mode', *Journal of Pragmatics,* 8: 595-606.

Hudson, A. (1994), 'Diglossia as a special case of register variation', in: D. Biber and E. Finegan (eds.) *Sociolinguistic perspectives on register.* New York: Oxford University Press. 294-314.

Johansson, S., G. Leech and H. Goodluck. (1978), *Manual of information to accompany the Lancaster-Oslo/Bergen Corpus of British English, for use with digital computers*. Oslo: University of Oslo Department of English.

Joseph, J. E. (1987), *Eloquence and power: The rise of language standards and standard languages.* New York: Basil Blackwell.

Kim, Y.-J., and D. Biber. (1994), 'A corpus-based analysis of register variation in Korean', in: D. Biber and E. Finegan (eds.) *Sociolinguistic perspectives on register.* New York: Oxford University Press. 294-314.

Kurzon, D. (1985), 'Signposts for the reader: A corpus-based study of text deixis'. Text 5: 187-200.

Labov, W. (1972), *Sociolinguistic patterns*. Oxford: Basil Blackwell.

Labov, W. (forthcoming), 'Quantitative reasoning in linguistics'. http://www.ling.upenn.edu/~wlabov/Papers/QRL.pdf

Lambrecht, K. (1994), *Information structure and sentence form: Topic, focus, and the mental representations of discourse*. Cambridge: Cambridge University Press.

Lee, D. Y. W. (forthcoming), *Modelling variation in spoken and written English*. Oxford: Routledge.

Ochs, E. (1979), 'Planned and unplanned discourse', in: Givón, T. (ed.) *Syntax and Semantics 12: Discourse and syntax*. New York: Academic Press. 51-80.

Poole, M. E., and T. W. Field. (1976), 'A comparison of oral and written code elaboration', *Language and Speech,* 19: 305-311.

Prince, E. (1981), 'On the inferencing of indefinite-*this* NPs', in: A. K. Joshi , B. Webber & I. Sag (eds.) *Elements of discourse understanding*. Cambridge: Cambridge University Press. 231-250.

Scheibman, J. (2000), 'I dunno: A usage-based account of the phonological reduction of don't in American English conversation', *Journal of Pragmatics,* 32: 105-124.

Scheibman, J. (2001), 'Local patterns of subjectivity in person and verb type in American English conversation', in J. Bybee and P. J. Hopper (eds.), *Frequency and the emergence of linguistic structure*. Philadelphia: John Benjamins. 61-89

Simpson, R. C., S. L. Briggs, J. Ovens, and J. M. Swales. (2000), *The Michigan Corpus of Academic Spoken English*. Ann Arbor, MI: The Regents of the University of Michigan.

Svartvik, J. and R. Quirk (eds.) (1980). *A corpus of English conversation*. Lund: CWK Gleerup.

Thompson, S. A., and A. Mulac. (1991a), 'The discourse conditions for the use of the complementizer *that* in conversational English', *Journal of Pragmatics* 15: 237-251.

Thompson, S. A. and A. Mulac. (1991b), 'A quantitive perspective on the grammaticization of epistemic parentheticals in English'. In E. Closs Traugott and B. Heine (eds.), *Approaches to grammaticalization, vol. 1*. Amsterdam: John Benjamins. 313-329.

Wald, B. (1983), 'Referents and topic within and across discourse units: Observations from Current Vernacular English', in: F. Klein-Andreu (ed.) *Discourse Perspectives on Syntax*. New York: Academic Press. 91-116.

Wells, R. (1960), 'Nominal and Verbal Style', in: T. A. Sebeok (ed.) *Style in Language*. Cambridge, MA: MIT Press. 213-220.

Appendix
This appendix contains some of the data used in the pilot study.

Table 1. Basic information about each text used in the test corpus.

Text	Spkr Gender	Lecture Type	Subject Matter	Word count
COL200MX133-S3	M	Colloquium	Chemical Biology	8641
COL285MX038-S1	F	Colloquium	Education	4985
COL385MU054-S3	M	Colloquium	Public Math	6718
COL605MX039-S5	F	Guest Lecture	Women's Studies	5184
COL605MX132-S1	F	Colloquium	Christianity and the Modern Family	10367
COL999MX059-S2	M	Colloquium	Problem Solving	5387
DEF305MX131-S2	F	Defence	Fossil Plants	8993
LEL115JU090-S1	F	Lecture	Intro Anthropology	11018
LEL220SU073-S1	F	Lecture	Intro Communication	5190
LES115MU151-S1	F	Lecture	Archaeology of Modern American Life	9939
LES315SU129-S1	M	Lecture	African History	7772
SEM365VO029-S1	M	Seminar	Professional Mechanical Engineering	12346

Table 2. Raw data from the pilot study.

Text	3rd person pronouns (Original)	3rd person pronouns (Corrected)	Dem adjs (Original)	Dem adjs (Corrected)
COL200MX133-S3	58	44	207	193
COL285MX038-S1	256	200	39	26
COL385MU054-S3	93	79	137	129
COL605MX039-S5	123	68	46	38
COL605MX132-S1	230	169	121	96
COL999MX059-S2	126	118	62	43
DEF305MX131-S2	82	69	142	92
LEL115JU090-S1	322	262	113	71
LEL220SU073-S1	152	126	43	43
LES115MU151-S1	113	98	96	68
LES315SU129-S1	166	124	134	111
SEM365VO029-S1	89	80	210	94

Table 3. Calculating the envelope of variation.

Text	1st pers pros	2nd pers pros	All specific pros	Indefinite articles	Dem adjs & indefinite articles
COL200MX133-S3	237	44	325	253	446
COL285MX038-S1	130	11	341	132	158
COL385MU054-S3	186	33	298	231	360
COL605MX039-S5	112	20	200	181	219
COL605MX132-S1	166	11	346	260	356
COL999MX059-S2	253	59	430	157	200
DEF305MX131-S2	284	54	407	156	248
LEL115JU090-S1	221	52	535	268	339
LEL220SU073-S1	82	32	240	131	174
LES115MU151-S1	176	107	381	329	397
LES315SU129-S1	169	139	432	204	315
SEM365VO029-S1	334	37	451	369	463

Table 4. Calculated frequencies for each feature, according to each method.

Text	3rd pers pros per word	Dem adjs per word	3rd pers pros per envelope	Dem adjs per envelope
COL200MX133-S3	0.00509	0.02234	0.135	0.433
COL285MX038-S1	0.04012	0.00522	0.587	0.165
COL385MU054-S3	0.01176	0.01920	0.265	0.358
COL605MX039-S5	0.01312	0.00733	0.340	0.174
COL605MX132-S1	0.01630	0.00926	0.488	0.270
COL999MX059-S2	0.02190	0.00798	0.274	0.215
DEF305MX131-S2	0.00767	0.01023	0.170	0.371
LEL115JU090-S1	0.02378	0.00644	0.490	0.209
LEL220SU073-S1	0.02428	0.00829	0.525	0.247
LES115MU151-S1	0.00986	0.00684	0.257	0.171
LES315SU129-S1	0.02136	0.01724	0.287	0.352
SEM365VO029-S1	0.00648	0.00761	0.177	0.203

Using Singular-value Decomposition on Local Word Contexts to Derive a Measure of Constructional Similarity

Paul Deane and Derrick Higgins

Educational Testing Service

Abstract

This paper presents a novel method of generating word similarity scores, using a term by n-gram context matrix which is compressed using Singular Value Decomposition, a statistical data analysis method that extracts the most significant components of variation from a large data matrix, and which has previously been used in methods like Latent Semantic Analysis to identify latent semantic variables in text. We present the results of applying these scores to standard synonym benchmark tests, and argue on the basis of these results that our similarity metric represents an aspect of word usage which is largely orthogonal to that addressed by other methods, such as Latent Semantic Analysis. In particular, it appears that this method captures similarity with respect to the participation of words in grammatical constructions, at a level of generalization corresponding to broad syntacticosemantic classes such as body part terms, kin terms and the like. Aside from assessing word similarity, this method has promising applications in language modeling and automatic lexical acquisition.

1. Overview

A number of tasks in computational linguistics involve assessing the similarity of words, according to their syntactic or semantic properties. This list includes:

- word clustering for use as conditioning events in tasks like language modeling
- automatic acquisition of new lexical entries
- numerous information retrieval applications
- automated scoring of free-response test items

In this paper, we describe a new method for calculating word similarity based on a very simple sort of information: the local n-gram contexts in which a word is found. In principle, there is a difference between assessing the degree to which words share the same syntactic behavior, and assessing the similarity in their meaning, but the work of Dekang Lin (Lin, 1998; Pantel and Lin, 2002), among others, has shown that distributional similarity is a good cue to semantic relatedness. Since we do not use a parser, we do not have direct access to the selectional preferences on which Lin's similarity scores are based. As we shall discuss below, however, local context can be very informative about the grammatical *constructions* (Goldberg, 1995; Fillmore et al., 1988) in which words are used. This semantic similarity metric, which we refer to as SVD on Contexts, offers promise in the applications described above, because it not only allows an assessment of the similarity of word pairs, but also the appropriateness of a word in a given context. Critically the SVD on Contexts method makes use of an association strength statistic, the Rank Ratio statistic, which identifies those n-gram contexts that appear more frequently with any particular word than one would expect for any word taken at random (cf. Deane 2005 for an application of the rank ratio statistic to the problem of identifying idioms and collocations).

In the present paper we focus on describing the method, offering impressionistic results based on the word similarity rankings, and evaluating quantitative results on various synonym test sets employed elsewhere in the literature. We employ standard natural language processing techniques for evaluating the relative effectiveness of alternative methods. In such methods, a statistical algorithm is trained (or attuned to the data) using a corpus, often quite large. A smaller test set of texts are reserved or some other source of data (in our case, tests of synonym knowledge originally designed for humans) is provided, and a standard of performance is set. The effectiveness of alternative methods can then be assessed by examining precision (the percent of items correctly identified) and recall (the percent of the total number of correct items that were actually identified by the method).

While the synonym test results of SVD on Contexts lag behind those of the highest-scoring method, this is at least in part due to the specific properties of words chosen as distractors in the tests. Furthermore, analysis suggests that the dimension of word similarity which it captures is largely orthogonal to that captured by other methods. In particular, the method appears to provide useful information about constructional patterning, e.g., the extent to which words belong to classes that fill particular slots in grammatical constructions. This method of analysis has certain advantages for particular applications, such as finding appropriate words for Cloze-like verbal assessment tasks where test-takers are expected to judge how well words fit into particular blanks in a sentential context.

2. Previous work

A number of authors have produced semantic similarity measures for words which can be trained on language corpora. A detailed comparison of these, as well as semantic similarity measures based on resources such as WordNet and *Roget's Thesaurus* can be found in (Jarmasz and Szpakowicz, 2003). As mentioned above, Dekang Lin has addressed the issue of scoring the similarity of word pairs based on their distributions. Lin (1998) applies a parser to the training corpus to extract triples consisting of two words and the grammatical function by which they are linked, and then constructs an information-theoretic measure on the basis of these triples, which serves as a word similarity score. Since grammatical functions (such as *subject-verb* and *verb-object*) are the basic datum of this method, these scores are based in large part on the selectional properties of verbs.

A number of other approaches to word similarity are based on the idea of situating each word in a high-dimensional vector space, so that the similarity between words can be measured as the cosine of the angle between their vectors (or a similar metric). Latent Semantic Analysis (LSA) (Landauer and Dumais, 1997) is the most widely cited of these vector-space methods. It involves first constructing a term-by-document matrix based on a training collection, in which each cell of the matrix indicates the number of times a given term occurs in a given document (modulo the term weighting scheme). Given the expectation that similar terms will tend to occur in the same documents, similar terms ought to have similar term vectors in this scheme. Singular Value Decomposition (SVD) is then applied to this matrix, a dimensionality reduction technique which blurs the distinctions between similar terms and improves generalization. Typically, around 300 factors are retained. See Section 3 below for more details on SVD.

Schütze (1992) and Lund & Burgess (1996) have also produced vector-based methods of assessing word similarity. The primary differences between these methods and LSA are, first, that they use a sliding text window to calculate co-occurrence, rather than requiring that the text be pre-segmented into documents, and second, that they construct a term-by-term matrix instead of a term-by document matrix. In this term-by-term-matrix, each cell represents the co-occurrence of a term with another term within the text window, rather than the occurrence of a term within a document. The methods remain very similar to LSA, however; in each case, a vector is constructed to represent the meaning of a word based on the content words it occurs with, and the similarity between words is calculated as the cosine between the term vectors.

Another vector-based word similarity metric is produced by Random Indexing (Kanerva et al., 2000; Sahlgren, 2001). Sahlgren's application of this method involves first assigning a *label vector* to each word in the vocabulary, an 1800- row sparse vector in which the individual rows are meaningless, and words are distinguished by randomly assigned vectors in which a small number of elements have been randomly set to 1 or -1. The *index vector* for each word is then derived as the sum of the label vectors of all words occurring within a certain distance of the target word in the training corpus (weighted according to their distance from the target word). Sahlgren uses a window size of 2-4 words on each side of the target word. This is similar to the other vector-based approaches mentioned here, but it is more scalable because it does not require a computationally intensive matrix reduction step like SVD. Also, Sahlgren reports slightly better results than LSA on the 80-question TOEFL synonym test introduced by Landauer & Dumais (1997).

Finally, Turney's PMI-IR (Turney, 2001) approach to word similarity should be mentioned, since it currently has the best performance (73.75%) on the TOEFL synonym test of any word similarity metric automatically derived from corpus data. PMI-IR is based upon a slightly different set of assumptions than the other word similarity metrics mentioned here; rather than assuming that similar words will have similar distributional properties (i.e., they will occur around the same other words), PMI-IR assumes that similar words will occur near *each other*. Somewhat surprisingly, this assumption seems to be borne out by the results of the method, which involves using a web search engine to collect statistics on the relative frequency with which words co-occur in a ten-word window. Unfortunately, the use of a search engine makes this metric quite slow to apply, so that it is only feasible at present for very small vocabulary tasks. It should be noted that the PMI-IR has one definite advantage over the other methods studied here (corpus size), and another possible advantage in the nature of the corpus, which makes its performance somewhat incommensurable with the other two methods we examine. The web is by definition a much larger corpus than the Lexile corpus, and performance of almost any cooccurrence-based analysis system is strongly impacted by corpus size: usually, the larger the corpus, the better the performance. In addition, web documents tend to be short and very much focused around single topics, which makes them likely to contain the kind of data needed by the PMI-IR method.

3. Technical description

The method of assessing word similarity introduced here is technically very similar to the other vector-based methods cited above, but it differs from these in two primary respects. Firstly, the data on which our co-occurrence matrix is built involve local n-gram contexts, rather than whole documents or text windows. This means that our similarity scores will be more heavily influenced by words' syntactic parallelism than these other methods. Secondly, we use a different statistic in constructing this matrix (the *log rank ratio*), rather than the co-occurrence count or some weighted form of it. We first construct a *term-by-context* matrix, in which each row corresponds to a word in the vocabulary, and each column to an n-gram context in which these words may be found in the training data. For instance, *"toward __"* might be one of our bigram contexts, and *"we quickly __"* could be a trigram context.

At present we use only bigram and trigram word contexts in our matrix, but in principle we could use longer contexts as well, or higher-level linguistic contexts such as parse tree fragments. For the experiments described here, the data for this matrix was derived from the Lexile corpus, which comprises about 400 million words of general fiction from a variety of reading levels. Of course, for this matrix to be manageable, we cannot include every word and context which occurs in such a large corpus. In practice, we have limited the vocabulary to the 20,000 most frequent words in the corpus, a set that included all words that appeared more than 100 times in the corpus, and included only those contexts for which a word in the corpus has a log rank ratio (see below) exceeding a threshold value. Contexts are also required to occur with at least three different words in the vocabulary. In the matrix cell corresponding to a given word–context pair, we record the log rank ratio value for the pair. To calculate this statistic, we must first define a few lower-order statistics:

- The context set X_w for a word w is the set of all bigram and trigram contexts in which the word occurs in the corpus.
- For a context *c*, the global count *Countg(c)* of the context is the number of times the context occurs in the corpus.
- For a context *c* and word *w*, the local count *Countl(c;w)* of the context is the number of times the word appears in the context in the corpus.
- The global rank *Rankg(c;w)* of a context *c* with respect to a word *w* is determined by sorting the contexts in the word's context set by their global count, from highest to lowest, assigning the average rank in case of ties.
- The local rank *Rankl(c;w)* of a context *c* with respect to a word *w* is determined by sorting the contexts in the word's context set by their local count, *Countl(c;w)*, from highest to lowest, assigning the average rank in case of ties.
- The rank ratio of a context–word pair *RR(c;w)* is defined as *Rankg(c;w)/Rankl(c;w)*. In fact, we use the log of this value, so that positive values indicate contexts which are typical for a word, and negative values contexts which are atypical.

While we could as well use the simple count *Countl(c;w)* of context–word pairs in constructing the matrix, exploratory analyses indicated that the log rank ratio value was more effective in discounting high-frequency contexts. For instance, a high-frequency context like "of the __" appears with very many words, and provides very little information that can discriminate one word from another (or at least, one noun from another) whereas a lower-frequency context that appears frequently with a few words, such as "sheer __" provides much more information that can discriminate those words from the rest of the vocabulary. We also experimented with inversely weighting *Countl(c;w)* by the number of word types appearing with the context c, or by the number of contexts appearing with the word w, but again, using the log rank ratio seemed to provide a better measure of word similarity

Each row of the matrix thus constructed could be taken as a vector representation of the corresponding word, and we could calculate the similarity between words as the cosine of the angle between their vectors. In practice, however, this measure of similarity is complicated by the fact that these vectors would be quite long (as there are about 250,000 distinct contexts represented in the matrix), and there is necessarily some noise in their composition, since the corpus does not provide a perfect reflection of the distributional properties of the words which occur within it. To reduce the noise in these representations, we apply Singular Value Decomposition (SVD) to our input matrix, a kind of dimensionality reduction also used in Latent Semantic Analysis. We used the **SVDPACKC** (Berry et al., 1993) software package to extract the 100 most significant factors from the matrix; while using a larger number of factors could potentially produce better representations, computational constraints presently prescribe an upper limit of 100 or so factors on this task. Singular Value Decomposition of the term-by-context matrix M produces three matrices T, S, and C. S is a diagonal matrix containing the top 100 singular values of M, and T and C allow term and context vectors respectively, to be mapped into the reduced space. The product T X S X C of these three matrices approximates the original matrix M. Now, in order to find the similarity between any two words, instead of calculating the cosine of the angle between row vectors from M, we first map these vectors into the 100-dimensional factor space, and calculate the cosine similarity metric on these reduced vectors.

4. Analysis and Evaluation

Impressionistically, using this method to measure similarity between words produces useful results. Figure 1 lists the most similar words to *house*, first using vectors from the full term-by-context matrix M, and then using the SVD reduction of that space. The similarity ranking induced by using the full matrix M is fairly good, including mainly words referring to enclosed spaces typically occupied by people. The similarity scores produced by the reduced vectors look somewhat clearer, though. Comparing the rankings, we see that the second

Full Matrix	**SVD on Contexts**
house 1	house 1
cabin 0.202	cabin 0.903
backyard 0.178	barn 0.862
farmhouse 0.177	cottage 0.862
campsite 0.174	inn 0.853
classroom 0.170	hut 0.847
cottage 0.168	store 0.844
apartment 0.168	lodge 0.840
building 0.167	restaurant 0.839
schoolhouse 0.166	shack 0.830
bungalow 0.166	office 0.829
neighborhood 0.162	tent 0.823
hut 0.156	room 0.823
barn 0.154	kitchen 0.821
igloo 0.140	shed 0.814
mansion 0.139	parlor 0.813
mailbox 0.138	farmhouse 0.807
courtroom 0.133	building 0.803
warehouse 0.133	hotel 0.801
bunkhouse 0.130	schoolhouse 0.796

Figure 1: Words most similar to *house*, in the full matrix and the reduced space obtained by SVD[1]

column lacks the words *classroom, backyard, campsite,* and *neighborhood* from the first column, which do not refer to buildings, and also the inappropriate *mailbox*. Considering the simplicity of the information which we use to construct this similarity measure (local n-gram contexts), and the fact that this information is largely syntactic, it is significant that we are able to extract information about semantic fields in this way.

There are two reasons why data reductions such as SVD are employed in a context like this. The first is simple practicality: manipulating vectors with a few hundred dimensions requires much less space and is computationally much more efficient than using the entire raw data matrix. The second, and more important reason, is that the data reduction step also creates generalizations over classes that are not explicitly present in the original matrix. That is, the data reduction step creates (in effect) the presumption that words that behave similarly in general will behave similarly even in cases where the (relatively sparse) original data matrix does not tell us there is similar behaviour. It is this cleaning-up effect that accounts for the fact that there are usually improvements in data representation for the reduced matrix in an appropriately constructed SVD analysis.

4.1 Comparing local context information to a more topic-based word similarity model

As noted, this metric is based on local syntactic information, and so its predictions regarding word similarity are heavily based on parallelism of local syntactic co-occurrence patterns. Note that since we are not stemming the input data as a pre-processing step, inflected forms may not always be given high similarity scores with their uninflected (or differently inflected) relations, if they differ significantly in certain ways. For example, "houses" does not appear near the top of the list in Figure 1, in part due to the systematic difference in verbal inflection following them. (While *house* may be highly associated with the context "__ *stands*", *houses* will instead have a high association with "__ *stand*".) Our decision not to stem the data reflects a desire to capture generalizations at a syntacticosemantic rather than a purely semantic level; if a particular inflected form is the correct one in a particular context, we desired to retain this information, since the ultimate application – judging which words are appropriate in a particular syntactic, Cloze-like context – is sensitive to morphosyntactic form.

Given the reliance of our method on syntactic information, it is worth comparing its behavior to alternate methods whose data is more topic-oriented, such as LSA or Random Indexing. These methods use co-occurrence of content words within documents or context windows as the basis for word similarity judgements. That is, they count content words (not common function words, which are placed on a stop list) and keep track of how many times content words appear within a given distance, whether that distance is 2 words or 100 words, without taking word order into account. They therefore tend to produce similarity rankings more influenced by the relatedness of the words to certain topics, rather than their suitability in a given syntactic frame. By contrast, the n-gram contexts used in SVD on Contexts are actual word sequences, and the same words used in a different sequence count as a different context. In Figure 2, we illustrate this difference between our method (SVD on Contexts) and Random Indexing, one of the more topic-based similarity scores.[2] In column 1, we present the words most similar to *bottle*, using our own implementation of Random Indexing according to Sahlgren (2001), with a context window of 3 words on each side of the target word, and 1800-length index vectors, and trained on around 30 million words of newswire text. Predictably, the words judged similar to *bottle* by this Random Indexing metric have a largely topical connection, relating loosely to drinking events or activities in which bottles are likely to play a part. The second column shows the words judged most similar to *bottle* by our SVD on Contexts method. This list is comprised of words for various types of containers, which is most likely the result of a few n-gram contexts which show up as highly significant for this class, such as *"a __ of"*. This list of words does not show a bias toward containers typically used for fluids. In column 3 of Figure 2, we present a simplistic method of combining these two word similarity measures, by simply summing the cosine scores assigned by each method.

Random Indexing	**SVD on Contexts**	**Combined Metric**
bottle 1	bottle 1	bottle 2
bottles 0.646	sack 0.940	jug 1.38
quart 0.542	box 0.903	bucket 1.23
tap 0.511	package 0.903	jar 1.21
jug 0.506	bucket 0.897	bag 1.14
drinking 0.492	basket 0.882	container 1.09
drink 0.488	jug 0.878	bottles 1.05
glasses 0.487	jar 0.870	carton 1.02
sparkling 0.482	bag 0.864	pail 1.01
pipes 0.475	bowl 0.855	pot 1.01
coolers 0.475	tray 0.852	tray 1.00
beer 0.468	cup 0.848	box 0.998
fresh 0.465	mug 0.843	glass 0.990
cannons 0.465	carton 0.837	basket 0.989
imported 0.464	pan 0.819	package 0.980

Figure 2: Words most similar to *bottle*, using three different word similarity metrics methods.

Even though this is a purely heuristic method of aggregation, the similarity ranking seems to be more heavily skewed than either of the others toward those words that we might intuitively see as most similar to *bottle*: nouns referring to containers used primarily for fluids.

Note that, in constructing a word-similarity metric, a minimum requirement is that near-synonyms or *plesionyms* (Edmonds and Hirst, 2002) should receive high similarity scores. Using this requirement as a basis for evaluation, a number of authors have evaluated their systems on synonym tests such as the 80-question TOEFL test used by Landauer & Dumais (1997). Jarmasz & Szpakowicz (2003) present results for various word similarity measures on the TOEFL synonym test, as well as two other tests, the 50-question ESL synonym test used by Turney (2001), and a larger set of synonym items from the *Reader's Digest* Word Power (RDWP) feature. On each of these tests, the test taker is presented with a target word followed by four options, and is instructed to choose the word which is most nearly synonymous with the target. (In the case of the 50 ESL items, there is also a sentence frame which the student may use to disambiguate the target word, in case it has multiple senses, but this test is not usable in evaluation of LSA-like spaces where multiple word senses are not represented.) The contrast in behavior between Random Indexing and SVD on Contexts suggests that the two metrics could fail to rank plesionyms highly for entirely opposite reasons: while SVD on Contexts could fail by giving too high a weight to non-synonyms from the same semantic field, Random Indexing could fail by giving too high a weight to topically related words which could not be substituted for the synonym in context. Note that on the synonym tests, this last possibility is not typically tested, as the test-taker is asked to select among words which can in fact be used in the sentential context; thus we expect that SVD on Contexts will probably not perform as well as topic-based methods where the task requires discriminating among synonyms, but that it is likely to perform better where the task requires identification of words which fit well in the same constructional contexts.

4.2 Extensibility: Inferring Vectors from Contexts

The initial vector space constructed using SVD on Contexts contains the 20,000 most frequent words in the Lexile corpus, which excludes many of the words that appear on the TOEFL synonym test and many of the other synonymy test sets. However, one of the key features of SVD on Contexts is that it establishes a direct link between words and contexts: both words and contexts are assigned vectors using the same basis, such that words which appear in a context tend to have high cosine values combined with that context. It is thus possible to infer vectors for words which did not take part in the original analysis by calculating a weighted combination of vectors for contexts with which the word is strongly associated.

In the simplest possible method for inferring vectors for words from context vectors, each word would be assigned a vector based upon the sum of the vectors for the contexts in which it appeared. However, better results were obtained by taking a weighted sum where each context vector was multiplied by the rank ratio for its association with the target word. Applying this method, a larger set of word vectors was obtained, yielding an extended vocabulary of

78,800 words, which covered all words appearing more than 40 times in the Lexile corpus.

This extensibility -- the potential to infer vectors for new vocabulary based upon its appearance in contexts which formed part of the original SVD analysis -- is one of the major potential advantages of the method. The usefulness of such inferred vectors was evaluated by randomly selecting words at progressively decreasing frequencies and manually scoring whether highly correlated words (more than 0.55 cosine) in fact belonged to the same part of speech and the same narrow syntacticosemantic classes. The results were fairly stable for words that appeared more than 100 times in the Lexile corpus, and deteriorated rapidly below that point, though useful result sets continued to appear even with words that appeared as little as 40 times. The limiting factor appeared to be whether the most informative contexts associated with a word in fact had participated in the original singular value decomposition. Where they had not, less informative contexts dominated the inferred vectors, yielding less useful results.

4.3 Performance on Synonym Tests

In evaluating metrics of word similarity with respect to these tests, we choose the option which has the highest similarity with the target word. If this option is the key (the answer considered correct by the examiner), then full credit is given. If two or more options are tied for the highest similarity score with the target, partial credit is given. In presenting the results below, we also include a baseline model which simply randomly guesses at each item; clearly it would achieve 25% accuracy.

On the TOEFL, ESL, and RDWP test sets, Turney's (2001) PMI-IR method has produced the best results of any system which does not make use of a thesaurus or other manually-created resource. Table 1 shows that our SVD on Contexts metric fares about the same as Random Indexing but significantly worse than PMI-IR on all three test sets.

In Table 1, the results reported are for our reimplementation of Random Indexing and PMI-IR, and differ slightly from those reported by Sahlgren (2001) and Turney (2001), respectively. Our Random Indexing implementation follows Sahlgren, using vectors of length 1800, and a context window of 3 words on either side of the target word, but we use a different training corpus, consisting of 30 million words of *San Jose Mercury-News* text. Our implementation of PMI-IR follows Turney's exactly, and the small performance gain we report can only be attributed to changes in the web content indexed by AltaVista. We report this new set of results for ease of comparison with the performance achieved by combining all three methods. Also note that the results for Random Indexing are averaged over five training runs, because of the stochastic nature of the algorithm.

In part, the generally lower performance of our SVD on Contexts model may be due to the design of the synonym tests; our metric is designed to identify words which occur in the same characteristic set of linguistic constructions, which includes among other things grouping words according to part of speech.

Since synonym test items almost never include options which belong to a different part of speech, our metric does not get any credit for making this distinction. This fact also helps the scores of more topic-based word similarity metrics such as LSA and Random Indexing. Since a test item will never ask whether *horse* and *canter* are synonyms, these methods are not handicapped by assigning a high similarity score to such a word pair.

Part of the difference can also be ascribed to the fact that PMI-IR gathers its statistics from the entire world-wide web, a much larger corpus than that available to the other two models. This advantage is also a hindrance for practical applications, though; the use of web search in PMI-IR makes it too slow for most uses.[3]

Table 1: Comparison of word similarity results across three synonym tests

	TOEFL	**RDWP**	**ESL**	**Overall**
Baseline	20/80 (25%)	75/300 (25%)	12.5/50 (25%)	107.5/430 (25%)
SVD onContexts	58/80 (73%)	107/300 (35.7%)	17/50 (34%)	172.25/430 (40.1%)
Random Indexing	54/80 (67.5%)	109.2/300 (36.4%)	19.6/50 (39.2%)	182.8/430 (42.5%)
PMI-IR	64.25/80 (80.0%)	216.83/300 (72.3%)	33/50 (66.0%)	314.08/430 (73.0%)

The SVD on Contexts metric was run under two conditions involving slightly different weighting schemes for inferring vectors for words not part of the original 20,000 word vocabulary derived by SVD. When vectors for contexts below a threshold value were excluded, performance was as shown. When all vectors were included in the weighted summation scheme which yielded vectors for words beyond the original set, performance on the TOEFL test set went down to 60%. These results suggest that the methods for combining information from contexts require further examination in order to optimize the results.

Analysis of the items in which SVD on Contexts produced higher cosines for an incorrect answer suggests that SVD on Contexts is indeed measuring constructional/grammatical equivalence. A number of incorrect answers involved pairs of words such as *enough/sufficient* or *solitary/alone* where there are major differences in grammatical patterning between synonyms; of the remaining items, the majority involved sets like *tranquility/happiness/peacefulness* or *consumed/supplied/eaten* where the incorrect words (*happiness, supplied*) belong to the same narrow syntacticosemantic classes as the correct choices.

4.4 Beyond word similarity

The SVD on Contexts word-similarity measure seems to produce intuitively reasonable similarity rankings, as exemplified by Figures 1 and 2. The performance of this metric on the synonym test sets, while below the standard of PMI-IR and other methods, is still significantly better than the baseline, and appears to provide preferential access to information about compatibility of words in local syntactic contexts. However, the analysis of word similarity, while one application of SVD on Contexts, does not exploit its full potential.

The performance of SVD on Contexts can be elucidated further by considering the relationship between the n-gram contexts used in this method and full grammatical constructions. Grammatical constructions generally consist both of a syntactic structure, such as the verb–noun phrase–noun phrase pattern of ditransitive sentences ([give]$_{V}$[him]$_{NP}$[the ball]$_{NP}$), and a set of semantic generalizations (e.g., that ditransitive verbs are most typically verbs of giving, with the indirect object being the recipient and the direct object the possession being transferred). These generalizations have salient reflexes in ngram language patterning. For instance, n-gram contexts like *"__ him the"*, *"__ her a"* and the like are direct reflexes of the basic syntactic generalization for the ditransitive construction, and are very strongly associated with verbs of giving. Similar observations can be extended to a wide range of other argument structure constructions, which typically involve both characteristic syntactic patterns and strong semantic selectional constraints on which predicates and arguments can be combined. This correlation yields interesting results when SVD on Contexts is applied, because the method not only induces a similarity metric across words using the term matrix, but also a similarity metric of words to contexts, and of contexts to contexts using the context matrix.

Note first that SVD on Contexts allows the calculation of cosine similarity between words and contexts and between pairs of contexts. In the former case, given a context, such as *"__ of mine"* or *"__ me of"*, we can calculate a strength of association between word and context vectors, as shown in Figures 3 and 4:

confidante	0.88
friend	0.82
partner	0.81
cousin	0.80
girlfriend	0.80
daughter	0.79
son	0.79
nephew	0.78
sidekick	0.77
grandson	0.77
playmate	0.77

Figure 3: Words whose vectors are most similar to the vector for the context *"__ of mine"*

accuses	0.89
apprise	0.88
assures	0.85
deprives	0.85
deprive	0.83
informs	0.83
convinces	0.83
disabuse	0.81
told	0.81
warned	0.78
remind	0.77

Figure 4: Words whose vectors are most similar to the vector for the context "__ *me of*"

It is possible, similarly, to take a context and calculate the most similar contexts using vectors from the context matrix. The rankings which result often group together contexts which indicate the same constructional pattern. For instance, the contexts most similar to "__ *him the*" are presented in Figure 5.

__ her the	0.994	__ me your	0.982
__ me his	0.993	__ us one	0.982
__ them the	0.992	__ her his	0.982
__ him his	0.991	__ you the	0.981
__ me this	0.990	__ them his	0.981
__ her her	0.990	__ us her	0.980
__ him my	0.990	__ them their	0.980
__ him her	0.989	__ them her	0.979
__ me her	0.989	__ you my	0.979
__ us the	0.989	__ us our	0.979
__ her my	0.988	__ me stuff	0.978
__ us his	0.987	__ her anything	0.978
__ me something	0.987	__ us these	0.978
__ us this	0.986	__ you those	0.977
__ myself the	0.985	__ everyone the	0.977
__ me nothing	0.984	__ her something	0.977
__ them something	0.984	__ me all	0.976
__ me the	0.983	__ him something	0.976
__ me these	0.982	__ them what	0.975

Figure 5: Most similar contexts to "__ *him the*"

In this example, the most similar contexts are also instances of the same syntactic structure ("__ + *pronoun* + *pronoun*" *or* "__ + *pronoun* +

determiner", which instantiate a general syntactic context "__ **NP NP"**). There is thus strong reason to believe that the method could be applied to induce generalizations over word sequences rather than word-word similarity alone.

Exploiting the potential of SVD on Contexts to induce context-context similarity and estimates of word-context fit is arguably one of the most fruitful directions for future research with this method, as it would most effectively exploit the relationship between word meanings and constructions that is at the heart of the information provided by local n-gram contexts. However, our results in this area are still largely exploratory.

5. Future directions

We believe that this method of using singular-value decomposition to characterize similarities between words based on the linguistic contexts that are most predictive of them shows promise. At present, however, our implementation could be improved in a number of ways. First, the current implementation of our system extracts only the top 100 singular values from the term-by-context matrix, due to computational limitations. LSA, another application of SVD, has obtained optimal results with the number of factors set around 300 on some tasks, so we hope that in future work we will be able to increase the number of factors used in our SVD on Contexts model. Second, there is nothing necessary about our decision to limit the word contexts considered to local bigram and trigram contexts. We hope that we will be able to improve upon the current model by considering other contexts, such as longer n-gram contexts, and contexts involving richer linguistic structure, such as parse tree fragments. In addition to extending our current SVD on Contexts model, another important area for further research is pursuing possible applications of this method. The most important such area, in our opinion, is in language modeling. While the mathematical details of such an application remain to be worked out, using SVD in the estimation of the probability of a word's occurrence in a language model could help to address smoothing issues, as well as alleviating the necessity of using word clustering to estimate conditional probabilities.

Notes

1 One effect of the data reduction, by reducing the dimensionality of the data and eliminating sparsely populated dimensions from the vector, is to raise the overall cosine similarity of the most highly similar forms; thus the much higher cosines for the top-ranking associates of *house* in Figure 1.

2 Since PMI-IR (Turney, 2001) performs so well on the synonym tests described below, it might seem reasonable to include this model in the comparisons of this section as well. Unfortunately, PMI-IR is much too

slow to use it to calculate a similarity score between all pairs of words in the vocabulary. The fact that PMI-IR is based on time-consuming web queries, and depends on an external data source, makes it impractical for almost any application.

3 One of the significant differences between the TOEFL test and the other two synonym test sets, is that the distractors (alternatives to the correct answer) presented in the TOEFL items appear very often to be attractive in terms of their meaning but not in terms of their syntactic properties. Since both SVD on Contexts and Random Indexing use nearby words (which reflect syntactic similarity as well as semantic similarity) to define their vectors, they are at a disadvantage when all the choices presented belong to the same close syntactic/semantic classes as the correct answer.

6. References

Berry, M., T. Do, G. O'Brien, V. Krishna, and S. Varadhan (1993*), SVDPACKC (version 1.0) user's guide*. University of Tennessee.

Bishop.C. M. (1995), *Neural networks for pattern recognition*. Oxford University Press.

Deane, Paul (2005). A nonparametric method for extraction of candidate phrasal terms. In *43rd Annual Meeting of the Association for Computational Linguistics: Proceedings of the Conference, 25-30 June 2005, University of Michigan*, pp. 605-613.

Edmonds, P. and G. Hirst (2002), 'Nearsynonymy and lexical choice', *Computational Linguistics*, 28(2):105–144.

Fillmore, C. J., P. Kay and M. C. O'Connor (1988), Regularity and idiomaticity in grammatical constructions, *Language*, 64(3):501–538.

Goldberg, A. (1995), *Constructions: A construction grammar approach to argument structure*, Chicago: University of Chicago Press.

Jarmasz, M. and S. Szpakowicz (2003), Roget's thesaurus and semantic similarity, *in* Nicolov, N., K. Botcheva, G. Angelova, and R. Mitkov, R., (eds.) *Recent advances in natural language processing III: Selected papers from RANLP 2003*, Amsterdam: John Benjamins, pp. 111-120.

Kanerva, P., J. Kristoferson, and A. Holst (2000), Random indexing of text samples for latent semantic analysis, *in* L. R. Gleitman and A. K. Josh (eds.), *Proc. 22nd annual conference of the cognitive science society* Mahwah NJ: Lawrence Erlbaum Associates, p. 1036

Landauer, T. K. and S. T. Dumais (1997), A solution to Plato's problem: The latent semantic analysis theory of acquisition, induction, and representation of knowledge, *Psychological Review*, 104(2):211–240.

Lin, D (1998), An information-theoretic definition of similarity, *in* Jude Shavlik (ed.), *Proc. 15th international conference on machine learning*, San Francisco: Morgan Kaufmann, pp. 296–304.

Lund, K. and C. Burgess (1996), Producing high-dimensional semantic spaces from lexical cooccurrence, *Behavioral research methods, instruments and computers*, 28(2):203–208.

Pantel, P. and D. Lin (2002), Document clustering with committees, *in*: *Proceedings of the 25th annual international ACM SIGIR conference on research and development in information retrieval*, New York: ACM Press, pp. 199-206.

Sahlgren, M. (2001), Vector based semantic analysis: Representing word meanings based on random labels, *in* Lenci, A., Montemagni, S. and Pirrelli, V. (eds.) *Proceedings of the ESSLLI 2001 workshop on semantic knowledge acquisition and categorisation.* Helsinki, Finland, http://www.helsinki.fi/esslli/, pp. 27-36.

Schütze, H. (1992), Dimensions of meaning, *in: Proceedings of supercomputing '92,* Los Alamitos: IEEE Computer Science Press, pp. 787–796.

Turney, T. (2001), 'Mining the Web for synonyms: PMI–IR versus LSA on TOEFL', *in* DeRaedt, L. and Flach, P. *Proceedings of the 12th European conference on machine learning*, Berlin: Springer Verlag, pp. 491–450.

Problematic Syntactic Patterns

Sebastian van Delden

University of South Carolina Upstate

Abstract

Several re-occurring problematic syntactic patterns which were encountered during the implementation of a partial parser and natural language information retrieval system are presented in this paper. These patterns cause syntax-based partial parsers, which rely on initial part-of-speech tags, to make errors. We analyze two types of partial parsing errors: 1) errors due to incorrect part-of-speech tags, and 2) errors made even though the parts-of-speech have been identified and present some novel solutions to avoiding these errors.

1. Introduction

Partial parsers attempt to produce *partial* tree structures of natural language sentences, avoiding complex structural decisions which often require extra information that is not available to the partial parser – like verb sub-categorization and semantic knowledge. The complexity of the tree structure that is created depends on the desired application for which the partial parser is intended. In a *shallow* partial parse, a flat tree structure is created in which a few syntactic attributes such as noun, verb and prepositional phrase are recognized. In a *deep* partial parse, an information-rich tree structure is created in which more complex syntactic relations such as relative, subordinate, and infinitival clauses are also identified.

There have been many proposed approaches to partial parsing: *Finite State* (van Delden and Gomez 2003, 2004a; Ait-Mokhtar and Chanod, 1997; Abney 1996; Vilain and Day 1996; Kupiec 1993), *Memory-Based* (Daelemans et al. 1999; Tjong Kim Sang and Veenstra 1999; Veenstra 1998), *Transformation-Based* (Ramshaw and Marcus 1995), *Stochastic* (Church 1988); *Linguistic* (Voutilainen and Jarvinen 1995); and *Hybrid* (Dienes and Dubey 2003; Frank et al. 2003; Park and Zhang 2003; Schiehlen 2003).

Most of these partial parsing systems rely on part-of-speech tag information that is initially assigned by a part-of-speech tagger. The current state-of-the-art and most-widely-used taggers are Statistical, based on Hidden Markov Models (Brants 2000), and Rule-based (Ngai and Florian 2001). However, there are several other approaches to part-of-speech tagging that are also capable of producing state-of-the-art results: *Neural Network* (Ma et al. 1999; Schmid 1994a), *Decision Tree* (Schmid 1994b), *Maximum Entropy* (Ratnaparkhi 1996), *Support Vector Machines* (Gimenez and Marquez 2003; Nakagawa et al. 2001), and *Hybrid* (Ma et al. 2000; van Halteren et al. 1998) approaches. A popular set of part-of-speech tags[1] has been defined by the Penn Treebank Project (Marcus et al. 1993), and is commonly used by natural language processing systems since they can be assigned relatively accurately by these part-of-speech taggers and offer enough information to facilitate a higher level analysis of a natural language sentence.

Despite the large number of papers written on part-of-speech tagging and partial parsing, few describe, in detail, the types of re-occurring, unavoidable errors that are made. *Problematic syntactic patterns* that cause either the part-of-speech tagger or the partial parser to produce an error are discussed in this paper. These errors were encountered during the implementation of a finite-state partial parser which relies on part-of-speech information assigned by a Rule-Based tagger (Brill 1994, 1995). Several sources were examined during this implementation, including the Encarta and Britannica encyclopedias, the New York Times, and the Wall Street Journal Section of the Penn Treebank III. These errors occur not due to a lack of rules or automata that are encoded by the tagger or the partial parser, but by inadequacies in the approaches themselves.

The remainder of this paper is organized as follows: Section 2 presents errors that are commonly made by part-of-speech taggers and shows how these errors affect a partial parser; Section 3 presents errors that are made by partial parsers even though the part-of-speech tag information is correct; and Section 4 concludes the paper. Sections 2 and 3 also present some novel solutions to these re-occurring errors.

2. Part-of-speech Tagging Difficulties

Several re-occurring tagging errors were observed during our implementation of a partial parsing system (van Delden, 2005) and natural language information retrieval system (van Delden and Gomez, 2004b). A Rule-based tagger (Brill, 1995) was used *as is* without any retraining, a very time consuming process. Therefore, the errors discussed below are typical errors that one would find when downloading such taggers and using them without re-training them on the particular domain. Even if the tagger is properly trained, these errors will still occur, but in a lesser number. The errors are classified here into two levels of severity: *Inter-Phrase* and *Intra-Phrase* errors.

2.1 Inter-Phrase Tagging Errors

Inter-Phrase tagging errors are more severe that Intra-phrase ones. They are defined here as occurring when an incorrect part-of-speech tag is assigned to a word that belongs to a phrase that *cannot* contain that tag. The most commonly occurring instances were:

NNS and *VBZ* - plural noun versus 3rd person singular verb
JJ and *VBN/VBG* – adjective versus present/past participle
NN and *VB* - base noun versus base verb

There are several ways the tagger can make these errors. First, if the word is unknown, then lexical clues are used by the tagger to assign a part-of-speech tag. For example, consider the following sentence and assume that *blahblahs* is not in the tagger's lexicon (i.e. it is an unknown word): *The container blahblahs many artifacts*. In this case, *blahblahs* is a *3rd person singular verb*. Lexical clues may suggest that it is actually a plural noun (because of the *–s* suffix). Contextual information must then be used to realize that it is actually a verb. If the tagger fails to realize this, an error will occur.

Second, another situation arises when the word is known, but it requires a part-of-speech tag that has not been observed during training, i.e. the required target tag is not associated with the word in the lexicon. This results in terrible tagging errors. For example, consider the following sentence that occurred during testing: *The pitted bearing needed to be replaced.* The word *pitted* only has *VBN* and *VBD* tags (types of verbs) associated with it in the lexicon that was acquired during training. Even though *pitted* is obviously not a verb in the above sentence, it will be tagged as one since the appropriate target tag (adjective - *JJ*) is not a possible tag according to the lexicon. A novel solution to this problem is to supplement the tagger with a new contextual transformation that changes a part-of-speech tag whether or not the target tag is in the lexicon. This transformation would minimize such obvious errors. Adding this capability to our tagger resulted in 94% of such errors being corrected in our tests.

Third, another common error occurs when the target tag is in the lexicon, but is not the most likely tag, and an appropriate contextual rule has not been learned that would choose it for the new context in which it currently appears. In this case, the most likely tag is assigned which is, of course, not always correct. For example, consider the above sentence once more: *The pitted bearing needed to be replaced.* The word *bearing* could be a noun (NN) or a present participle verb (VBG). If VBG is the most likely tag, it will be assigned to *bearing* in this sentence, resulting in an error if no contextual rule has been learned that would change it to its correct tag (NN).

Inter-Phrase tagging errors usually result in errors being made by secondary systems (like (partial) parsers) which rely on them. A partial parser could be supplemented with heuristic rules that assume tagging errors are possible. These heuristic rules are skeptical of the part-of-speech tags and rely on information that is usually beyond the scope of the tagger. For example, consider the following heuristic rule that was added to our system: *If the tagged sentence has no verb, then find the words in the sentence that could also be verbs and switch the most likely one to its verb tag.* This rule corrected just over 80% of such errors in our tests.

2.2 Intra-Phrase Tagging Errors

An Intra-Phrase tagging error is defined here as occurring when an incorrect part-of-speech tag is assigned to a word that belongs to a phrase that *can* contain that tag. The most commonly occurring instances were:

VBN and *VBD* - past tense versus past participle
JJ and *NNP* - adjective versus proper noun

VBN and *VBD* are both found in verb phrases and *JJ* and *NNP* are both found in noun phrases (JJ can also comprise a predicate). When their tags are confused, a system which relies on part-of-speech tag information may or may not contain an error - it depends on the particular situation. For example, in the following sentence, it would not be difficult to still recognize the verb phrase even though *walked* should be tagged *VBN* (past participle): *I/PRP have/VB ,/, of/IN course/NN ,/, walked/VBD the/DT dog/NN ./.* Such tagging errors sometimes occur when the past participle form of the verb does not directly follow the auxiliary verb.

However, in the following sentence, correctly identifying the relative clause depends on which forms of the morpho-syntactic verb tags are assigned to *ran* and *stumbled*: *The horse raced past the barn stumbled.* If *raced* is tagged *VBD* and *stumbled VBN*, then it is likely that a computer will incorrectly identify the relative clause as beginning at the second verb. Had the sentence been *The horse raced past the barn painted red* then this would have been a correct decision. Note that the classic garden-path example *The horse raced past the barn fell* would not cause a problem since *fell* can only be a past tense verb.

Minor tagging errors can also cause problems with noun phrase recognition. In the following sentence, *British* has been incorrectly tagged as an adjective: *The/DT British/JJ agreed/VBD to/TO sign/VB the/DT treaty/NN ./.* This may result in a noun phrase recognition system making an error since the tagger has identified no noun in the potential noun phrase *The British*. *British* in this case is incorrectly tagged as a *JJ*, but *JJ* could be a possible tag for it: *The/DT British/JJ army/NN agreed/VBD to/TO sign/VB the/DT treaty/NN ./.*

Heuristic rules could also be added to the noun phrase recognition system to handle such tagging errors. For example, *IF determiners 'a' or 'the' are followed by a verb, THEN include the verb in the noun phrase* or *IF determiners 'a' or 'the' are followed by an adjective then this will be a noun phrase regardless of whether a noun follows*.

Adding heuristic rules that treat the part-of-speech tags with scepticism is a quick and easy fix to many re-occurring problems that are encountered. However, this is a confusion of two separate problems - part-of-speech tagging and (partial) parsing. A (partial) parser should focus on rules that assume the part-of-speech tags are correct. Future advances in part-of-speech tagging will hopefully produce a tagger that is very accurate across multiple domains without the need for re-training. This tagger would definitely enhance the practical value of any system that relies on part-of-speech tags.

3. Partial Parsing Difficulties

The partial parsing difficulties presented here were encountered during the implementation of a finite-state partial parser. These difficulties are not due to a lack of automata but to ambiguous syntactic patterns that require more complex semantics or verb sub-categorization to be correctly identified.

3.1 Subordinate Clauses

Post-verbal noun phrases are usually grouped with their preceding verb by a partial parser. This can cause a problem when a subordinate clause introduces a sentence but is not concluded with a comma, as in: *Since Mary jogs a mile seems a short distance*. In this sentence, *a mile* is actually the subject of the main clause, but may be grouped with the subordinate clause since it appears directly to the right of the verb. This error could be avoided by adding extra arcs to the automaton to ensure that a verb phrase does not directly follow the apparent noun phrase object.

Verb sub-categorization information would not have been useful in the previous example since *jogs* can take a distance noun phrase as a direct object. However, it may be useful when an ambiguous subordinate conjunction which could also be a preposition is present. Consider the following sentences: *I located the customer after you went looking for him.* and *I thought the customers before you were very rude*. In the first sentence, the verb *located* takes the noun phrase complement *the customer* and is then followed by a subordinate clause - *after you went looking for him*. The second sentence is syntactically very similar causing a finite-state partial parser to make the same grouping: *before you were very rude* would be incorrectly identified as the subordinate clause. However, this would mean that the verb *thought* was taking a noun phrase complement. If verb sub-categorization information had been available, this incorrect classification could have been avoided since the verb *to think* does not take a single noun phrase complement. In our parsing methodology, we are interested in a system of independent components that are applied in sequence to input sentences, achieving a full parse in the end. Instead of complicating the syntactic partial parser with verb sub-categorization information, a second system of automata augmented with semantic rules would be applied to the output of the purely syntactic partial parser.

Another error may occur when multiple *IN* tags (preposition or subordinate conjunction) appear consecutively separated by noun phrases. For example, *I waited after work until nighttime before the client finally called*. The difficulty here lies in determining whether the subordinate clause starts at *after*, *until* or *before* – which could all be prepositions or subordinate conjunctions. In this case it begins at the final *IN (before)* in the sentence, but this is not always the case. Semantic rules are needed to determine which *IN* actually starts the subordinate clause. A possible solution is to isolate the subject candidates for the verb *called*, and then use a semantic analysis (like one proposed by Gomez 2004) to identify which candidate can fill a thematic role as the subject in the sentence. The most likely candidate is chosen as the starting position of the subordinate clause.

There is another problematic syntactic pattern when attempting to distinguish between particular types of complement and relative clauses. Consider the following sentence: *Mary told Peter I was coming to dinner.* A complement clause should be identified: *I was coming to dinner.* However, this cannot correctly be accomplished without verb sub-categorization information. For example consider the sentence: *Mary found the book I lost in the library.* This sentence is syntactically almost equivalent to the earlier one, but now there is a relative clause – *I lost in the library* - which is modifying the noun phrase object *the book.* Syntactic clues will not be able to resolve these ambiguities. Verb sub-categorization could be used here to realize that the verb *told* (from the first sentence) takes a noun phrase complement followed by a clause complement, and the verb *found* in the second sentence only takes a single noun phrase object.

3.2 Noun Phrases

There are several types of problematic syntactic patterns that occur when trying to identify noun phrases. First consider the following sentence: *By 1950 many people had left the area.* The problem occurs when a prepositional phrase introducing a sentence and containing a year is directly followed by a noun phrase that is not a pronoun and does not contain a determiner. Grouping the pattern *CD JJ NNS* is not a bad choice, since such a pattern could very well be a valid noun phrase: *12/CD red/JJ apples/NNS.* This very specific error was quite easily minimized when we added a lexical feature to the automaton that looks for such a pattern containing the year part of a date, resolving 100% of such errors during our testing.

Another possible error can occur when two noun phrase objects are located next to each other. For example: *Peter gave [NP Mary books]. Mary books* will be incorrectly grouped as a single noun phrase. This is not a very bad decision since such a pattern (*NNP NNS*) could very well be a single noun phrase, for example: *Peter gave [NP Calculus books] to Mary.* As with previous examples in Section 3.1, this error could possibly be corrected by including verb sub-categorization information in the automaton. A similar situation can be found in the following sentence: *I told Mary Peter was coming.* This situation is similar to the subordinate clause problems discussed in Section 3.1. *Mary Peter was coming* could very easily be misidentified as a subordinate clause because the NP automaton is unable to recognize that there are actually two noun phrases and not one. Such a sequence is possible however: *I said Peter Henderson was coming.*

Again, verb sub-categorization can be used here to realize that *told* does not take a clause complement alone whereas *said* does.

Another less-frequent error is made when a predicate is directly followed by a comma and a noun phrase, as in: *After the poor man turned green, many medics finally came to his aid.* The sequence *green, many medics* is mistaken as a noun phrase since *JJ, JJ NNS* is a likely noun phrase pattern. We did not add a separate rule to fix this problem since in our tests *JJ, JJ NNS* was a noun phrase over 99% of the time.

Finally, a time noun phrase could be mistaken for a regular noun phrase when one of the lexical tokens is being used in a proper noun phrase, for example: *USA Today sold over 14 million copies last year. Today* in this sentence is part of the noun phrase *USA Today*. However, in the sentence *Today John sold over 14 million copies*, *Today* is a time noun phrase and should not be grouped with *John*.

3.3 Coordination

Attempting to resolve coordination leads to many problematic syntactic patterns. However, the task can be simplified by fully resolving clausal coordination ambiguity and only partially resolving phrasal coordination ambiguity. When a conjunction coordinates two clauses, there is usually only one pre-conjunct coordination site, making the full disambiguation of such conjunctions relatively accurate, for example: *I saw that Mary ate an apple and that Peter bought a book*. Determining that two subordinate clauses are being coordinated is rather straightforward. However, when phrases are in coordination, there are usually several pre-conjunct sites, making it difficult to determine the correct one, for example: *I bought a car with a sunroof and a boat.* versus *I bought a car with a sunroof and a navigation system*. versus *I bought a car with a sunroof and a stereo*. Semantic information is needed to determine that *car* and *boat* are being coordinated in the first sentence and *sunroof* and *navigation system* in the second. In the third sentence, *stereo* could be in coordination with *car* or *sunroof* depending on whether the stereo is in the car or not. Coordinated phrases, however, can be relatively accurately *partially* disambiguated. Partial disambiguation is defined here as identifying only the post-conjunct of the sentence. Argarwel and Boggess (1992) have defined a well-known algorithm which uses semantic information for determining the pre-conjunct. Therefore, identifying only the post-conjunct of coordinated phrases at the time of partial parsing is worthwhile since the pre-conjunct could be identified later using the semantically-based algorithm. Based on this idea, van Delden (2002) developed an algorithm which combines both syntactic and semantic information to determine where the pre and post conjuncts in a sentence start. This algorithm was tested on the sources listed in section 1 and, on average, correctly disambiguated 90.8% of coordinating conjunctions.

However, some problematic patterns still arise with this approach. Consider the following example: *I saw Mary eat an orange and read a book.* This sentence is ambiguous, but the ambiguity is diverted to the part-of-speech tagger. If the tagger says that *read* is a present tense verb, then two coordinated subordinate clauses are grouped as: *I saw [CC-SUB [SUB Mary eat/VB an orange] [CC-VC and read/VB a book]]*. If the tagger says that *read* is a past tense verb, then the two coordinated verb clauses are identified as: *I [CC-VS saw/VBD Mary eat an orange [CC-VC and read/VBD a book]]*. A problem with a tagger that assigns a single tag to each word is that only one parse of an ambiguous sentence can be captured. There are taggers that assign multiple tags to each word; however, Charniak et al. (1996) report that single tag taggers deliver the best results for parsers.

Some ambiguity simply cannot be resolved. Consider the following sentence: *We see/VB that the girls read/VB books and know/VB that the boys do/VB not.* Base verb tags (VB) would be assigned to each verb in the sentence, so the tagger does not resolve any ambiguity and verb tense information does not help in this case. Choosing the rightmost pre-conjunct is a possibility, but there is no way of knowing if this is actually the correct classification. Either grouping could be possible: *We see ... and (we) know …* or *the girls read ... and (the girls) know*

3.4 Lists and Appositions

Errors occur when attempting to distinguish between lists of noun phrases and comma-enclosed appositions. Whenever an apposition contains a coordinate conjunction, there is the possibility of confusing it with a list: *The assignment was given to John Smith, the president of the company and the manager of the restaurant.* This sentence is ambiguous – there is no way of knowing if the assignment was given to one person or three separate people based on this sentence alone. However, in the WSJ Section of the Penn Treebank III, these patterns were usually appositions containing coordinated noun phrases. To identify these, a small semantic rule can be added to look for the following pattern:

proper-noun , noun-phrase(not proper) or
noun-phrase(not proper) , proper-noun

where the WordNet (Miller 1993) hypernyms of the head noun in noun-phrase must contain the super-concept "person", "region" or "organization". The motivation behind this rule is the fact that a proper noun is usually used to name a person, place, or organization. Because at least one of the noun phrases must be proper, this solution corrects most errors without producing many of its own, correcting over 98% of such cases in the Wall Street Journal Section 23 of the Penn Treebank III. This rule will, however, not resolve all cases, for example: *This morning I ate an apple, a fruit high in iron, and a bowl of cereal.* In this sentence, it is likely, although not absolutely necessary, that *a fruit high in iron* apposes *apple*. However, consider the sentence: *I ate an apple, a cereal high in iron, and a banana*. This is definitely a list of noun phrases since *an apple* is not *a cereal*. A very careful semantic analysis needs to be performed to resolve these ambiguities.

Elliptical constructions will also cause false lists of noun phrases or appositions to be identified, for example: *Athens was famous for its decorated pottery, Megara for woolen garments, and Corinth for jewelry and metal goods*. The omission of the verb phrase *was famous* would make this pattern appear to be a list of noun phrases. A detailed analysis of the entire sentence is needed to resolve elliptical constructions and is beyond the capabilities of finite state approaches like partial parsing.

Determining the boundary of a list of noun phrases is also a problem for partial parsers and can only be fully resolved using semantic information. For example, an incorrect grouping will more than likely be made in the following sentence: *Beth brought the strawberries that were freshly picked by [LIST-NPS the neighbors, the bananas, and the apples]*. Semantics is needed to realize that *the strawberries* is actually the first item in the list and it is being modified by a relative clause. Such lists cannot correctly be identified, but fortunately they occur relatively infrequently. Relative clauses that are attached to noun phrases within the list (for example to *bananas* in the sentence above) do not cause a problem with boundary identification.

Finally, another ambiguity that cannot be resolved occurs when a list of noun phrases is confused with a single noun phrase containing a list of noun modifiers. For example, a list of post-verbal noun phrases is identified in the following sentence when actually there is only one post-verbal noun phrase: *The terrorists targeted [LIST-NPS the FBI, CIA and Capitol buildings]*. This example could be corrected by noticing the syntactic dissimilarity, and would result simply in designing another automaton that would recognize such patterns as single noun phrases. Again, this will not resolve the noun phrases that do not contain syntactic dissimilarity - semantics is required.

4. Conclusions

When designing and implementing a partial parser that serves as a component in full parsing system, careful consideration needs to be given to the format of the partial tree structure that is created. A syntactic partial parser should not attempt to make explicit attachment decisions which usually require semantic knowledge. Leaving certain ambiguities caused by problematic syntactic patterns in the output could result in a better full parse by considering semantic and verb sub-categorization information as a secondary step to partial parsing.

Even though many problematic syntactic patterns exist, finite state approaches that attempt to produce a deep partial tree structure are capable of rather good performance on correctly tagged text. Approximately 88% sentence level accuracy was achieved by both van Delden and Gomez (2003) and Abney (1996) during a comparative analysis of their two systems.

We conclude this paper by listing some sentences which were encountered during testing and were correctly handled by our finite-state partial parsing system. These example sentences are a good indication of the complexity that can be achieved be a finite-state partial parser, despite the problematic syntactic patterns that can occur. Refer to van Delden (2003) for a complete list of the partial parsing categories used below.

(NP Other/JJ successful/JJ writers/NNS) (PP in/IN (NP this/DT school/NN)) ,/, (REL including/VBG (LST-NP (NP Catherine/NNP Aird/NNP) ,/, (NP Reginald/NNP Hill/NNP) ,/, (NP Patricia/NNP Moyes/NNP) ,/, and/CC (NP June/NNP Thomson/NNP))) ,/, (VP have/VBP) (PP at/IN (NP the/DT center/NN)) (PP of/IN (NP their/PRP$ works/NNS)) (NP an/DT imperfect/JJ) (PP though/IN (NP sensitive/JJ sleuth/NN)) (REL whose/WP$ (NP life/NN) (CC-NP and/CC (NP attitudes/NNS)) (VP are/VBP)) (PP of/IN (ADV almost/RB) (NP equal/JJ importance/NN)) (PP to/TO (NP the/DT mystery/NN)) ./.

(NP Other/JJ useful/JJ medical/JJ substances/NNS) (REL now/RB manufactured/VBN) (PP with/IN (NP the/DT aid/NN)) (PP of/IN (NP recombinant/JJ plasmids/NNS)) (VP include/VBP) (LST-NP (NP human/JJ growth/NN hormone/NN) ,/, (NP an/DT immune/JJ system/NN protein/NN) (REL known/VBN) (PP as/IN (NP interferon/NN)) ,/, (NP blood-clotting/JJ proteins/NNS) ,/, and/CC (NP proteins/NNS)) (REL that/WDT (VP are/VBP used/VBN)) (ING in/IN making/VBG (NP vaccines/NNS)) ./.

(CO-PP (PP In/IN (NP large/JJ paintings/NNS)) (REL often/RB encrusted/VBN) (PP with/IN (LST-NP (NP straw/NN ,/, (NP dirt/NN) ,/, or/CC (NP scraps/NNS))) (PP of/IN (NP lead/NN))) ,/, (NP Kiefer/NNP) (VP depicted/VBD) (ING devastated/VBN (NP landscapes/NNS)) (CC-NP and/CC (NP colossal/JJ ,/, bombed-out/JJ interiors/NNS)) ./.

(NP It/PRP) (VP seems/VBZ) (SUB that/IN (NP even/JJ actors/NNS) (REL who/WP (VP speak/VBP) (NP AAVE/NNP)) (PP at/IN (NP home/NN)) (VP recognize/VB)) (PP on/IN (NP some/DT level/NN)) (SUB that/IN (NP the/DT grammar/NN) (PP of/IN (NP the/DT vernacular/NN)) (VP would/MD not/RB be/VB understood/VBN)) (PP by/IN (NP the/DT general/JJ public/NN)) ./.

Acknowledgements

This work has been partially supported by the University of South Carolina Research and Productivity Scholarship Fund.

Notes

1 Refer to Santorini (1995) for a detailed description of these part-of-speech tags.

References

Abney, S. (1996), 'Partial Parsing via Finite State Cascades', In Proceedings of the 1996 *European Summer School on Logic, Language and Information Robust Parsing Workshop*, Czech Republic, 8-15.

Ait-Mokhtar, S., and J. Chanod (1997), 'Incremental Finite-State Parsing', In Proceedings of the *5th Conference on Applied Natural Language Processing*. date, 72-79.

Argarwel R., and L. Boggess (1992), 'A Simple but Useful Approach to Conjunct Identification', In Proceedings of the *30th Annual Meeting of the Association of Computational Linguistics*, Newark, Delaware, 15-21.

Brants, T. (2000), 'TnT - A Statistical Part-of-Speech Tagger', In Proceedings of the *6th Applied Natural Language Processing Conference*, Seattle, Washington, 224-231.

Brill, E. (1995), 'Transformation-Based Error-Driven Learning and Natural Language Processing: A Case Study in Part of Speech Tagging', *Computational Linguistics*, 21(4):543-565.

Brill, E. (1994), 'Some Advances in Transformation Based Part-of-Speech Tagging', *National Conference on Artificial Intelligence*, 722-727.

Charniak, E., Carroll, B., Adcock, J., Cassandra, C., Gotoh, Y., Katz, J., Littman, M., and J. McCann (1996) 'Taggers for Parsers', *Journal of Artificial Intelligence*, 85(1-2):45-57.

Church, K. (1988), 'A stochastic parts program and noun phrase parser for unrestricted text', In Proceeding of the *2nd Conference on Applied Natural Language Processing*, Austin, Texas, 136-143.

Daelemans, W., Buchholz, S., and J. Veenstra (1999), 'Memory-Based Shallow Parsing', In Proceedings of *the 1999 Conference on Natural Language Learning*, Bergen, Norway, 53-60.

Dienes, P., and A. Dubey (2003), 'Deep Syntactic Processing by Combining Shallow Methods', In Proceedings of *the 41st Annual Meeting of the Association of Computational Linguistics*, Sapporo, Japan, 431-438.

Frank, A., Becker, M., Crysmann, B., Kiefer, B., U. Schäfer (2003), 'Integrated Shallow and Deep Parsing: TopP meets HPSG', In Proceedings of the *41st Annual Meeting of the Association of Computational Linguistics*, Sapporo, Japan, 104-111.

Gimenez, J., and L. Marquez (2003), 'Fast and Accurate Part-of-Speech Tagging: The SVM Approach Revisited', In Proceedings of the *2003 International Conference on Recent Advances in Natural Language Processing*, Borovets, Bulgaria, 158-165.

Gomez, F. (2004), 'Building Verb Predicates: A Computational View', In Proceedings of *the 42nd Annual Meeting of the Association of Computational Linguistics*, Barcelona, Spain, 359-366.

Kupiec, J. (1993), 'An Algorithm for Finding Noun Phrase Correspondences in Bilingual Corpora', In Proceedings of the *31st Annual Meeting of the Association of Computational Linguistics*, Columbus, Ohio, 17-22.

Ma, Q., Uchimoto, K., Murata, M., and H. Isahara (2000), 'Hybrid Neuro and Rule-based Part of Speech Taggers', In Proceedings of the *18th Conference on Computational Linguistics*, Saarbrucken, Germany, 1:509-515.

Ma, Q., Uchimoto, K., Murata, M., and H. Isahara (1999), 'Elastic Neural Networks of Part of Speech Tagging', In Proceedings of *the IEEE-INNS International Joint Conference on Neural Networks*, Washington, DC, 2991-2996.

Marcus, M., Santorini, B., and M. Marcinkiewicz (1993). 'Building a Large Annotated Corpus of English: the Penn Treebank', *Computational Linguistics*, 19(2):313-330.

Miller, G. (1993), 'Introduction to WordNet: An On-line Lexical Database', Princeton, *CSL Report 43*.

Nakagawa, T., Kudoh, T., and Y. Matsumoto (2001), 'Unknown Word Guessing and Part-of-Speech Tagging Using Support Vector Machines', In Proceedings of the *6th Natural Language Processing Pacific Rim Symposium*, Tokyo, Japan, 325-331.

Ngai, G., and R. Florian (2001), 'Transformation-Based Learning in the Fast Lane', In Proceedings of the *North American Chapter of the Association for Computation Linguistics*, Pittsburgh, Pennsylvania, 40-47.

Park, S., and B. Zhang (2003), 'Text Chunking by Combining Hand-Crafted Rules and Memory-Based Learning', In Proceedings of the *41st Annual Meeting of the Association of Computational Linguistics*, Sapporo, Japan, 497-504.

Ramshaw, L., and M. Marcus (1995), 'Text Chunking using Transformation-Based Learning', In Proceedings of the *3rd Workshop on Very Large Corpora*, Somerset, New Jersey, 82-94.

Ratnaparkhi, A. (1996), 'A Maximum Entropy Model for Part-of-Speech Tagging', In Proceedings of *Empirical Methods in Natural Language Processing*, Pittsburgh, Pennsylvania, 133-142.

Santorini, B. (1995) 'Part-of-speech Tagging Guidelines for the Penn Treebank Project', 3rd Revision, 2nd Printing.

Schmid, H. (1994a), 'Part-of-speech Tagging with Neural Networks', In Proceedings of *1994 Conference on Computational Linguistics*, Kyoto, 172-176.

Schmid, H. (1994b), 'Probabilistic Part-of-Speech Tagging Using Decision Trees', In Proceedings of the *International Conference on New Methods in Language Processing*, Manchester, 44-49.

Schiehlen, M. (2003), 'Combining Deep and Shallow Approaches in Parsing German', In Proceedings of the *41st Annual Meeting of the Association of Computational Linguistics*, Sapporo, Japan, 112-119.

Tjong Kim Sang, E., and J. Veenstra (1999), 'Representing Text Chunks', In Proceedings of *European Chapter of the Association of Computational Linguistics*, Bergen, Norway, 173-179.

van Delden, S. (2005), 'Simple but Useful Algorithms for Identifying Noun Phrase Complements of Embedded Clauses in a Partial Parse', In Proceedings of the *10th International Conference on Applications of Natural Language to Information Systems*. Alicante, Spain, 357-360.

van Delden, S., and F. Gomez (2004a), 'Cascaded Finite-State Partial Parsing: A Larger-first Approach', *Current Issues in Linguistic Theory*, John Benjamin Publishers, Amsterdam, 260:402-413.

van Delden, S., and F. Gomez (2004b), 'Retrieving NASA Problem Reports: A Case Study in Natural Language Information Retrieval', *Journal of Data and Knowledge Engineering*, Elsevier Science , 48(2):231-246.

van Delden, S., and F. Gomez (2003), 'A Larger-first Approach to Partial Parsing', In Proceedings of the *2003 International Conference on Recent Advances in Natural Language Processing*, Borovets, Bulgaria, 124-131.

van Delden, S. (2003), 'Larger-First Partial Parsing', Ph.D. Dissertation, University of Central Florida.

van Delden, S. (2002). 'A Hybrid Approach to Pre-Conjunct Identification', In Proceedings of the *2002 Language Engineering Conference*, University of Hyderabad, India, 72-77.

van Halteren, H., Zavrel, J., and W. Daelemans (1998), 'Improving Data Driven Word Class Tagging by System Combination', In Proceedings of the *Combined Conference on Computational Linguistics and the Association of Computational Linguistics*, Montreal, Quebec, 491-497.

Veenstra, J. (1998), 'Fast NP Chunking Using Memory-Based Learning Techniques', In Proceedings of *1998 BENELEARN*, Wageningen, The Netherlands, 71-78.

Vilain, M., and D. Day (1996), 'Finite-State Phrase Parsing by Rule Sequences', In Proceedings of *1996 Conference on Computational Linguistics*, Copenhagen, Denmark, 274-279.

Voutilainen, A., and T. Jarvinen (1995), 'Specifying a Shallow Grammatical Representation for Parsing Purposes', In Proceedings of the *7th Meeting of the European Chapter of the Association for Computational Linguistics*, Dublin, 210-214.

Towards a Comprehensive Survey of Register-based Variation in Spanish Syntax

Mark Davies

Brigham Young University

Abstract

This study is based on a recent 20 million word corpus of Modern Spanish (1900-1999), containing equivalent sizes of conversation, fiction, and non-fiction. To date, this is the only large, tagged corpus of Spanish that contains texts from a wide range of registers. Nearly 150 syntactic features were tagged, and the frequency of these features in the 20 different registers was calculated. This data is now freely available to researchers via the web. Researchers can examine the frequency of any of the 150 features across the 20 different registers, or examine which of the 150 features are more common in one register than in another. Hopefully this detailed data will be used by teachers and materials developers to provide students of Spanish with a more realistic and holistic view of register variation than has been possible to this point.

1. Introduction

To date there have been no large-scale investigations of register variation in Spanish syntax. It is true that there have been some articles dealing with register variation involving individual grammatical constructions (e.g. Davies 1995, Davies 1997, Torres Cacoullos 1999, Davies 2003a). There have also been some reference books that provide studies of a wide range of syntactic phenomena in Modern Spanish, but the attention to register differences is often limited and somewhat ad-hoc (e.g. deBruyne 1995, Bosque and Demonte 1999, Butt and Benjamin 2000). In addition, none of the studies that look at more than one syntactic phenomenon is based on a large corpus of Spanish that is composed of many different types of registers. Part of the reason for this is that until very recently, there were no large publicly-available corpora of Spanish that could be used for such analyses.

The lack of in-depth investigations into register variation across a wide range of syntactic phenomena in Spanish is somewhat disappointing, when one considers the range of materials that are available and the studies that have been carried out in other languages. English, for example, has the 1200+ page Longman Grammar of Spoken and Written English (Biber et al 1999), which is based on a 40+ million word corpus of speech, fiction, newspaper, and academic texts. This grammar is replete with detailed register-based analyses and insightful charts and tables that compare the frequency of hundreds of syntactic constructions and phenomena in four different registers (conversation, fiction, news, and academic writing) The goal, of course, would be to make similar materials available for other languages.

In this paper, we will consider the progress that has been made in compiling data for the first large-scale investigation of register differences in Spanish grammar. This study has been carried out with the support of a grant from the National Science Foundation, and it will eventually result in a large multi-dimensional analysis of register variation in Spanish (similar to Biber 1988). These results from Spanish will allow comparison with multi-dimensional analyses of other languages such as English, Tuvaluan, Somali, and Korean (cf. Biber 1995).

Section 2 of this paper briefly introduces the 20+ million word corpus that is the basis for the study. Section 3 discusses the way in which the corpus has been annotated and tagged to enable extraction of the needed data. Section 4 considers a freely-available web-based interface that allows users to examine variation for nearly 150 different syntactic features in 20 different registers. Finally, Section 5 discusses some of the more salient and interesting findings from the study in terms of register-based variation in Spanish syntax.

2. The corpus

The corpus that was used in this study is the largest annotated corpus of Spanish, and the only annotated corpus of Spanish to be composed of texts from spoken, fiction, newspaper, and academic registers. The corpus contains 20 million words of text and comprises the "1900s" portion of the NEH-funded Corpus del Español (www.corpusdelespanol.org), which contains 100 million words of text from the 1200s-1900s (for an overview of this corpus and its architecture, see Davies 2002 and Davies 2003b). Table 1 provides some details of the composition of the 20 million word corpus used in this study.

As can be seen, some care was taken to ensure that the corpus adequately represents a wide range of registers from Modern Spanish. The corpus is divided evenly between speech (e.g. conversations, press conferences, broadcast transcripts), fiction, and non-fiction (e.g. newspapers, academic texts, and encyclopaedias).

Table 1. Composition of 20 million word Modern Spanish corpus

	# words	Spain	# words	Latin America
Spoken	1.00	España Oral[1]	2.00	Habla Culta (ten countries)
	0.35	Habla Culta (Madrid, Sevilla)		
3.35	**1.35**		**2.00**	
Transcripts and plays	1.00	Transcripts/Interviews (congresses, press conferences, other)	1.00	Transcripts/Interviews (congresses, press conferences, other)
	0.27	Interviews in the newspaper ABC		
	0.40	Plays	0.73	Plays
3.40	**1.67**		**1.73**	
Literature	0.06	Novels (BV[2])	1.60	Novels (BV[2])
	0.00	Short stories (BV[2])	0.87	Short stories (BV[2])
	0.19	Three novels (BYU[3])	1.11	Twelve novels (BYU[3])
	2.17	Mostly novels, from LEXESP[4]	0.18	Four novels from Argentina[5]
			0.20	Three novels from Chile[6]
6.38	**2.42**		**3.96**	
Texts	1.05	Newspaper ABC	3.00	Newspapers from six different countries
	0.15	Essays in LEXESP[4]	0.07	Cartas ("letters") from Argentina[5]
	2.00	Encarta encyclopedia	0.30	Humanistic texts (e.g. philosophy, history from Argentina[5)]
			0.30	Humanistic texts (e.g. philosophy, history from Chile[6)]
6.87	**3.20**		**3.67**	
Total	**8.64**		**11.36**	

Sources:

1. Corpus oral de referencia de la lengua española contemporánea (http://elvira.lllf.uam.es/docs_es/corpus/corpus.html)
2. The Biblioteca Virtual (http://www.cervantesvirtual.com)
3. Fifteen recent novels, acquired in electronic form from the Humanities Research Center, Brigham Young University
4. Léxico informatizado del español (http://www.edicionsub.com/coleccion.asp?coleccion=90)
5. From the Corpus lingüístico de referencia de la lengua española en argentina (http://www.lllf.uam.es/~fmarcos/informes/corpus/coarginl.html)
6. From the Corpus lingüístico de referencia de la lengua española en chile (http://www.lllf.uam.es/~fmarcos/informes/corpus/cochile.html)

3. Annotating the corpus

3.1 There were essentially three stages in the annotation and tagging of the corpus. The first stage was to identify the register for each of the 4051 texts in the corpus. The list of registers includes the following:

SPOKEN: 1. contests 2. debate 3. drama 4. formal conversation 5. formal telephone conversation 6. informal conversation 7. institutional dialogue 8. interviews 9. monologue 10. news 11. sports
WRITTEN: 12. academic texts 13. business letters 14. editorials 15. encyclopedias 16. essays and columns 17. general nonfiction 18. literature 19. general news reportage 20. sports reportage

3.2 The second stage was to identify the syntactic features that we felt might be of interest from a register-based perspective. The following is a partial listing of the nearly 150 features (the full listing is given at www.corpusdelespanol.org/registers/) that were tagged and analyzed as part of the study (only a partial listing is given for the final category of [Subordinate Clauses]):

GENERAL: 1. type/token ratio 2. avg. word length
NOUNS: 3. NPs without articles, determiners, or numbers, 4. singular nouns, 5. plural nouns, 6. derived nouns (e.g. -azo, -ión, -miento), 7. proper nouns, 8. Diminutives (-ito), 9. Augmentatives (-isimo)
PRONOUNS: 10. 1st person pronouns, 11. 2nd person tu pronouns, 12. 2nd person ud. pronouns, 13. 1st person pro-drop, 14. 2nd person pro-drop, 15. all 3rd person pronouns except 'se', 16. reflexive se, 17. emoción se, 18. se, not passive, reflexive, or matización, 19. conmigo/contigo/consigo, 20. lo de, la de, etc., 21. lo + ADJ, 22. all clitics 23. pronominal possessives (e.g., la mía), 24. emphatic possessive pronoun (e.g., hija mía), 25. demonstrative pronouns (e.g., ése)
ADJECTIVES: 26. premodifying adjectives, 27. postmodifying adjectives, 28. predicative adjectives, 29. Color adjectives, 30. Size/quantity/extent adjectives, 31. Time adjectives, 32. Evaluative adjectives, 33. Classificational adjectives, 34. Topical adjectives, 35. quantifiers (e.g., muchos, varias, cada)
OTHER NOUN PHRASE ELEMENTS: 36. definite articles, 37. indefinite articles, 38. premodifying possessives, 39. premodifying demonstratives (e.g., ese)
ADVERBS: 40. Adverbs--Place, 41. Adverbs--Time, 42. Adverbs--Manner 43. Adverbs--Stance, 44. Other -mente adverbs, 45. Other adverbs--not -mente
OTHER NON-VERBAL PARTS OF SPEECH: 46. single-word prepositions, 47. multi-word prepositions, 48. general single-word conjunctions, 49. other single-word conjunctions, 50. multi-word conjunctions,

51. Causal subordinating conjunctions (e.g. puesto que, ya que), 52. Concessive subordinating conjunctions (e.g. aunque, a pesar de que), 53. Conjunctions of condition and exception (e.g. si, con tal que), 54. exclamations (any exclamation mark)

VERBS: 55. Indicative, 56. Subjunctive, 57. Conditional, 58. Present, 59. Imperfect, 60. Future, 61. Past, 62, Progressive, 63. Perfect, 64. Aspectual verbs, 65. Existential 'haber', 66. ir a, 67. Verbs of mental perception, 68. Verbs of desire, 69. Verbs of communication, 70. Verbs of facilitation/causation, 71. Verbs of simple occurrence, 72. Verbs of existence/relationship, 73. Verb + infinitive, 74. Haber + que/de, 75. Other obligation verbs: e.g. deber, tener que, 76. Ser passive with 'por', 77. Agentless ser passive, 78. Se passive with 'por' , 79. Agentless se passive, 80. All main verb 'ser' , 81. All main verb 'estar', 82. Infinitives without preceding verb or article, 83. infinitives as nouns, 84. 'ser' + ADJ + 'que' + SUBJUNCTIVE , 85. 'ser' + ADJ + 'que' + INDICATIVE, 86. 'ser' + ADJ + INFINITIVE , 87. modal + present participle

SUBORDINATE CLAUSES: 88. Sentence initial el que, etc., 89. non-sentence initial el que, etc., 90. relative pronoun que, 91. verb complement que, 92. noun complement que, 93. adjective complement que, 94. comparative que, 95. temporal que, 96. Que clefts with indicative ... 141. Donde relatives w/ conditional, 142. Que verb complements with conditional, 143. CU verb complements, 144. CU questions, 145. Yes/No questions, 146. tag questions

3.3 The third stage was to actually tag the 20 million words in the 4051 texts for each of these 150 parts of speech. This was of course the most time-consuming part of the project. The first step was to create a 500,000 word lexicon for Spanish, which was assembled from various sources. The second step was to carry out a traditional linear scan and tagging of the entire corpus. The general schema that we used to design the tagger was the same as that used to create the English tagger that Biber used to tag the 40 million word Longman corpus (see Biber et al. 1999). The tagger relied on a sliding ten word window of text with both left and right checking to resolve ambiguity, and it was a hybrid between a strictly rule-based system and a probabilistically-based tagger. During a period of several months, the automatic tagging was revised manually and corrections were made to the tagger. Although we did not carry out exhaustive calculations of the accuracy of the tagger, the manual revision of several 500 word excerpts in the final stages of tagging suggested that the tagger achieved between 98% and 99% accuracy.

The following selection shows a short sample of what the tagged output looks like. Each of the 20 million lines of text contains 1) the word form 2) part of speech (primary and secondary; e.g. imperfect verb/3pl) 3) miscellaneous features 4) feature tag (e.g. 'que complement' or 'multi-word preposition') and

5) lemma:

(1)
y ^con+coor+++++_gensingcon_+y+
me ^p1cs+per+++++_1pro_+yo+
enfrenté ^vm+is+1s++++_1prod_indicat_preter_+enfrentar+
otra ^d3fs+ind++++!!+_quant_+otro+
vez ^nfs+com+++++_singn_+vez+
con ^en++++++_1wrdprep_+con+
ella ^p3fs+per+++++_3pro_+ella+
y ^con+coor+++++_gensingcon_+y+
con ^en++++++_1wrdprep_+con+
su ^d3cs+pos+++++_prepos_+su+
vela ^nfs+com++++!!+_singn_+vela+
encendida ^jfs+++++!!+_postadj_+encendido+

After the traditional linear tagging, we imported the data into a relational database (MS SQL Server) where additional disambiguation was carried out. Again, this disambiguation was both rule and probability-based. An example of the probabilistic tagging was the way in which we handled Noun+Past Participle strings, where it is unclear whether the past participle is an adjective (*niños cansados* "tired children", *ventanas rotas* "broken bottles") or the verb in a passive sense (*libros publicados en 1974* "books published in 1974", *dinero gastado ayer* "money spent yesterday"). Using the relational database, we calculated the relative frequency with which each past participle form was used with *ser* "to be" (implying the norm) or *estar* "to be" (implying change from the norm). Typically, past participles occurring more with *estar* lent themselves more to an adjectival interpretation in N+PP sequences, whereas those that occurred more with *ser* lent themselves more to a passive interpretation. In this case, then, the data from one table (relative frequency of PP + *ser/estar*) was used to probabilistically tag sequences in another table (N + PP). Many such updates and corrections to the corpus were made over a period of three months.

4. Web-based interface to register-based differences in syntax

Once the 20 million words in the 4000+ text files were tagged, we then created statistics to show the relative frequency of the 150 features in each of the 20 registers. This data was then imported into a MS SQL Server database, where it was connected to the web. The interface that was created as a result of this process (now located at http://www.corpusdelespanol.org/ registers/) allows for a wide range of queries by end-users.

4.1 The most basic type of query asks for the relative frequency of one of the 150 syntactic features in each of the 20 registers. Using a drop-down list, users select one of the 150 features and they then see a table like the following (note that all figures for the following four tables have been normalized for frequency per thousand words):

Table 2. Register differences for [first person pronouns]

REG	PER 1000	TOKENS	# WORDS IN REG
SP-informal conversation	19.41	12828	660750
SP-drama	18.76	9419	502044
SP-contests	16.97	1100	64817
SP-formal conversation	16.77	49363	2942861
SP-debate	14.73	1640	111328
SP-formal telephone conversation	11.25	98	8708
WR-literature	10.10	92998	9210325
SP-interviews	9.42	14551	1544067
SP-institutional dialogue	7.63	4026	527345
WR-business letters	7.62	335	43979
SP-monologue	7.28	2919	401145
SP-news	6.17	516	83664
WR-editorials	4.78	394	82511
SP-sports	4.56	273	59857
WR-essays and columns	3.62	7941	2192407
WR-news reportage	2.28	4767	2094657
WR-general nonfiction	1.57	3608	2293820
WR-academic texts	0.72	146	202943
WR-encyclopedias	0.08	231	2852860

The table shows the actual number of tokens in each register, as well as the normalized value (per thousand words) in each of the 150 registers, and then sorts the results in descending order of frequency.

As the preceding table shows, the use of first person pronouns is the most common in informal conversation and drama and least common in academic texts and encyclopaedias (which is probably not too surprising). Often the findings are less intuitive, as in the following table, which shows the relative frequency of conditional verbs.

As Table 3 shows, the use of the conditional verb tense tends to be more common in the spoken registers than in the written registers, although there are some spoken registers where it is not very common (e.g. sports broadcasts and informal conversation) and some written registers where it is relatively more common (fiction and essays).

4.2 The website offers an alternative way of searching the data as well. Users can select any two of the twenty registers, and then see which of the 150 syntactic features are used more in Register 1 than in Register 2. For example, Table 4 shows the listing that compares academic texts to formal conversation. The table shows the frequency (per thousand words) in the two competing registers, and the

Table 3. Register differences for [conditional verbs]

REGISTER	PER 1000	TOKENS	# WORDS IN REG
SP-formal telephone conversation	2.30	20	8708
SP-interviews	2.20	3399	1544067
SP-debate	2.12	236	111328
SP-drama	2.01	1010	502044
SP-monologue	1.90	764	401145
WR-literature	1.85	17004	9210325
SP-institutional dialogue	1.80	947	527345
WR-essays and columns	1.74	3819	2192407
SP-formal conversation	1.70	4994	2942861
WR-news reportage	1.69	3535	2094657
WR-editorials	1.55	128	82511
SP-contests	1.47	95	64817
WR-general nonfiction	1.45	3327	2293820
SP-news	1.35	113	83664
SP-informal conversation	0.97	642	660750
SP-sports	0.97	58	59857
WR-academic texts	0.80	162	202943
WR-encyclopedias	0.63	1805	2852860
WR-business letters	0.00	0	43979

difference between the two. For example, the first line of the chart indicates that postnominal past participles (*los libros escritos* "the (written) books (written)") occur more than eleven times as frequently in the academic register as in conversation.

Table 4. Syntactic features: [ACADEMIC] vs. [FORMAL CONVERSATION]

FEATURE	DIFF	ACAD	CONV
postnominal past participles	11.17	2.14	0.18
ser passive with 'por'	5.73	0.45	0.07
agentless *ser* passive	4.74	1.70	0.35
topical adjectives	3.08	5.20	1.68
derived nouns (e.g. –azo, -ión, -miento)	3.02	53.22	17.62
postmodifying adjectives	2.87	39.24	13.65
se passive with 'por'	2.83	0.29	0.09
premodifying adjectives	2.38	11.47	4.81
time adjectives	2.29	3.68	1.60
consigo	2.27	0.04	0.01
ser + ADJ + INFINITIVE	2.18	0.30	0.13
infinitives as nouns	2.16	0.64	0.29
agentless se passive	2.16	4.68	2.15
NPs without articles, determiners, or numbers	1.97	101.02	51.39

As Table 4 indicates, [ACADEMIC] texts have (in relative terms) many more passives, nouns, adjectives, and prepositions than [FORMAL

CONVERSATION], due to the more "informational" nature of academic texts vis-a-vis the "interactive" nature of conversation (cf. Biber 1993).

Conversely, one would find the following features to be more common in conversation than in the academic register. Note that many of these features reflect a more "interactive", "people-oriented" type of speech (note also that when the academic figure is .00, it has been smoothed to .01 to avoid division by zero)

Table 5. Syntactic features: [FORMAL CONVERSATION] vs [ACADEMIC]

FEATURE	DIFF	CONV	ACAD
tag questions	295.02	2.95	0.00
2nd person ud. pronouns	143.57	1.44	0.00
exclamations (any exclamation mark)	90.72	1.80	0.01
2nd person tu pronouns	49.86	4.18	0.07
diminutives (-ito)	30.45	0.90	0.02
augmentatives (-isimo)	28.26	0.56	0.01
ir a	23.09	2.39	0.09
1st person pronouns	23.00	16.77	0.72
emphatic possessive pronouns (e.g., hija mía)	19.37	0.19	0.00
yes/no questions	9.74	4.99	0.50
progressives	9.03	1.60	0.17
existential 'haber'	8.30	3.85	0.45
adverbs – Place	8.09	4.35	0.53
CU questions	6.77	0.23	0.02
conmigo	6.59	0.07	0.00
1st person pro-drop	5.39	12.13	2.24

One would probably expect to see clear-cut differences in syntactic features between dissimilar registers such as conversation and academic texts. It is interesting, though, to compare more similar types of speech or writing, and still see what syntactic features differentiate the two registers. For example, one might expect [newspaper editorials] to be almost identical with [newspaper essays and columns], but in fact there are subtle differences. Table 6 shows some of the syntactic features that are more common in editorials than in essays. As we see, because of the persuasive nature of editorials we find more emphatic constructions, verbs of desire, and (perhaps due to the need to build up complex series of argumentation) more clefting types of constructions. In summary, because there are 20 different registers in the corpus and because users can compare any two registers in the list, nearly 400 different pair-wise comparisons of registers in Spanish can be made.

Finally, in addition to being able to see the frequency of 150 different features in all 20 registers, as well as being able to compare two registers directly, the website also allows users to see a KWIC (keyword in context) display for any of these data. For example, if users want to see examples of the [verbs of desire] that are more common in editorials than in essays (the query just discussed), they

Table 6. Syntactic features: [editorials] vs. [essays and columns]

FEATURE	DIFF	EDIT	ESSAY
emphatic possessive pronouns (e.g., hija mía)	2.49	0.16	0.05
pronominal possessives (e.g., la mía)	2.47	0.21	0.07
augmentatives (-isimo)	2.14	0.51	0.23
existential 'haber'	2.13	2.52	1.17
temporal que	2.07	0.08	0.03
other el que with subjunctive	1.78	0.46	0.25
other el que with indicative	1.76	5.49	3.11
verbs of desire	1.73	2.64	1.51
que clefts with indicative	1.72	0.11	0.05
causal subordinating conjunctions (e.g. porque, ya que)	1.66	2.97	1.78
non-sentence initial el que, etc.	1.64	3.03	1.84
que headless & sentence relative clauses (INDIC)	1.55	0.13	0.08

simply click on the [verbs of desire] entry in the listing, and they then see a KWIC display for the first fifty occurrences in that register (in this case editorials), as in the following:

1. del asesinato de estas palabras. Quiero ser presidente , pero no a
2. cinismo fácil y divertido . No quiero decir que lo sea , cínico
3. vez valga la comparación , pero prefiero otros recuerdos personales . Va para
4. del grupo . Cuántos Sharnu desearíamos ? Cuántos son ? Leo las
5. a obra es muy valiosa y necesitábamos tenerla . Mi juicio es a
6. Amaba y odiaba su obra . espero arruinar el apetito de cada hijo
7. carta a su hijo , pero prefiero escribir de Ana y para Ana
8. impide que veamos lo que no queremos ver , y nos vamos corriendo

To summarize, this is the first and only corpus interface that allows researchers of Spanish to directly examine register differences in Spanish on such a large scale. Because the data is freely available to all researchers, this data will hopefully be used by many people to create more detailed descriptions of Spanish, which can then be used to develop more useful materials for the classroom.

5. Examples of register variation in Spanish

In this section, we will briefly provide two examples of ways in which a cluster of features is distributed differently in competing registers of Spanish. In order to simplify the presentation, we have grouped the 20 individual registers into three "macro" registers – conversation, fiction, and non-fiction.

The first table shows the relative frequency of different parts of speech in these three registers.

Table 7. Relative frequency of different parts of speech

	Percent		
	Spoken	Fiction	Non-fiction
noun	19.5	24.7	32.4
verb	19.4	18.6	12.0
adjective	4.0	4.5	7.2
adverb	10.5	5.8	3.1
pronoun	9.3	7.2	3.1
conjunction	7.0	6.1	5.0
determiner	3.5	3.5	2.7
preposition	12.1	15.0	18.4
article	9.0	11.5	13.9
question word	3.5	2.7	1.6

Table 7 shows, for example, that there are roughly as many nouns as verbs in spoken Spanish (about 19.5 percent of all tokens for each of these two parts of speech). In non-fiction texts, however, there are many more nouns than verbs – almost three times as many. Not surprisingly, the "noun-heavy" non-fiction texts also have more adjectives and more prepositions, while the "verb-heavy" spoken register has more adverbs. This difference is a result of the general "information-oriented" nature of non-fiction texts, compared to the "interactive nature" of conversation (cf. Biber 1993). Note also that the fiction texts in general occupy a position between conversation and non-fiction. Finally, we note that these data tend to agree quite well with the relative frequency of different parts of speech in English (for example, cf. Biber et al. 1999: 65-69).

The second example of register variation deals with the relative frequency of the different verb tenses in each of the three macro registers; the data for these features are found in Table 8.

This data provides a number of insights into register variation in Spanish. First, it shows that the two primary past tenses (preterit and imperfect) account for more than 50% of all verbs in fiction, which is more frequent than in non-fiction texts and more than twice as common as in conversation. This compares nicely with the data for English (found in Biber 1993), who explains that fiction texts of course contain more past tense verbs because they are more oriented towards narrated past events, whereas conversation is oriented more towards the present. Finally, this basic distinction between the present and the past also carries over into compound verb tenses, such as the perfect (present-oriented) and the pluperfect (past-oriented).

The second major difference deals with aspect – specifically the relative frequency of the progressive. As Table 8 indicates, the progressive is most frequent in spoken Spanish, followed by fiction, and finally by non-fiction, where it has only about one-seventh the frequency of spoken texts. According to Biber et al. (1999: 461-62) this is due to the "ongoing, here-and-now" nature of conversation, as opposed to non-fiction texts, which tend to deal more with general relationships outside of any particular temporal frame.

Table 8. Relative frequency of different verb tenses

	Percent		
	Spoken	Fiction	Non-fiction
indicative			
present	61.3	33.6	45.8
preterit	11.0	23.8	30.2
imperfect	13.6	26.8	13.4
future	0.8	1.5	0.7
conditional	1.4	1.9	1.0
perfect	3.9	1.4	3.1
pluperfect	0.7	2.8	1.4
subjunctive	5.8	7.4	4.3
present	4.2	3.3	2.9
imperfect	1.3	3.6	1.3
perfect	0.1	0.1	0.1
pluperfect	0.2	0.6	0.1
progressive	1.4	0.7	0.2

The third major difference deals with mood in Spanish, which of course is much more marked (via the subjunctive) than it is in English. As the table indicates, the subjunctive mood is the most common in fiction, then speech, and then non-fiction. This distinction is perhaps somewhat less intuitive than the preceding two features. The higher frequency of the subjunctive in fiction may be due to the need to explicitly spell out the feelings, desires, and opinions of the protagonists in the story (and these types of verbs are the primary triggers for the subjunctive in Spanish), vis-a-vis conversation, where these are implied as part of the speech act. Finally, the higher frequency of the subjunctive in fiction and conversation as opposed to non-fiction texts may be due to the "people-oriented" nature of the first two texts, where the attitudes and feelings of one person affect a second person, which is a major motivation for the subjunctive (cf. Butt and Benjamin, 246-56).

6. Conclusion

While other languages such as English have detailed studies of register differences (e.g. Biber et al 1999), such insights have not been readily available for Spanish. To this point, students, teachers, and materials developers for Spanish have had to simply rely on intuition to understand how spoken Spanish differs from written texts, and how the different registers (formal and informal conversation, fiction, academic texts, etc.) relate to each other. With the data from the present study, however, researchers and students of Spanish finally have access to a wealth of information – via a free and simple web-based interface –

which will provide them with a much-improved understanding of the precise nature of syntactic variation in Spanish.

Acknowledgement

This study has been carried out with the support of a grant from the National Science Foundation #0214438.

References

Biber, D. (1988), *Variation across speech and writing.* Cambridge: Cambridge University Press.

———. (1993), 'The multi-dimensional approach to linguistic analyses of genre variation: an overview of methodology and findings', *Computers and the Humanities* 26: 331-45.

———. (1995), D*imensions of register variation: A cross-linguistic comparison.* Cambridge: Cambridge University Press.

———. S. Johansson, G. Leech, S. Conrad, E. Finegan. (1999), *The Longman grammar of spoken and written English.* London: Longman.

de Bruyne, J. (1995), *A Comprehensive Spanish Grammar*. Oxford: Blackwell.

Bosque, I. and V. Demonte. (1999), *Gramática descriptiva de la lengua española.* 3 vols. Madrid: Espasa Calpe.

Butt, J. and C. Benjamin. (2000), *A New Reference Grammar of Modern Spanish.* New York: McGraw-Hill.

Davies, M. (1995), 'Analyzing Syntactic Variation with Computer-Based Corpora: The Case of Modern Spanish Clitic Climbing', *Hispania* 78:370-380.

———. (1997) 'A Corpus-Based Analysis of Subject Raising in Modern Spanish', *Hispanic Linguistics* 9: 33-63.

———. (2002), 'Un corpus anotado de 100.000.000 palabras del español histórico y moderno', in: *SEPLN 2002* (Sociedad Española para el Procesamiento del Lenguaje Natural). (Valladolid). 21-27.

———. (2003a), 'Diachronic Shifts and Register Variation with the "Lexical Subject of Infinitive" Construction. (Para yo hacerlo)', in: S. Montrul and F. Ordóñez (eds.) *Linguistic Theory and Language Development in Hispanic Languages*. Somerville, MA: Cascadilla Press. 13-29.

———. (2003b), 'Relational n-gram databases as a basis for unlimited annotation on very large corpora', in: K. Simov (ed.) *Proceedings from the Workshop on Shallow Processing of Large Corpora* (Lancaster, England, March 2003). 23-33.

Torres Cacoullos, Rena. (1999), 'Construction frequency and reductive change: diachronic and register variation in Spanish clitic climbing', *Language Variation and Change* 11:143-170.

Between the Humanist and the Modernist: Semi-automated Analysis of Linguistic Corpora

Gregory Garretson and Mary Catherine O'Connor

Boston University

Abstract

This paper promotes a semi-automated approach to corpus studies of discourse phenomena and other phenomena that do not easily lend themselves to computational methods. The approach involves the following components: (a) use of "linguistic proxies" for the phenomena under study, which allow finding and coding tokens in a corpus, (b) automated methods of identifying tokens and adding codes to them, and (c) manual analysis of the tokens, aided by appropriate software tools. In particular, the use of alternating passes of automated and manual analysis is advocated. These methods are illustrated through description of three sub-studies within a project examining the English possessive alternation conducted by the authors. Several advantages of a semi-automated approach are presented, including (a) an improved cycle of exploratory analysis, (b) high levels of accuracy coupled with reasonable levels of speed and consistency, (c) increased explicitness in coding methodology, and (d) the creation of reusable tools.

1. Introduction

There is no question that technology has changed—and continues to change—the way we study language. The profusion in recent years of possibilities for collecting, recording, and analyzing data has led to the blossoming of "corpus linguistics." However, we still have a long way to go before we will be able to realize the full potential of computers (if we can even imagine what that may be) in linguistic research. This paper directly addresses the nature of the compromises that are currently necessary in order to use technology to good effect in our linguistic studies without losing the sophistication that characterizes the manual analysis of data. Specifically, we will advocate a method for studying discourse phenomena that employs alternating passes of automated and manual analysis.[1]

1.1 The debate

We would like to introduce two characters to help us with this discussion. They are voices that will probably sound familiar to anyone who has worked on a research team of any size in the past decade. Let us call them simply "the Humanist" and "the Modernist." The Humanist is a solid researcher of the "old school," who believes that linguistic analysis requires the sagacious exercise of the trained mind, which alone will uncover the subtle patterns in the data that are the goal of analysis. The Humanist harbors reservations about computers and the potentially facile focus on quantitative analysis they seem to promote.

Across the table sits the Modernist, an optimistic believer in progress and new technology. The Modernist has great admiration for the achievements of past research but is fairly certain that now, "there must be an easier way to do it." The Modernist is very comfortable using computers, and believes that just as these have changed the way we communicate, they must surely change the way we conduct our research. The Modernist exhibits great enthusiasm for arcane programming languages and complex software, but has remarkably little patience for repetitive manual work.

The debate across the table goes roughly as follows: The Modernist suggests that several thousand tokens of the phenomenon under study are required, in order to give statistical power to the analysis. The Humanist balks at this idea, insisting that the coding must be done manually to reach an acceptable level of accuracy, and therefore a smaller data sample will have to suffice. The Modernist exclaims that it will take far too long to perform the coding manually; it must be automated. The Humanist cannot imagine how such coding could possibly be done automatically. Besides, the software required would be expensive. The Modernist points out that even undergraduate researchers are not cheap these days, and besides, how would they all be trained to conduct coding of sufficient quality to make it worthwhile? The debate continues…

Having been through our own versions of this discussion, we have come to an appreciation of both points of view. The solution we advocate is a compromise between the two extremes represented by these characters. While hardly novel, this compromise, we believe, is not one that all research teams discover, or learn to implement. We therefore propose to share the lessons we have learned in the hope that others may be guided to see similar solutions—more quickly—for their own research.

1.2 Types of linguistic data

A critical factor in the choice of a research method is the type of data under analysis. Some linguistic phenomena lend themselves much more readily than others to a computational solution. For example, a study of lexical frequency is extremely easy to automate, given a little bit of programming experience or the right corpus software tools. In fact, it would be foolish to attempt to count words in a document manually, since it would take a great deal of time and almost certainly result in a lower level of accuracy. On the other hand, a study of a phenomenon such as metaphor would be extremely difficult to implement automatically, given the current state of our knowledge.

If we imagine a continuum of linguistic phenomena with lexical frequency near one end and metaphor near the other, we can see that a great many phenomena fall somewhere in the middle. Phenomena such as discourse status, topic, animacy, and politeness exhibit a certain degree of surface regularity and identifiability, although not as much as we might usually consider necessary for a computational approach. These phenomena in the middle are precisely the ones that we consider suited to a combined manual-and-automated analytical approach. In Section 2 we will present a case study involving three such phenomena, in order to illustrate different forms such an approach might take. First, however, we will paint a general picture of the method and the nature of the compromises involved.

1.3 The notion of "linguistic proxy"

Central to the question of how amenable a phenomenon is to corpus methods is the degree to which it is realized in identifiable and predictable surface forms. Pronouns and other closed classes, for example, are quite easy to identify in a corpus of untagged text, until we run into complications such as subject drop. But even phenomena such as subject drop and null complementizer use can be approached easily enough using a parsed corpus, by identifying *potential* sites of occurrence. However, there are many phenomena, especially under the general rubric of "discourse," that do not involve closed-class items, or even consistent syntactic categories, but rather occur in a variety of forms, in unpredictable locations, and even spanning utterance boundaries. For example, if one were to study the speech activity of "joking" in a corpus of spoken English, how would one go about finding instances of joking?

In the case of these phenomena that do not correspond directly to surface forms found in a text, a compromise is necessary to enable corpus-based studies. Often enough, although the phenomenon itself is elusive, we are able to identify *linguistic proxies*: surface forms that indicate rather than embody the phenomenon. In the case of joking, an obvious type of proxy would be strings like *joke*, *kidding*, *funny*, *good one*, etc. A better proxy—though not strictly linguistic—might be laughter, if it has been transcribed in the corpus. While not all joking is accompanied by laughter, and not all laughter results from joking, it nevertheless serves as a reasonably good index of the phenomenon, at least good enough to be used as a starting point.

We have found that to the extent that such proxies can be identified, methods of analysis can be automated. Although automated analysis is rarely sufficient, it can be highly useful when combined with one or more stages of manual review.

1.4 Combined manual-and-automated coding

The method that we have found to be most productive in studying these phenomena involves alternating passes of automated and manual analysis. By "manual analysis," we mean item-by-item analysis by a human, using some sort of software. By contrast, "automated analysis" involves a computer program selecting or coding the tokens all at once without human intervention. Given a large corpus and a linguistic phenomenon to study, the first step is to identify the proxies of the phenomenon that make identifying tokens of it possible. Usually, these proxies are searched for automatically, and the results are checked manually. The safest method is generally to cast the widest net possible in the automated stage, and then to discard irrelevant tokens in the manual stage.

Once a set of tokens has been identified, the stage of coding begins, in which a set of codes is used to classify the tokens. This may take several forms: The tokens may be extracted from the corpus and coded in a database, or they may be left in place and annotated using in-line codes, or the data may be left untouched and annotated using stand-off markup, with the annotations located in a separate file along with pointers to the text. We will use the term "coding" to refer to the general activity, regardless of which system is used. Of course, anyone who has coded linguistic data has quickly learned that any set of codes must be revised as new data present unanticipated complexities. We have found that our alternating cycles of automated and manual coding facilitate this unavoidable process, as we will discuss further in Section 4.

For now, let us suppose that there is a clearly identifiable set of codes to apply to the tokens based on some identifiable features. The coding then proceeds in two passes. First, an automated pass is made using software programmed to apply the codes on the basis of word form, part-of-speech tags, or some other heuristic. Second, human coders review the analysis performed by the software, making changes to the codes as necessary. If necessary, the cycle is repeated, drawing on discoveries made during the manual pass. At every stage, efforts should be made to satisfy the desires of both the Humanist and the Modernist; the algorithms created for the automated coding should to the greatest extent possible encode knowledge of the subtleties of the phenomenon in question. Meanwhile, the manual coding should be facilitated as much as possible by technology.

We have concluded that this basic pattern yields very good results, provided that (a) the team has access to the tools or programming expertise necessary to conduct the automated analysis, (b) the number of tokens is sufficiently large that the time saved in manual work is greater than the time taken in tool preparation (though see Section 4 for further considerations), and (c) the phenomenon has reliable enough linguistic proxies that the automated pass has a success rate significantly greater than chance.

2. A case study: the possessive alternation in English

The context of our methodological experiments was a project investigating, among other things, the English "possessive alternation."[2] In order to illustrate some of the ways manual and automated coding may be combined, after giving some background to the study, we will describe our approach to the coding of linguistic weight, animacy, and discourse status.

2.1 Background

Since Jespersen, linguists have tried to determine the factors that influence the choice between the Saxon s-genitive (*the ship's captain*, henceforth *X's Y*) and the of-genitive (*the captain of the ship*, henceforth *Y of X*). Proposed factors have included possessor animacy (e.g., Leech et al. 1994, Rosenbach 2002), relative animacy of possessor and possessee (e.g., Hawkins 1981, Taylor 1996), topicality or information status of possessor (e.g., Deane 1987, Anschutz 1997), and possessor weight or "processability" (e.g., Kreyer 2003; cf. Arnold et al. 2000). In addition, a number of observers have suggested that the semantics of the possessee may be the greatest determinant of the choice (e.g., Barker's (1995) analysis, which assigns a determinative role to the relationality of the possessee), while still others have suggested that the two constructions represent inherently different semantic relations (e.g., Stefanowitsch 2000).

Because of the large number of factors that may determine the choice of construction, a very large sample is needed to identify tendencies and control for confounds. But any researcher who wishes to assemble a large sample of *X's Y* and *Y of X* tokens is faced with several obstacles in getting to that core set.

First, many semantic relations allow *Y of X* but do not allow *X's Y* at all. These "non-reversibles" include partitives (*some of the students/*the students' some*), measure/container phrases (*a cup of coffee/*coffee's cup*), collective classifiers (*a flock of geese/*geese's flock*), and others. Fixed phrases such as *Bachelor of Science* and titles such as *Satan's L'il Lamb* are non-reversible in another sense: speakers have no choice if they wish to convey the special semantics of those expressions. Such invariant cases need to be eliminated or tagged as non-reversible so that they will not contaminate the study of the factors influencing choice of construction when there truly is a choice.

Second, the effects of the proposed explanatory dimensions, especially animacy, topicality, and weight, are difficult to disentangle. For example, human referents tend to be topical, thus discourse old, thus pronominal, thus light/short. Are there independent effects associated with these dimensions, or can the contribution of weight, for example, be derived from discourse status or pronominality? Generally, previous studies have not included enough data to disentangle the confounds and answer these questions.

For this study, our goal was to assemble a database of 10,000 tokens of these two constructions (*X's Y* and *Y of X*) taken from the Brown Corpus (Francis and Kucera 1979) and representing five different genres. These tokens would therefore involve 20,000 noun phrases. These large numbers would allow us to control for a number of possible confounds to a degree not possible in previous studies.

Given the large number of tokens of the two genitive constructions that we had to code and the number of dimensions we wished to investigate, the task appeared rather daunting. The research team for this part of our project consisted of only a few members, one of whom (the first author) had some computer programming experience. We had access to a corpus that had been part-of-speech tagged but not parsed.[3] It became increasingly clear that the Modernists among us would be able to justify the position that we needed electronic help. Automating as many of these processes as possible was clearly desirable.

All of the programming and tool development made use of free, open-source resources, thereby keeping costs low. The first stage involved designing software tools to identify in the corpus a sufficient number of tokens of the constructions *X's Y* and *Y of X*, taking care to avoid any instance of *of* phrases modifying a verb (*think of her*), an adjective (*afraid of women*), etc. Thanks to the use of part-of-speech tags, it was not especially difficult to automate the collection of 10,000 tokens.

After we had extracted our initial set of tokens, we had to identify and set aside all non-reversible tokens. We wrote programs to identify all "hard" non-reversibles such as measure phrases and partitives, and some "soft" non-reversibles such as idioms (*first of all*), nominal compounds (*dog-eared men's magazines*), and deverbal nominal heads that do not preserve argument assignment upon reversal (*fear of him*). Our automatic retrieval of these tokens depended on our ability to identify lexical heads that had some likelihood of being in non-reversible tokens, such as *sort* (*some sort of mistake*), *bunch* (*a bunch of kids*), and so on. Many other tokens that, for idiosyncratic reasons, would not easily reverse were identified by hand. After this thorough filtering, our sample of 10,000 tokens had been reduced to approximately 6,500.

In the following sections we will describe our approach to finding proxies and automating the coding of three dimensions of importance to the study: weight, animacy, and discourse status. The first of these even a staunch Humanist would admit should be automated. The second, even a Modernist would hesitate to automate. And the third is an example of a compromise making a difficult task far easier.

2.2 Linguistic weight

How to code for linguistic weight, or "heaviness," is by no means obvious. Suggestions have variously been made to code for orthographic words, syntactic nodes, and syllables. Clearly, whatever the precise nature of linguistic weight is, we must abstract away from our corpus data to measure it. Put another way, we require a proxy for weight in our data. Fortunately, Wasow (1997) compares several metrics and concludes that they yield very similar results; therefore, we may opt for the one that is easiest to implement. In this case, we selected orthographic words as a reasonable proxy for linguistic weight.

Counting words is a simple task for a computer. Starting with a plain-text database in which all *X's Y* and *Y of X* tokens had been identified, we wrote a Perl script (program) to run through the database, counting the orthographic words in the *X* and the *Y* of each token and adding codes to the token reporting these numbers. Such scripts can run through a million-word corpus in less than one minute. Once the tokens had word-count codes, this information could be studied as a factor in later analyses without having to count the words again in each analysis.

Although this is not really an issue in the case of weight, a generally important reason for adding codes to the individual tokens (either as in-line or as stand-off markup) is that the codes applied to a given token may later be changed manually if they are found to be incorrect. That is, the results of each stage of analysis are open to inspection, before the final analyses—say, comparing the relative importance of various factors—are performed.

In short, given a satisfactory proxy for weight, automation of the coding was relatively simple and extremely rapid, and manual coding of the data was unnecessary.

2.3 Animacy

Though animacy may be counted among the phenomena in the middle of the continuum of tractability, it is certainly located toward the difficult end. In contrast to coding for weight, coding for animacy was neither simple nor rapid. We encountered two principal difficulties, which we will briefly describe.

The first difficulty derives from the fact that animacy is a property of *referents*, not of *referring expressions*. The word *head* may be expected to refer to a physical part of a human or animal, but examples like *the head of the Democratic party* and *the head of the stairs* show that it can be used to refer to a whole person, or to something decidedly non-human. Therefore, when we encounter a noun phrase in a corpus, we must first decide whether it is a referring expression, and if it is, we must decide what entity it refers to.

Establishing the intended referent of a noun phrase is often far more difficult than might be supposed; for instance, consider the examples below, all taken from our corpus material.

(1) a line running down the length of the South
(2) the persistent Anglophilia of the Old South
(3) the Northern liberal's attitude toward the South

In (1), the noun phrase *the South* appears to refer to a physical region in the world. By contrast, in (2), *the Old South* must have a human referent, but does it refer to a set of individuals or a special collective entity? More difficult still, what is the referent of *the South* in (3)? Is it a physical region, a set of individuals, a collective entity, or something else, such as a set of traditions or a worldview? Sometimes the context available does not allow us to choose with confidence among a variety of interpretations.

The second difficulty has to do with the nature of the phenomenon itself: it is not clear what the relevant animacy categories *are*. Although there is little doubt that the animacy of referents does play a part in discourse choices made in English, we do not know *a priori* how many distinctions are necessary to describe patterns within a given linguistic system. At one extreme, we might posit a binary system of HUMAN vs. NON-HUMAN (cf. Dahl and Fraurud 1996). On the other hand, there is evidence (Leech et al. 1994) that speakers distinguish several categories, including ORGANIZATION, PLACE, and TIME.

We made the tactical decision to code for the largest number of categories we could feasibly manage, with the possibility of collapsing categories later, and created a schema of seven codes as shown (not strictly ordered) in (6). For further discussion of this schema, see Zaenen et al. (2004).

(6) HUMAN, ANIMAL, ORGANIZATION, TIME, PLACE, CONCRETE INANIMATE, NON-CONCRETE INANIMATE

After much testing and discussion, we developed a set of criteria for applying the animacy codes to tokens and developed a decision tree to aid the coders in making judgments. The question then became whether any automation might be possible, given the abundance of examples like (1)–(3) above.

The Modernists on the team believed that the animacy coding could profit from an automated pass. The Humanists expressed grave skepticism. How, if humans themselves could hardly decide how to apply the categories, could a computer program be expected to do it? After some discussion, it was decided that the Modernists would make an attempt.

The method used was as follows: A frequency list containing all the words in the corpus material was produced, from which all nominal forms (nouns and pronouns) were extracted automatically. This was simple, since the corpus was part-of-speech tagged. A list was made of the 500 most frequent of these, and the team went through the list manually, assigning to each one *the animacy category most likely to correspond to the most probable referent* of the noun.[4] For example, the noun *head*, despite its many referential possibilities, was assigned to the category CONCRETE INANIMATE, on the assumption that it would most often refer to the actual head of a human or animal (it had been decided that animacy is not inherited in cases of meronymy—that is, the parts of a human are not themselves HUMAN).

A computer script was written that iterated over all the tokens in the database, comparing each *X* and *Y* to the list of 500 words (which accounted for approximately 50% of the tokens). In the case of a match, it would assign the associated code; otherwise, it would assign as an "elsewhere condition" the code NON-CONCRETE INANIMATE, by far the most common in the data as shown by our tests.

The result was a database with each noun phrase coded for an animacy category; this database was the starting point for the manual pass of coding. Each code was checked manually and changed if necessary. By examining the database *before* and *after* manual checking, we were able to establish a measure of accuracy for the automated coding. This came out to roughly 75%, meaning that only one in four codes needed to be changed. This is in fact rather successful, when one considers that with a set of nine codes (the seven listed above plus MIXED for coordinate NPs of mixed category, and OTHER for non-referring NPs) chance performance would yield 11% accuracy if each category had roughly equivalent numbers of tokens—and far worse given that they do not.[5]

We have found that researchers tend to have strong feelings about whether it is better for human coders to apply codes to the data "from scratch" or to check and possibly change previously applied codes, such as those produced by the automated pass. An understandable concern of Humanist types is that coders might become complacent when merely checking codes and thus be less exacting in their judgments than they would be if coding from scratch. Modernists tend to argue that there is no guarantee that coding from scratch results in more accuracy than post-hoc checking. Our tests convinced us that the Humanists have nothing to fear from taking the approach of automating the coding and subsequently checking the codes. At least for our research team, checking codes was no more likely to result in errors than applying codes was; moreover, checking codes was significantly faster. Applying codes "from scratch" proved to be a more laborious and tiring task, resulting in a higher proportion of errors. We do not claim that this will be true for all research teams and all phenomena, but for our purposes it was clear that, given 20,000 noun phrases to code, checking codes was the more efficient procedure.

One difficulty remained, however: 20,000 tokens is still a large number to check manually. How could this manual pass of analysis best be facilitated, to improve accuracy and efficiency, and reduce fatigue? Poring over a part-of-speech tagged corpus in a word processor is not an activity most people relish. Investigation of existing corpus tools turned up none that seemed capable of facilitating the type of analysis we needed to perform—applying animacy codes in context—and therefore we designed our own tool.

The Corpus Coder, discussed in greater detail in Section 3, is a program with a graphical interface that allows a user to page through the tokens one by one with part-of-speech tags hidden, view them in context, and add codes to them simply by clicking on the desired code. This program greatly facilitated the manual coding, allowing the researchers to code hundreds of tokens per hour.

In summary, once a set of categories for animacy was arrived at, the coding was made considerably faster and easier by (a) an initial pass of automated analysis and (b) the use of special software for facilitating manual coding.

2.4 Discourse status

The category of discourse status proved to lie roughly in the middle of the continuum, between weight and animacy. As with animacy, discourse status is not a property of words, but rather a property of referents. Whether a given discourse referent is highly accessible to the speaker and hearer (or writer and reader) cannot be read directly off the data, but rather must be inferred. One way of doing this is to create a model of the discourse that tracks referents, noting each mention of each referent and determining the accessibility of a referent at a given point by calculating the time elapsed (or amount of discourse) since the last mention of that referent. Such systems have been created (e.g., Givón 1983), but they are not without their problems; for example, how oblique can a reference to an entity get before it is no longer counted as a mention? And of course, such a system is fairly difficult to implement.

Another approach, and one sanctioned by a great deal of literature on discourse (e.g., Prince 1992, Gundel et al. 1993, and Ariel 2003, among others) is to treat the form of a noun phrase as a proxy for the discourse status of its referent. It has long been observed that, generally, pronouns refer to highly activated, or discourse-old, entities, while indefinite noun phrases, for example, refer to new discourse entities. While such generalizations have many exceptions, they enable us to make a first-order classification of referring expressions into discourse categories, thus mapping a rather elusive phenomenon onto a very tractable set of surface distinctions.

The procedure we adopted was to use a combination of definiteness and noun phrase form (expression type) as a proxy for discourse status, using the categories shown in (7) and (8) below.[6]

(7) Definiteness categories: DEFINITE, INDEFINITE

(8) Expression type categories: PRONOUN, PROPER NOUN, COMMON NOUN, KINSHIP NOUN, COMMON NOUN, GERUND, etc.

These categories are by no means straightforward to identify, even in a part-of-speech tagged corpus. As has been noted in the computational literature (e.g., Nelson 1999), proper names in particular present challenges for automatic recognition. To mention just one example, consider proper names that themselves consist entirely of common nouns (and function words), such as *the House of Representatives*. Nevertheless, clues in written language such as capitalization can be pressed into service when making guesses about the expression type of noun phrases.

In coding for discourse status, we employed the same two-pass method used for animacy, first running a computer script on the data to apply codes based on heuristics, and then checking all of the codes manually. The script for automatically assigning definiteness and expression type codes contained a fairly complicated algorithm combining word lists (e.g., definite determiners, indefinite determiners, pronouns, kinship terms), and heuristics based on word form (e.g., capitalization, derivational affixes). Comparison of the results before and after manual coding showed that the automated coder achieved a success rate of over 95%, meaning that only one in twenty codes was deemed incorrect by the human coders.

Certainly, for some applications, and depending on the amount of data, an accuracy rate of 95% may be considered sufficient. However, we desired the highest possible level of accuracy; therefore, all tokens were manually checked. The use of the Corpus Coder and our decision-tree materials made this process quite rapid and comparatively undemanding.

In sum, using proxies for discourse status made coding the database relatively simple, with one important caveat: The proxies used may or may not accurately reflect the true discourse status of the referents. However, the literature on this topic strongly supports the relevance of such proxies and underwrites our decision to use this approximation to discourse status in our analysis.

Although the purpose of this paper is not to discuss the possessive alternation, but rather to use it as a source of examples for dealing with various phenomena, we would perhaps be remiss not to report briefly the findings of the three sub-studies discussed above. Using our 6,500 filtered and coded tokens, we calculated the ratio of *X's Y* tokens to *Y of X* tokens and found three separable effects. The *X's Y* construction was strongly favored in cases of animate possessors, in cases of possessors expressed in forms that imply discourse-old status, and in cases where possessors are light in weight. The *Y of X* construction was strongly favored in cases of inanimate possessors, in cases of possessors expressed in forms that imply discourse-new status, and in cases where possessors are heavy in weight. Perhaps most important, the size of our sample and the fact that we had removed all instances of inapplicable tokens allowed us to control for confounding of these three variables. We found that holding weight constant, the effect of discourse status still held, as did the effect of animacy. Controlling for animacy, we found that discourse status still had an independent effect, as did weight. And controlling for discourse status, animacy and weight appeared to have independent effects. We are currently preparing the data for a more powerful statistical study to quantify the degree to which these effects are independent.

3. Tools developed

One of the results of the study described above was the production of a publicly available database consisting of the aforementioned 10,000 pairs of nouns in the constructions *X's Y* and *Y of X*. Known as the Boston University Noun Phrase Corpus, this is freely accessible via our Web interface at http://npcorpus.bu.edu. The website has an incorporated search tool that is modeled after our Corpus Coder (though it is not a stand-alone application); this allows the user to search tokens from up to five genres by text string or by code, using all of the categories discussed above and several others.

Although the Corpus Coder itself is not currently publicly available, as it was designed for one particular application, it may be of some utility to describe some of the design features we found to be especially beneficial for the coding of corpus data. The Coder, pictured in Figure 1 of the Appendix, was written in the Perl programming language with the Tk graphical interface. Perl is an open-source language with excellent text-manipulation capabilities and with an abundance of available open-source code modules, allowing relatively simple and rapid development.[7] The Corpus Coder has two main functions: adding or changing the codes on corpus tokens, and searching the tokens for text or code combinations. Figure 2 of the Appendix shows the Coder's search window.

The Coder shows the tokens in the database one by one, in the context of the sentence they occur in. If more context is desired, the "View Context" button opens another window in which that sentence is shown with a few sentences preceding and following. If more context is desired, the "window size" can be increased indefinitely. Also, the part-of-speech tags may be toggled on and off.

A panel of checkboxes and radio buttons serves two functions: displaying the codes currently assigned to the current token and allowing the user to change these codes simply by clicking alternative codes. An important part of the tool's design which is not apparent is that the program generates the radio buttons and checkboxes *automatically* on the basis of an array of choices typed at the top of the program code; this array can easily be changed in order to offer other categories and other codes. For example, if the user decided to start coding for active/passive voice, one line of code added to the array would mean that the program, when re-launched, would display a new line of radio buttons (with values such as "active" and "passive," or whatever was specified) allowing the user to begin adding these codes to the tokens. The codes would also be added automatically to the search interface, shown in Figure 2. At no point is data ever lost due to changes in the interface.

We have found that such a highly adaptable program can be a tremendous asset in the stage of designing coding schemas to apply to the data—for example, as when attempting to come up with a set of animacy categories to cover all of the data. Of course, there must come a point at which the categories have been finalized, and all data are coded from the same set of options. However, this point tends to come after some experimentation with the data.

It is similarly helpful to have a highly flexible search function. The Corpus Coder's "Fancy Search" allows the user to specify a combination of textual and categorial search terms, connected with Boolean "and" or "or," and with the option of negating a search term in order to search for its inverse. Once a search has been performed, the resulting set of tokens may be paged through and coded as usual using the main window. This allows the user to code or check codes quite selectively if, for example, a certain problem area is discovered. Features such as this contribute toward the goal of having the results of the coding be open to inspection and possible revision at every stage.

The other significant category of tool used in the analysis was the "autocoder" scripts that were run in the automated passes. These were useful in two ways: First, they allowed the first pass of automated analysis, which made it possible for the manual analysis to be based on already existing codes. Second, they could easily be rewritten to effect global changes to the database, if for example, it were decided to collapse two categories into one. This is an ideal task for a computer script, since it requires little discernment and would be highly laborious to perform manually.

4. Advantages of a combined method

To return to our two characters, the Humanist and the Modernist, our view is that they both make reasonable requests: The Humanist wants the coding of corpus data to be as meticulous and as insightful as possible, while the Modernist wants to use technology to enable analysis on a scale previously unattainable. Judicious use of technology and human labor allows, we believe, a compromise that retains the advantages of both manual and automated analysis, while mitigating their respective disadvantages. In this section, we will elaborate on some of the advantages, both obvious and not-so-obvious, of such an approach.

Briefly, the approach advocated here makes use of some or all of the following: (a) proxies for the phenomena under study, which make it possible to find tokens in a corpus, (b) automated methods of identifying tokens in the corpus, (c) automated methods of adding codes to the tokens, and (d) manual analysis of the tokens, aided by well-designed coding tools. Above all, a cyclical application of automated and manual coding passes seems to yield highly favorable results. Below we discuss the effects of this method on the cycle of analysis, the speed, accuracy and consistency of the coding, the question of explicitness, and the design of reusable tools.

4.1 The cycle of analysis

As mentioned above, it is rare for a research team to create a list of tokens, start coding at the top, work straight through to the end, and then go on to write up the results. Linguistic analysis is generally not that simple. Instead, it is often necessary to start with pilot studies on test corpora or a subset of the data, poring over the data several times, revising hypotheses and reworking the coding schema until it both covers all foreseeable cases and is free of unnecessary categories.

This process can be greatly facilitated by the right software tools, ones that make it simple to add, review, and change codes on the data, especially if the categories may be changed at any point without losing data. Also, as mentioned above, "autocoder" scripts that can automatically change the codes on the data can be very helpful in adjusting coding schemas, since they allow codes to be changed categorically with great ease when the schema changes.

With such tools in place, a research team can go over a set of data a number of times, coding it in various ways, reviewing the results, making changes, and fine-tuning the system. We have found that moving back and forth between the data and the proverbial drawing board is the surest way to develop an analysis of which one can be reasonably confident.

4.2 Speed, accuracy, and consistency

Obviously, we all want our data coding to be both rapid and correct. But what we mean by "correct" is worth considering: We want each token to be coded for the most appropriate category, and we also want similar tokens to be coded in the same way. In other words, we require both accuracy and consistency. Generally, humans tend to be more accurate, while computers tend to be more consistent. A computer program gives the same results every time it is run on the same data. Humans, by contrast, suffer from fatigue, boredom, flagging motivation, and other conditions. Yet a human coder is able to bring to bear a far greater amount of inferential power than a computer. This is why we have said that there are certain tasks—the high-inference tasks—that are best done manually.

Nevertheless, it would be false to assert that computers are less accurate than humans in coding. A computer program is as good as the instructions it contains. If a highly subtle complex of conditions are written into the algorithm, the program can perform with a high degree of accuracy, even mimicking human judgment. Everything depends on the extent to which clear instructions for coding the data can be written; in fact, as will be discussed below, this is just as desirable for human coders as for automated ones.

As for speed, there is no question that computers can perform thousands of times faster than humans the tasks they are able to do. Few would argue against the assertion that purely mechanical tasks should be automated whenever possible. We have claimed here that it is also worthwhile automating more complex tasks, such as making a first pass of coding corpus data. It must be recognized that preparing the software to do this takes time, thereby reducing the time savings. As we will see, however, there are good arguments for putting a fair amount of time into tool development.

Where does this leave us? Computers are both faster and more consistent than humans. Humans have a greater capacity for subtle judgment and the drawing of inferences. However, to the extent that this capacity can be translated into instructions for a machine, coding software can be made quite accurate as well. In the case of relatively high-inference phenomena such as those discussed above, we believe that a combined method, having a computer do the easy parts and humans do the difficult parts, results in an acceptable level of speed and consistency coupled with a high level of accuracy. The more the coding process can be facilitated, the greater the amount of data that can be analyzed, and the greater the empirical validity of the analysis.

4.3 Explicitness

Consistency in data coding is highly desirable for two reasons: First, we want our data set to be internally consistent. Second, we want our study to be repeatable. Science is based upon the reproducibility of results, and the increasingly wide availability of linguistic corpora makes it easier and easier for scholars to test the assertions made by others based on corpus data. In an ideal case, when presenting the results of a study, a researcher should present the methodology in a sufficiently clear fashion that another researcher should be able to go to the same data, perform the same study, and get the same results. In practice, however, this is not usually the case. Not only are the data used by many researchers not available to others, but also the methodology is often reported in a vague fashion that leaves much open for interpretation. Obviously, space in publications is limited, but there are ways in which research teams might make publicly available detailed information about their methods, as through the World Wide Web.

In fact, many researchers might be hard pressed to explain their methodology in detail, because a great deal of intuition and guesswork is often involved. For example, asking a series of coders to apply animacy codes to corpus tokens will almost always result in variation, due to the different ways in which individuals interpret the tokens. Such is language. Nevertheless, a crucial goal of one's methodology should be to reduce to a minimum any arbitrary and individual variation in the coding. How can this be done? We have found that in the case of human coders, having a coding manual as a reference, with descriptions of the codes and instructions for applying them, is of great value. Furthermore, we have had a great deal of success with flowchart-style decision trees, designed to help coders with some of the trickier phenomena. Such measures can make dramatic improvements in both consistency and accuracy.

The use of automated coding procedures takes this even further. Computers are extraordinarily literal; the instructions they are given must be perfectly explicit. This is often a source of frustration for the user, but in this case it serves us well. If we are to program a computer to perform a coding task, we must understand that task perfectly. The more conditions we build into the algorithm, the more explicit our statement of the coding methodology becomes. In this way, using a computer forces us to be explicit about our methods, which in turn increases our understanding of our results, their reproducibility, and our accountability to our colleagues.

4.4 Reusable tools

Finally, let us return to an issue raised earlier. Consider this scenario: A researcher needs to code 1,000 tokens in a corpus. Going through the corpus manually and coding them would take ten hours. Alternatively, the researcher could spend six hours writing a program to perform the coding, and then four hours checking the results produced by the program (the program takes one minute to run). In other words, both methods will take the same amount of time. The Humanist might argue that using a computer is not worth the effort, since no time is saved. However, the Modernist would certainly point out that the next week, when another 1,000 tokens are needed, the coding will take only four hours, resulting in an overall time savings of one-third.

This hypothetical scenario makes the point that tools are inherently reusable. Moreover, well-designed tools are particularly reusable, in two ways. First, to the extent that they are adaptable, they can be used for a variety of tasks. Second, to the extent that the source code is encapsulated well (i.e., functions for performing different tasks are kept separate), they can serve as the basis for other tools. For example, all of our "autocoder" scripts were based on the same model, with minor or major changes, depending on the task at hand. But only one was written from scratch. Good programming makes use of previous solutions to problems.

Going one step further, once a research team has designed and used a tool, that tool may be shared with others. The distribution of free and open-source tools is one of the great developments of the technological revolution of recent years. The more researchers contribute to open collections of tools, the greater the chances that in the future, the tool one happens to need will not have to be designed from scratch. We support this collaborative model of the use of technology in research.[8]

5. Conclusion

In the end, the Humanist and the Modernist both make valuable contributions to the research project. The complex understanding of phenomena that is the province of the scholar is not under threat from technology—but perhaps the traditional methods of analysis are. The existence of new tools calls for a re-evaluation of the ways in which we conduct research, but it need not result in a lowering of standards. Quite the opposite; to the extent that computers allow us to perform our analyses more carefully and on larger quantities of data, they are all to the good. And until the day when our understanding of the elusive phenomena in the middle of the continuum is such that we can state it with the explicitness that computers require, a division of labor between man and machine seems the best course of action.

Acknowledgements

This material is based on work supported by the National Science Foundation under Grant No. 0080377. The support of NSF is gratefully acknowledged. Any opinions, findings, and conclusions or recommendations expressed in this material are those of the authors and do not necessarily reflect the views of the National Science Foundation. Thanks are also due to a number of individuals for advice and contributions to the study of the possessive alternation in English that is the basis for this paper. These include Annelie Ädel, Marjorie Hogan, Joan Maling, Barbora Skarabela, Arto Anttila, Vivienne Fong, and John Manna. We would also like to thank several people for helpful comments on our presentation at the Fifth North American Symposium on Corpus Linguistics, including Eileen Fitzpatrick, William Fletcher, Angus Grieve-Smith, David Lee, JoAnne Neff, Steve Seegmiller, Sebastian van Delden, and Longxing Wei.

Notes

1 Please address correspondence to Gregory Garretson: gregory@bu.edu.

2 Optimal Typology of Determiner Phrases (NSF grant No. 0080377 to M. C. O'Connor, PI); see Acknowledgements.

3 We are grateful to Fred Karlsson of the University of Helsinki, who granted us the use of his English Constraint Grammar-tagged version of the Brown Corpus.

4 It should be pointed out that these assignments were based entirely on intuition. A more principled method would be to code a test corpus and use actual statistics as the basis for matching words and categories. However, it is not clear that the end result would be any different.

5 The simplest way to use such an "autocoder" would be to have it always assign the same code: whichever is most frequently correct across the data. In our case, this would have resulted in over 40% accuracy, had we applied the code NON-CONCRETE INANIMATE to each nominal.

6 These are in fact simplifications of the coding schemas used. For more information, see the documentation on the BU Noun Phrase Corpus website at http://npcorpus.bu.edu.

7 See the Perl Directory at http://www.perl.org.

8 Building on many of the successful aspects of the Corpus Coder, we are currently developing a system of coding tools known as Dexter. These tools will be open-source and available for free online at http://www.dextercoder.org. This project, supported by the Spencer Foundation (Grant No. 200500105), is initially focusing on the analysis of spoken-language transcripts, although in the future it may well be expanded to include corpus tools of various types.

References

Anschutz, A. (1997), 'How to Choose a Possessive Noun Phrase Construction in Four Easy Steps', *Studies in Language*, 21: 1-35.

Ariel, M. (2003), 'Accessibility Theory: An Overview', in: T. Sanders, J. Schilperoord and W. Spooren (eds.) *Text Representation: Linguistic and Psycholinguistic Aspects*. Amsterdam: John Benjamins. 29-87.

Arnold, J. E., T. Wasow, A. Losongco, and R. Ginstrom (2000), 'Heaviness versus newness: The effects of structural complexity and discourse status on constituent ordering', *Language*, 76: 28-55.

Barker, C. (1995), *Possessive Descriptions*. Stanford, CA: CSLI.

Dahl, O. and K. Fraurud, (1996), 'Animacy in Grammar and Discourse', in: T. Fretheim and J. K. Gundel (eds.), *Reference And Referent Accessibility*, Amsterdam: John Benjamins. 47-64.

Deane, P. (1987), 'English Possessives, Topicality, and the Silverstein Hierarchy', *BLS 13*. Berkeley, California: Berkeley Linguistic Society.

Francis, W. N. and H. Kucera (1979), *Manual of Information to Accompany a Standard Sample of Present-day American English*. Providence, RI: Brown University Press.

Givón, T. (1983), *Topic continuity in discourse: A quantitative cross-language study*. Amsterdam, Philadelphia: John Benjamins.

Gundel, J. K., N. Hedberg and R. Zacharski (1993), 'Cognitive Status and the Form of Referring Expressions in Discourse.' *Language*, 69: 274-307.

Hawkins, R. (1981), 'Towards an account of the possessive constructions: *NP's N* and *the N of NP*', *Journal of Linguistics*, 17: 247-269.

Kreyer, R. (2003), 'Genitive and of-construction in modern written English. Processability and human involvement', *International Journal of Corpus Linguistics*, 8: 169-207.

Leech, G., B. Francis and X. Xu (1994), 'The Use of Computer Corpora in the Textual Demonstrability of Gradience in Linguistic Categories', in: C. Fuchs and B. Victorri (eds.) *Continuity In Linguistic Semantics*. Amsterdam: John Benjamins. 57-76.

Nelson, M. (1999), 'What Are Proper Names and How Do We Identify Them?', *Copenhagen Studies in Language*, 23: 83-103.

Prince, E. F. (1992), 'The ZPG Letter: Subjects, Definiteness, and Information-Status', in: W. C. Mann and S. A. Thompson (eds.) *Discourse Description: Diverse Linguistic Analyses of a Fund Raising Text*. Amsterdam: John Benjamins. 295-325.

Rosenbach, A. (2002), *Genitive variation in English: Conceptual factors in synchronic and diachronic studies*. Berlin, New York: Mouton de Gruyter.

Stefanowitsch, A. (2000), 'Constructional semantics as a limit to grammatical alternation: The two genitives of English', *CLEAR (Cognitive Linguistics: Explorations, Applications, Research)*, 3.

Taylor, J. R. (1996), *Possessives in English*. Oxford: Oxford University Press.

Wasow, T. (1997), 'Remarks on grammatical weight'. *Language Variation and Change*, 9: 81-105.

Zaenen, A., J. Carletta, G. Garretson, J. Bresnan, A. Koontz-Garboden, T. Nikitina, M. C. O'Connor, and T. Wasow (2004), 'Animacy Encoding in English: why and how', in: D. Byron and B. Webber (eds.) *Proceedings of the 2004 ACL Workshop on Discourse Annotation, Barcelona, July 2004*. 118-125.

Appendix

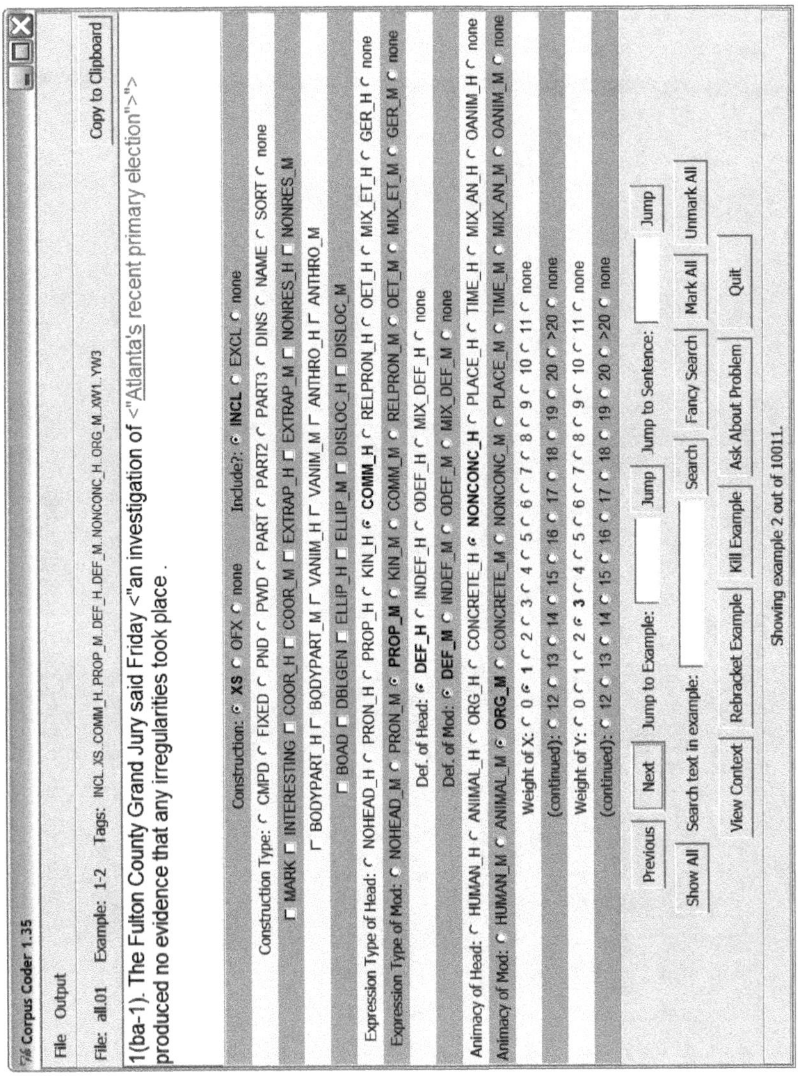

Figure 1. The Corpus Coder, main window

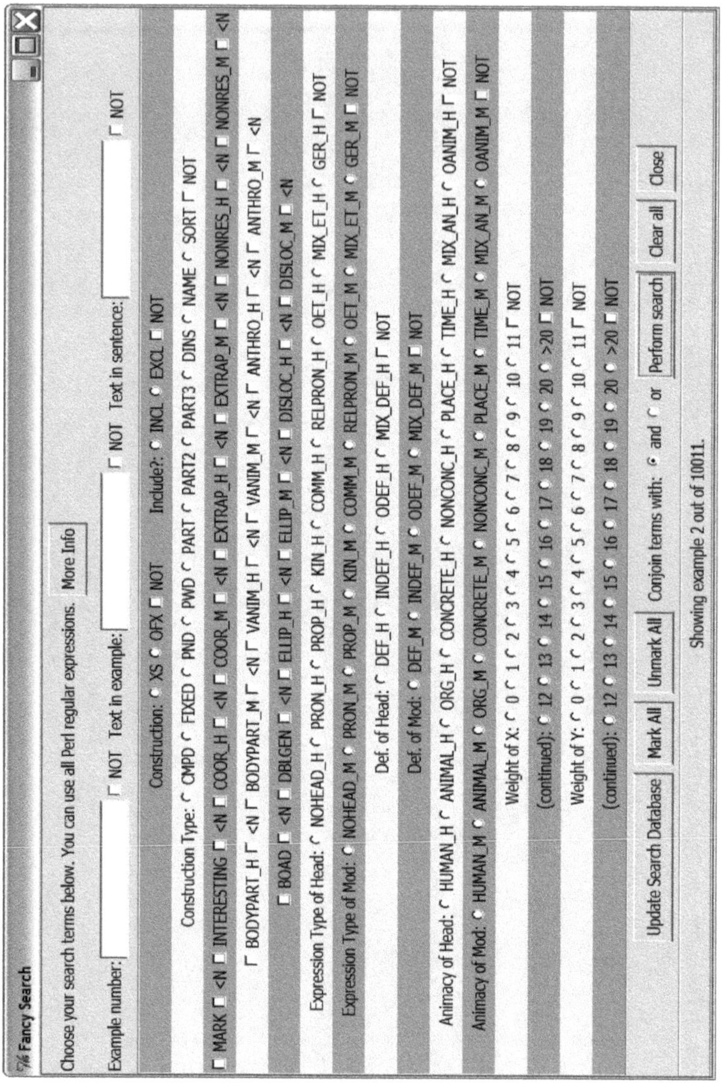

Figure 2. The Corpus Coder, search window

Pragmatic Annotation of an Academic Spoken Corpus for Pedagogical Purposes

Carson Maynard and Sheryl Leicher

University of Michican

Abstract

The Michigan Corpus of Academic Spoken English (MICASE) has quickly become a valuable pedagogical resource, inspiring a new approach to the creation of teaching materials. In addition to, and perhaps more novel than, materials relating to lexis and grammar, the transcripts in the corpus offer a wealth of authentic examples of interactional and pragmatic phenomena that ESL teachers otherwise find very difficult to obtain. However, as the corpus currently exists, the transcripts must be searched manually for these kinds of discourse features. The present project reports on ongoing efforts to annotate the corpus in order to make pragmatic information more readily accessible, thereby enhancing the value of the corpus for teachers. First, for each speech event, brief informative abstracts have been compiled, summarizing content and describing salient discourse features. Secondly, additional metadata has been encoded in the headers of the transcripts which describes the relative frequency of 25 pragmatic features, including features involving classroom management (e.g., assigning homework), discourse style and lexis (e.g., humor, technical vocabulary), interactivity (e.g., student and teacher questions, group work), and content (e.g., defining or glossing terms,and narratives). Finally, a representative subcorpus of fifty transcripts has been manually tagged for 12 of the 25 pragmatic features (e.g., advice, disagreement) and will be computer searchable in the near future. In this paper, we describe this pragmatic annotation, including an overview of the features we decided to tag, and discuss benefits and limitations of the annotation scheme. We consider some pedagogical applications that utilize this additional mark-up and argue that despite the limitations and labor-intensive nature of this type of pragmatic mark-up, these innovative enhancements will be of value to both teachers and researchers.

1. Introduction

Historically, teachers of English as a Second Language and teachers of English for Academic Purposes have relied heavily on written discourse and/or on their own intuitions about how language functions in academia to create teaching materials that help prepare their students for the oral and aural demands of interacting and participating at the university level. Fortunately, with the emergence of specialized spoken corpora, we now have authentic examples available of the very kinds of interactions that these teachers wish to target. The opportunity now exists for teachers to be guided by *what really exists;* that is, authentic examples, rather than just what has been taught in the past, or some ideal.

An excellent source for these kinds of examples is MICASE (The Michigan Corpus of Academic Spoken English), which is unique in being not only a corpus of academic English, but of American English as well. MICASE is a spoken language corpus of approximately 1.7 million words focusing on contemporary university speech within the microcosm of the University of Michigan in Ann Arbor. This is a typical large public research university with about 37,000 students, approximately one-third of whom are graduate students. Speakers represented in the corpus include faculty, staff, all levels of students, and native, near-native, and non-native speakers. The 200 hours of speech were recorded at 152 different events between 1997 and 2001. The project was funded by the English Language Institute at the U of M, and since its ultimate aim was to benefit non-native speakers, it was important to capture the variety of contexts in which English is spoken in order to reflect what actually happens on American university campuses.

Unfortunately, although these massive amounts of speech data are now available, specific examples of the language that is actually used to accomplish things in the academic community (e.g., explaining, defining) are still not readily accessible. Teachers must continue to rely on some degree of intuition in order to search for specific phrases with which they are familiar or that they suspect fulfill the functions they wish to investigate. Alternatively, they could spend countless hours poring over the transcripts individually, hand-searching for suitable examples of speech and model interactions.

In order to ameliorate this intimidating task and to allow a data-driven (rather than intuition-driven) discourse analysis of this valuable corpus, in 2001 the MICASE team embarked on a new coding project: an on-site pragmatic analysis of the corpus. This effort has resulted in the creation of three different analytical tools for accessing some interactional and pragmatic phenomena that ESL/EAP teachers otherwise find very difficult to obtain: 1) a compilation of abstracts for each of the 152 speech events in MICASE; 2) an "inventory" of the pedagogically interesting pragmatic content of each speech event; and 3) a pragmatically-tagged sub-corpus of 50 transcripts. These three tools facilitate data collection by providing three different entry points into the corpus, thus accommodating different research approaches or styles (e.g., top-down vs bottom-up) and allowing access to different groupings of information or vantage points from which to view a single event or the entire corpus.

The aim of our project is not to make sweeping generalizations about any particular pragmatic function or its prevalence or realization in academic discourse, but rather to simply expose interesting linguistic phenomena that occur in our corpus, so that teachers and researchers can easily locate examples of functional language they are likely to be interested in for their own purposes.

2. Methods

As we began to plan for the pragmatic analysis of MICASE, we recognized that it would be a very labor- and time-intensive endeavor, fraught with problems and controversy, but one that would hopefully pay future dividends. Over the last few years, the work has been carried out by a team consisting of the project director and two part-time research assistants. The project director and one of the researchers have been working on the project for the duration, while four different graduate students have filled the position of the second research assistant. In this section, we outline our procedures and discuss some of the many challenges we encountered.

We began by compiling metadata and writing abstracts for each speech event. For each event, a researcher listened to the recording as s/he read through the transcript. This encouraged a holistic view of the event and revealed certain insights into the event that would not be obvious from the transcript alone. In order to do this, we devised a checklist, or inventory, of 25 linguistic/pragmatic functions and discourse features of relevance (the metadata) with the goal of making the transcripts more useful to people who are studying a particular pragmatic feature, such as expressing sarcasm or assigning homework. These features are listed below.

Inventory of Pragmatic Features

Advice/direction, giving or soliciting
Assigning Homework
Definitions
Disagreement
Discussion
Dramatization
Evaluation (positive and negative)
Examples
Group/pair work
Humor
Speaker Introductions
Introductory roadmap
Large group activity
Logistics/announcements
Narratives
Problem solving
Questions
Referring to handout
Requests
Returning or going over homework or an exam
Reviewing for an exam
Sarcasm

Tangents, personal topics
Technical vocabulary
Visuals

Our selection of these features was motivated by the data; we chose features that appeared to be interesting, salient, productive, important in academia, and of use to the largest number of potential users. The researcher noted the presence and/or relative frequency (*none*, *few*, or *numerous*) of these features in each transcript. This pragmatic inventory serves as a general guideline so that users can determine which transcript(s) will provide the most evidence of the features they are studying.

Our decisions about what to include in the abstracts were motivated by the content and context of the event. For the abstracts, we wanted a "thick" description of the event that would make details surrounding the event available. Each abstract, of approximately 200-250 words, provides a general overview of the speech event, outlines its content or subject matter, and describes what transpired in that venue throughout the recorded period, including salient interactional and pragmatic features. We used a worksheet to keep a rough log of events and topics to aid us in writing the abstract. One very attractive feature of the abstracts is that they bring to light some of the relevant classroom culture within the culture of the academic community of discourse by providing interactional and ethnographic details that give insight into the setting, tone, participants, and other salient features. The abstracts encourage utilization of the corpus for content-based language instruction by providing a way for users to get at specific content. This is an approach that is very compatible with form-focused instruction, which emphasizes the connection between units of language and culture.

Included with each abstract is a concise summary of information regarding the class/audience size and academic level, primary speaker demographics (sex, academic role, native speaker status), academic division (e.g., humanities, physical sciences), primary discourse mode (e.g., monologic or interactive), and date and length of recording. Figure 1, although shorter than most, typifies our abstracts:

An instructor, after reading the abstract, might be inspired to examine the ways in which the instructor manages the classroom and guides the discourse, or s/he might create a lesson for ESL/EAP students contrasting the language of the smaller discussion section with that of more formal settings such as large lectures. A savvy student could investigate the abstracts and access a transcript in order to observe how students interact with each other and their instructor during discussion sections.

We have finished writing the abstracts and coding the metadata for each event. All of this information, along with some very valuable indices and additional resources, are included in *The MICASE Handbook*, published by the University of Michigan Press (Simpson-Vlach and Leicher, in press). We are still

Intro Anthropology Discussion Section (DIS115JU087)

Discussion section, undergraduate, social sciences, mixed monologic and interactive, 22 students, 1 graduate student instructor, 18 speakers, recorded winter 1999, 51 minutes, recording complete.

The graduate student instructor begins by telling the class the topic for the session: power, social organization, and both societal and personal aspects of social control. The instructor asks numerous probing, open-ended questions, allowing lengthy "wait time" after most questions. She paraphrases or summarizes students' responses and writes them on the chalkboard. Many of her questions expand on responses to the previous question(s). Students' raised hands are acknowledged and responses are followed by positive feedback from the instructor (e.g., "good point"). The instructor gives analogies and examples from the textbook and makes references to the professor's lecture. At the end of class, she directs students to turn in their papers, and three students stay after to ask questions.

Figure 1: Sample abstract

in the process of creating our third tool, a pragmatically-tagged corpus. While the abstract gives a general overview of each event and the pragmatic inventory gives an overview of the pragmatic features, pragmatic tagging identifies specific instances or examples of language clearly performing any of a set of various pre-determined pragmatic functions.

The ultimate goal of this phase is to produce XML marked-up transcripts that can be searched for a variety of features using an online search engine. Because the process is so labor-intensive, we decided to restrict this phase to a subcorpus of fifty transcripts. The subcorpus was selected as a representative sampling of all speech events, drawn evenly from the academic divisions; however, this selection process was not entirely random because we deliberately chose transcripts that we thought were pragmatically the richest. Our purpose was not to enable statistical claims about these data, but to improve the value of the corpus for EAP teachers, to facilitate qualitative research, and to make the corpus more attractive to users who are not trained in corpus linguistics.

This database has been created using XML markup, which has enabled us to tailor the tags for our particular purposes. Most of our pragmatic tags include only a starting point, because the beginning of a pragmatic feature is often much easier to determine than the end. The exception to this is questions, which almost always have a relatively clear beginning and end; these are coded with both start and end tags. In cases where a particular feature appears throughout a passage—for example, advice in an advising session—we have chosen only to mark the first instance rather than tag every one. Our intention is to point the users to the occurrence and let them determine the scope.

Pragmatic tagging is done in two stages. To ensure a higher level of accuracy, each transcript is analyzed by two readers. The first reader goes through it methodically, marking any instances of the pre-selected target categories. After the transcript has been thoroughly annotated it is passed to the second reader, who double-checks the tags and enters them into the database.

We used three primary criteria to select a subset of the 25 features in the pragmatic inventory for tagging. First, we wanted to focus on features that are not easily searchable; this eliminated categories such as examples, which are often signaled by particular words and phrases like "for example." Secondly, and more importantly, we wanted to include features that are prevalent in the data so that people interested in studying them could be assured of having a decently large sample size. However, we had to strike a balance between features that were prevalent and features that were ubiquitous; for example, instances of metalanguage and humor were simply far too numerous for us to code all instances, so we excluded those categories from our coding. Third, we wanted to focus on features that were relatively unambiguous. Our goal was to achieve a high degree of precision rather than total recall, so we make no claims of having an exhaustive listing of these features; what we do want to be able to claim is that our list is accurate. If we came across an instance that was questionable, we generally excluded it. This not only makes the existing dataset more reliable, it also considerably reduces the time we spend debating the categorization of phrases. Figure 2 shows the final list of tagged pragmatic features.

		Pragmatic Tags
1.	ADV	Advice (giving, soliciting)
2.	AHW	Assigning homework
3.	DEF	Defining / glossing terms
4.	DIR	Directives
5.	DIS	Disagreement
6.	EVN	Evaluation (positive, negative)
7.	IRM	Introductory roadmap
8.	NAR	Narrative
9.	Q	Questions
10.	REQ	Requests
11.	SPI	Speaker introductions
12.	TAN	Tangents

Figure 2 Pragmatic Tags

Certain categories turned out to be far more complex than we had originally envisioned. A good example of this is evaluation. From the outset, we made the decision to only tag language that was very clearly evaluative and to mark each one as either positive or negative. In some cases this was easy—"this is a pleasure" is clearly positive and "this doesn't do a lot for me" is clearly negative. However, we soon discovered that there were numerous evaluative comments that we could not categorize immediately; although the words or phrases were evaluative, we had to look at the surrounding context to understand whether they were positive or negative. We called this *contextual evaluation*, which includes "this is a very interesting process" and "yeah, what a great housemate she is." From these sentences alone, we cannot tell whether the speaker actually *likes* or *dislikes* the process or the housemate, we only know that he or she finds them in some way worthy of comment. We also considered instances in which the speaker expressed *hypothetical evaluation*, such as this example from the Social Psychology Dissertation Defense: "would you expect Koreans to say boy that's hogwash, that's really dumb, i think that's a horrible, reaction to the situation, would you expect that to be the case?" After coding evaluations for some time, we realized that the majority of the evaluative language in our transcripts was made up of the same few words, such as *good*, *bad*, *cool*, *funny*, *interesting*, and *nice*, all of which are very common and easily used as search terms. Once we realized how pervasive evaluative utterances were, and how difficult they were to define, we decided to drastically modify the category. We have now eliminated the category of hypothetical evaluation and restricted the tagging to unexpected or unusual adjectives, and phrases which are metaphorical, uncommon, or otherwise of interest pedagogically.

We went through a similar process with our *advice* category. We originally thought that recommendations, directions, and commands were similar enough to group them under one umbrella category of *advice*, but we eventually realized that the situation was more complex. An utterance such as, "We're going up to the head of the stairs here if you wanna follow me" is a command but the polite phrasing makes it sound more like a suggestion. Eventually, we decided on three separate categories: *advice*, *requests*, and *directives*. The *advice* category now includes suggestions and recommendations only ("you should go see Linda Donohue" and "so you might want to think about that"). *Requests* generally require some kind of action to be performed but are phrased in such a way that they can be declined, usually due to a status differential between the speaker and the addressee ("if I could ask you to fill this out" and "I'd love to hear from you"), whereas *directives* tell someone to do something (sometimes politely) and cannot be declined if the addressee wants to maintain face ("put your cup back there and come here" and "don't get brains on the tables okay?").

Finally, we should briefly mention the *question* code, which is unique among our tagged features in that it is also a syntactic category; however, our interest is not primarily in syntactic form but in how this form intersects with pragmatic function. We decided to tag questions after preliminary research on WH- questions in the classroom showed noteworthy trends in their pragmatic use. For example, WH- questions are used more by teachers than students. The question code expanded enormously from our original guidelines as we realized how many subtle variations we had not yet accounted for. Primarily, we divide questions into seven major types: *wh-*, which means that it contains a WH- word;

polar, which means it is answerable by *yes* or *no*; *declarative*, a subtype of polar which is syntactically not a question, but its interrogative function is signaled by its intonation and interactional effect; *negative*, a polar question which begins with a negative particle; *alternative*, which means that a predefined set of possible answers is provided; *request*, whether for repetition or comment; and *tag*, which includes positive, negative and lexical tags. Within these seven primary types, we devised a subcategorization system to indicate if the question was fully formed, ellipted, incomplete, or otherwise remarkable.

3. Discussion

Our hope is that the tagged categories will be multifunctional and useful for a variety of purposes. Our work, of course, reflects the needs and goals of the English Language Institute (ELI) at the University of Michigan, but we believe that these needs and goals will mesh well with those of other potential users.

To give one example, we could consider the pragmatic tag for questions and how it might be used as a resource by different groups, which can be represented by the members of the ELI community, who mainly fall into at least one of four groups: researchers, testers, teachers, and learners. Each of these groups has a different goal, and can use the pragmatically tagged subcorpus to suit their own purposes. Researchers may be interested in studying the effect of demographic or status differences on how speakers phrase questions, or looking at how pre-questions, discourse markers, or false starts are used. Testers may want to determine the types of questions students can expect to encounter, especially questions that have a purpose other than simply asking for information, and incorporate them into listening tests. Teachers can use pragmatic tagging to demonstrate to their students how questions are structured, paying particular attention to less-frequently-taught strategies such as hedging or indirectness. Use of the pragmatic tags can also be helpful in teacher training to show how teachers represented in the corpus ask questions of students and which questioning strategies are the most productive.

We may also try to make this subcorpus available to students, but this has yet to be finalized. If the database does become accessible to students, they would be able to use the tagged corpus as a self-access learning resource. For example, they might be interested in learning how rhetorical questions structure the discourse of lectures and how interactive questions structure the discourse of discussion sections.

These, of course, are only a few quick examples of the sorts of things one might do with the question tag, and there are many other possibilities for the other tags. Teachers might be interested in the structure of introductory roadmaps, researchers could look at the way spoken academic definitions differ from definitions in written discourse, and students might benefit from looking at the ways in which requests for advice or suggestions are framed.

4. Conclusion

In the best of all possible worlds, if our pragmatic annotation is completed and found to be useful, teachers will finally have easy access to a corpus of spoken pragmatic data, to guide them by what actually exists as they plan their lessons. The annotated version of MICASE will be useful for teachers of academic English, and the methods we have applied here can be used with other corpora as well. Having access to a pragmatic analysis enhances the value of MICASE by facilitating data collection, thus enabling a data-driven discourse analysis by researchers, teachers, teacher trainers, testers, linguists, and others. The forthcoming MICASE Handbook will increase the value of the corpus even further by allowing people to make use of the abstracts and pragmatic inventory, which encourages in-depth, qualitative use of a single transcript rather than, or in addition to, quantitative or comparative cross-corpus investigations. The work that we are doing will enable teachers and researchers to further their own agendas by facilitating access to the corpus in a variety of ways.

Our primary goal at this point is simply to finish tagging our subset of transcripts and make it available, at which point we also want to encourage people to actually use it. We also hope to create a relatively simple search interface, similar to what already exists for MICASE but that also incorporates a category for pragmatic codes. At a minimum, we would like this interface to enable cross-searches with pragmatic codes and some of the other existing categories, such as speech event type and speaker variables. We hope that this paper will also provide some inspiration for how to apply pragmatic tagging to other specialized corpora.

Using Oral Corpora in Contrastive Studies of Linguistic Politeness

María José García Vizcaíno

Montclair State University

Abstract

Oral corpora constitute excellent sources of real data with which to undertake pragmalinguistic inductive research into politeness phenomena. The purpose of this paper is to demonstrate the importance and the main advantages of two oral corpora, the British National Corpus and a Peninsular Spanish Spoken Corpus (Corpus Oral de Referencia del Español Contemporáneo), in contrastive studies on linguistic politeness. In particular, this work aims to explain how these corpora can be used in general and specific qualitative as well as quantitative studies to analyze politeness strategies in English and Spanish. The results of the analyses shed light on the nature of politeness phenomena and on the functions of politeness strategies in four different domains of social interaction. Also, some pedagogical implications for the fields of teaching Spanish and English as foreign languages are discussed.

1. Introduction

Many traditional studies of linguistic politeness are based primarily on theoretical grounds or on examples taken from personal experience, conversations or anecdotes from real life (Lakoff, 1973, 1975; Leech, 1983; Haverkate, 1994; Sifianou, 1989, 1992a, 1992b; Wierzbicka, 1985; Hickey, 1991; Hickey and Vázquez Orta, 1994). Within this trend, the work undertaken by Brown & Levinson (B&L hereinafter) in 1987 is one of the few that uses multiple languages to demonstrate the existence of linguistic politeness strategies. However, not even in this work is it clear how the authors arrive at the repertoire of strategies. We do not know if B&L examined examples of those languages first and then, out of these examples, concluded that there were certain politeness strategies or if they had a prior hypothesis about the strategies and then tested that hypothesis by examining them in three languages: English, Tamil and Tzeltal. Likewise, in recent studies on linguistic politeness, except for some works based on oral corpora,[1] most of the research done is more deductive than inductive. In other words, scholars try to prove the existence of certain linguistic mechanisms in speech instead of analyzing the speech to see what strategies speakers use in social interaction.

Spoken corpora are an excellent source of authentic empirical data on which to base pragmalinguistic studies because this type of corpora allows the researcher to analyze how people really talk and how politeness phenomena are present in the speech that we use every day in different situations. There are three main advantages to using oral corpora for research in pragmatics. First, they can represent a wide range of genres. Therefore, they are suitable for studying spoken language in diverse communicative contexts. Second, these corpora offer information about the speakers: sex, age, education level, and social distance and power relationships among the participants. This is important when trying to study how social factors affect the use of linguistic politeness mechanisms. Finally, these corpora contain prosodic information.

In the field of politeness studies, prosodic information such as intonation, pitch, hesitations in speech, or laughs is truly relevant for analyses of linguistic strategies since, for example, it is very different to utter a request with rising intonation than with falling intonation. When using rising intonation (Can I borrow your car?↑), the speaker leaves the request and its performance open to the hearer and thus takes into account the hearer's freedom of action (his negative face -- see below). In contrast, uttering the request with falling intonation (Can I borrow your car?↓), implies to some extent that the hearer will comply with the request and hence, the speaker impedes the addressee's freedom of action and threatens his negative face.

In this paper, I will demonstrate how oral corpora can be used to study politeness phenomena in two languages and also why it is important to use an inductive approach to analyze speech in order to find out what potential linguistic politeness mechanisms exist in the usage of spoken language. For this purpose, the main features of these corpora will be discussed as well as the modifications that were made to fit the purpose of this study. In addition, I will explain how these corpora were used to undertake both general and specific qualitative analyses having these sources of data. I will also illustrate how these corpora can be an excellent source of data for quantitative studies since they offer a wide range of genre types and include information about participants. Finally, some of the results and conclusions obtained together with some pedagogical implications of the study will be presented.

2. Linguistic Politeness and Interactional Domains

The theoretical framework of this paper is based mainly on two models of politeness: Brown and Levinson's politeness model (1987) and Spencer-Oatey's rapport management proposal (2000, 2002). B&L's model represents one of the most detailed and complete studies of politeness phenomena undertaken so far.[2] To briefly summarize their proposal, two key concepts must be explained: face and face-threatening act. The concept of 'face' was taken from Goffman (1967) and refers to the group of basic social needs and desires of human beings. These needs can be of two different types. On the one hand, all human beings need their thoughts, opinions, and likes to be respected, approved of, understood and admired by others. This is what B&L call 'positive face'. On the other hand, human beings also need their freedom of action to be unimpeded by others ('negative face').

Taking into account this notion of face, in social interaction there are certain acts that may 'threaten' the participants' positive and negative face such as requests, disagreements, and apologies. These acts are called FTAs: "face threatening acts" (B&L, 1987:25). In order to perform these acts without damaging the face of others, there are particular strategies that participants can use in verbal interaction. These strategies are linguistic means that are used to achieve certain goals while at the same time protecting the participants' face. These strategies can be oriented towards the positive face (positive politeness strategies) or the negative face (negative politeness strategies).

Spencer-Oatey's model of rapport management (2000) constitutes another relevant contribution to the field of linguistic politeness. In this model, the author contends that language is used to foster, maintain, or even threaten social relationships. This idea of rapport or social relations management involves two essential elements: the concept of 'face' and the notion of 'sociality rights'. Whereas 'face' is associated with personal/social values and is concerned with people's sense of worth, dignity and so on, 'sociality rights' are connected to personal/social expectations, and reflect people's concerns over fairness, consideration and so on. (Spencer-Oatey 2000:14).

In this model of rapport management, there are five interrelated domains. These are: the illocutionary domain, which is related to the strategies used to perform certain FTAs such as requests, apologies, etc., the discourse domain, which is related to the structure and choice of topic of the discourse, the participation domain, which is related to the procedural aspects of the interaction such as turn-taking, overlapping or listener responses, the stylistic domain, which is related to the stylistic aspects of interaction such as choice of tone and choice of genre-appropriate terms, and the non-verbal domain, which is related to gestures, eye contact, and body movement. These five domains play a crucial role in the management of rapport since they handle different aspects of social interaction. One of these aspects is the concept of face, which is responsible for the illocutionary domain in verbal interchange and which will be identified in the present study as an important motivation for the use of politeness strategies. However, there are other components also crucial in the management of "harmony-disharmony" (Spencer-Oatey 2000:13) that influence the choice of politeness as will be shown below. These are the previously mentioned 'sociality rights'. These rights are related to various aspects of verbal interchange such as discourse content and structure, turn-taking procedures, style, and gestures and body-language, which in turn constitute the discourse, participation, stylistic and non-verbal domains respectively.

3. Oral corpora as a data source for contrastive studies of linguistic politeness

3.1 *Corpus Oral de Referencia del Español Contemporáneo* (COREC)

The *Corpus Oral de Referencia del Español Contemporáneo* (COREC hereinafter) was a project that took place at the Universidad Autónoma de Madrid (Spain) in 1992 under the supervision of Professor Francisco Marcos Marín. This corpus is a spoken language corpus transcribed from audio tapes. It includes 1,100,000 words transcribed in electronic format. It is called '*de referencia*' (reference) because this corpus offers extracts, not whole texts or documents. This is a public corpus accessible to anyone.[3]

The main features of the COREC make it a particularly good source of data with which to study politeness phenomena in Peninsular Spanish. The corpus has a broad variety of texts ranging from informal conversations among friends to academic and formal lectures. The representation of each genre is determined according to specific frequency bands previously established in Marcos Marín (1994). The COREC also offers explicit information about the speakers such as sex, age, occupation and place of birth as well as implicit information about the social distance and power relationships among participants. The corpus also contains prosodic information that can be recovered from the audio tapes. Finally, the structure of the files in the COREC is very user-friendly making the transcripts easy to handle. The structure of the files consists of a header and the body of the transcript itself as shown in the following example:

<cinta 015>
<PCIE015D.ASC>
<24-01-92>
<fuente=grabación directa en domicilio privado>
<localización=Madrid>
<términos=dinosaurio, cromosoma, gen, célula, A.D.N., D.N.A., A.R.N., nucleótido, polinucleótido, proteína, célula, neurona, genotipo, fenotipo, organismo, mamífero, era terciaria, ilirio>
<H1=varón, 28 años, biólogo, madrileño>
<H2=varón, c. 28 años, paleontólogo, madrileño>
<H3=varón, 25 años, ingeniero técnico agrícola, madrileño>

<texto>
<H1> ¿Leíste el domingo lo de... lo del periódico, lo que hablaba de los dinosaurios?
<H2> Hombre, sí... lo que pasa es que... dices eso de... coger y...
<H1> Sí <simultáneo> que...
<H2> ...introducir <simultáneo> material genético y...
<H1> Eso, eso... <simultáneo> <fático=duda>
<H2> ...fabricar </simultáneo> dinosaurios... No me parece muy serio.

<H3> ¿En qué se basaba?
</texto>
<texto>

The header is made up of several elements. First, there is a tag with the number of the audio tape where the speech is recorded (three digits). After that, comes the identification file tag. Within this, first there is the initial of the researcher who recorded and transcribed the text (P for Pedro in our example); the next three letters stand for the type of text transcribed (CIE means 'científico', "scientific"); then, the number of the tape where the text is recorded and the position it occupies in the tape marked by the letters of the alphabet (in our example, the text would be on the 015 tape and in the fourth position since letter D occupies the fourth position in the Spanish alphabet); finally, there is .ASC indicating that the file is written in ASCII code. Immediately after that, there are tags related to speech including information about the date (*fecha*), source (*fuente*) (TV, radio, natural conversation, academic lecture, etc.) and place (*localización*), which is the place where the text was recorded (in our example, Madrid). Next, there is a tag with keywords that give us an idea of the topic of the text. Finally, there are tags corresponding to information about the speakers. Each participant has his/her own tag which specifies the sex, age, occupation and place of birth of the speaker. If a speaker's age is approximate, you find c. (*circa*) before the age, for example, "varón, c. 45 años" meaning "male, approx. 45 years old".

After the header, the body of the text itself appears, limited by the tags <texto> ('texto' meaning 'text') at the beginning and </texto> at the end. The transcripts of the texts in the COREC are orthographic, not phonetic or phonological. This means that although the COREC offers tags related to paralinguistic features such as hesitations (<vacilación>), laughs (<risas>), whispering (<murmullo>), silences (<silencio>), and overlapping or simultaneous speech, it offers no information about pitch, intonation and tone of voice. These prosodic features are relevant in this study since it is not the same thing to utter "Sit down" in a friendly tone of voice (invitation) as with the strong tone of voice of an imperative sentence "Sit <u>**DOWn**</u>" (command). Because of this, I decided to re-transcribed a second group of conversations, which made up the general qualitative study data:[4] I listened to them carefully and transcribed them again noting all the prosodic aspects of the speech, following the guidelines given by Langford (1994) concerning the transcription of spoken interaction.

To illustrate the importance of the prosodic information in a study like this, let us examine three examples taken from my own phonetic transcriptions of a telephone conversation between a woman (<H1>) who is ordering some office supplies and the owner of a stationary store. In (1), the woman is not sure about the technical words for the things she needs, so she uses rising intonation (the convention is ↑) to leave her requests open for the hearer to correct if necessary. At the same time, she takes the hearer's opinions into account and does not impose on him.

<H1> Yo le voy a dar las dimensiones de uno que no tiene:: ↑aníllas↑, o sea:: <vacilación> taládros↑ (.)

(1) <H1> I am going to give you the size of one that ha::s no ↑rings ↑, I mea::n, <hesitation> holes↑ (.)

In (2), the owner is tentative in his request by making the sound of some vowels longer than usual (the convention is :). In this way he mitigates and attenuates the request since he gives her options. The effect is to not impose on his client.

(2) si tuviera uste:d (.) para decirme la:s (.)
(2) if you ha:d (.) to tell me the: (.)

Finally, the speaker sometimes uses a low tone of voice (marked by ° °) as a strategy to protect the addressee's positive face. In (3), the woman is ordering a folder with the letters of the alphabet. Notice how she utters the letters of the alphabet a, b, c in a quick (italics) and low tone of voice (°*abc*°) so that she does not threaten the positive face of the owner of the store who is more than likely to know that the letters of the alphabet are a, b, c. If she had not used this specific tone of voice, it would have been impolite to make such a clarification on her part.

(3) ↑quisiéra ahora:: (1.0) separadore::s er (.) de abecedários↑ (.) *o sea* (1.0) separadores co:n (.) <fático=duda>°las letras del abecedario °*abc*° (1.0) é:so es (.) para <vacilación>

(3) ↑I would like no::w (1.0) folde::rs er (.) of the alphabet↑ (.) *I mean* (1.0) folders wi:th (.) <doubting> the letters of the alphabet °*abc*° (1.0) tha:t's right (.) to <hesitation>

The addition of prosodic annotations was one of the main adaptations made to the COREC for the purpose of the qualitative studies.

3.2 The British National Corpus (BNC)

The British National Corpus (BNC hereinafter) is a corpus of 100 million words of modern English, both written and spoken.[5] The written part contains 90 million words and the spoken part has 10 million. For the purpose of this study, I only focused on the spoken part, whose main features are very similar to those of the COREC. First, it offers a wide variety of genres divided into two groups. One group is the so-called 'demographic part', which contains transcripts of spontaneous natural conversations. The other group is the 'context-governed part', which contains transcripts of speech recorded in non-spontaneous or semi-spontaneous communicative situations. This context-governed part includes four broad categories or 'domains' of genres: educational and informative (lectures, news broadcasts, class discussions, tutorials), business (sales demonstrations, trade union meetings, interviews), institutional and public (political speeches, council meetings), and leisure (sports commentaries, club meetings, radio phone-ins).

The second feature of the BNC is that it offers information about the speakers: sex, age, speaker's first language, dialect, education, social class, occupation, and aspects of the relationship between the participants such as who is the active or passive participant in a 'mutual' (symmetrical relationship) or 'directed' (asymmetrical) relationship. These participants were selected from different sex and age groups, and different regions and social classes in a demographically balanced way. Third, the BNC also includes some prosodic and paralinguistic information.

Finally, the structure of the files is very similar to the COREC. BNC files are made up of a header and a body. The header contains all the information related to the content, including the setting and the participants. The header also contains tags with information about the whole BNC project such as bibliographic information, electronic data, and distribution aspects. This general information about the BNC was not needed for this study and besides, all these tags make the BNC headers unnecessarily long. Thus, I decided to eliminate them and just leave in the header those tags related to aspects of the speech itself, its degree of spontaneity (spont) marked with different codes such as H (high spontaneity), L (low), M (medium) or U (unknown), the speech setting and information about the speakers.

With regard to the body of the transcript itself, the files in the BNC are coded using SGML tags. In addition to these syntactic and morphological tags, the corpus offers information about some paralinguistic features such as pauses, laughs, hesitations, change in tone of voice (<shift>), overlapping (<ptr t> where 'ptr' marks the exact point where the overlapping starts and 't' the participant who overlaps), etc. Since this study involved only prosodic features, I eliminated the SGML tags and only kept those tags containing prosodic and paralinguistic information. The following example shows a file in t he spoken BNC already adapted for the purpose of the study. In other words, the long general header has been deleted (it would be too long to reproduce here anyway) and also the SGML tags of the body of the transcript have been eliminated.

```
(. . .)
<header type=text creator='dominic' status=new update=1994-11-27>
Justice and Peace Group meeting -- an electronic transcription
<date value=1994-11-27>
<rec date=1993-04-12 time='19:30+' type=DAT>
<creation date=1993-04-12>
   <partics>
```

<person age=3 educ=X id=PS1VH n=W0001 sex=m soc=UU>
Age: 40
Name: Charlie
Occupation: tradecraft worker
</person>
<person age=3 educ=X id=PS1VJ n=W0002 sex=f soc=UU>
Age: 40
Name: Moira
Occupation: tradecraft worker
</person>
<person id=G3UPS000 n=W0003>
No further information available
</person>
<person id=G3UPS001 n=W0004>
No further information available
</person>
<relation active=PS1VH desc=husband mutual=N passive=PS1VJ>
<relation active=PS1VJ desc=wife mutual=N passive=PS1VH>
</partics>
<settDesc>
<setting county='North Yorkshire' n=088601 spont=M who='PS000 PS1VH PS1VJ G3UPS000 G3UPS001 G3UPS002 G3UPS003 G3UPS004 G3UPS005 G3UPS006'>
<locName>
York
</locName>
<locale>
meeting room
</locale>
<activity>
meeting of the Justice and Peace Group
speeches and group discussion
</activity>
<keywords>
<term>
economics
</term>
<term>
furthering fair trade with Thirld World countries
</term>
</keywords>

Person: PS1VH
Line: 0001

Good evening.
Line: 0002
Are we ready?
Line: 0003
(pause dur=34) Can I say two minutes for what I think might happen and where we've derived some of the (pause) authority from.
Line: 0004
Then maybe (pause) we could introduce ourselves seeing as (pause) there's some folk here who haven't met everybody before.
Line: 0005
(pause) And after that er we shall be taking the running order which is then a sketch next, (pause) which is not cast yet
Person: PS000
(ptr t=G3ULC001) (vocal desc=laugh) (ptr t=G3ULC002)
Person: PS1VH
Line: 0006
(ptr t=G3ULC001) because we didn't know who was coming and who (ptr t=G3ULC002) wasn't.
Line: 0007
(pause) But I'm sure we'll man we'll manage that okay.

The main features of the spoken BNC presented here make it a very suitable and useful oral corpus for analyses of politeness. Yet, the size difference between the BNC and the COREC meant that something had to be modified to fit our purpose. The COREC contained 1 million words and the spoken part of the BNC had 10 million. In order to undertake a contrastive study between politeness strategies in English and Spanish, the *tertium comparationis* had to be equal. So, since 1 million words constitutes a figure representative enough to carry out qualitative analyses, I selected 1 million words of the BNC transcripts and created my own subcorpus out of the 10 million words of the spoken part.

However, in order to undertake the contrastive study in a reliable and balanced way not only did the corpora have to contain the same number of words but they also had to have the same percentages of each genre, especially if quantitative studies were to be conducted in a later stage to analyze the influence of discourse type and situation with respect to a particular linguistic strategy. If genres were not represented in the same percentages and 1 million words were randomly extracted from the BNC, incorrect conclusions could be reached by saying, for example, that a certain strategy X is more frequent in informal spontaneous conversations in Spanish. If in the 1 million-word COREC, the percentage of informal conversations is 25%, that is, there are about 265,000 words that make up informal conversations, and in the 1 million-word BNC selected randomly it happened that the percentage of informal conversations was just 5%, the result would be biased and the conclusion that speakers of Peninsular Spanish use strategy X more often than British English speakers would be ill-founded since the *tertium comparationis* were not equal. Only when the percentage of informal conversations is the same in English and Spanish can that type of conclusion be drawn, since "it is only against a background of sameness that differences are significant" (James 1980).

Therefore, I proceeded to create a subcorpus of 1 million words out of the 10 million words of the spoken BNC with the same proportion of genre types as in the COREC. This was one of the most difficult tasks in the adaptation of the BNC for this work: first, to select BNC files that matched particular percentages in the COREC, and then, to extract these files out of the 10 million words to create a subcorpus. The first step of selecting the files was done by using the bibliographic index of the BNC.[6] This index consists of a bibliographic database, which contains information about every file. Each entry in each file of the corpus has a code of letters and numbers that specify all the information related to that particular file: spoken or written, demographic or context-governed, domain of context-governed and number of words in the transcript. Unix tools helped in the matching of transcripts of the correct length and type.

4. Qualitative studies of politeness.

Once the corpora had been chosen and adapted for the purpose of the study, all data was ready for the analysis. The analysis of the data involved two different stages: a general qualitative study and several specific qualitative studies. In both stages, the analyses were performed on both the COREC and the BNC.[7] The general qualitative study consisted of the analysis of a number of texts in the subcorpora. This analysis revealed the presence of particular strategies that were used to protect and enhance speakers' negative and positive face respectively. Once these transcripts were analyzed and certain linguistic politeness mechanisms were identified, these mechanisms were studied in more detail in the specific qualitative studies. These specific analyses consisted of an analysis of the part of speech, speech act, and pragmatic functions of each individual strategy in a representative number of instances.[8]

4.1 Methodology of the general qualitative study

The main justification for the qualitative study was that my approach was meant to be inductive, not deductive. Rather than demonstrating the existence of certain linguistic strategies, I wanted to analyze oral discourse in general to identify what strategies speakers use in social interaction depending upon the specific communicative context. In other words, the aim was to analyze whether there are particular linguistic mechanisms that people use for particular purposes in different situations, and if such mechanisms exist, how they function in each context. In this sense, the present study can be framed by a specific trend within the broad field of Discourse Analysis (DA hereinafter), which Schiffrin (1994) calls 'Interactional Sociolinguistics' (IS hereinafter). In general, DA adopts the perspective of studying language as discourse, which entails focusing on the functionality of language: what the speaker intends to obtain and what he actually obtains by using certain linguistic mechanisms. IS is based on this general view as well as on two key concepts: situated meaning and context.

The notions of 'situated meaning' and 'context' involve studying the meanings of an utterance by situating it in its context. It is precisely the contextualization of an utterance that motivates its use: the context in which an utterance is used explains why it is used in the first place. IS intends to explain why people say certain things, not by analyzing the motivation behind that utterance but by analyzing the discourse strategy used for that purpose.[9] Thus, the context of an utterance plays an analytically crucial role in IS.

The approach in this study is the IS approach: to explain the use of language by analyzing the discourse strategies (politeness strategies being one particular type) employed by speakers in specific contexts. If the role of context is so important in a study of this nature, then one cannot determine *a priori* what linguistic mechanisms, acts or expressions will be considered to be polite or if some of them are more polite than others. Therefore, it was necessary to undertake a general qualitative study first in order to analyze discourse in context and to identify what potential politeness strategies seem to be frequently used in each communicative situation and how they function in each specific context. The frequency and functioning of these 'potential' politeness strategies were examined in detail at a later stage in the specific qualitative studies.

The general qualitative study involved two stages: adaptation of the transcriptions and analyses of the transcriptions themselves. As discussed in section 3.1, the orthographic transcriptions in the COREC were adapted to capture the prosodic and paralinguistic features required for this study. Likewise, section 3.2 covers the modifications made to the BNC files in order to eliminate syntactic and morphological information and focus on other aspects more relevant for the present analysis. These adaptations in the transcriptions can be considered to be the first stage in the general qualitative study because this process itself involved a great amount of analytical work. While the transcriptions were edited and modified, I was able to observe important aspects of discourse that may be unnoticed when working on transcripts that are complete and ready to analyze. As Atkinson and Heritage (1984) state, the production and use of transcripts are research activities themselves since they "involve close, repeated listenings to recordings which often reveal previously unnoted recurring features of the organization of talk." Therefore, the first stage of the general qualitative study was very beneficial and actually supplemented the second stage in the general qualitative study, which was the analysis of the discourse itself in order to identify potential linguistic politeness mechanisms.

Following the functional approach to discourse analysis adopted by IS, the analysis of the modified transcriptions consisted of identifying particular discourse strategies that seemed to be related to face-maintenance phenomena such as protecting the negative face or fostering the positive face of the discourse participants, and to the sociality rights of the interaction. With these transcriptions analyzed and some particular politeness devices identified, I proceeded to carry out the specific qualitative studies.

4.2 Methodology of the specific qualitative studies

The specific qualitative studies were necessary in order to test whether those 'potential' politeness strategies spotted in the general qualitative study were actually politeness mechanisms and to examine the function of these actual politeness mechanisms in different contexts. These specific qualitative studies involved several stages.

The first stage was to search for the linguistic strategies. For this purpose, the search program Microconcord (Oxford University Press) was used. This program allows you to search for entries containing the requested word or phrase (for example, *sort of*, *well*, or *you know* among the English strategies and *bueno*, *eso es*, and *efectivamente* among the Spanish mechanisms). Also, it allows you to see the larger context in which that search entry is found. Microconcord offers a maximum of 1695 entries but you can restrict the number and the program selects that number of entries randomly (100 in our studies). This program was chosen because it offers the frequency averages for the entries requested and it can expand the searches to their wider contexts. This latter attribute was very useful since during this stage I was interested in analyzing how a particular linguistic strategy functioned in a particular context.

The second stage consisted of the specific qualitative studies of those 100 examples of each strategy selected randomly by Microconcord. These studies involved three main steps. First, I analyzed the part of speech of the item where the strategy was found. This step was only applied to those morphosyntactic strategies whose grammatical category can affect the way the strategy functions in the context. For example, the diminutive suffix *–ito* in Peninsular Spanish can be affixed to nouns, adjectives and adverbs. In its specific qualitative study, the 100 samples of the diminutive were classified according to the part of speech to which the *-ito* was affixed. The results of the specific qualitative study showed that most of the samples of *–ito* were attached to either nouns (44.5%) or adverbs (42.5%). Also, the results of the analysis of the speech acts where this diminutive was found showed that more than half of those percentages were evaluative or exhortative speech acts. The diminutive functioned here as an attenuation device, mitigating the illocutionary force of the speech act and focused on the noun in the case of the evaluatives and on the adverb in the exhortatives: 'Fue un *poquito* como un pequeño engaño' (It was a little bit like a small deceit), 'Tienen que marcar ahora *mismito* el teléfono' (You should call this number just right now).[10] In other words, the analysis of the part of speech where the strategy appeared proved to be very useful in these studies since it was often directly related to the pragmatic function of that particular strategy.

The second step in the specific qualitative studies involved analyzing the type of speech act in which the strategy was found. To this end, Searle's taxonomy of illocutionary acts (1976) was followed with some adaptations. For example, within the category of representatives, I distinguished between those acts that just describe an aspect of the external world (descriptives) from those that express an evaluation or opinion by the speaker about an aspect of the world (evaluatives). Likewise, within the commissives, offers or invitations were differentiated from promises. In the same way that the part of speech analysis proved to be useful for the analysis as a whole because of the influence of the part of speech on pragmatic functions, the analysis of the type of illocutionary acts in which the politeness strategies were found also helped to clarify their pragmatic behavior. For example, in the specific qualitative study of the discourse marker *well*, it was observed that the illocutionary acts in which this marker appeared were closely related to its pragmatic functions. In 23 out of 34 cases of *well* as a transition marker, *well* was found in descriptives, such as '*Well*, anyway it was coal tokens', used as a conclusive marker to end a conversation.[11] However, in 16 out of 19 cases of *well* as an attenuation marker, this marker appeared in evaluatives (critiques, opinions, disagreements) such as 'That's not quite the same thing as fairly traded though', and the answer: '*Well*, it is in a way because...' Therefore, the type of speech act in which the discourse marker appeared (descriptive or evaluative) affected its pragmatic function (transition or attenuation).[12]

Finally, the third and most important step in the specific qualitative studies was the analysis of the pragmatic functions of the strategies. Taking into account the part of speech and the illocutionary speech act where the strategy was found, all the pragmatic functions of the particular strategy in every context were analyzed. By doing so, I was able to determine if all the functions had to do with politeness phenomena or with something else. In other words, I wanted to determine if all the 'potential' politeness strategies identified in the general qualitative study were actually politeness strategies or if they were strategies related to other domains of social interaction.

5. Using oral corpora in quantitative studies

Spoken corpora constitute not only an excellent source of data for qualitative studies that analyze how certain linguistic politeness strategies function in different contexts; they can also be used in quantitative studies that examine how social and contextual factors influence the use of those strategies. Although the study described here did not involve quantitative analysis, I did explore the possibilities that the COREC and the BNC offer to carry out such analysis and found that although both corpora are suitable for quantitative studies since they offer information about the participants and the setting, this information needs to be prepared beforehand.

The corpus data needs to be prepared for quantitative analysis because the information about participants that both the COREC and the BNC offer is not always explicitly given, so, it is necessary first to identify and extract all the variables related to the speakers and, then, to group and prepare that information in order to handle participants' attributes in an efficient manner. Among all the factors related to the speakers, there are three traditionally considered as relevant to the use of politeness strategies: sex (Lakoff, 1973, 1975; Zimin, 1981; Nichols, 1983; Smith, 1992; Holmes, 1995; García Vizcaíno, 1997), social distance, and power relationships (Brown and Gilman, 1960; Leech, 1983; Brown and Levinson, 1987; Slugoski and Turnbull, 1988; Blum-Kulka et al., 1989; Holmes, 1990). Information about these three factors can be found either explicitly or implicitly in the COREC and BNC.

With respect to the social factor of sex, both corpora give explicit information about the gender of the speaker in the header of the file, so, this variable can be handled very easily just by dividing the participants in two groups: male and female. Regarding social distance and power relationships among the speakers, some studies agree on separating these variables (Holtgraves, 1986; Slugoski and Turnbull, 1988; Brown and Gilman, 1989) while others believe they should be treated under the same category (Brown and Levinson, 1987; Watts et al., 1992; Spencer-Oatey, 1996). In future quantitative studies, I would not separate these variables since I agree with Watts et al. (1992) that power relationships among participants (vertical relations) will affect the social distance (horizontal relations) among them and vice versa. Needless to say, the communicative and contextual situations have to be taken into account when pondering these factors. For example, if the participants are a professor and a student but they happen to be brothers, the distance and power relations will be asymmetrical when these speakers are in a professional context such as the classroom and symmetrical when they are in a familiar setting such as having a meal with their parents.

The corpora used here differ with respect to the explicitness of the power relationships among the speakers. The BNC offers explicit information about the type of relationship among the speakers in most of the headers of its files. The BNC specifies if the relationship is 'mutual' (symmetrical), that is, if all the participants are on an equal footing, or if it is 'directed' (asymmetrical), in which the roles of the participants are described differently. The roles applicable to a 'directed relationship' are classed in the BNC as either 'passive' or 'active'. For example, the relationships "colleague" or "spouse" would be classed as mutual, while "employee" or "wife" would be classed as directed. Unfortunately, the COREC does not offer explicit information about the relationship among speakers in the headers of the files. However, the social distance and power relations among the participants can be determined by examining the whole context and situation of that particular communicative exchange. Therefore, in both corpora, information about the type of relationship among the speakers can be retrieved either explicitly or implicitly and classified into two categories: symmetrical and asymmetrical relationships.

Apart from the social factors of sex, distance and power relationships among the speakers, there are other participants' attributes that are offered in the headers of the files in both corpora: age and occupation. Regarding age, speakers can be divided according to the six groups suggested in the BNC: under 15 years of age, 16-24, 25-34, 35-44, 45-59, and over 59. With respect to participant occupation, since the corpora offer specific information about professions, speakers can be divided into three main groups by level of education: low, medium or high.

The second major adaptation of the COREC and BNC for quantitative studies has to do with the information these corpora offer about setting and type of discourse. As Freed and Greenwood (1996) point out, the type of discourse (degree of spontaneity, topic, and requirements of the contextual situation as a whole) plays a crucial role in social interaction and in the linguistic mechanisms that speakers use, so this information should be considered an important social variable to take into account in quantitative studies on politeness strategies. As in the case of participant attributes, the information about discourse type and setting also needs to be prepared beforehand.

As previously mentioned, one of the advantages of using oral corpora is the wide range of discourse types that they offer since this allows us to study politeness strategies in a wide array of situations. Also mentioned above were the different genres and domains that the COREC and the BNC embrace, making them very suitable for our purpose. In the BNC, the information about the type of discourse and the degree of spontaneity of the interaction is given explicitly in the file headers, whereas the COREC only explicitly specifies the discourse type in the header, leaving implicit in the text the information about the degree of spontaneity of the setting. However, when analyzing the COREC and BNC subcorpora in the general qualitative study, I realized that the information given in the file headers about the discourse type and setting was not very reliable since the classification of discourse types seems to merge the formal aspects of the speech with the topic it deals with.

In the COREC, as mentioned earlier, the second identification tag in the header gives information about the discourse type of the file. However, it is not clear whether the information given in that tag refers to the topic of the discourse or to its structure. For example, there are files whose discourse type tags are identified as CON (for conversations) and other files identified as CIE (for scientific), yet in the COREC one may find conversations that have a high degree of specialization in content because that particular conversation is among friends who are expert in molecular biology and they are identified as CON and not CIE. The reverse also occurs: there are scientific texts that have a non-rigid format very similar to that of conversations and they have been classified as CIE and not CON. Besides, the criteria used to differentiate texts identified as DEB (debates), DOC (documentaries) and ENT (interviews) are not very clear, especially when there are texts categorized as DOC in which you find the typical question-and-answer structure of interviews.

The BNC presents the same problem. As noted previously, within the context-governed part of the spoken corpus, there are four domains: educational and informative, business, institutional and public, and leisure. However, in the general qualitative study of the BNC subcorpora, I realized that some discourse types were shared by these four domains, so they did not seem to be that different. For example, within the domain of business you may find interviews, yet there are interviews classified under the domain of leisure too, so it seems that again two criteria are being mixed: topic of discourse and formal structure. Also, sometimes the degree of spontaneity specified in the headers does not seem to match the particular setting. For instance, some academic lectures were assigned a high degree of spontaneity (<spont=H>), when this type of discourse situation is often prepared somehow in advance and so should be characterized as having at least a medium degree of spontaneity.

Therefore, due to these anomalies, when using these corpora in quantitative studies, one must prepare the information provided by the COREC and BNC regarding discourse type and setting according to a more coherent taxonomy that does not mix aspects related to form with those related to content. The model of diatypic variations proposed by Gregory (1967) provides such a taxonomy.[13]

A description of discourse varieties and their broad choice of language usage should take into account which aspects of discourse are related to and influence the wide range of communicative situations and contexts in which spoken language is used. These aspects are the situational categories of purpose, medium and addressee relationship, which in turn represent the contextual categories of field, mode and tenor of discourse. These contextual categories constitute the diatypic variety differentiation in language, i.e., the contextual categories suggested by Gregory's model, which can be used as criteria to distinguish the different aspects involved in spoken discourse in order to reach a more reliable taxonomy of discourse types in the corpora. Taken individually, field, mode, and tenor each apply to the COREC and BNC with special considerations.

The field of discourse relates to the purpose of the addressor in that particular speech event. According to Gregory, the purposive roles of the speakers may be specialized or non-specialized. In the COREC and BNC data, the identification tags may give us an approximate idea of the degree of specialization of the texts, but as was said before, one should not simply rely on these tags. In the COREC, there are texts categorized as CIE (scientific) which *prima facie* could be classified as 'specialized' since one would assume they use very technical and specialized language, but they turn out to have very neutral non-specialized language. Likewise, the COREC uses the tag EDU (education) and the BNC uses the educational and informative domain to include texts as different as university lectures and classes to 6-year-old children. Although these types of situations are related to the topic of education, they are very different with respect to the field of discourse and the purpose of the speaker. Whereas the former could be classified as having a specialized field of discourse, the latter would definitely be non-specialized. Hence, one needs to analyze the whole discourse and its context in order to determine the field of discourse of each speech situation.

Mode of discourse deals with the degree of spontaneity of a spoken discourse. The BNC offers explicit information about the degree of spontaneity of the discourse and the COREC leaves implicit this information in its discourse type identification tags. However, one should again use these explicit and implicit data cautiously just as hints to determine the real and actual degree of spontaneity after having analyzed the discourse in its entirety. The reason for this is that not all the speech situations in these spoken corpora have the same degree of spontaneity and, hence, fall under the same category of mode of discourse. For example, informal conversations among friends and interviews both constitute spoken discourse situations. However, casual conversations are much more spontaneous than interviews,[14] so these two discourse types cannot simply be identified as spontaneous; they need to be differentiated according to their particular mode of discourse. For both corpora, one could use three categories: spontaneous (as in informal conversations), non-spontaneous (as in political speeches or sermons which are written to be spoken) and semi-spontaneous (as in interviews).

Finally, tenor of discourse results from the mutual relations between the language used and the relationships among the speakers (Gregory 1967: 188). These relations vary depending on the degree of formality or informality among the participants. Therefore, this category is directly related to the social distance and power relationships of the speakers. In this sense, the information about the participants provided in the headers of the corpora explicitly, as well as the implicit information that can be obtained while carrying out the qualitative studies, will help to determine if the tenor of discourse in that situation is formal or informal.

Once the situational and contextual categories of spoken interaction - field, mode and tenor of discourse, according to Gregory's model -- have been defined and applied to the corpora, cases of at least 12 different diatypic varieties can be found in the COREC and BNC (see Tables 1 & 2). Yet, these varieties of discourse types relate to the formal features of spoken interaction. They do not relate to the content or topic of the exchange. Hence, in order to identify what percentage of discourse types exist in each diatypic variety according to the topic, one can simultaneously establish five domains of text topics: education/information, journalism, institutions, conversations, and leisure. So, for example, you may have two texts that belong to the education domain but one is AEF and the other is ADG. The difference lies in the fact that the first one is non-spontaneous mode and formal tenor (for example, a lecture on taxes given to a group of ministers) and the second is semi-spontaneous mode and informal tenor (for example, a private Spanish lesson between friends). To present the diatypic variety and topic domains of the texts in which specific politeness strategies occur, charts can be used as in Figure 1, which shows an example of a linguistic politeness strategy in the BNC: *sort of*. This strategy occurs primarily in the diatypic variation BCG, that is, non-specialized field, spontaneous mode and informal tenor. Within this variety, the topic or content domain where most instances of *sort of* were found was leisure and conversations among friends and relatives.

Table 1. Situational and Contextual Categories of Spoken Interaction

A=Field specialized
B = Field non-specialized
C = Mode spontaneous
D = Mode semi-spontaneous
E = Mode non spontaneous
F = Tenor formal
G = Tenor informal

Table 2. Types of Diatypic Varieties in the Corpora

ACF	Field specialized – Mode spontaneous- Tenor formal
ACG	Field specialized – Mode spontaneous - Tenor informal
ADF	Field specialized – Mode semi-spontaneous - Tenor formal
ADG	Field specialized – Mode semi-spontaneous-Tenor informal
AEF	Field specialized – Mode non-spontaneous-Tenor formal
AEG	Field specialized – Mode non-spontaneous – Tenor informal
BCF	Field non-specialized – Mode spontaneous – Tenor formal
BCG	Field non-specialized – Mode spontaneous – Tenor informal
BDF	Field non-specialized – Mode semi-spontaneous – Tenor formal
BDG	Field non-specialized - Mode semi-spontaneous -Tenor informal
BEF	Field non-specialized - Mode non-spontaneous - Tenor formal
BEG	Field non-specialized - Mode non-spontaneous - Tenor informal

6. Results of the analyses

Different results were obtained from each type of analysis, demonstrating the benefits and usefulness of undertaking two different types of qualitative studies and of using these oral corpora as a data source for the study. On the one hand, the general qualitative study revealed some aspects of the nature of politeness phenomena. On the other hand, the specific qualitative studies gave a better understanding of how politeness strategies work in English and Spanish.

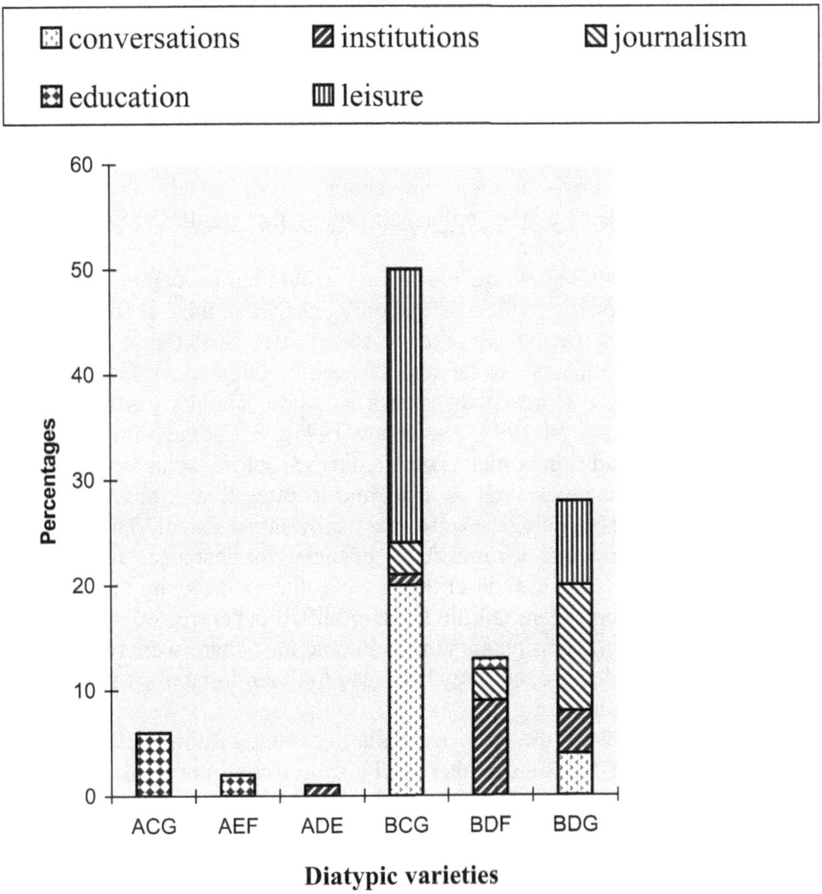

Figure 1. Distribution of *sort of* according to Topic and Oral Discourse Typologies

The analyses done in the general qualitative study showed that, in general terms and in both languages, politeness entails a series of linguistic strategies used by speakers in order to achieve certain social goals in particular contexts and communicative situations. For example, in Spanish the particle *¿no?* after evaluative speech acts is used as a positive politeness strategy to show interest towards the addressee's opinion and to invite him to express his own opinion; at the same time the speaker leaves his ideas open and does not impose them on the interlocutor. Likewise, half of the cases of *you know* studied in the BNC show that this marker is used as a positive politeness strategy to achieve solidarity and empathy with the addressee. The fact that politeness strategies function as means towards ends show that politeness is not a motivation in itself, as has sometimes been claimed when relating indirectness to politeness phenomena (Leech 1983; B&L 1987; Thomas 1995), but the means speakers use to attain their objectives. Participants in social interaction do not use certain strategies to be more polite, but to obtain specific social aims. In this sense, politeness strategies are used to 'modify' or 'correct' certain speech acts or communicative situations that may threaten participants' goals in social interaction. It is precisely this 'corrective' aspect of politeness that leads us to the next finding that resulted from the general qualitative study.

If politeness strategies are the means to ameliorate certain FTAs (face threatening acts), linguistic politeness will only exist when there is something that may threaten social interaction. In other words, if there is no threat, then there is no point in using politeness strategies. Therefore, linguistic politeness is not something that is always present in speech as some scholars have pointed out (Hickey and Vázquez Orta 1994, Haverkate 1994), but something that is only present when this condition is met: a threatening aspect in social interaction. For example, in discourse types such as academic lectures it was observed in both corpora that politeness strategies were practically non-existent. The reason for this is that in an academic lecture about glaciers, for instance, almost all the illocutionary speech acts are descriptives. In other words, in that particular communicative situation there is little to be modified or 'corrected' since there is no apparent threat to the participants in the interaction. There were other types of strategies used in the lecture, but they belonged to other domains of interaction as will be explained below.

On the other hand, the specific qualitative studies showed that politeness strategies as a whole function neither in the same scope nor in the same way. Speakers use different types of linguistic mechanisms and orient them differently, that is to say, they may choose to protect the positive face of the participants by using positive politeness mechanisms or respect the negative face of the addressee by resorting to negative politeness strategies. As B&L (1987) maintain, strategies may be oriented towards the positive face of the addressee (to get closer to his/her likes, interests and common knowledge) or to his/her negative face (to protect the addressee's freedom of action). This was perceived in the specific qualitative studies conducted. The same linguistic mechanism may sometimes function as a positively-oriented strategy or as a mechanism used to attenuate imposition, that is, as a negatively-oriented strategy. For example, in the specific qualitative study of the Spanish diminutive suffix *–ito* in the COREC, it was observed that the suffix could be oriented towards the positive face of the addressee to make a compliment and enhance solidarity with the interlocutor such as in 'Y esta falda con vuelec**ito**. Es que en las fotos quedan muy bien' (And this sort of nice swirl of the skirt. It looks so cute in the pictures) or it could be oriented towards the negative face of the addressee to attenuate the imposition of a request, for instance: 'Espera un moment**ito**' (Wait a little bit, please).

However, one aspect that B&L do not mention is that, apart from this positive or negative orientation, within the scope of positive politeness, strategies can be oriented towards the protection of someone's positive face or its enhancement; contrary to what happens within the scope of negative politeness in which strategies are always oriented towards the protection of the addressee's negative face, not its enhancement. For example, in the same case of the diminutive suffix *–ito* apart from the two main functions or orientations mentioned above, attenuation of an exhortative or affective solidarity with the addressee in a compliment, the diminutive can be also used in evaluative speech acts such as the criticism 'Estabas un poqu**ito** despistado' (You were a little bit absent-minded) to protect the positive face of the addressee. Although this orientation of the strategy is also towards the positive face of the addressee such as in the example of the compliment there is an important difference between both examples. In the evaluative act, the diminutive aims to protect the addressee's positive face by attenuating the meaning of the adjective 'despistadito' (a little bit like absent-minded) in the criticism. However, in the case of the compliment, *-ito* functions as a strategy to foster affect and closeness with the hearer, that is, to enhance her positive face, not to protect it.

Apart from the positive or negative face orientation of politeness strategies, in the specific qualitative studies undertaken, face did not seem to be the only motivation for participants to use certain strategies in social interaction.[15] For example, in the analysis of *bueno* and *well* in the COREC and BNC, two main pragmatic functions were identified: attenuation and transition. In their attenuation function, these markers are used to mitigate the illocutionary force of a potentially threatening act such as a request or a criticism: '*Well*, I think it's absolutely necessary to do this in supermarkets but erm you know that maybe fair trading in our country supermarkets erm are not the only way to shop' or '*Bueno*, a mí me parece impresionante' (*Well*, I think it is unbelievable) and hence, they are used to save participant face in the interaction. However, in the transition function, *bueno* and *well* contribute to starting, continuing or concluding a conversation or statement in a less abrupt manner than if the marker had been omitted: '*Well* now, what can we do for this lady?' or '*Bueno*, ¿me va diciendo su nombre?' (*Well*, can you start by giving me her name?). They are politeness strategies not oriented directly to the illocutionary force of the FTA, but rather to the discourse structure itself: topic changes and organization. Therefore, in this transitional function, these discourse markers are used as strategies to develop a better rapport management in the interaction, not in the sphere or scope of face maintenance (illocutionary domain) but in a different domain: the discourse domain (García Vizcaíno & Martínez-Cabeza 2005). In the specific qualitative studies, it was observed that politeness strategies fell under four of the domains pointed out by Spencer-Oatey (2000) and explained in section 1: illocutionary, discourse, participation and stylistic domains.

7. Conclusion

This paper has presented the different uses and advantages of using spoken corpora as a data source for pragmalinguistic research. In particular, it has been shown how two corpora of Peninsular Spanish and British English, the COREC and the BNC respectively, can be adapted to the needs and purpose of contrastive studies in linguistic politeness. Although there can be many different ways of using these corpora, in this study I have focused on the use of these corpora in qualitative studies and a potential application of them to quantitative analyses.

The results obtained in qualitative analyses show that in general the nature of politeness phenomena is very similar between both languages because both use linguistic strategies as means towards ends. However, the specific qualitative studies demonstrate that although some politeness strategy functions are the same in Spanish and English, there are also particular differences in pragmatic behavior between them. For example, the specific qualitative studies of *bueno* and *well* reveal that their two main functions (attenuation and transition) are the same in Spanish and English, so students of Spanish and English may use *bueno* and *well* similarly in illocutionary and discourse domains. However, the qualitative studies also revealed that there are other pragmatic functions that exist in one language and not in the other such as the expressive function in *bueno*. The discourse marker *bueno* is sometimes used as an expressive marker with the values of impatience or resignation. This function was not identified in the use of *well* in the BNC. Consequently, native speakers of Spanish studying English as a foreign language often tend to reproduce the expressive function of *bueno* in *well*, producing ill-formed utterances from the pragmatic point of view since by doing so they convey mere transition in discourse structure instead of a choice of style on the part of the speaker. In other words, they use the same marker, but in the wrong domain of interaction.

These results may have interesting pedagogical implications in fields such as the study of Spanish or English as a Foreign Language since students of Spanish and English need to learn not only how to speak or write the language properly, but also how to interact in different social contexts. In other words, students sometimes are successful in their linguistic competence, but fail in their social skills and performance in a foreign language.

Notes

1 The most outstanding case is the Conversations Corpus created by the research group Val. Es. Co (Briz, 2001a). This corpus has been and is currently being used as a data source for empirical studies on linguistic politeness (Briz, 2001b, 2002; Zimmerman, 2002).

2 There have been, however, several critics of the B&L model including critics of their concept of 'face' (Matsumoto 1988, Ide 1989, Gu 1990) and critics of their hierarchy of strategies (Haverkate 1983, 1994, Blum-Kulka 1987, Fraser 1990, Hickey 1992), to name a few.

3 The corpus can be found at: ftp://ftp.lllf.uam.es/pub/corpus/oral/corpus.tar.Z. The following website is useful for extracting the oral corpus: http://www.terra.es/personal/m.v.ct/iei/elcorpus.htm.

4 I was allowed to record the audio tapes at the Computational Linguistics Laboratory in the Universidad Autónoma in Madrid (*Laboratorio de Lingüística Computacional de la UAM*).

5 The BNC can be accessed through the following website: http://www.natcorp.ox.ac.uk/.

6 This index is available at ftp://ftp.itri.bton.ac.uk/bnc/.

7 By COREC and BNC it will now be understood the subcorpora created out of these corpora.

8 A brief presentation of some of the results of the specific qualitative studies may be found in García Vizcaíno (2001).

9 The term 'discourse strategy', covers a wide range of expressions that can satisfy a broad variety of interpersonal purposes (Schiffrin 1994).

10 The translations into English intend to convey not only the same meaning as the original examples in Spanish, but also the same pragmatic illocutionary force. For example, in the case of 'Tienen que marcar ahora *mismito* el teléfono', the diminutive suffix *–ito* is used to mitigate the illocutionary force of the request. Therefore, the translation into English should not just convey the literal meaning ('You have to call this number right now'), but also the pragmatic polite force of the utterance. This is why instead of 'have to' (meaning literally 'tienen que') I have chosen the modal verb 'should', which imposes less on the addressee ('You should call this number just right now').

11 The other 11 cases of *well* as a transition marker appeared in directives, commissives and expressives.

12 For more information about the pragmatic behavior of the discourse markers *well* and *bueno* see García Vizcaíno and Martínez-Cabeza (2005).

13 By "diatypic variation", Gregory means the linguistic perception of language usage by speakers in communicative situations.

14 The interviewer often prepares the questions in advance and many times even gives an outline of the question to the person to be interviewed.

15 In this matter, I have taken into account the theory of relevance by Sperber and Wilson (1986). Hence, although one can never be positive about speakers' intentions since one cannot get inside someone's mind, we can analyze what is said by the inferential process followed in ostensive communication.

References

Atkinson J.M. and J. Heritage (eds.) (1984), *Structures of Social Action*. Cambridge: Cambridge University Press.

Blum-Kulka, S. (1987), 'Indirectness and politeness in requests: same or different?', *Journal of Pragmatics*, 11: 131-146.

Blum-Kulka, S., House, J., and Kasper, G. (1989), *Cross-Cultural Pragmatics: Requests and Apologies*. New Jersey: Ablex.

Briz, A. y Grupo Val.Es.Co (eds.) (2001a), Corpus de conversaciones coloquiales. Anejo de la Revista *Oralia*. Madrid: Arco Libros.

Briz, A. (2001b), *El español coloquial en la conversación: esbozo de pragmagramática*. Barcelona: Ariel Lingüística.

Briz, A. (2002), 'La estrategia atenuadora en la conversación cotidiana española', in Bravo, D. (ed.) Actas del Primer Coloquio del Programa EDICE: La perspectiva no etnocentrista de la cortesía: identidad sociocultural de las comunidades hispanohablantes. Estocolmo: Institutionen för spanska, portugisiska och latinamerikastudier. 17-46.

Brown, R. and A. Gilman (1960), 'The pronouns of power and solidarity', in Sebeok, T. (ed.) Style in Language. Cambridge, MA: M.I.T. Press. 253-276.

Brown, R. and A. Gilman (1989), 'Politeness theory and Shakespeare's four major tragedies', Language in Society, 18: 159-212.

Brown, P. and Levinson, S.C. (1987), Politeness: Some Universals of Language Usage. Cambridge: Cambridge University Press.

Fraser, B. (1990), 'Perspectives on politeness', Journal of Pragmatics, 14: 219-236.

Freed, A. F. and A. Greenwood (1996), 'Women, men, and type of talk: What makes the difference?', Language in Society, 25: 1-26.

García Vizcaíno, M.J. (1997), Review of Holmes, J. Women, Men and Politeness (1995), Miscelánea, 18: 366-371.

García Vizcaíno, M.J. (2001), 'Principales estrategias de cortesía verbal en español', Interlingüística, 10: 185-188.

García Vizcaíno, M.J. and Martínez-Cabeza, M.A. (2005), 'The pragmatics of well and bueno in English and Spanish', Intercultural Pragmatics, 2(1): 69-92.

Goffman, E. (1967), Interaction Ritual: Essays on Face to Face Behaviour. Garden City, New York: Doubleday.

Gregory, M. (1967), 'Aspects of varieties differentiation', Journal of Linguistics, 3(2): 177-198.

Gu, Y. (1990), 'Politeness in modern Chinese' Journal of Pragmatics, 14: 237-57.

Haverkate, H. (1983), 'Los actos verbales indirectos: El parámetro de la referencia no específica', Lingüística Española Actual, 5: 15-28.
Haverkate, H. (1994), La cortesía verbal: estudio pragmalingüístico. Madrid: Gredos.
Hickey, L. (1991), 'Comparatively polite people in Spain and Britain', Association for Contemporary Iberian Studies, 4 (2): 2-6.
Hickey, L. (1992), 'Politeness apart: Why choose indirect speech acts?', Lingua e Stile, 37: 77-87.
Hickey, L. and I. Vázquez Orta (1994), 'Politeness as deference: A pragmatic view', Pragmaligüística, 2: 267-286.
Holmes, J. (1990), 'Apologies in New Zealand English', Language in Society, 19: 155-199.
Holmes, J. (1995), Women, Men and Politeness. London: Longman.
Holtgraves, T. (1986), 'Language structure in social interaction: Perceptions of direct and indirect speech acts and interactants who use them', Journal of Personality and Social Psychology, 51(2): 305-313.
Ide, S. (1989), 'Formal forms and discernment: Two neglected aspects of universals of linguistic politeness', Multilingua, 8(2/3): 223-48.
James, C. (1980), Contrastive Analysis. London: Longman.
Lakoff, R. (1973), 'The logic of politeness; or minding your p's and q's', in Papers from the ninth regional meeting of the Chicago Linguistics Society. 292-305.
Lakoff, R. (1975), Language and Woman's Place. New York: Harper Colophon.
Langford, D. (1994), Analysing Talk: Investigating Verbal Interaction in English. London: MacMillan.
Leech, G.N. (1983), Principles of Pragmatics. London: Longman.
Marcos Marín, F.A. (1994), Informática y Humanidades. Madrid: Gredos.
Matsumoto, Y. (1988), 'Reexamination of the universality of face: Politeness phenomena in Japanese', Journal of Pragmatics, 12: 403-26.
Nichols, P.C. (1983), 'Linguistic options and choices for black women in the rural south', in Thorne, B., Kramarae, C. and N. Henley (eds.) Language, Gender, and Society. Rowley, MA: Newbury House. 54-68.
Schiffrin, D. (1994), Approaches to Discourse. Oxford: Blackwell.
Smith, J. (1992), 'Women in charge: Politeness and directives in the speech of Japanese women', Language in Society, 21: 59-82.
Searle, J.R. (1976), 'A classification of illocutionary acts', Language in Society, 5: 1-23.
Sifianou, M. (1989), 'On the telephone again! Differences in telephone behaviour: England versus Greece', Language in Society, 18: 527-544.
Sifianou, M. (1992a), 'The use of diminutives in expressing politeness: Modern Greek versus English', Journal of Pragmatics, 17: 155-173.
Sifianou, M. (1992b), Politeness phenomena in England and Greece: A cross-cultural perspective. Oxford: Clarendon Press.

Slugoski, B.R. and W. Turnbull (1988), 'Cruel to be kind and kind to be cruel: Sarcasm, banter and social relations', Journal of Language and Social Psychology, 7(2): 101-121.

Smith, J. (1992), 'Women in charge: Politeness and directives in the speech of Japanese women', Language in Society, 21: 59-82.

Spencer-Oatey, H. (1996), 'Reconsidering power and distance', Journal of Pragmatics, 26: 1-24.

Spencer-Oatey, H. (ed.) (2000), Culturally Speaking. Managing Rapport through Talk across Cultures. London: Continuum.

Spencer-Oatey, H. (2002), 'Developing a Framework for Non-Ethnocentric 'Politeness'Research', in Bravo, D (ed.) Actas del Primer Coloquio del Programa EDICE: La perspectiva no etnocentrista de la cortesía: identidad sociocultural de las comunidades hispanohablantes. Estocolmo: Institutionen för spanska, portugisiska och latinamerikastudier. 86-96.

Sperber, D. and D. Wilson (1986) Relevance, Communication and Cognition, Oxford: Basic Blackwell.

Thomas, J. (1995), Meaning in Interaction: An Introduction to Pragmatics, London: Longman.

Watts, R., I. Sachiko and E. Konrad (eds.) (1992), Politeness in Language: Studies in its History, Theory and Practice. Berlín: Mouton de Gruyter.

Wierzbicka, A. (1985), 'Different cultures, different languages, different speech acts: Polish vs. English', Journal of Pragmatics, 9: 145-178.

Zimin, S. (1981), 'Sex and politeness: factors in first- and second-language use', International Journal of the Sociology of Language, 27: 35-58.

Zimmerman, K. (2002), 'Constitución de la identidad y anticortesía verbal entre jóvenes masculinos hablantes de español', in Bravo, D. (ed.) Actas del Primer Coloquio del Programa EDICE: La perspectiva no etnocentrista de la cortesía: identidad sociocultural de las comunidades hispanohablantes. Estocolmo: Institutionen för spanska, portugisiska och latinamerikastudier. 47-59.

One Corpus, Two Contexts: Intersections of Content-Area Teacher Training and Medical Education

Boyd Davis and Lisa Russell-Pinson

University of North Carolina-Charlotte

Abstract

This chapter explores the use of one corpus in two different contexts: content-area K-12 teacher preparation and medical education. The corpus, the Charlotte Narrative and Conversation Collection, consists of over 500 oral interviews and narratives; all of the speakers in the corpus reside in and around Mecklenburg County, NC, and span a range of ages, ethnicities, cultures and native languages. This collection is drawn upon to sensitize content-area public school teachers to the backgrounds of their increasingly diverse student population and to serve as a resource for creating and adapting content-area lessons. Associated with this corpus is a smaller corpus of on-going conversations with speakers diagnosed with dementia; the language in the dementia corpus and that of the elderly speakers in the primary corpus are used as the basis for research on disordered speech and for teaching prospective health care providers how to communicate more effectively with the elderly. Using the primary corpus for two different educational initiatives has saved time and effort for language researchers.

1. Introduction

While pedagogical corpora are usually created for second and foreign language contexts (Biber et al. 1998, 1999; Hunston 2002; Hyland 2000), other disciplinary uses of corpora have been noted. For example, Davis and Russell-Pinson (2004) report the challenges and successes of using corpora to train content-area public school teachers; in addition, Shenk, Moore and Davis (2004) draw on corpora in training healthcare professionals and caregivers to recognize and employ strategies for effective communication with people with dementia of Alzheimer's type (DAT).

This article will describe how one corpus has been able to support both content-area teacher training and medical education initiatives. The Charlotte Narrative and Conversation Collection (CNCC) has been used for two purposes: to support certain teacher-training initiatives and, in conjunction with a collection of conversations with cognitively impaired speakers, to augment the DAT research.

The CNCC represents speakers from greater Mecklenburg County, NC by embodying the varied ethnicities of the region and containing materials in multiple varieties of English, Spanish, Chinese and other languages spoken in the area. The corpus is synchronic and has approximately 500 interviews in two dozen languages and at least that many varieties of English, with speakers comprising different ages and cultures. Another multicultural collection consists of longitudinal conversations with persons diagnosed as having cognitive impairment, particularly DAT. Web access to the CNCC is sponsored by Special Collections, Atkins Library at University of North Carolina – Charlotte, as part of its new digital collection, New South Voices, at http://newsouthvoices.uncc.edu. Storage, access and retrieval of the DAT corpus are currently being designed to meet standards of the Health Insurance Portability and Accountability Act (HIPAA) of 1996.

From 2001-2005, Project MORE (Making, Organizing, Revising and Evaluating Instructional Materials for Content-Area Teachers) was funded by the Office of English Language Acquisition of the U.S. Department of Education as a Training All Teachers initiative. It drew on the CNCC for two purposes:

- To promote curricular change within university courses that support and extend prospective and practicing content-area teachers' understanding of the diverse learners in the region.
- To develop content-area lessons appropriate for K-12 English language learners (ELLs) and corresponding teacher-training materials as exemplars of how to use authentic oral narrative material in the adaptation or creation of subject-specific lessons.

Since narrative can be used as a "linguistic crossroads of culture, cognition and emotion" (McCabe 1997, quoted in Silliman and Champion 2002: 146), the authentic narratives in the CNCC have helped teachers to better understand and respond to their learners' needs (Davis and Russell-Pinson 2004; cf. Fenner 2003) and to produce rich, multi-layered and imaginative curricula (cf. Egan 1995).

In the same vein, conversational excerpts from the cohort of elderly speakers in the CNCC, augmented by selected clips from the DAT collection, have recently served as the foundation of a new gerontology course. The course, team taught by faculty from gerontology, nursing and applied linguistics, centers on sensitizing current and future health care providers to the communication needs of the elderly, including those with DAT. In addition, it features communication interventions developed from research on the DAT corpus and spurs cultural awareness by asking students to examine and compare their own backgrounds and attitudes to those of the speakers in both corpora.

This article will explore the efficacy of corpus-based materials in two areas, teacher preparation and healthcare/medical education, by providing rationales for the use of corpora in these contexts, examples of materials created from the CNCC and DAT corpora for both venues, and some initial assessment by trainees and trainers of the value of corpus-based materials for their own learning and for their delivery of instruction to others.

2. The Charlotte Narrative and Conversation Collection and the DAT Collection

The CNCC is part of the first release of the American National Corpus (ANC: Reppen and Ide 2004). The CNCC is more modest in scale than the ANC; still, developers of both corpora strive to attain a common, if challenging, goal of constructing representative collections of authentic language use. Specifically, the CNCC aims to deliver a corpus of conversation and conversational narration characteristic of speakers in the New South region of Charlotte, NC and surrounding areas at the beginning of the 21st century. To achieve this end, the CNCC contains interviews of and conversations between long-time residents and new arrivals, including first- and second-language English speakers of all ages, races and ethnicities prominent in the region. The speakers tell personal stories, most often about early reading and schooling experiences, pastimes and past times, life-changing events, or challenges and barriers they have overcome; they also have informal conversations about their families, professions, beliefs and cultures.

Because such a corpus can appeal to a number of different types of users, both content and accessibility must be suitable to K-12 content-area and second-language teachers creating linguistically appropriate materials for their students, medical educators developing culturally-competent training materials for caregivers, budding and seasoned historians studying local or oral histories, and a host of other professionals.

The CNCC, and its host site, the digital New South Voices (NSV) collection, must also be congruent with other web-delivered collections of oral language. We adhere to principles noted by Kretzschmar (2001) in an overview of the American Linguistic Atlas Project. Kretzschmar (162) maintains that interviews must be presented in ways that address the needs of speech science (therapy and speech recognition) and natural language processing, that are "compatible" with current sociolinguistic research and survey research, and that are "planned in expectation of quantitative processing." Accordingly, all interviews and conversations have either been digitized from analog tapes or collected in digital format to support acoustic analyses, such as those typically conducted on vowel sounds. Transcripts for each interview are transcribed, reviewed by two editors, and then encoded, using the Text Encoding Initiative (TEI) guidelines, available at http://www.tei-c.org. Metadata for each transcript adhere to the Dublin Core (DC) standard, found at http://dublincore.org. The CNCC and the NSV use the fifteen DC elements with an additional nine elements necessary to describe more adequately the features of these audio resources. Our subsequent discussion will focus on the CNCC.

The interviews, conversations and conversational narratives in the CNCC are not traditional sociolinguistic interviews, as described by Labov (1984), in that they are not a standard length, and do not include features such as word elicitation, reading passages, oral sentence completions, or the reading of a word list. They are, however, congruent with other sociolinguistic data collection techniques. Sampling techniques for obtaining sociolinguistic data, and the types of data themselves, are now seen as being multiple, ranging from telephone interviews for the forthcoming *Atlas of North American English* (http://www.ling.upenn.edu/phono_atlas/home.html) to piggybacking on community economic polls, such as the Texas Poll (Tillery, Bailey and Wikle 2004). Like the interviews and conversations conducted by students for Johnstone's study of conversations referencing time and place (Johnstone 1990), CNCC interviews are typically conducted by a person, almost always a university student, who is known by the respondent, and who seeks to elicit narratives of personal experience or opinion along lines that the respondent seems to prefer.

To date, we support three search strategies. Online searching includes a Quick Search, which allows single or multiple keyword searches over the entire collection of interviews. Content searching allows the user to find interviews containing up to three particular keywords within limited contexts: person, place, organization or building, and a date range. Content-and-demographic searching allows the user to perform content searching over the text of specific interviews and narratives selected by the age, gender, language or country of origin of the speaker, and may be further limited by type of narrative: monologue, speech, interview, conversation (dialogue) or multiparty conversation.

Similar strategies will be used to search the DAT collection, but it will be accessed separately, and will include:

- Aliases for names of all speakers.
- Anonymization of details as appropriate.
- Password-protected access to transcripts, audio and video.

Not only is such protection enjoined by federal regulation through HIPAA, but there are also further reasons for carefulness. Our permissions to record the conversants in the DAT collection are typically given by a relative, spouse, or legal guardian, and their privacy must be guarded as well. First, because of the stigma still attached to any form of cognitive impairment, some family members do not want it to be known that their family includes an impaired person. Second, the conversants may speak candidly, giving information which could identify or even give revealing information about others, sometimes to their detriment. Thus, in order to protect the privacy of DAT speakers and their families, we envision putting in place a password-protection system that provides access to transcripts and the audio and video components of the DAT collection only to those who have registered with the Special Collections Unit of UNC-Charlotte's Atkins Library or the Library at the Medical University of South Carolina, and have proffered researcher or scholarly credentials, and documented approval by a Human Subjects Research review.

The conversations are transcribed, edited, and encoded like the narratives and conversations in the CNCC. A pilot effort has begun on discourse-tagging DAT conversations, coordinated by Canadian members of the international study group working with this corpus (cf. Ryan, Orange, Spykerman and Byrne 2005).

A second pilot to implement inverse indexing as part of the search has been initiated by Stephen Westman of UNC-Charlotte's Atkins Library (Westman and Davis 2005).

3. Rationale for Using the CNCC in Content-Area Teacher Training and Medical Education

The CNCC is an ideal tool for assisting content-area teachers in broadening their perspectives beyond the typical native English-speaking students who once populated their classes. First, the CNCC contains oral language materials in a number of languages, including multiple varieties of English, Spanish and Chinese and single varieties of Hmong, Vietnamese, Korean, Russian and Japanese. Because the proportion of non-English languages in the CNCC reflects the demographic make-up of the ELLs currently enrolled in local school systems, content-area teachers can review translated transcripts of conversations and interviews to learn more about the backgrounds of these speakers and those of similar origins. Second, the English portion of the CNCC features a number of non-native English speakers talking about the educational systems in and customs and histories of their homelands, the speakers' challenges in adjusting to life in the U.S. and the process through which they acquired English. This subsection of materials has helped to sensitize teachers to the cultural differences between students' native countries and the U.S. as well as the circumstances that ELLs often encounter when they enter a monolingual classroom setting in the U.S. Finally, the CNCC contains a wide array of subject matter suitable to be drawn upon for many K-12 content areas; for example, India-native Shavari Desai talks about her father's account of the partition of India, a story that can complement both history and social studies lessons, while Preeyaporn Chareonbutra's narrative about her Thai family and their travels around the globe can supplement world geography instruction. These and other narratives in CNCC have been used to deepen content-area teaching, for such materials add a personal voice to the subject matter and motivate students to invest more in the lesson, especially when instructors link these narratives to their students' own experiences (cf. Freeman and Freeman 2003).

Both the main collection of the CNCC, with its interviews and conversations with non-impaired speakers in multiple age cohorts, and the DAT corpus of conversations with aging persons having cognitive impairments are useful for healthcare and medical education for much the same reasons. First, the CNCC narratives expand content through the introduction of authentic voices of elderly persons, motivating students and trainees to link corpus speakers to their own knowledge base. Second, the diverse ethnic and linguistic range of the narratives in the CNCC promotes cultural awareness and helps to strengthen curricula about the communication needs and expectations of different populations. Finally, because the CNCC has been used for on-going studies on the discourse of Alzheimer's (e.g., Green 2002; Moore and Davis 2002; Davis

2005), students have an opportunity to examine the data collected for such research and used as the basis for several communication interventions designed for DAT speakers, as well as review publications on these studies, a process that stimulates trainees to bridge the gap between research and practice. Below we describe on-going teacher-training and medical education initiatives tied to the CNCC.

4. Enhancing Content-Area Teacher Training through the CNCC: Project MORE

With 121,640 students and 148 schools, the Charlotte-Mecklenburg School System (CMS) is one of the largest school districts in the U.S. (CMS Fast Facts 2005). CMS has seen a rapid increase in the enrollment of ELLs over the past decade; in the 2004-2005 academic year, the number of ELLs enrolled in CMS rose to 11,510, while the total number of students who do not speak English as a home language grew to 16,631 (CMS ESL Fast Facts 2005). This trend is mirrored in the surrounding counties and, indeed, throughout NC. Hakuta (2000: 2) attributes the rise in non-native English speakers in the state to two factors:

- Large numbers of migratory families [that] are choosing to settle in North Carolina rather than move on to follow the growing season. . . [This trend] has induced friends and extended family members of these previously migratory families to relocate to North Carolina from other states and countries.
- The textile, poultry and furniture industries. . . [which] have increased production in recent years.

Although NC schools continue to hire increasing numbers of ESL teachers to staff language support classes, it is often difficult to retain qualified and experienced teachers. "As a result, students are being placed into content-area classes sooner than the two years typically recommended in this region, and often without the benefit of adequate ESL instruction" (Davis and Russell-Pinson 2004: 148). Adding to this challenging situation is the fact that licensed content-area teachers in the state are still not required to complete coursework or have practical experience in understanding or addressing the diverse language, cultural and educational needs of ELLs, despite the unprecedented 200% growth in the number of ELLs enrolled in NC public schools over the past decade (U.S. Department of Education 2002).

These circumstances prompted the U.S. Department of Education to fund a training-all-teachers grant for this region. Project MORE, an initiative designed to help content-area teachers to better recognize and respond to the needs of the ELLs in their classes, began in 2001. It drew on the CNCC for two main objectives.

First, the CNCC was used to expose practicing and prospective teachers to the varied linguistic and cultural backgrounds of public school students in the area. Because the corpus can be searched by the language background, country of origin, gender and age of each speaker, the CNCC allowed those participating in Project MORE activities (a) to explore the local populations that were of interest to them; (b) to learn more about the growing diversity of southern NC and (c) to link the content of certain narratives to a range of school subjects, such as language arts, social studies and health.

Second, the oral language materials in the corpus were used to develop exemplar content-area lesson plans suitable for instructing ELLs and native English speakers alike; these model lessons were then used to teach current and future teachers how to adapt and develop classroom materials for their own students' needs. These two goals are detailed below by describing two teacher-training exercises that used the CNCC in different but effective ways.

4.1 Technology-Based Teacher In-Service Courses

As we have noted elsewhere (Davis and Russell-Pinson 2004), content-area teachers may show resistance to using corpora and associated technologies, such as concordancers. Through our teacher-training initiatives, we identified several obstacles that we faced when introducing content-area teachers to corpora and corpus-related tools, including the teachers' ambivalence about using authentic language and perception of information overload. However, there was one challenge that we had not expected to encounter when training public school teachers. To our surprise, we found that many of the content-area teachers with whom we worked – especially those who have been practicing for some time – are intimidated by technology. "Because the teachers may not have access to technology in the classroom and most have not been trained to use it with students, this lack of experience makes them reluctant to try unfamiliar forms of technology, such as corpora and concordancing" (154). To help remedy this situation, Project MORE held several technology-based in-services that gave participants one hour of license-renewal credit upon completion.

The in-services covered a number of basic computer-related techniques, such as online searching for content-area materials and participating in online discussions, and then culminated in using a range of corpora, including the CNCC, and corpus-based tools to produce one lesson appropriate for both their first- and second-language students. The teachers whom we trained responded favorably to the introduction of corpora in this manner. In evaluations of the in-services, all of the participants indicated that they had learned more about technology in general, and corpora and concordancing in particular; furthermore, most remarked that they felt more comfortable with computers as a result of the technology-based workshops.

In order to receive their technology credit, teachers had to develop corpus-based materials suitable for their students. Tarra Ellis, a seventh-grade social studies teacher at Northridge Middle School in Charlotte, NC, created the "Open

Sesame" lesson presented below in Table 1. Because all NC public school instruction must follow the North Carolina Standard Course of Study (NCSCOS) goals according to grade and subject, Ellis chose these goals from the NCSCOS standards for Middle School Social Studies to guide her lesson:

- Describe similarities and differences among people of Asia and Africa.
- Compare the physical and cultural characteristics of regions in Asia and Africa.
- Identify examples of cultural transmission and interaction within and among regions in Africa and Asia.
- Identify people, symbols and events associated with the heritage of African and Asian societies.
- Acquire information from a variety of sources.
- Use information for problem solving, decision making and planning.
- Develop skills in constructive interpersonal relationships and in social participation.

Table 1: "Open Sesame" Lesson for Social Studies

Open Sesame:
A Lesson for 7th Grade Social Studies
By Tarra Ellis

Objectives: Students will create a Chinese history booklet in which they:

- Retell a Chinese folktale from the CNCC
- Apply it to a major event in Chinese history
- Compare/contrast it with a Middle Eastern folktale

Materials: copy of narrative, computers with internet access, construction paper, computer paper, crayons/markers/colored pencils, scissors, glue

Procedures: Working in pairs, students will be asked to create a booklet on Chinese history. The booklet will contain 3 parts:

- Retelling the "Open Sesame" story from Mei Wen Xie's CNCC interview
- Selecting a major feature on China from "Mr. Dowling's Electronic Passport" website to summarize and explain how those involved should have heeded the lesson taught in "Open Sesame"
- Comparing and contrasting "Open Sesame" with "Ali Baba and the Forty Thieves" in a Venn Diagram

In addition, students will draw pictures and/or print them from the internet. (As an alternative, students may choose to create a PowerPoint presentation instead of a paper booklet.)

Ms. Ellis came to the workshop knowing her students' needs: her first and second-language students required materials that would hold their interest while giving them sufficient content with which to practice reading and writing skills. With both the NCSCOS goals and her students' needs in mind, Ms. Ellis searched the CNCC database and found Jia Kim's interview of Mei Wen Xie, which touches on a number of similarities and differences between Chinese and Korean culture. In the interview, Xie retells the Chinese folktale of "Open Sesame." In a feedback form accompanying her lesson, Ellis wrote that she chose to use this excerpt because:

> *China is part of my 7th grade social studies curriculum. The story 'Open Sesame' is an interesting story that my students would enjoy. The narrative provides other examples of Chinese culture, such as oral tradition and teaching values. Plus, it includes a little comparison between China, Korea and other nations.*

From Xie's story in the CNCC, Ellis created a number of activities related to needs she perceived for her students (Table 2). This and other teacher-developed, corpus-based lessons are on the Project MORE website, which is used in teacher-training courses and is available as a resource to teachers across the state, and, indeed, around the world.

Table 2: Needs-based Rationale for the Design of "Open Sesame"

Teacher's Perceived Needs of Students	**How The Lesson Addresses these Needs**
Students need practice to become better readers and writers.	Asks students to listen to, read, and retell a narrative; to focus on writing conventions; to conduct computer research; to enhance critical literacy
Students need variety that can address different language abilities and learning styles.	Provides students with options for creating the material and integrating reading, writing, art, computer skills and teamwork
Students need hands-on and interactive activities to sustain interest and focus.	Incorporates different websites, art work and creative expression

4.2 University-Level Teacher-Preparation Courses

Project MORE also sponsored mini-grants for UNC-Charlotte Arts and Science Faculty who typically had 50% or more teacher-licensure candidates in their courses and agreed to use the CNCC to supplement their teacher-preparation courses. The competitive mini-grants were awarded to faculty in American studies, applied linguistics, art education, educational research, English education, history, rhetoric and composition, English literature, American literature and Spanish. The mini-grants allowed the faculty to introduce the CNCC to their students, link the content of CNCC narratives and interviews to the content of the course, and create activities and lessons based on the CNCC, all while equipping the prospective teachers with the technological tools needed to sustain continued corpus-based learning and practice.

One mini-grant recipient was Susannah Brown, an assistant professor in UNC-Charlotte's Art Department. The theme of Brown's Art Education Methods course was personal narrative in and through art. She began the semester by asking students to connect their own personal narratives to those of classmates, community members and professional artists through a series of short interviews. Brown then introduced her students to the CNCC and assigned them to design lesson plans that combined CNCC narratives with art production; she also encouraged her students to create original artwork to illustrate the kinds of work their future students might produce. One of Brown's students chose Rosalia Cruz's narrative as the basis of her lesson plan, which addressed a number of NCSCOS goals for middle school art, such as:

- Using a variety of media and techniques in an expressive manner
- Recognizing and discussing the use of multiple senses in visual arts
- Understanding and discussing that ideas from reality and from fantasy may be used to create original art
- Understanding the use of life surroundings and personal experiences to express ideas and feelings visually

Figure 1, below, presents an example of a student-produced poster collage based on Cruz's narrative.

Brown remarked that the assignment makes prospective teachers more aware of their future students' needs, especially those of non-native English speaking students, and helps prospective teachers to understand what a personal narrative is and to use personal narratives in art education, especially in lesson planning and production of artwork.

In addition, Brown conducted a pre-test and a post-test to measure how her students' understanding of personal narratives and the teaching of art to ELLs evolved from the beginning to the end of the course. The pre-test results revealed that most of her students had little familiarity either with personal narratives or teaching ELLs. However, her post-test showed that her students had increased their understanding of both concepts. Based on her students' progress, Brown believes that her use of personal narratives from the CNCC was crucial to expanding her students' knowledge of both the major theme of her course and the educational, cultural and linguistic backgrounds of their future students.

Figure 1: Collage Based on Rosalia Cruz's Narrative

5. Using the CNCC to Enhance Medical Education: DAT Discourse

Since 2000, a small team has been collecting discourse from speakers with dementia of the Alzheimer's type (DAT); the discourse collected occurs in spontaneous conversation in natural settings and is recorded in assisted living facilities in urban and rural NC. The collection team is comprised of UNC-Charlotte faculty in applied linguistics, nursing, and gerontology and on occasion, includes other researchers from Johnson C. Smith University, as well as visiting faculty from the University of Dortmund (Germany) and the University of Canterbury (New Zealand). A larger multi-disciplinary team of faculty, including specialists in applied linguistics, gerontology, geriatric nursing, computer science, communication studies and communications disorders from universities in NC and SC, Canada, Germany, and New Zealand, analyzes the discourse.

Team members use portions of the CNCC to promote curricular change and to enhance student research experiences in courses on discourse and aging. The team also draws on the audio and transcripts from the CNCC for continued collaborative research on DAT discourse; the research results are then presented in professional development sessions designed for those working with aging persons. The sections below explore the wide-ranging applications of the CNCC to these on-going initiatives.

5.1 Enhancing Curricula and Student-Research Experiences

One curricular application of the CNCC corpus, augmented by an excerpt from the DAT collection, was an intensive interdisciplinary course for graduate and undergraduate students offered as the first state-wide, Internet-delivered course sponsored by the NC Gerontology Consortium in Summer 2003. The course was team-taught by three UNC-Charlotte faculty, Dena Shenk (Gerontology), Boyd Davis (Applied Linguistics), and Linda Moore (Nursing). It included students who were in various locations across the state and reflected different cultural backgrounds and professional experiences. The course, Gerontology 5050/Nursing 4050/English 5050: *Communicating with Older Persons with Alzheimer's Disease*, drew on the DAT subcomponent of the CNCC several times during the six weeks of the online course. Each week had a specific theme and a set of full group and small group assignments keyed to the course CD, which incorporated transcripts and audio files from the CNCC as well as instructor-authored articles and reports that were keyed to conversations in it and in the DAT collection. Students reviewed both print (research-based articles and excerpts from CNCC transcripts) and audio material (CNCC files) in the thematic modules on the course CD and responded to discussion questions posted on the main Internet site. The collection supported students in

- Comparing the speech in the DAT collection to non-disordered speech of other elderly interviewees in the larger corpus of the CNCC
- Examining strategies and techniques developed from analysis of CNCC and DAT conversations, to be adapted for effective communication with aging speakers, including those with DAT
- Expanding awareness of cultural diversity as a shareable resource among formal caregivers
- Reading and discussing articles outlining research keyed to conversations in the CNCC

Each week, students read and discussed in their online groups a set of articles on different approaches to defining language in dementia, provision of care, and delivery of services. They were then asked to try one or more of the approaches and techniques individually, at their worksite or with family members. One example of a research-based technique that the students used during the six-week session is "quilting." Developed initially from the conversations with DAT speakers, quilting conversation requires a collaboration between the caregiver and the DAT-speaker to construct meaning through a story (Davis and Moore 2002; Moore and Davis 2002). In quilting, the caregiver is encouraged to follow up on a detail in a story, typically by repeating as well as paraphrasing what the DAT speaker says, and then to wait patiently for a response. Waiting gives the DAT-speaker greater opportunity to "play back" what was said. Below is a brief example of disordered speech that illustrates the repetition of '*dry goods*' and offers the DAT-speaker the opportunity to expand on this idea.

> Caregiver: *Is that your award for working at Belk?*
> DAT-speaker: *It is on the wall. My, oh, dry goods.*
> Caregiver: *You worked in dry goods.* [pause]
> DAT-speaker: *This material* [touches housecoat]. *We had lots of cotton. I was young in the picture.*

After examining similar discourse strategies in conversational excerpts from the CNCC and reading related articles, students were asked to try quilting techniques in their own interactions with older speakers, including some DAT speakers. More than one student reported an experience similar to "Chuck's," when he took his father fishing:

> *We found a couple of other little places and wound up staying most all of the day exploring and quilting. It was really amazing how he became so much more alert and aware after remembering these old places. I really think the environment somehow stimulated his ability to identify and 'reclaim'... memories that I had previously thought long gone. And these were new stories, not the same old WWII stories.*

Examining the discussions in articles about conversation with older speakers and comparing them to their own experiences led new professionals first to discuss cultural differences and then to research them. Reflective writings, shared in the small and full-class online discussion groups, began with shared personal and family experiences and reflected the diversity of the class membership (Shenk, Moore and Davis 2004):

> ... *Vietnamese culture is based entirely around the family, and right now, my mom is going through some tough times...Us kids have become very Westernized to the point where it annoys...her situation is special because she doesn't speak English fluently....A nursing home is really not an option.*
>
> ... *Because everybody is talking about nursing care for elderly, I wanted to add few points about my own culture (I am from India)...Where do the elderly go in India? Well, elderly stay with their families only.*

Subsequent discussions suggested that students were connecting conversation with workplace experience and research.

> ... *With episodic memory, one retrieves episodes or events in life from memory. In conversations with my Granny (93), she is an example of having a strong episodic memory... one resident I met who had Alzheimer's showed evidence of retrieving episodic memory-- as I read the Bible, she started quoting...*
>
> ... *It has been my experience with my own family and working in a long term care facility that many minorities do not even know about various resources that are available to them*

At the end of the course, 18 of the 24 participants completed an online evaluation, noting that "they 'learned a lot in this course' (mean response of 4.41 on a 5-point scale). Specifically, they felt they 'learned to value new viewpoints' (mean response of 4.4 on a 5-point scale) and that the course effectively challenged them to 'think' (mean response of 4.75 on a 5-point scale)" (Shenk, Moore and Davis 2004: 234). Perhaps more importantly, the diversity among the students and the diversity presented by the corpus-based materials and instructional experiences "offered an important way to focus discussion on the diversity within the aging experience, particularly in terms of communicating with people with dementia" (231).

A second curricular intervention is the infusion of web-delivered instructional multi-media into courses at different levels and at different educational institutions, thanks to a grant from the National Alzheimer's Association for 2005-2008. Currently, materials on communication, aging and dementia are first evaluated for their cultural sensitivity as well as their technical content and usability by students taking courses in the four-year curriculum of the gerontology major at Winston-Salem State University. Undergraduate and graduate students taking nursing and gerontology courses at this historically black university use the materials in different courses and write reviews of the materials. For example, students work with materials about aging, language, and dementia that have been developed from a number of conversational interviews in the CNCC, such as the set from Bellefonte Presbyterian Church, which includes the oldest African Americans in the collection, "Miss Clarissa," "Miss Janie," and "Mr. George," none of whom is impaired. Occasionally the materials also include excerpts from conversations with speakers who are significantly impaired. Because the materials are developed to promote cultural sensitivity in dementia care, students are asked to use and then to review complementary materials, such as Table 3, to see if these materials present useful culture-specific generalizations without stereotyping a gender or an ethnicity, and to offer suggestions for their improvement.

Table 3: Dementia Issues for African Americans

• First-degree relatives of African Americans with Alzheimer's Disease have a higher cumulative risk of dementia than do those of whites with AD. Thus, there is a greater familial risk for dementia (Greene et al. 2002). • African Americans may be four times more likely than whites to develop Alzheimer's Disease by age 90 (http://www.ethnicelderscare.net). • Many African American caregivers view memory deficits and behavioral difficulties as an expected consequence of normal aging. Symptoms of dementia may cause little concern until the disease advances and the person cannot fulfill social roles within the family. AD may be stigmatized as a form of mental illness. • Perhaps some of the behavior disorders in dementia may resemble culturally-specific syndromes, such as those called *worriation* and *spells* (http://www.diversityresources.com/rc_sample/african.html).

After reviewing the materials, students completed web-based evaluations that allowed them to rate issues about both content and presentation. The materials have been well received (an average of 4 on a 5-point Likert scale for questions pertaining to content, usability, and cultural sensitivity) by students at Winston-Salem State University and are currently being redesigned for web-based delivery in coursework for first- and second-language adults seeking certification as Nursing Assistants at Central Piedmont Community College.

5.2 Researching DAT Discourse

A third curricular intervention is the use of the CNCC and selected portions of the DAT-collection for honors-undergraduate and graduate projects at team-members' universities, chosen and supervised by research faculty who are part of the collection and research protocols. In 2003, Amanda Cromer completed a capstone project under Linda Moore (Nursing) and Dena Shenk (Gerontology) for her graduate degree in Nursing at UNC-Charlotte; she reviewed examples of co-constructed conversation in the CNCC, and chose to apply the quilting technique across two cohorts of older persons with different ethnicities, finding that the technique worked well with both. Jenny Towell's 2004 Graduate Internship in Applied Linguistics under Boyd Davis at UNC-Charlotte was designed to give her experience in the community. She reviewed conversations in the CNCC in order to redesign materials on communication and dementia for the local Alzheimer's chapter. In 2005, McMaster University honors student Annmarie O'Leary worked under Ellen Bouchard Ryan to use selected conversations for her honors project; the Speech and Language Pathology student investigated conversational breakdown and repair in a set of conversations with DAT-speaker "Robbie Walters", as illustrated below in Table 4. All three of the students are using the experience and the resulting materials in their professional and educational lives: Cromer, to deliver training on communication interventions with DAT speakers, and O'Leary and Towell, to continue with graduate work in speech disorders and in textual studies, respectively.

Table 4: Analytic Strategies for Conversational Repair

Repetition	The trouble source is repeated following a signal.
Elaboration	The trouble source is repeated and additional information is presented.
Rephrase	The trouble source is uttered differently following a signal.
Confirmation	The speaker confirms that the listener who signaled the repair understands.
Maintenance of Conversational Flow	The problem is ignored and the speaker continues speaking.
Self-Correction	The trouble source is repeated in the absence of a signal.

Based on their analysis, O'Leary et al. (2005) conclude in their poster that "an individual in the moderate stage of AD has the capacity to accomplish repair during spontaneous conversations."

Other collaborations among international team members have led to a series of articles on discourse with and by older persons, supported by material drawn both from the CNCC, for non-impaired speech, and from the DAT collection. A recent collection of research articles, *Alzheimer talk, text and context: Identifying communication enhancement* (Davis, 2005), focuses primarily on DAT discourse, using the CNCC corpus for comparisons of DAT and non-impaired speech. One article in the book focuses on the pragmatic functions of so-called 'empty words' in DAT and normal speech in the CNCC. Davis and Bernstein (2005) studied concordances of *thing/anything/something/everything* by DAT-speaker "Annette Copeland" and compared the usages to those produced by non-impaired women of the same age and background in the CNCC. The functions of one of the words examined, *thing*, is illustrated in Table 5.

Table 5: Functions of *thing* in non-impaired speech

Functions of *thing*	**Examples from the CNCC**
Clichéd (formulaic) phrase	*(all) that sort of* ***thing*** [see extender]
Patient/direct object pro-form, typically substituting for: action event/situation discrete, countable object abstraction or mental activity	 *I thought we'd have time to explore and do* ***things****...* *...and one Christmas,* ***things*** *were really difficult [things = circumstances due to financial hardship]* *I was going to sell the* ***things*** *in Mother's house* my, that **thing** hurt, honey [thing = heartbreak]
Euphemism [sexual]	*well, it was his* ***thing***
Extender	*and all that kind of/sort of* ***thing***
Emphasizer-evaluator phrase	*and of all* ***things*** *I had my tonsils out that was the surprising* ***thing****, you know*
Colloquial: pro-form within phrase	*she jus' the meanest* ***thing*** *you ever saw*
Fronted/anticipatory pro-form/phrase	*The* ***thing*** *is, we.. ; ...the only* ***thing*** *I could say was...*
Depersonalization/reduction of humanness	*No, I think that was some, some* ***thing*** *that we saw...*

Davis and Bernstein's review of the functions identified for *thing* and other 'empty words' from the main CNCC corpus of non-impaired speakers supports their identification of similar functions in the conversations of several cognitively impaired speakers in the DAT collection. DAT speech, by and large, showed little difference for functions of 'thing' for the speakers reviewed; several team members are currently studying connections between empty speech, formulaic phrases and extenders in Alzheimer discourse as compared to non-impaired speakers in the CNCC (Maclagan and Davis 2005a, 2005b).

6. Conclusions: Promoting Professional Development

In his 2004 annual address to the American Dialect Society, society President Charles Meyer asked, "Can you really study language variation in linguistic corpora?," and followed that question with another that speaks directly to the challenges we face: "Can a single corpus be reliably used as the basis of studies examining many different language phenomena?" (Meyer 2004:339). He reviewed what have so far been the two major approaches to creating a representative corpus; he remarked that one approach includes texts chosen to represent a range of genres and the other uses "proportional sampling" (Biber 1993) to create a corpus containing "the most frequently used types of spoken and written English" (348-349). Meyer also mentions a third way, and it is the way we have chosen to proceed with the CNCC – developing corpora with a specific focus. As examples of the focused corpus (350), Meyer lists four that are regional:

- York Corpus, which contains speakers of the York, England, dialect
- Northern Ireland Transcribed Corpus, which combines region and age group
- Bergen Corpus of London Teenage Language
- MICASE, which is named for a region (Michigan), but focuses on the genre of academic English

The CNCC seeks to represent the region surrounding a recently urbanized New South metropolis by collecting conversations and stories representing typical demographic characteristics: age cohorts, genders, census-recognized ethnicities, and languages or language varieties. New studies keyed to the 2000 Census, such as the Administration on Aging's "Older Americans 2000," analyze new patterns of immigration plus changing projections for increased lifespan and retirement in Southern states. Across the South, the Census shows that homes speaking languages other than English are expanding rapidly, and at the same time, the region is attracting new cohorts of retirees. For example, the NC Division of Aging and Adult Services (n.d.) reports, "North Carolina ranks tenth among states in the number of persons age 65 and older and eleventh in the size of the entire population. . . . NC was ranked fourth nationally in the increase of the number of older persons age 65+ (47,198 in NC) between April 2000 and July 2003." We see a need to expand our collections of language to include our burgeoning cohorts of second-language newcomers, so that they and their children can be culturally and linguistically represented and supported. Additionally, we need to include and preserve the voices of the aging, so that medical education can incorporate their voices and their needs, and their health care providers can learn how to hear them (cf. Davis and Shenk 2004).

The CNCC is satisfying the need that pre-professionals and practitioners have to hear and see real people speaking in real voices. This has been borne out in many of the in-services held by Project MORE for practicing and prospective teachers, who describe an increased understanding of the linguistic and cultural needs of ELLs after reviewing materials in the CNCC and curricular interventions developed from CNCC materials. Much of the data for geriatrics that has been warehoused are quantitative in nature and format. Data that are qualitative take a much longer time to assemble, standardize, format, and make accessible. Medical researchers are simply not used to making their recordings or transcripts available. We endorse Meyer's (2004:353) call to scholars assembling corpora "for individual research projects to consider making their corpora publicly available. This would make important data sets available to a wider group of linguists, permit replications of already conducted research, and ultimately make the task of data collection simpler." In this way, corpora can contribute to further professional development for a range of specialties, while also advancing research in a number of domains.

7. Future Directions

ESL teachers in the U.S. understand the impact of statistical projections for ELLs in their schools. They have relatively little trouble adapting authentic materials to their students: using *realia* is one of the traditions in second-language instruction and training, especially as it expands vocabulary or reinforces listening and paraphrasing. What is problematic is the lack of training for the majority of teachers who are taught to impart their content area to language majority students, but without any instruction in how to do this with new language learners. Continued corpus-based, narrative-keyed training for content-area teachers, such as that described above, will allow them to effectively involve first- and second-language learners with each other as well as with course content. We call upon teacher trainers to learn about the diverse uses of corpora, which, in addition to being a resource for language and content-area instruction, can serve as a gateway to learning about technology and computerized media (cf. Davis and Russell-Pinson 2004). Furthermore, we challenge content-area teachers to find additional ways to incorporate corpus-based materials in their classrooms. For example, involving students in creating their own recorded narratives and conversations to complement ones in the CNCC and then drawing upon them in subsequent lessons can potentially increase student literacy, motivation and retention (cf. Fenner 2003; Fine 1987; Freeman and Freeman 2003; Heath 1982; Saracho 1993).

We also call upon researchers to develop corpus-based, narrative-keyed training for healthcare that underscores and goes beyond current notions of cultural competence. This training should include the development of corpus-based healthcare materials for the following populations:

- Professionals in medicine and gerontology
- Low literacy paraprofessionals in health care, e.g. direct care workers

- Second language direct care workers in health professions, such as Nurse Assistants
- Family caregivers

The creation of materials for each of these distinct groups requires a multidisciplinary approach. For example, as Russell-Pinson and Moore (2005) point out in their discussion of lay audience texts on Alzheimer's, the collaboration of linguists and professionals from other disciplines can produce more nuanced analyses of DAT discourse and, as a result, better instructional materials. Furthermore, they write that partnerships among researchers from different specialties are vital to conducting effective outcomes research, which uncovers how the use of health information affects "the ability to relate to health care providers and...perceived self-efficacy to cope with illness" (Bauerle Bass 2003: 23).

By focusing on how community members can benefit from research based on the CNCC, we demonstrate our adherence to what Wolfram (1993:227) calls the *Principle of Linguistic Gratuity*: "Investigators who have obtained linguistic data from members of a speech community should actively pursue ways in which they can return linguistic favors to the community." We can begin by adding more corpus-based, authentic materials to curricula for prospective and practicing content-area teachers, who need additional instruction in linguistic and cultural awareness. Corpus-based healthcare materials produced for paraprofessionals inform the trainees about regional styles, which may be unfamiliar to non-native speakers. Such materials can also help these workers gain insight into the pronunciation, lexicon and discourse structure of the medical profession in general, and are part of the approach we are currently taking in creating new materials for Nursing Assistants and other direct care workers. Since "practitioner awareness of obvious differences in meaning of words or phrases and grammatical differences...is not always matched by awareness of the types of indirect interpersonal communication failure that can occur" (Robinson and Gilmartin 2002), insights gained from corpora can increase understanding about authentic language use in medical contexts, which stands to improve communication among healthcare providers and clients.

Corpus-based materials hold great promise for sustained advances in both teacher preparation and medical education. With attention from a diverse group of scholars and practitioners, we can continue to make strides in both domains and corpus-based educational initiatives can specifically benefit teachers and students, providers and patients, while serving the community as a whole.

References

Administration on Aging (2002), *Older Americans 2000,* retrieved 16 October 2004 at http://www.aoa.gov/prof/adddiv/adddiv.asp.

Bauerle Bass, S. (2003), How will internet use affect the patient? A review of computer network and closed internet-based system studies and the implications in understanding how the use of the internet affects patient populations, *Journal of Health Psychology,* 8 (1): 23-36.

Biber, D. (1993), Representativeness in corpus design, *Literary and Linguistic Computing*, 8: 243–57.

Biber, D., S. Conrad and R. Reppen (1998), *Corpus linguistics: Investigating language structure and use*, Cambridge: Cambridge University Press.

Biber, D., S. Johansson, G. Leech, S. Conrad, and E. Finegan (1999), *Longman grammar of spoken and written English,* Harlow, UK: Pearson Education.

Charlotte-Mecklenburg Schools (2005), CMS ESL Fast Facts.

Charlotte-Mecklenburg Schools (2005), CMS Fast Facts.

Davis, B. (ed) (2005), *Alzheimer talk, text and context: Enhancing communication*, New York and Houndsmills, UK: Palgrave-Macmillan.

Davis, B and C. Bernstein (2005), Talking in the here and now: Reference and narrative in Alzheimer conversation, *in* B. Davis (ed), *Alzheimer talk, text and context: Enhancing communication*, New York and Houndsmills, UK: Palgrave-Macmillan.

Davis, B. and L. Moore (2002), Though much is taken, much abides: Remnant and retention in Alzheimer's discourse, *in* J. Rycmarzck and H.Haudeck (eds), "In search of the active learner" *im Fremdsprachenunterricht, in bilingualen Kontexten und ausinterdisziplinärer Perspektive,*Dortmund, Germany: University of Dortmund, pp. 39-54.

Davis, B. and L. Russell-Pinson (2004),Corpora and concordancing for K-12 teachers: Project MORE, *in* U. Connor and T. Upton (eds), *Applied corpus linguistics: A multidimensional perspective,* Amsterdam: Rodopi, pp.147-160.

Davis, B. and D. Shenk (2004), Stylization, aging, and cultural competence: Why health care in the South needs linguistics, LAVIS (Language Variety in the South) III: Historical and Contemporary Perspectives, Tuscaloosa, AL, 15-17 May 2004.

Egan, K. (1995), Memory, imagination, and learning: Connected by the story, *The Docket: Journal of the New Jersey Council for the Social Studies,* Spring: 9-13.

Fenner, D. (2003), Making English literacy instruction meaningful for English language learners, *ERIC/CLL News Bulletin*, 26 (3): 6-8.

Fine, M. (1987), Silencing in public schools, *reprinted in* B.M. Power and R.S. Hubbard (eds), (2002), *Language development: A reader for teachers*, Upper Saddle River, NJ: Merrill/Prentice Hall, pp. 195-205.

Freeman, Y. and D. Freeman, (2003), Struggling English language learners: Keys for academic success, *TESOL Journal*, 12 (3): 5-10.

Giles, H. and P. Powesland (1997). Accommodation theory. In N. Coupland and A. Jaworski, eds. *Sociolinguistics: a reader*. New York: St. Martin's Press, 232-239.

Green, N. (2002), A virtual world for coaching caregivers of persons with Alzheimer's Disease, *Papers from the AAAI 2002 workshop on automation as caregiver: The role of intelligent technology in elder care*, Menlo Park, CA: AAAI Press, pp. 18-23.

Greene, R., L. Cupples, R. Go, K. Benke, T.Edeki, P. A. Griffith, M. Williams, Y. Hipps, N. Graff-Radford, D. Bachman and L. Farrer for the MIRAGE Study Group (2002), Risk of dementia among White and African American relatives of patients with Alzheimer Disease, *Journal of the American Medical Association*, 287: 329 - 336.

Hakuta, K. (2000), Hispanic and limited English proficient (LEP) population growth in North Carolina, retrieved 10 September 2003 at http://www.stanford.edu/~hakuta/LAU/States/NorthCarolina/NCPopGrow.htm#Top.

Heath, S.B. (1982), A lot of talk about nothing, *reprinted in* B.M. Power and R.S. Hubbard (eds), (2002), *Language development: A reader for teachers*, Upper Saddle River, NJ: Merrill/Prentice Hall, pp. 81-88.

Hunston, S. (2002), *Corpora in applied linguistics*, Cambridge: Cambridge University Press.

Hyland, K. (2000), *Disciplinary discourses: Social interactions in academic writing,* London: Longman.

Johnstone, B. (1990), *Stories, community, and place: Narratives from Middle America*, Bloomington, IN: Indiana University Press.

Kretzschmar, W. (2001), Linguistic databases of the American Linguistic Atlas Project, *in* S. Bird, P. Buneman and M. Liberman (eds*), Proceedings of the IRCS workshop on linguistic databases*, Philadelphia: University of Pennsylvania, pp.157-66.

Labov, W. (1984), Field methods of the project in linguistic change and variation, *in* J. Baugh and J. Sherzer (eds), *Language in use*, Englewood Cliffs, NJ: Prentice-Hall, pp. 28-53.

Maclagan, M. and B. Davis (2005a). Fixed phrases in the speech of patients with dementia. With Gina Tillard. Presentation, PHRASEOLOGY 2005 The many faces of Phraseology. Université catholique de Louvain (Belgium), 13-15 October 2005.

Maclagan, M. and B. Davis (2005b).Extenders, intersubjectivity, and the social construction of dementia. Presentation, New Ways of Analyzing Variation 34, New York University, October 20-23, 2005.

Meyer, C. (2004), ADS annual lecture: Can you really study language variation in linguistic corpora?, *American Speech*, 79: 339-55.

Moore, L. and B. Davis (2002), Quilting narrative using repetition techniques to help elderly communicators, *Geriatric Nursing,* 23 (5): 262-266.

North Carolina Division of Aging and Adult Services (n.d.), retrieved 4 February 2005 at http://www.dhhs.state.nc.us/aging/cprofile/ncprofile.htm.

O'Leary, A., E. Ryan and A. Anas (2005), Language changes in Alzheimer's Disease: Conversational breakdown and repair, Honours Undergraduate thesis, McMaster Faculty of Health Sciences and Gerontology, McMaster University.

Reppen, R. and N. Ide (2004). The American National Corpus: overall goals and the first release. *Journal of English Linguistics*, 32: 105-113

Robinson, M. and J. Gilmartin (2002), Barriers to communication between health practitioners and service users who are not fluent in English, *Nurse Education Today* 6: 457-465.

Russell-Pinson, L. and L. Moore (2005), Understanding text about Alzheimer's Dementia, *in* B. Davis (ed), *Alzheimer talk, text and context: Identifying communication enhancement*, New York and Houndsmills: Palgrave-Macmillan.

Ryan, E., J. Orange, H. Spykerman and K. Byrne (in press for 2005), Evidencing Kitwood: Personhood strategies in conversing with Alzheimer's speakers, *in* B. Davis (ed), *Alzheimer talk, text and context: Identifying communication enhancement*, New York and Houndsmills: Palgrave-Macmillan.

Saracho, O. (1993), Literacy development: The whole language approach, *in* O.N. Saracho and B. Spodek (eds), *Language and literacy in early childhood education*, New York: Teachers College Press, pp. 42-59.

Shenk, D., L. Moore and B. Davis (2004), Teaching an interdisciplinary distance education gerontology course: Benefits of diversity, *Educational Gerontology*, 30 (3): 219-235.

Shenk, D., B. Davis and B. Alexander (2005), Teaching about caring for people with dementia and issues of cultural competence, Association for Gerontology in Higher Education 31, Oklahoma City, OK, 24-27 February 2005.

Silliman, E.R. and T. Champion (2002), Three dilemmas in cross-cultural narrative analysis: Introduction to the special issue, *Linguistics and Education*, 13 (2): 143–150.

Tillery, J., G. Bailey, and T.Wikle (2004), Demographic change and American dialectology in the twenty-first century, *American Speech*, 79: 227-50.

U.S. Department of Education (2002), The growing numbers of limited English proficient students: 1991/1992-2001/2002, Washington, DC: Office of English Language Acquisition.

Westman, S. and B. Davis (2005), Approaches to searching for language and diversity in a "Whitebread City" digital corpus: The Charlotte Conversation and Narrative Collection, ACH/ ALLC (Association for Computers and the Humanities/Association for Literary and Linguistic Computing) 2005, University of Victoria, Victoria, BC, 15-18 June 2005.

Wolfram, W. (1993), Ethical considerations in language awareness programs, *Issues in Applied Linguistics* 4: 225-255.

"GRIMMATIK:" German Grammar through the Magic of the Brothers Grimm Fairy Tales and the Online Grimm Corpus

Margrit V. Zinggeler

Eastern Michigan University

Abstract

The rationale for GRIMMATIK *(coined from the brothers* Grimm *name and the German word for grammar* 'Grammatik;' *textbook forthcoming) is to offer a learner-oriented, research-based German grammar to intermediate and advanced students of German. Bringing together German grammar and the brothers Grimm fairy tales offers a different approach to learning and reviewing German grammar and it introduces students to the original German texts of the world-known and beloved fairy tales which were first published in 1812 as* Kinder- und Hausmärchen *(KHM). The* GRIMMATIK *method addresses a variety of grammatical elements in the analysis of selected brothers Grimm fairy tales. It is the student who finally constructs a reasonably simple form of German grammar, consecutively isolating the parts of speech, phrases, and sentence structure. Recognition of language patterns leads to paradigm segmentation and classification and eventually to internalisations of language rules and the acquisition of grammatical competence. This paper presents methods for using the Online Grimm corpus for German grammar learning.*

1. Introduction

Exploiting concordances and corpora as tools for foreign language teaching and learning has become more attractive and widespread with the availability of computers and online services for every student (Leech, 1997; Botley, McEnery, Wilson, 2000; Godwin-Jones, 2001; Granger, Hung, Petch-Tson, 2002; Sinclair, 2004). This approach is well documented for English language teaching and is based on the thesis that by researching the language students will learn the language; this is also known as data-driven learning (Johns, 1991). It was Dodd's article 'Exploiting a Corpus of Written German for Advanced Language Learning' (Dodd, 1997) that inspired me to look at the large selection of corpora of the German language that have been assembled by the *Institut für deutsche Sprache* (IDS), in Mannheim, Germany. The Grimm corpus is an ideal data set with a manageable and significant amount of data for research by students who already have intermediate knowledge of German. The 7th edition of 1978 contains 201 stories and ten legends for children, which have been translated into over 160 languages. Today, the Internet offers many tools for studying the brothers Grimm fairy tales, e.g. *Project Gutenberg,*[1] alphabetically displays over 300 electronic texts of the brothers Grimm. Comprehensive grammatical and structural analysis of the brothers Grimm fairy tales, however, can best be accomplished with the

Grimm Corpora. It can be downloaded from the COSMASII webpage[2] of the "Institut für Deutsche Sprache" in Mannheim, Germany. It is available at no charge. The concentration in GRIMMATIK is on the 200 *Kinder- und Hausmärchen*, omitting the 585 legends and 10 children's legends of the Grimm corpus.

2. What is *GRIMMATIK*?

German grammar books are rather boring, especially for more advanced students of the German language. Although the traditional grammar books include helpful drill exercises, oral and written application tasks, and vocabulary lists, they generally focus – in each chapter – on one specific grammatical topic or element of speech only, such as German nouns (weak and strong) and the case system, German verbs (weak, strong, irregular, modal, reflexive, and the tenses), the German prepositions and conjunctions, German adjectives, pronouns, adverbs, the passive voice, the subjunctive mood, with other chapters on negation and interrogatives, the imperative, spelling, punctuation, time expressions, word order, infinitives, numerals etc.. By the time students reach the chapter on the subjunctive, they have forgotten the rather complicated rules for adjective endings dependent on gender, number, and case. Grammar rules are presented using tables that the students have to learn by heart and they must remember grammatical structures based on drill exercises, which is indeed counterproductive. Standard, traditional grammar teaching methodology removes grammar from cognitive thinking and language *per se*. Besides, traditional grammar is descriptive, omitting cognitive and autonomous learning processes. Furthermore, grammar and literature are rarely combined in a true fashion. The dichotomy between literature and grammar/linguistics – between *Germanistik* and *Philologie* – has a long history in Europe. The brothers Grimm, Wilhelm – the poet and narrator – and Jacob – the philologist and father of modern German linguistics – represent themselves this dichotomy between the study of structural language rules and laws on the one hand and the narration and interpretation of a story on the other hand.

Some years ago, I had the idea to write a new German grammar book using the original brothers Grimm fairy tales – the *Kinder und Hausmärchen* (KHM) – as the basic text corpus and a methodology with which the students review all parts of speech in every selected fairy tale and by which they recognize and find structural patterns themselves. When students analyse and collect grammatical data and establish their own tables and charts, language structures evolve in a revealing manner and something magical happens. The students are ultimately learning German grammar while they are reading and analysing the original brothers Grimm, often very grim, fairy tales!

I coined this approach and the title of the forthcoming textbook from the German word for grammar – *Grammatik* – and the name of the fairy tale collecting brothers – Grimm – into the term *GRIMMATIK*. The methodology is based on text grammar and current research in second language acquisition and it builds on the principles of *Produktionsgrammatik* which is a receptive grammar[3] as well as communicative approaches to foreign language teaching. *GRIMMATIK* is not a descriptive German grammar including all exceptions and derivations. Its main objective is that students gain a general grammatical competence acquired through cognitive paradigm structures and reflective learning through selection criteria.

GRIMMATIK requires that students of German review grammatical terms such as the parts of speech, phrases, and elements of a sentence. This objective is accomplished with exercises also focusing on examples from the brothers Grimm fairy tales not discussed in this article. Students in a fourth year *Advanced German Syntax and Composition* class at Eastern Michigan University were the subjects of the *GRIMMATIK* pilot project. During the third week of the semester, the class met in the computer lab and they received an introduction to the COSMASII system and the Grimm corpora.

3. COSMAS and the Online Corpus of the Brothers Grimm Fairy Tales

The corpus of the GRIMM-Database includes 201 fairy tales (KHM; 7th edition, 1978), 585 legends and 10 children's legends (3rd edition, 1891) collected by the brothers Jacob and Wilhelm Grimm[4] and consisting of 1,342 pages or a total of 518,827 word forms. Yoshihisa Yamada and Junko Nakayama of Ryukoku University in Kyoto, Japan, established the electronic corpus. It is available online via the Website of the Institute for German Language (IDS), Mannheim, Germany, with a system called COSMAS (the Corpus Search, Management and Analysis System: http://www.ids-mannheim.de/cosmas2). The sophisticated COSMASII system is now available as version 3.6 at no charge; students and researchers just need to sign up with a password. The website offers extensive explanations and online help on how to download and use COSMASII. Personalized user support is promptly available via e-mail. *GRIMMATIK* makes direct use of corpora in teaching.

3.1 COSMAS Exercises

Since not all undergraduate and graduate students in the Advanced German Syntax class at Eastern Michigan University know what a concordance or a corpus is, the best way to introduce them to these concepts is to work with COSMAS and show them how to open the search window and search for words, nouns and verbs, some familiar words and all the new vocabulary of three very short fairy tales (*Der goldene Schlüssel, Der Großvater und sein Enkel, Die Sterntaler)* that we had already analysed syntactically defining nuclear sentences, or independent clauses (*Kernsatz*), frontal sentences, or imperative and interrogative clauses which have the verb as the first element (*Stirnsatz*), brace sentences, or dependent clauses (*Spannsatz*), and prepositional phrases (see appendix, example 6). Students learned how to navigate around COSMAS and how to get results with KWIC (Key Word in Context) and display a more extended context defined by the number of words, sentences, and paragraphs before and after a keyword. As mentioned above, we generally limit the searches to the GRI – Brüder Grimm corpus containing the 201 fairy tales thus optimising critical hits and ensuring didactic benefits.

3.2 Word Frequencies: Nouns

How many times a word appears and in which particular Grimm fairy tales not only offers interpretative fuel,[5] but for German, a highly inflected language, the word lists resulting from this exercise reveal patterns of case structures, and various plural forms as well as information on how these morphological suffixes are structured and how the preceding words behave. Since all nouns are capitalized in German, this feature is a distinctive marker for language learners. Another feature of German is compound nouns, which can be listed with a COSMAS search option called *Lemmatisierung*. This means that compound words are not broken down. These options are highly beneficial for vocabulary building.

No student in my class knew the word *Hirse*. They searched COSMAS by entering *&Hirse* into the search window (*Zeileneingabe*) and getting the forms *Hirse, Hirsen, Hirsenbrei*. These words appear 8 times in the KHM. With the selected context results (one sentence before and one sentence after the key word), it was obvious to them without consulting a dictionary that it must be a grain. Students will find that German word endings with –e are generally feminine (*Hirse* has the same declension as e.g. *Blume*). A basic method of *GRIMMATIK* is to offer tables to the students so they can enter the structural information and recognize morphological and syntactical patterns. Then, students use a dictionary to find the gender of a noun before determining the case, which is dependent on the function in the sentence: subject, direct, indirect or genitive object, or the preceding preposition.

Key-Word + previous word	**Gender, sg./pl.**	**Case**	**Rule for sg./pl.**	**Meaning**
voll Hirsen	f., pl.	Dat.	-n for pl. dat.	full of millet
den Hirsen	f., pl.	Acc.	-n for pl. acc.	millets
(und) Hersche (Hirse)	f., sg.	Acc.	-e for sg. acc.	millet
guten süßen Hirsenbrei	m. sg.	Acc.	-Ø (brei)	good sweet millet gruel
mit Hirsen	f. pl.	Dat.	-n	with millet
den Hirsen	f. pl.	Acc.	-n	the millets
größer als Hirsen	f. pl.	Nom.	-n	larger than millets
Hirsenbrei	m. sg.	Acc.	-Ø (brei)	millet gruel

Jammer (lamentation, misery) was another word that was new for the students. With the search *&Jammer*, they found 5 word forms and 19 occurrences in the KHM (*Jammer, Jammern, jammerschade, jammervoll, jammervolles*). Of course, the capitalized forms are nouns, yet from the context (*ihr Schreien und Jammern/Heulen und Jammern*) it can be deduced that *Jammern* is a verb used in the text as a noun. The morpheme *–(e)n* is the marker for a verb infinitive (*schreien, heulen, jammern*). The students also figured out that *jammerschade* is an adverb and that *jammervoll* is used as an adverb and an adjective, the latter because of the morphological suffix *–es* which indicates (in KWIC-list from the Grimm legends) that the described noun is neuter and accusative because it is the direct object. (See appendix, example 4[6].)

The beauty – or I call it the magic – of such student analyses with COSMAS is that the students actively and automatically will use the new vocabulary which they researched in the corpus in other oral and written assignments, e.g., when writing their own fairy tales in the creative writing section or in class discussions about the content and meaning of the fairy tales. Indeed, many students used *Hirse* and *Jammer* in their stories.

3.3. Verbs

An introductory exercise familiarizes students with verb searches using three verbs of the first three tales that they analyzed: *drehen* (turn), *lassen* (let), and *fließen* (flow). Since the command & in front of the searched word lists all occurring forms, it is ideal for reviewing German verb forms: inflected forms in various tenses and moods, including past participles and infinitives (see appendix, examples 2 and 7). Students enter their findings into a table such as follows.

Form in tale	Infinitive	Tense, Mood	Person: Sg./Pl.	Translation of infinitive
drehte … herum	herumdrehen	Simple past, Indicative	3.pers.sg.	turn (around)
floss	fließen	Simple past, Indicative	3.pers.sg.	flow
ließen	lassen	Simple past, Indicative	3.pers.pl.	let

A distinctive feature of German verbs is a prefix (*an-, auf-, mit-, heraus-*, etc.) that can occur with many different verbs, sometimes changing the basic meaning of the verb considerably, e.g. *ankommen, auffahren, anlassen, mitkommen, mitfahren, mitlassen, zurückkommen, zurückfahren, zurücklassen, abkommen, abfahren, ablassen*, etc. The prefix "jumps" to the end of an independent clause in the present and simple past tense and it often looks like a regular preposition for students, yet in a dependant clause where the finite verb is in final position, this element is a verb prefix as also in the past participle.

(*Rumpelstilzchen kam jede Nacht zurück. / Weil Rumpelstilzchen jede Nacht zurückkam,….*) Students had to search for *herumdrehen* and get the KWIC-results and the full texts to see how and where the prefix is positioned. This can be accomplished with a command searching for verbs with separable prefixes: &drehen /+s0 herum. Students will find seven occurrences in which the prefix jumps to the end of a clause and that the verb is used six times in the past tense (the marker is: *–t-e*) and once in present tense 3pers. Sg form. In one instance – in KHM 112 – *herum* is indeed a preposition in the same sentence, yet it does not belong to the verb *drehen.* (See appendix, example 2.)

Since *lassen* is a strong, very high frequency verb (1138 in the Grimm Corpus) with 16 different forms, occurring 636 times in 148 KHM (some forms only appear in the legends), it seems to be ideal to show students large-scale possibilities on how to analyze verb forms structurally in a group exercise. *Lassen* is mostly used with another infinitive or a preposition. (*Der König ließ den Befehl ausgehen,... Laßt Gnade für Recht ergehen! Da ließ Rapunzel die Haarflechten herab, ... Laß mir dein Haar herunter.*') When translating the examples into English, students see even greater discrepancies, because "let" basically occurs only in two morphological varieties in English (let, lets).

LASSEN	**Morphological variations**	**Possible functions**	**Meaning in text**
gelassen	ge-	Past participle	(had) let
lasse	-e	Possibilities: ich lasse (pres.) er lasse (subjunctive I)	I let, or he would let
lassen	-en	infinitive or 1st and 3d pers.pl.	to let, they let
lassest	-est	2d pers. sg. subj.I	you would let (sg.)
Lasset	-et	2d pers.pl. imperative	Let…
lasset	-et	2d pers. pl.subj.II	you would let (pl.)
Laßt	-t	2d pers.pl. imperative	Let…
Läßt	(ä)-t	2d pers.pl., present	you let
laßt	-t	2d pers.pl., imperative	…, let….
läßt	(ä)-t	2d pers.pl., present	you let (pl.)
Ließ	(ie)-Ø	2d pers.pl., past	you let
ließ	(ie)-Ø	2d pers.pl., past	you let
ließe	(ie)-e	3d pers.sg, subj. II	he would let
ließen	(ie)-en	1st or 3d pers.pl.,past	they let
ließest	(ie)-est	2d pers.sg. sub.II	you would let

Students also review orthographical characteristics with this example. After a long stem vowel, the double *ss* changes into -ß-. Since the search is sensitive to upper/lower case in this example, some forms occur in frontal position, generally indicating an imperative or interrogative (sometimes a conditional sub-clause without conjunction), which is ideal for reviewing syntactical rules. (See appendix, example 7.) Not only new verbs but also familiar words are didactically valuable for reviewing tenses.

Since the Grimm fairy tales are mostly narrated in the simple past, students review many strong and irregular verb forms, grammatical elements that often need extensive review.

3.4 Adjectives

In German, attributive adjectives have morphological endings dependent on gender, number, and case of the noun(s) which they describe. Adjectives can also be used as adverbs or predicates (subject completion); then they do not have any endings. One COSMAS-based task asks the students to find the adjective *mitleidig* (compassionate) in the KHM, to enter the various forms and functions into a table, and to find grammatical rules.

GRI/KHM, Brüder Grimm: Kinder- und Hausmärchen

erst frieren und zappeln." Und weil er **mitleidig** war, legte er die ...
e so elend umkommen müßten. Weil er ein **mitleidiges** Herz hatte, so ...
n dem Bach ausgeruht hätte. Weil er ein **mitleidiges** Herz hatte, so ...
ich nicht bleiben: ich will fortgehen: **mitleidige** Menschen werden mir ...
sein Lebtag nicht wieder heil." Und aus **mitleidigem** Herzen nahm es ...
hrte er sich um und sprach "weil ihr so **mitleidig** und fromm seid, so ...
zimmer ein lautes Jammern. Er hatte ein **mitleidiges** Herz, öffnete die ...
Stückchen Brot in der Hand, das ihm ein **mitleidiges** Herz geschenkt ...
kt hatte und ihn forttragen wollte. Die **mitleidigen** Kinder hielten ...
en halb Ohnmächtigen erblickte, ging er **mitleidig** heran, richtete ihn ...
sich in einer Höhle versteckt oder bei **mitleidigen** Menschen Schutz ...

Form in text	Ending	Part of speech	Case, Number	Meaning
mitleidig	-Ø	adverb (predicate)	-	he was compassionate
ein mitleidiges (Herz)	-es	adjective (after ein-word)	acc. sg. neuter	he had a compassionate heart
mitleidige (Menschen)	-e	adjective (no article)	nom., pl., masc.	compassionate people
mitleidigem	-em	adjective (after preposition, no article)	dat. sg., neuter	(out) of a compassionate heart

(die) mitleidigen (Kinder)	-en	adjective (after der-word)	nom.,pl. neuter	the compassionate children
(bei) mitleidigen (Menschen)	-en	adjective (after preposition, no article)	dat.pl. masc.	(with) compassionate people

It would have been ideal if there had been an accusative sg. neuter form with a definite article (*das mitleidige Herz*) in a text to show that the -s ending of the definite article will be added to the adjective if preceded by an "ein-word" (indefinite article and possessive pronouns, such as *mein, kein, unser* etc.). The same rule applies to phrases like "aus dem mitleidigen Herz". Since *GRIMMATIK* is for more intermediate and advanced students of German, they generally verify and consolidate grammatical rules with these COSMAS-based exercises that require analysing occurrences of vocabulary and searching for morphological and syntactical rules. However, it is also possible that students will find grammatical rules that are new to them.

3.4 Sentence Structure

Before completing tasks with COSMAS, students had to classify the most salient clauses of fairy tale sentences when working with the *GRIMMATIK* project. Based on current grammar approaches by German grammarians (Duden, 1998; Sommerfeldt, 1999; Helbig, 1999, 2001; Kürschner, 2003). German sentences can be divided into *Kernsatz* (nuclear clause), *Stirnsatz* (frontal clause), *Spannsatz* (brace clause), and prepositional phrases.[7] In a German main or independent clause, defined as a nuclear sentence, the finite verb is the second element. The finite verb is in final position in a dependent clause (brace clause), and in a frontal clause, the finite verb is the first element, such as in an imperative or interrogative sentence without a question word. Of course, in a fairy tale or any (poetic) text, occasional variations occur. Since key words are in bold print in the selected COSMAS text segments, it is easy for students to determine or rather verify syntactical rules for German verbs. These pattern finding exercises indeed help to consolidate syntactical rules so that English-speaking students actively put the German finite verbs into the correct second or final position, especially in writing, a more reflective language modality than speaking.

Other, more complex grammatical issues can well be analyzed with COSMAS (Zinggeler, forthcoming), such as e.g. the subjunctive form used with the conjunction *ob* (if, whether). The search ob /w15 wäre reveals e.g. 29 hits in the KHM; ideal for a didactical exercise.

4. Points to Consider in Teaching with Corpora

Certain issues arise when using corpora for grammar teaching in the classroom. Other issues come to the fore when the grammar exercises are intended for publication.

4.1 Classroom Approach

It is advisable to slowly walk the students through each step of the online corpora searches in a laboratory setting and to design easy, yet stimulating tasks and provide intelligent tables into which students can enter their findings. Since the students already possess a considerable grammatical understanding in an intermediate or advanced German language course, they generally enjoy the new approaches with *GRIMMATIK* for reviewing grammar and often they come up with their own findings about morphological and syntactical language patterns.

Because there are many structural, functional, and contextual repetitions in the brothers Grimm Fairy Tales, these stories are ideal for reviewing a host of critical elements. After the students participating in the *GRIMMATIK* pilot project had written their own creative fairy tales (one fairy tale was assigned as a group exercise: three partners had to come up with characters and then each student wrote one part, taking up where the other had left the story), a COSMAS-based exercise consisted of finding particular words and motives, which they had used in their own tales, in the corpus of the original Grimm fairy tales.

4.2 A Publication Concern

Since I have been working on *GRIMMATIK*, the online version of COSMAS has already changed several times; currently version 3.6 is most recent as of the writing of this article. Textbook publishers have become reluctant to include such quickly changing, additional technology in textbooks, unless they have a certain control over the Website. Although the basic search method with COSMASII has not changed, new versions are more user-friendly but at the same time some aspects have become more sophisticated. The online corpora of the Institute for German Language, which is supported by the German government, will most certainly be available for a long time and benefit our foreign language students because of the vast possibilities these tools offer for language teaching and research.

5. Conclusion

Although corpora could be used for foreign language teaching in first and second year college courses (Möllering 2001; St. Johns 2001), they are ideal for intermediate and advanced students of a foreign language because they allow students to build and test their already acquired grammatical understanding. The exercises and tasks provide ownership. Students love the detective work as they become language researchers.

There is a wealth of potential grammatical tasks that can be deduced from the possibilities with online corpus technology. The quest and question is how can we best design tasks and tables for students learning a foreign language?

Notes

1 http://gutenberg.spiegel.de/autoren/grimm.htm

2 http://www.ids-mannheim.de/cosmas2

3 A receptive grammar is perceived from the viewpoint of the recipient, the learner and his/her grammatical understanding. Grammatical understanding is a cognitive process. See: Hans Jürgen Heringer, *Lesen lehren lernen: Eine rezeptive Grammatik des Deutschen.* Tübingen: Niemeyer, 1988.

4 Jacob Grimm (1785-1863) and Wilhelm Grimm (1786-1859) both studied law and eventually became professors at the University of Göttingen and later in Berlin. They had published the first collection of German fairy tales in 1812 as *Kinder- und Hausmärchen* (KHM). Jacob is known as the father of German philology and the author of many books on the German language and also of the "Grimm's Law" of sound patterns and changes in Indo-European and Germanic languages.

5 These characters of the KHM occur with the following frequency:

König (king)	734	Königin (queen)	160 (~ 1/5)
Prinz (prince)	23	Prinzessin (princess)	16
Königssohn (king's son)	137	Königstochter (king's daughter)	213
Vater (father)	369	Mutter (mother)	223
Sohn (son)	104	Tochter (daughter)	196
Junge (boy)	101	Mädchen (girl)	314

We can speculate and say that the king is more important than the queen, yet a king's daughter is much more relevant than a king's son. Furthermore, the father figure is more frequent than the mother, yet the girl and daughter seem to be of greater importance than a boy or son. Hence, the father-daughter relationships in the Grimm fairy tales are statistically more significant than issues regarding mothers and sons.

6 All examples from the Grimm corpus of COSMAS are abbreviated for this article.

7 German language textbooks do not make this distinction.

References

Biber, D., S. Conrad and R. Reppen (1994), 'Corpus-based approaches to issues in applied linguistics. *Applied Linguistics*', 15: 169-189.

———. (1998), *Corpus Linguistics. Investigating Language Structure and Use.* Cambridge, UK: Cambridge University Press.

Botley, S., T. McEnery, and A. Wilson (2000), *Multilingual Corpora in Teaching and Research.* Amsterdam, Atlanta: Rodopi.

Conrad, S. (2000), 'Will corpus linguistics revolutionize grammar teaching in the 21st century?', *TESOL Quarterly*, 3: 548-560.

Dodd, B. (ed.) (2000), *Working with German Corpora.* Birmingham, UK: Birmingham University Press.

Dodd, B. (1997), 'Exploiting a Corpus of Written German for Advanced Language Learning', in: A. Wichman, S. Fligelstone, T. McEnery and G. Knowles (eds.) *Teaching and Language Corpora.* London, New York: Longman. 134-145.

Duden-Grammatik (1998), *Grammatik der deutschen Gegenwartssprache.* 6. Auflage. Mannheim: Dudenverlag.

Figelstone, S. (1993), 'Some reflections on the question of teaching, from a corpus linguistics perspective', *ICAME Journal*, 17: 97-109.

Götze, L. (1999), 'Eine funktionale Grammatik für Deutsch als Fremdsprache', in: Skibitzki, B. and B. Wotjak (eds.), *Linguistik und Deutsch als Fremdsprache.* Tübingen: Niemeyer. 80-94.

Godwin-Jones, B. (2001), 'Emerging Technologies: Tools and Trends in Corpora Use for Teaching and Learning', *Language Learning and Technology*, Vol. 5, Nr. 3: 7-12.

Granger, S., Hung, J. and Petch-Tson, S. (eds.) (2002), *Computer Learner Corpora, Second Language Acquisition and Foreign Language Teaching.* Amsterdam, Philadelphia: John Benjamins.

Helbig, G., L., Götze, G. Henrici and H.J. Krumm (eds.) (2001), *Deutsch als Fremdsprache. Ein internationales Handbuch.* Berlin, New York: Walter de Gruyter.

Heringer, H.-J. (1988), *Lesen lehren lernen: Eine rezeptive Grammatik des Deutschen.* Tübingen: Niemeyer.

Kennedy, G. (1998), *An Introduction to Corpus Linguistics.* New York: Longman.

Küschner, W. (2003), *Grammatisches Kompendium.* Tübingen: UTB.

Leech. G. (1997), 'Teaching and Language Corpora – A Convergence'. in: A. Wichman, S. Fligelstone, T. McEnery and G. Knowles (eds.) *Teaching and Language Corpora*. London, New York: Longman.1-23.

Lewandowska-Tomaszczyk, B. and P.J. Melia (eds.) (1997), *International Conference on Practical Applications in Language Corpora . Proceedings.* Lódź: Lódź University Press.

McEnery, T. and A. Wilson (1996), *Corpus Linguistics.* Edinburgh: Edinburgh University Press.

Meyer, R., M.E. Okurowski and T. Hand (2000), 'Using authentic corpora and language tools for adult-centered learning', in: Botley, S., T. McEnery and A. Wilson. *Multilingual Corpora in Teaching and Research.* Amsterdam, Atlanta: Rodopi. 86-91.

Möllering, M. (2001), 'Teaching German Modal Particles: A Corpus Based Approach', *Language Learning and Technology*, Vol. 5, Nr. 3: 130-151.

Schmidt, R. (1990), 'Das Konzept einer Lerner Grammatik', in: Gross, H. and K. Fischer (eds.), *Grammatikarbeit im Deutsch-als Fremdsprache-Unterricht.* Iudicium Verlag. 153-161.

Sinclair, J. (1991), *Corpus, Concordance, Collocation.* Oxford UK: Oxford University Press.

———. (2004), *How to Use Corpora in Language Teaching.* Amsterdam, Philadelphia: John Benjamins.

Sommerfeldt, K.E. and G. Starke (1999), *Einführung in die Grammatik der deutschen Gegenwartssprache.* 3d ed. Tübingen: Niemeyer.

St. John, Elke (2001), 'A case for using a parallel corpus and concordancer for beginners of a foreign language', *Language Learning and Technology*, Vol. 5, Nr. 3: 185-203.

Zinggeler, M. (forthcoming), 'Wieviel Sekunden hat die Ewigkeit: Der Interrogativ in den KHM mit Antworten aus der *"GRIMMATIK"* und Grimm Corpora COSMAS', in: B. Lauder (ed.) *Jahrbuch Brüder Grimm-Gesellschaft.* Kassel: Brüder Grimm-Gesellschaft.

Appendix

1. Samples of introductory exercise using the online Grimm Corpus.

Zur Winterszeit - KHM 200

1. How many times does *Schlüssel* and *Winter/Winterszeit* occur in the brothers Grimm KHM? (Answer: 37 in KHM)
2. Which different articles/words precede the word *Schlüssel* in the other KHMs? Determine the case!
3. Exchange *Winter/Winterszeit* with another season in the *KWIC-Übersicht*! Does the grammatical structure change?
4. What is Hirse? Find out all the word forms and, from your reading in KWIC, the meaning.
5. How many times and in what form does *drehen* occur? With the prefix *herum*?
6. What other prefixes occur with *drehen?*

Der Großvater und sein Enkel - KHM 78

1. How many word forms of *lassen* are available? What is the simple past pl. form and how many times does it occur with an infinitive?
2. Search for *&fließen* and its prepositions!

2. Search example for *herumdrehen*:

Suchanfrage: &drehen /+s0 herum
Ergebnis-Übersicht; Sortierung: textweise
1+7:GRI/KHM, Brüder Grimm: Kinder- und Hausm 7 7

Belege
GRI/KHM.00054 Der Ranzen, das Hütlein und das Hörnlein, S. 311
Nach dem Essen sprach der Kohlenbrenner "da oben auf der Kammbank liegt ein altes abgegriffenes Hütlein, das hat seltsame Eigenschaften: wenn das einer aufsetzt und **dreht** es auf dem **Kopf herum**, so gehen die Feldschlangen, als wären zwölfe nebeneinander aufgeführt, und schießen alles darnieder, daß niemand dagegen bestehen kann.
GRI/KHM.00054 Der Ranzen, das Hütlein und das Hörnlein, S. 312
Er stellte noch mehr Volk entgegen, und um noch schneller fertig zu werden, **drehte** er ein paarmal sein Hütlein auf dem Kopfe **herum**; da fing das schwere Geschütz an zu spielen, und des Königs Leute wurden geschlagen und in die Flucht gejagt.
GRI/KHM.00060 Die zwei Brüder, S. 347
Dann riß er dem Jäger den Kopf wieder ab, **drehte** ihn **herum**, und der Hase heilte ihn mit der Wurzel fest. Der Jäger aber war traurig, zog in der Welt herum und ließ seine Tiere vor den Leuten tanzen.

GRI/KHM.00092 Der König vom goldenen Berg, S. 468
Da ward der Sohn zornig und **drehte**, ohne an sein Versprechen zu denken, den Ring **herum** und wünschte beide, seine Gemahlin und sein Kind, zu sich. In dem Augenblick waren sie auch da, aber die Königin, die klagte und weinte, und sagte, er hätte sein Wort gebrochen und hätte sie unglücklich gemacht.
GRI/KHM.00112 Der Dreschflegel vom Himmel, S. 548
"Wenn du da herabstürztest, das wär ein böses Ding," dachte er, und in der Not wußt er sich nicht besser zu helfen, als daß er die Spreu vom Hafer nahm, die haufenweis da lag, und daraus einen Strick **drehte**; auch griff er nach einer Hacke und einem Dreschflegel, die da **herum** im Himmel lagen, und ließ sich an dem Seil herunter.
GRI/KHM.00175 Die Eule, S. 719
Als nun der Hausknecht morgens in die Scheuer kam, um Stroh zu holen, erschrak er bei dem Anblick der Eule, die da in einer Ecke saß, so gewaltig, daß er fortlief und seinem Herrn ankündigte, ein Ungeheuer, wie er zeit seines Lebens keins erblickt hätte, säße in der Scheuer, **drehte** die Augen im Kopf **herum** und könnte einen ohne Umstände verschlingen.
GRI/KHM.00201 Der goldene Schüssel, S. 809
Er probierte und der Schlüssel paßte glücklich. Da **drehte** er einmal **herum**, und nun müssen wir warten, bis er vollends aufgeschlossen und den Deckel aufgemacht hat, dann werden wir erfahren, was für wunderbare Sachen in dem Kästchen lagen.

3. COSMAS search following a writing exercise:

Give a list of words that you used in your fairy tales and find out how many times, in which KHM, and in what form these words appear!

Nomen, Verben, Namen, Orte, etc.	**Anzahl Vorkommen**	**Welche KHM?**	**Welche Flexionsformen?**	**Andere Info.**

4. COSMAS search example for *Jammer*:
Result: 5 Wortformen zu Jammer: Jammer, Jammern, jammerschade, jammervoll, jammervolles

---

Ergebnis-Übersicht
Sortierung: textweise
1+12:GRI/SAG, Brüder Grimm: Deutsche Sagen 12
13+19:GRI/KHM, Brüder Grimm: Kinder- und Hausm 19

Kwic-Übersicht
GRI/KHM, Brüder Grimm: Kinder- und Hausmärchen

ein Jahr nach dem andern und fühlte den **Jammer** und das Elend der Welt.
hat schon sein Leben eingebüßt, es wäre **Jammer** und Schade um die schönen
Endlich ging sie in ihrem **Jammer** hinaus, und das jüngste Geißlein
einen großen Wald und waren so müde von **Jammer**, Hunger und dem langen
xe aber ward ins Feuer gelegt und mußte **jammervoll** verbrennen. Und wie sie zu
eine Wüstenei brachte, wo sie in großem **Jammer** und Elend leben mußte.
.Endlich sagte es zu ihr "ich habe den **Jammer** nach Haus kriegt, und wenn es
sie beklagt ihren **Jammer**,
beweint ihren **Jammer**,
n und hörten nicht auf ihr Schreien und **Jammern**. Sie gaben ihr Wein zu trinken,
ich die Hühner vom Feuer tun, ist aber **Jammer** und Schade, wenn sie nicht bald
h legen wollte, hörte er ein Heulen und **Jammern**, daß er nicht einschlafen konnte
goldene Straße sah, dachte er "das wäre **jammerschade**, wenn du darauf rittest," l
daraufgesetzt hatte, dachte er "es wäre **jammerschade**, das könnte etwas abtreten,
örte er in einem Nebenzimmer ein lautes **Jammern**. Er hatte ein mitleidiges Herz,
ihm da eine alte Frau, die wußte seinen **Jammer** schon und schenkte ihm ein
ugen herabflossen. Und wie es in seinem **Jammer** einmal aufblickte, stand eine
los, und sie erwachten alle wieder. "O **Jammer** und Unglück," rief der
Wie die Mutter das erblickte, fing ihr **Jammer** und Geschrei erst recht an, sie h

5. COSMAS search for: *&mitleidig*
Anz. Treffer = 16 (5 Sagen / 11 KHM)

GRI/KHM.00004 Märchen von einem, der auszog, das Fürchten zu lernen [zu: Kinder- und Hausmärchen, gesammelt von Jacob und Wilhelm Grimm; Erstveröffentlichung 1819], S. 54
Und weil er **mitleidig** war, legte er die Leiter an, stieg hinauf, knüpfte einen nach dem andern los, und holte sie alle siebene herab.
GRI/KHM.00017 Die weiße Schlange [zu: Kinder- und Hausmärchen, gesammelt von Jacob und Wilhelm Grimm; Erstveröffentlichung 1819], S. 131
Weil er ein **mitleidiges** Herz hatte, so stieg er vom Pferde ab und setzte die drei Gefangenen wieder ins Wasser. Sie zappelten vor Freude, streckten die Köpfe heraus und riefen ihm zu "wir wollen dirs gedenken und dirs vergelten, daß du uns errettet hast."
GRI/KHM.00018 Strohhalm, Kohle und Bohne [zu: Kinder- und Hausmärchen, gesammelt von Jacob und Wilhelm Grimm; Erstveröffentlichung 1819], S. 134

Weil er ein **mitleidiges** Herz hatte, so holte er Nadel und Zwirn heraus und nähte sie zusammen. Die Bohne bedankte sich bei ihm aufs schönste, aber da er schwarzen Zwirn gebraucht hatte, so haben seit der Zeit alle Bohnen eine schwarze Naht.

GRI/KHM.00031 Das Mädchen ohne Hände [zu: Kinder- und Hausmärchen, gesammelt von Jacob und Wilhelm Grimm; Erstveröffentlichung 1819], S. 200

Sie antwortete aber "hier kann ich nicht bleiben: ich will fortgehen: **mitleidige** Menschen werden mir schon so viel geben, als ich brauche."

GRI/KHM.00059 Der Frieder und das Katherlieschen [zu: Kinder- und Hausmärchen, gesammelt von Jacob und Wilhelm Grimm; Erstveröffentlichung 1819], S. 334

"Da sehe einer," sprach Katherlieschen, "was sie das arme Erdreich zerrissen, geschunden und gedrückt haben! das wird sein Lebtag nicht wieder heil." Und aus **mitleidigem** Herzen nahm es seine Butter und bestrich die Gleisen, rechts und links, damit sie von den Rädern nicht so gedrückt würden: und wie es sich bei seiner Barmherzigkeit so bückte, rollte ihm ein Käse aus der Tasche den Berg hinab.

GRI/KHM.00087 Der Arme und der Reiche [zu: Kinder- und Hausmärchen, gesammelt von Jacob und Wilhelm Grimm; Erstveröffentlichung 1819], S. 435

Als er in der Türe stand, kehrte er sich um und sprach "weil ihr so **mitleidig** und fromm seid, so wünscht euch dreierlei, das will ich euch erfüllen."

GRI/KHM.00101 Der Bärenhäuter [zu: Kinder- und Hausmärchen, gesammelt von Jacob und Wilhelm Grimm; Erstveröffentlichung 1819], S. 503

Er hatte ein **mitleidiges** Herz, öffnete die Türe und erblickte einen alten Mann, der heftig weinte und die Hände über dem Kopf zusammenschlug.

GRI/KHM.00154 Die Sterntaler [zu: Kinder- und Hausmärchen, gesammelt von Jacob und Wilhelm Grimm; Erstveröffentlichung 1819], S. 666

Es war einmal ein kleines Mädchen, dem war Vater und Mutter gestorben, und es war so arm, daß es kein Kämmerchen mehr hatte, darin zu wohnen, und kein Bettchen mehr, darin zu schlafen, und endlich gar nichts mehr als die Kleider auf dem Leib und ein Stückchen Brot in der Hand, das ihm ein **mitleidiges** Herz geschenkt hatte. Es war aber gut und fromm.

GRI/KHM.00162 Schneeweißchen und Rosenrot [zu: Kinder- und Hausmärchen, gesammelt von Jacob und Wilhelm Grimm; Erstveröffentlichung 1819], S. 682

Die **mitleidigen** Kinder hielten gleich das Männchen fest und zerrten sich so lange mit dem Adler herum, bis er seine Beute fahren ließ.

GRI/KHM.00178 Die Boten des Todes [zu: Kinder- und Hausmärchen, gesammelt von Jacob und Wilhelm Grimm; Erstveröffentlichung 1819], S. 725

Als er den halb Ohnmächtigen erblickte, ging er **mitleidig** heran, richtete ihn auf, flößte ihm aus seiner Flasche einen stärkenden Trank ein und wartete, bis er wieder zu Kräften kam.
GRI/KHM.00180 Die Gänsehirtin am Brunnen [zu: Kinder- und Hausmärchen, gesammelt von Jacob und Wilhelm Grimm; Erstveröffentlichung 1819], S. 735
Wenn ich denke, daß sie die wilden Tiere gefressen haben, so weiß ich mich vor Traurigkeit nicht zu fassen; manchmal tröste ich mich mit der Hoffnung, sie sei noch am Leben und habe sich in einer Höhle versteckt oder bei **mitleidigen** Menschen Schutz gefunden.

6. Example of syntactical exercise (Rapunzel (KHM 12):

Task: Determine first whether there are any prepositional phrases since they are most obviously recognizable and underline the preposition! Then find the finite verb(s) and the predicate(s); fill the clauses into the table. Determine the main clause(s) and the dependent clause (s) of the sentence.

Die Leute hatten in ihrem Hinterhaus ein kleines Fenster, daraus konnte man in einen prächtigen Garten sehen, der voll der schönsten Blumen und Kräuter stand; er war aber von einer hohen Mauer umgeben, und niemand wagte hineinzugehen, weil er einer Zauberin gehörte, die große Macht hatte und von aller Welt gefürchtet ward.

Prepositional Phrase(s)	*in ihrem Hinterhaus; in einen prächtigen Garten; von einer hohen Mauer; von aller Welt*
Nuclear clause(s)	*Die Leute hatten..., daraus konnte man..., er war...umgeben, niemand wagte...,*
Frontal clause(s)	
Brace clause(s)	*der voll der schönsten Blumen und Kräuter stand; weil er einer Zauberin gehörte; die große Macht hatte und von aller Welt gefürchtet ward.*
Comment	

7. COSMAS search:*&lassen*

Examples of selection of KWIC-overview (original/unsortiert).

GRI sies nicht gerne tat. Der Frosch **ließ** sichs gut schmecken, aber ihr
GRI Blut sollte vergossen werden, **ließ** in der Nacht eine Hirschkuh holen,
GRI "ich kann dich nicht töten **lassen**, wie der König befiehlt, aber
GRI Hirschkuh heimlich schlachten **lassen** und von dieser die Wahrzeichen
GRI hörte der König im Schlummer und **ließ** das Tuch noch einmal gerne fallen.
GRI der gnädige Gott wieder wachsen **lassen**;" und der Engel ging in die

GRI "Wo hast du die Gretel **gelassen**?" "Am Seil geleitet, vor die
GRI sie nicht vor Mitleiden und **ließen** ihn gehen. Sie schnitten einem
GRI aber war ohne Furcht und sprach "**laßt** mich nur hinab zu den bellenden
GRI Vater "wir wollen sie heiraten **lassen**." "Ja," sagte die Mutter, "wenn
GRI sie doch ihre Augen nicht müßig **lassen**, sah oben an die Wand hinauf und
GRI da aus Versehen hatten stecken **lassen**. Da fing die kluge Else an zu
GRI kann unmöglich wieder umkehren. **Laßt** mich nur hinein, ich will alle
GRI flicken." Der heilige Petrus **ließ** sich aus Mitleiden bewegen und
GRI noch hinter der Türe sitzt." Da **ließ** der Herr den Schneider vor sich
GRI wo die schönsten Kräuter standen, **ließ** sie da fressen und herumspringen.
GRI wäre satt, und hast sie hungern **lassen**?" und in seinem Zorne nahm er
GRI "so ein frommes Tier hungern zu **lassen**!" lief hinauf und schlug mit der
GRI mit dem schönsten Laube aus, und **ließ** die Ziege daran fressen. Abends,
GRI sättigen," sprach er zu ihr, und **ließ** sie weiden bis zum Abend. Da
GRI nicht mehr darfst sehen **lassen**." In einer Hast sprang er
GRI sie sahen, wie es gemeint war, **ließen** sich nicht zweimal bitten,
GRI an die Wand. Dem Wirte aber **ließen** seine Gedanken keine Ruhe, es
GRI ein ganzes Tuch voll Goldstücke. **Laßt** nur alle Verwandte herbeirufen,
GRI und bewegen können; und eher **läßt** er nicht ab, als bis du sagst
GRI gebe alles gerne wieder heraus, **laßt** nur den verwünschten Kobold wieder
GRI will Gnade für Recht ergehen **lassen**, aber hüte dich vor Schaden!"
GRI er "Knüppel, in den Sack!" und **ließ** ihn ruhen. Der Drechsler zog am
GRI meint, einen schlimmen Tanz, und **läßt** nicht eher nach, als bis er auf
GRI Brüdern abgenommen hatte. Jetzt **laßt** sie beide rufen und ladet alle
GRI einer großen Stadt für Geld sehen **ließen**: wir wollen ihn kaufen." Sie
GRI nichts draus machen, die Vögel **lassen** mir auch manchmal was drauf
GRI nicht, "vielleicht," dachte er, "**läßt** der Wolf mit sich reden," und

Assessing the Development of Foreign Language Writing Skills: Syntactic and Lexical Features

Pieter de Haan & Kees van Esch

Radboud University Nijmegen

Abstract

In de Haan & van Esch (2004; 2005) we outline a research project designed to study the development of writing skills in English and Spanish as foreign languages, based on theories developed, for instance, in Shaw & Liu (1998) and Connor & Mbaye (2002). This project entails collecting essays written by Dutch-speaking students of English (EFL writing) and Dutch-speaking students of Spanish (SFL writing) at one-year intervals, in order to study the development of their writing skills, both quantitatively and qualitatively. The essays are written on a single prompt, taken from Grant & Ginther (2000), asking the students to select their preferred source of news and give specific reasons to support their preference. Students' proficiency level is established on the basis of holistic teacher ratings.

A first general analysis of the essays has been carried out with WordSmith Tools. Moreover, the texts have been computer-tagged with Biber's tagger (Biber, 1988; 1995). An initial analysis of relevant text features (Polio, 2001) has provided overwhelming evidence of the relationship between a number of basic linguistic features and proficiency level (de Haan & van Esch, 2004; 2005).

In the current article we present the results of more detailed analyses of the EFL material collected from the first cohort of students in two consecutive years, 2002 and 2003, and discuss a number of salient linguistic features of students' writing skills development. We first discuss the development of general features such as essay length, word length and type/token ratio. Then we move on to discuss how the use of specific lexical features (cf. Biber, 1995; Grant & Ginther, 2000) has developed over one year in the three proficiency level groups that we have distinguished. While the development of the general features over one year is shown to correspond logically to what can be assumed to be increased proficiency, the figures for the specific lexical features studied do not all point unambiguously in the same direction.

1. Introduction

In order to get a detailed and systematic insight into the development of writing skills in English and Spanish as foreign languages, a research project was initiated at the University of Nijmegen in 2002, aiming at collecting a large number of foreign language student essays written at various stages in the curriculum. The project is described in some detail in de Haan & van Esch (2004; 2005). It is based on theories developed in Shaw & Liu (1998) and Connor & Mbaye (2002), and aims specifically to address the problem of relating text-internal features to holistic teacher assessment, with a view to ultimately assisting (non-native) teachers in assessing the development of non-native student writing.

Knowing how to communicate presupposes a number of distinct competences. In their model of communicative competence Canale & Swaine (1980) and Canale (1983) distinguish four different competences. The first is *grammatical competence*, by which is meant lexical, syntactic, semantic, morphological and phonological knowledge. The second is *discourse competence*, the ability to produce texts and significant text units appropriate to the level of the text. In this competence the major features are coherence, viz. the adequate combination of linguistic expressions, and cohesion, viz. the appropriate way of connecting these expressions. The third competence, the *sociolinguistic competence*, is the ability to communicate in a social and cultural context which is determined by such sociocultural factors as theme, roles, discourse participants, situation and norms of interaction. The fourth competence finally, *strategic competence*, is the ability to solve communication problems and compensate for deficiencies by verbal and non-verbal means.

Connor & Mbaye (2002) have proposed to adapt Canale & Swaine's (1980) communicative competence model for writing. They regard grammatical competence as the knowledge of grammar, vocabulary, spelling and punctuation. By discourse competence they mean the way the text is structured, especially with reference to how coherence and cohesion are established. Their sociolinguistic competence refers to the appropriateness of the genre, register and tone of the writing. Strategic competence, they feel, is the ability to assess the intended readership, to address them in the appropriate manner, and to present the appropriate arguments.

The advantage of Connor & Mbaye's proposal is that they associate the notion of communicative competence with writing skill. What still remains to be decided, however, is the relative weight of these four competences. If we want to be able to assess a writer's writing competence we would like to be able to assess each of these four competences relative to each other. In order to do this, we need to formulate a number of criteria to be used in the assessment of writing skills. Moreover, we will need to look into the similarities and the differences between native language (L1) writing on the one hand, and second language (L2) and foreign language (FL) writing on the other, both with respect to the quality of the written product, and to the characteristics of the writing process.

As far as the writing process is concerned, Silva (1993), on the basis of 72 studies on the differences between native English writing and L2 English writing, has shown that there is a certain amount of similarity between L1 and L2 writing. However, L2 writers do less in the way of advance planning, both on the global and the specific level, and devote less time to planning. L2 writers are also less creative in the generation of ideas. Producing a coherent text in L2 proves to be more difficult than in L1. The L2 writing process is more laborious, less fluent and less efficient than in L1. The most serious problem turns out to be the vocabulary needed: L2 writing speed is lower and L2 texts are shorter. Text revision in L2 is less frequent, less profound and less efficient.

With reference to L2 text characteristics, Silva notes significant differences in fluency, accuracy, quality and coherence. L2 texts are shorter, contain more errors, especially morphological and syntactic errors, and have less quality overall. As far as argumentation goes, L2 writers use different text structures and establish different logical relationships between parts of the text, which can be attributed to their different cultural backgrounds. This results in a different elaboration of arguments, a different way of connecting sentences and paragraphs, a different way of presenting and organising arguments and drawing conclusions, and in a less coherent text. Moreover L2 writers address their readers in a different way. L2 texts generally have a rather simple structure, are less complex, less mature, and stylistically less appropriate. Linguistically, L2 texts usually have fewer T-units, more coordinated sentences, and fewer passive voices, less lexical variety, fewer subordinators and reference words, and are less sophisticated overall.

Similarities between L1 and L2 writing have been shown by Roca de Larios, Murphy & Marín (2002), on the basis of an analysis of 65 studies with reference to factors relevant to the cognitive processes on which L2 writing is based. Apart from the differences found by Silva, and other differences related to the cognitive processes of writing and revising, they found similarities in the way in which efficient strategies were adopted, and in the global approach of the writing task, the setting of objectives, and the perception of writing as a complex task which can be broken down into a number of simpler tasks. They also found similarities in problem-solving strategies and in an interactive approach to text composition, in which there is a balance between the writing processes initiated and the time and mental effort spent to put the message across to the reader.

These differences and similarities have implications for the learning, the teaching, and the assessment of L2 and FL writing, not only with respect to grammatical and lexical aspects, but also to aspects of content, coherence and cohesion.

The study of the development of foreign language writing can benefit greatly from corpus research (Shaw & Liu, 1998), as collections of foreign language texts, collected at various intervals, can be looked upon as text corpora. The measures that can be used to establish this development (Polio, 2001) include those that point to linguistic maturity, such as sentence length, word length, and type/token ratio (Grant & Ginther, 2000).[1] All of these measures can be established fairly easily by means of standard corpus research tools (de Haan & van Esch, 2004; 2005).

It has been shown (Ortega, 2003) that in order to be able to measure substantial syntactic and lexical development, L2 or FL texts should not be collected from the same students at intervals shorter than nine to twelve months. Similarly, Shaw & Liu (1998) found that despite the fact that students in a group of L2 English writers from various language backgrounds wrote more formal texts at the end of a two-to-three-month EFL course, there were few changes in syntactic complexity, text organisation, lexical variety and the number of errors.

It would seem that features relating to the grammatical and discourse competences mentioned above can be studied on the basis of quantitative analyses of student essays. Features relating to the sociolinguistic and strategic competences, on the other hand, can be studied best on the basis of qualitative analyses. At this stage of our project we have not yet had occasion to perform any qualitative analyses. Therefore we will concentrate, in the current article, on the discussion of the grammatical and discourse features mentioned in section 2.2 (data analysis).

2. The research project

The research project that the current study forms part of is described in great detail in de Haan & van Esch (2004; 2005) and van Esch, de Haan & Nas (2004). It is envisaged to run from 2002 until 2008. In this period we aim to collect a large number of university student essays from the same students, at various intervals over a period of three years, and study these both quantitatively and qualitatively. The project is carried out at the departments of English and Spanish at the University of Nijmegen. Essays are collected from both Dutch-speaking students of English and Dutch-speaking students of Spanish. The combination is a deliberate one, for two reasons:

1. Students of English at Dutch Universities will have been taught English at primary and secondary school for a total of eight years when they enter university, which makes them fairly competent in English when they start their academic studies. Spanish, on the other hand, is not as a rule taught at Dutch primary or secondary schools, which means that Dutch university students of Spanish virtually all start at zero level. It is therefore to be expected that there will be huge differences between the development of the writing skills of the Spanish FL students and that of the English FL students.
2. English and Dutch are very closely related languages. Writing courses in English, especially at academic level, will need to concentrate far less on the mechanics of writing than the Spanish writing courses. This, again, will have an effect on the way in which writing skills develop in the two groups of FL students in the same period of time. It can also be expected that there will be significant differences in quality between the two groups.

2.1 Data collection

Data collection is outlined in de Haan & van Esch (2004; 2005). All the essays are written on a single prompt, taken from Grant & Ginther (2000), asking the students to select their preferred source of news and give specific reasons to support their preference. They are allowed 30 minutes to complete this task. The need to collect a new corpus of English and Spanish FL texts arises from the fact that to our knowledge, no suitable Spanish FL corpus is available, while for English the existing ICLE corpus (cf. Granger, 1998), although it contains a large collection of English FL essays written by Dutch-speaking university students, is not suitable as it does not contain any longitudinal data. In the project period we aim to collect three different essays from at least two cohorts of students.

It should be noted that our student population is quite different from the one used in Grant and Ginther. They collected essays written by L2 writers for the TOEFL Test of Written English (TWE). For their study they examined 30 essays from each of three different TWE scores, viz 3, 4 and 5 (TWE scores range from 1 to 6, 1 being the lowest score possible).

2.2 Data analysis

The data analysed for the current study are the essays written by the first cohort of English FL students (who started in September 2001) in March 2002 and in March 2003, i.e. when they were about seven months into their first year and second year respectively. It should be noted that these students were taught a specific course on academic writing during the first half of their second year. We will first discuss four general measures of fluency, viz. the average essay length, average sentence length, average word length and the standardised type/token ratio in 2002 and 2003.

We will then move on to discuss a number of more specific lexical features that have been suggested in the literature as having discourse function (cf. Grant & Ginther, 2000). First, conjuncts, such as *however* and *nevertheless*, are used to indicate logical relationships between clauses. Next, hedges (e.g. *sort of, kind of*) mark ideas as being uncertain and are typically used in informal discourse. Amplifiers, like *definitely* or *certainly*, indicate the reliability of the propositions or degree of certainty (cf. Chafe, 1985), while emphatics (e.g. *really, surely*) are used to mark the presence of certainty. Finally, demonstratives (*this, that, these* and *those*) are used to mark referential cohesion in a text, while downtoners (e.g. *barely, almost*) lessen the force of the verb, can be used to indicate probability, and can also mark politeness (cf. Biber, 1988; Reppen, 1994).

Essay lengths were calculated by means of the standard facility provided in Word; word lengths and standardised type/token ratios were provided by WordSmith Tools. Type/token ratios were standardised by calculating the ratio per 50 words of running text, after which a running average was calculated. Sentence lengths were calculated by hand. All of the specific lexical features mentioned above were identified automatically by Biber's (1988; 1995) tagger, as had been done in the Grant & Ginther (2000) study.[2] Frequency counts of these features were drawn up by means of SPSS.

In all, 66 English FL essays were studied. In 2002 the mean essay length amounted to 303 words, with a range from 133 to 528 words. One year later, in 2003, the mean essay length was 383 words, with a range from 215 to 604 words.[3] The students were divided into three proficiency classes on the basis of holistic teacher assessments of the 2002 essays, viz. best, middle and poor (cf. de Haan & van Esch, 2004; 2005). In the figures below we will present the development of the students in the three separate classes. All the essays were rated by three individual language proficiency teachers, after which an average ranking was calculated. Inter-rater reliability was fair ($r = .371$, $P < .05$).

2.2.1 General fluency

Figure 1 shows the mean essay length in terms of the number of tokens. It shows quite clearly that students in all proficiency level groups have increased their general fluency, and that the increase is most prominent in the group of poor students. We are clearly looking at a kind of "ceiling effect" here. There will be an upper limit to the number of words one can produce in 30 minutes' time, and the best students were obviously much closer to that ceiling already in their first year. Interestingly, Grant & Ginther (2000) found mean essay length figures that were much lower: ranging from 164 words for TWE level 3 to 253 words for TWE level 5. We will come back to this in the discussion section.

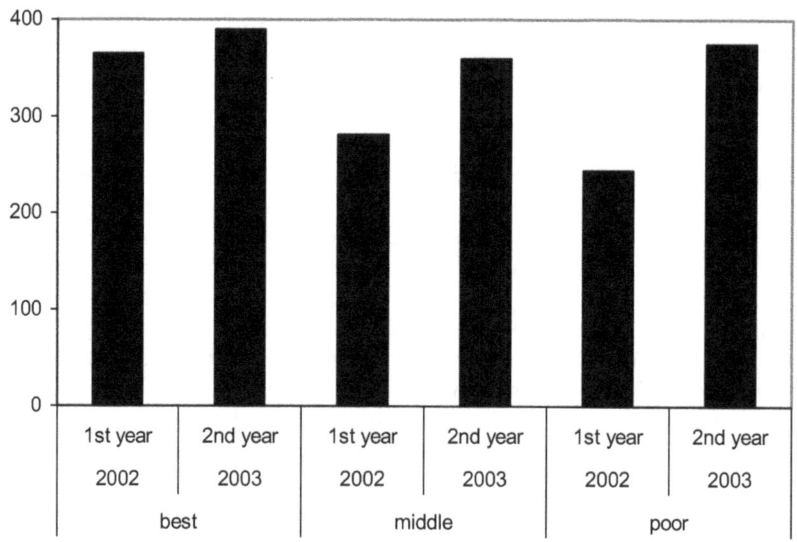

Figure 1: mean essay length in 2002 and 2003

Figure 2 shows the mean sentence length. Again, we see that students in all proficiency level groups write longer sentences, on average, in 2003 than in 2002. Sentence length has not been discussed much in the literature as a feature that can be indicative of general fluency. Still we find a steady increase of about 1.5 words per sentence overall. What we found rather puzzling at first (de Haan & van Esch, 2004) was the extreme mean sentence length that we found in the poor students' essays in 2002. When we studied these students' 2002 essays we found that they contained a fair number of run-on sentences, where comma splice errors had inevitably contributed to these extreme figures.[4] For this reason it might be better, perhaps, to count the number and the length of other text units, like finite or non-finite clauses, but these cannot be identified automatically at this stage.

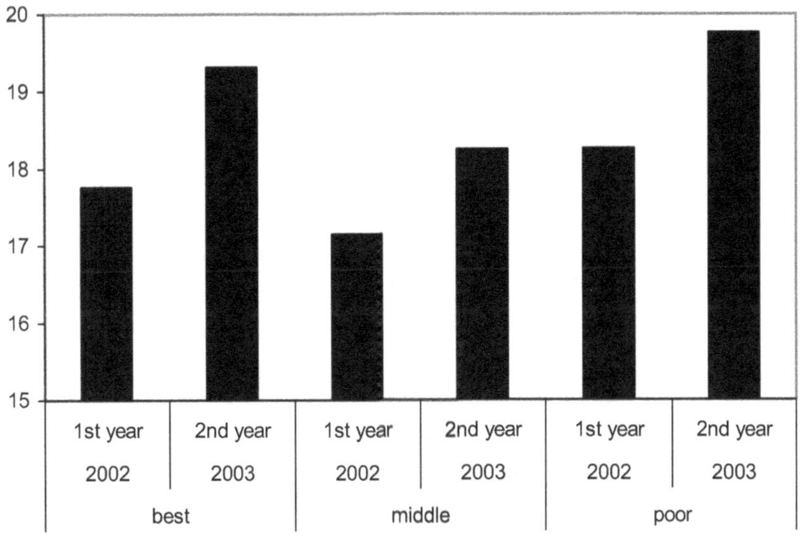

Figure 2: mean sentence length in 2002 and 2003

Figure 3 shows the mean word length. Grant & Ginther (2000) had found average word length scores ranging from 4.39 for TWE level 3 to 4.55 for TWE

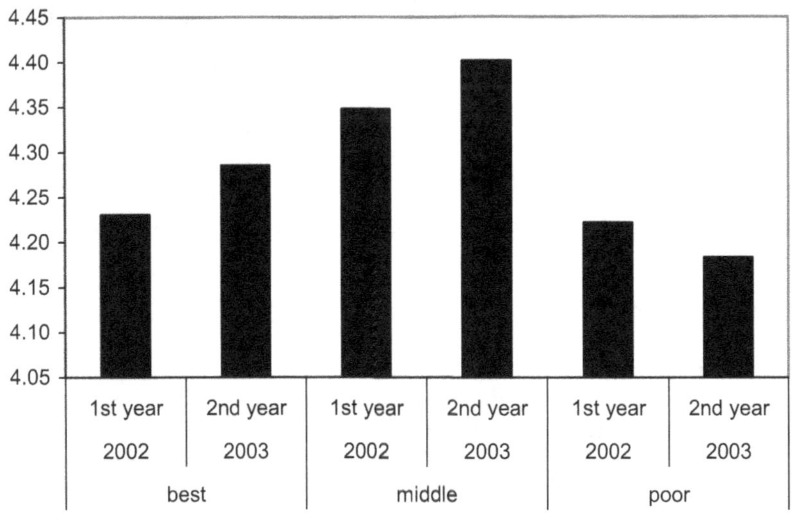

Figure 3: mean word length in 2002 and 2003

level 5. Our students do not come anywhere near those figures, not even in 2003. We will come back to this in the discussion section. We see a steady increase in word length for the best and middle students, but a decrease for the poor students. We also observe that the students in the middle group have a higher score than those in the best group, both in 2002 and in 2003. This is probably due to the fact that the students in the best group construct syntactically more complex sentences, which involves the use of relatively many short function words.

Figure 4 shows the standardised type/token ratios. These figures cannot be compared to Grant & Ginther's (2000) as they chose to count only the number of types in the first 50 words of the essays. Interestingly, what we see is a decrease in the type/token ratio from 2002 to 2003 in all proficiency level groups. We take this to be proof of the fact that, contrary to what is often assumed, a higher type/token ratio does not necessarily point to a better general proficiency. We will come back to this in the discussion section.

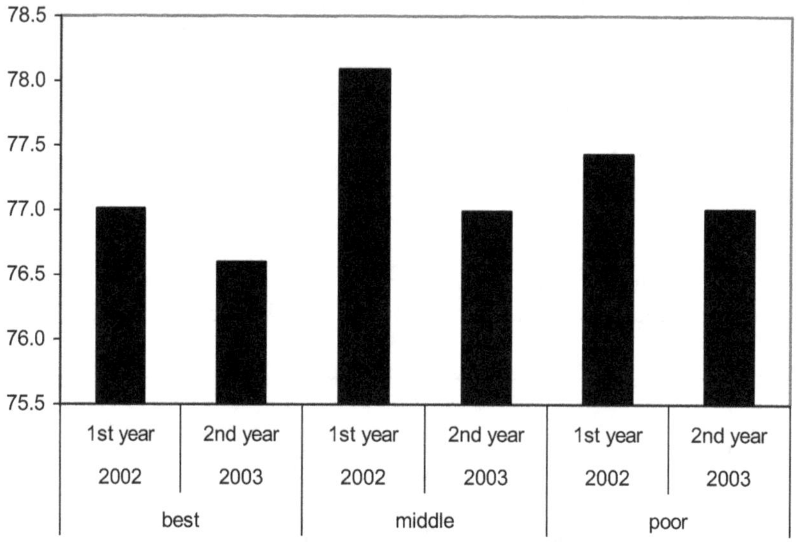

Figure 4: type/token ratio in 2002 and 2003 (standardised per 50 words)

2.2.2 Lexical features

Grant & Ginther (2000) note an overall increase[5] in the use of conjuncts, amplifiers, emphatics, demonstratives and downtoners from TWE level 3 to level 5, with a slightly different pattern for hedges, which do not occur very often in the first place. Given that hedges indicate uncertainly on the part of the speaker this makes sense, they claim, since the writers had been asked to write about their preferred news sources. The increased use of the other five features is taken to coincide with increased linguistic development, enabling the writers to use structures that make connections in the text. Grant & Ginther's findings support those of Ferris (1994) and Connor (1990), indicating that the overall use of these features increases as writers become more competent. Grant & Ginther point out, however, that the mere presence of the tagged features does not indicate whether or not they are used appropriately, a concern which was also raised by Ferris (1993).

There are a number of points we would like to raise before presenting our own data. First of all, it should be noted that Grant & Ginther (2000) apparently present the raw scores of the lexical features. Given the (considerable) differences in essay length (see above) we thought it better to calculate standardised scores per 1000 tokens for each essay. These are presented in the tables below. Secondly, Grant & Ginther take the observed increase in the mean scores from TWE level 3 to level 5 as a clear indication of increased competence. However, they completely ignore the huge standard deviation scores (which are often greater than the mean scores themselves), so that there is considerable overlap between the three levels distinguished. Finally, although with Ferris (1993) they express some concern as to the question of the appropriateness of use of the lexical features, it can be expected that if students had used the features inappropriately they would have been penalised for it by the raters, which should have been reflected in lower TWE scores.

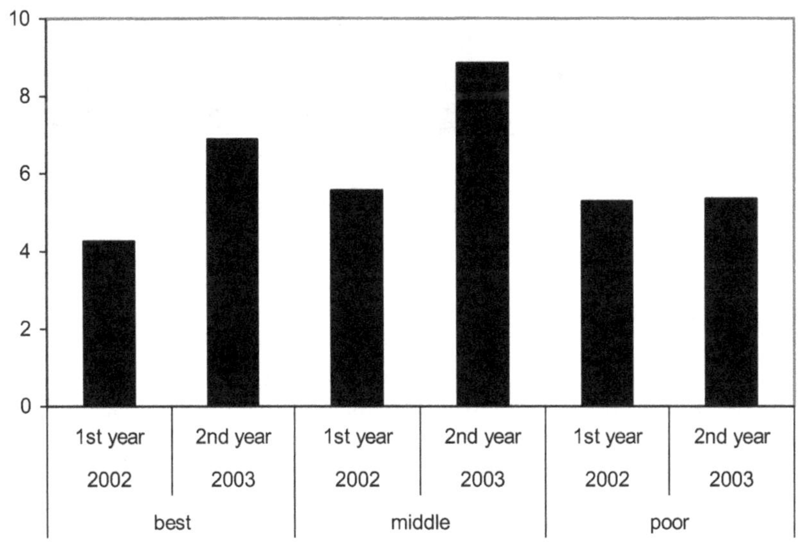

Figure 5: number of conjuncts per 1000 tokens

Figure 5 shows the number of conjuncts per 1000 tokens. Grant & Ginther (2000) make an explicit point about the difference between the level 5 students, who produce almost two conjuncts on average, and the level 3 students, who produce 0.47 conjuncts on average, and level 4 students, who produce even fewer: 0.33 conjuncts on average.[6] Contrary to what Grant & Ginther find, our best students do not produce the most conjuncts at all: in fact they produce the fewest in 2002. However, both the best and the middle students show an increase in the use of conjuncts from 2002 to 2003, whereas the poor students show no increase.

Figure 6 shows the number of hedges per 1000 tokens. Again, what we find for 2002 is completely different from what Grant & Ginther find, with the best students producing the fewest hedges. Interestingly, we see an increase in the number of hedges only for the best students and the poor students, while the middle students show a clear decrease.

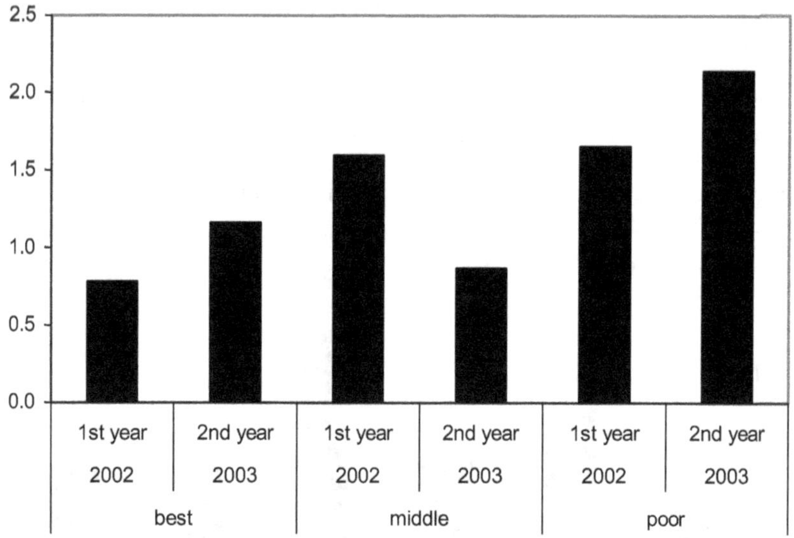

Figure 6: number of hedges per 1000 tokens

Figure 7 shows the number of amplifiers per 1000 tokens, while Figure 8 shows the number of emphatics per 1000 tokens. These two, as was suggested above, indicate the degree of certainty, or the mere presence of certainty. Figure 7 shows quite clearly that the number of amplifiers used does not necessarily correspond to the level of competence. First of all, the best and middle students show a decrease in the use of amplifiers. Secondly, the poor students not only use them more often than students in either of the other groups in their 2002 essays; they use them even more in their 2003 essays. Unless this were to mean that it is only the poor students who make progress (which is hard to assume in itself, although they might make more progress simply because there is more room for progress) this can only be taken to prove that Grant & Ginther's findings, again, must be considered with caution. Figure 8 shows a minimal increase in the number of emphatics in all three proficiency level groups. This does not refute Grant & Ginther's findings, but it does not provide very strong confirmation either.

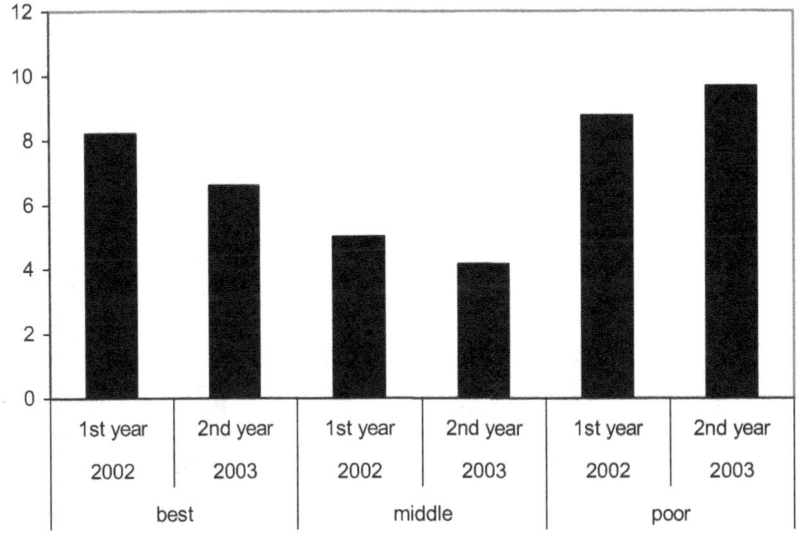

Figure 7: number of amplifiers per 1000 tokens

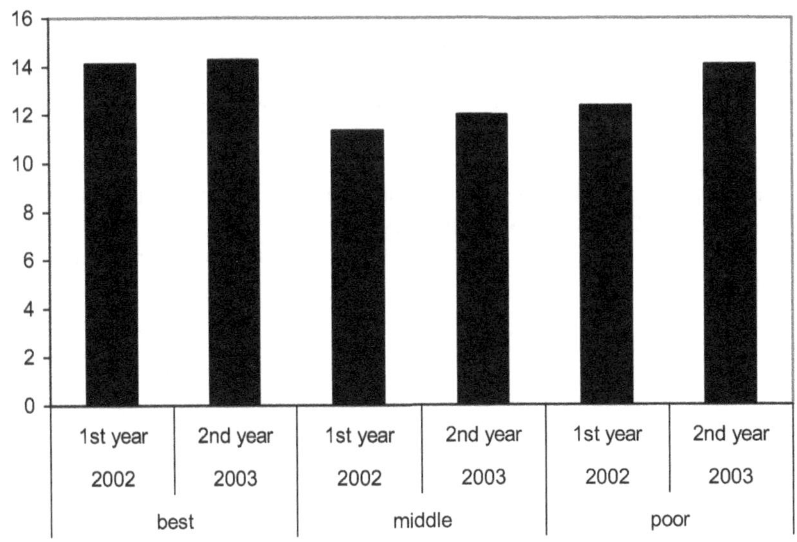

Figure 8: number of emphatics per 1000 tokens

Figure 9 shows the number of demonstratives per 1000 tokens. Demonstratives are taken to be markers of referential cohesion in the text. Both the best and the middle students use more demonstratives in 2003 than in 2002, possibly suggesting a better mastery of textual cohesion. However, the poor students, who produce twice as many demonstratives as the best students per 1000 tokens in 2002, drop their numbers to the same level as the middle students in 2003.

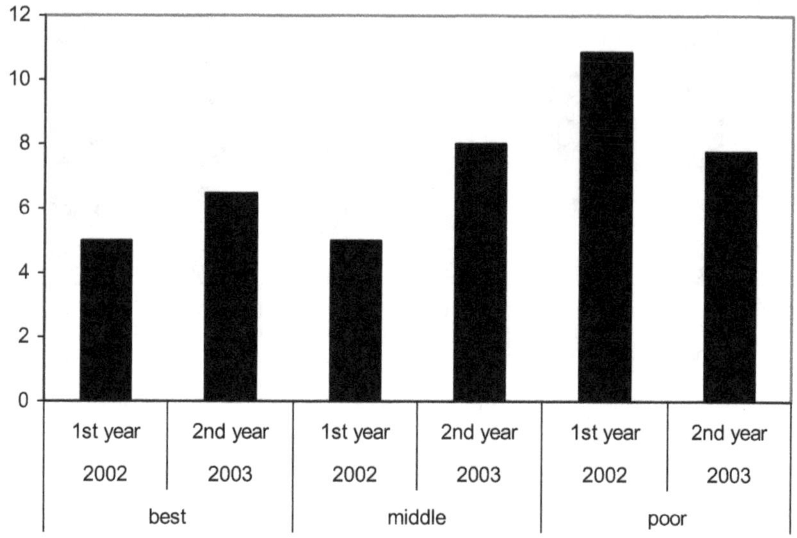

Figure 9: number of demonstratives per 1000 tokens

Figure 10, finally, shows the number of downtoners per 1000 tokens. Downtoners lessen the force of the verb, enabling writers to bring a certain amount of subtlety in the way they present their arguments, indicate probability, and mark politeness. What we see is a rather prominent decrease in the number of downtoners from 2002 to 2003 in the best and middle students, while the poor students remain fairly constant, and end up using the most downtoners in 2003.

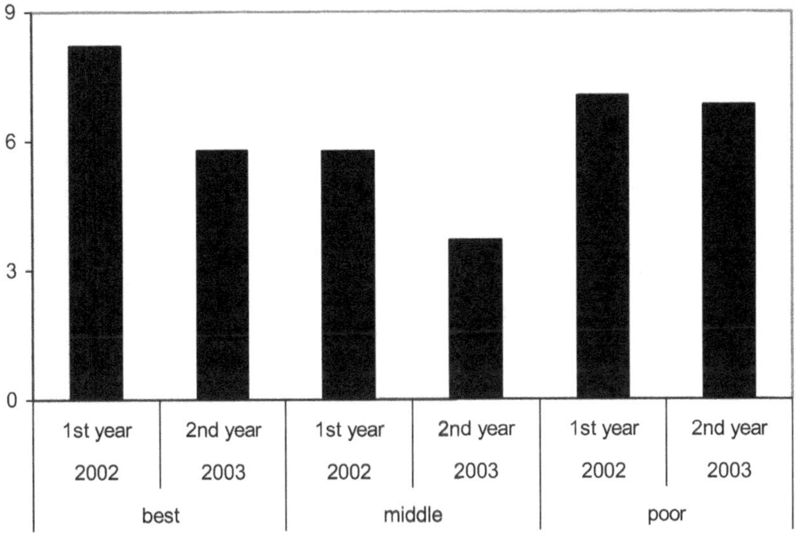

Figure 10: number of downtoners per 1000 tokens

3. Discussion

We will first discuss the results of the analysis of the features relating to general fluency. Three of these also occur in the Grant & Ginther (2000) study. We noticed that the essays in the Grant & Ginther study are far shorter than the ones produced by the Dutch students. On the other hand, there is a parallel between the TWE essays and ours, in that higher ratings correspond to longer essays. Moreover, our data show that development over time also corresponds to an increase in essay length. So it would be fair to conclude that essay length generally corresponds to general fluency, at least in relative terms.

This begs the question if we can at all relate essay length reliably to any kind of absolute level of competence. Given the great difference between the TWE essays and ours this is far more problematic. What needs to be taken into consideration is the paradoxical mismatch between essay length on the one hand and mean word length on the other. We found shorter words on the whole in the Dutch students' essays. If, as is often suggested, more mature writing is characterised by longer words on average we are faced with a problem: on the one hand the Dutch students seem to be far better than those who took the TWE test because of their greater essay lengths, but on the other, the TWE writers seem to be better because of their greater word lengths.

The question that must be answered, of course, is how mean word length can account for more mature proficiency. It stands to reason that a more mature student will have acquired more Latinate words for instance, and may for that reason more readily use a word like *consideration* instead of *thought*. On the whole it could be argued that lexical words tend to be longer than function words and that a student who masters the use of adjectives and adverbs to bring about shades of meaning, or derived nominalisations to increase the level of formality of his writing, is on his way to being a more proficient writer, so an increased use of these would account for an increase of the mean word length.

On the other hand, linguistically more mature students would also be able to produce syntactically more complex sentences, characteristic of a more formal style. De Haan (1987) found that it is especially the more formal texts that show a greater syntactic complexity, and that this syntactic complexity is brought about by embedding relatively simple structures into larger ones, which is typically achieved by means of (short) prepositions and subordinators, which would decrease the mean word length.

Finally, there is the decreased type/token ratio observed in our data, on all three proficiency levels, as opposed to the TWE data, which show an increase from level 3 to level 5. Bearing in mind that greater syntactic complexity is achieved by the use of relatively short and frequent[7] function words, such as prepositions and subordinators, a greater syntactic complexity will also be reflected in a lower type/token ratio. So we not only expect that there will be no straight positive relationship between mean word length and essay length, but also a possibly inverse relationship between type/token ratio and essay length, due to the greater syntactic complexity present in the longer, i.e. better, essays.

Therefore we are tempted to draw two conclusions with respect to general fluency. The first is that the Dutch essay writers are syntactically more advanced than the students who contributed essays to the TWE, which were studied by Grant & Ginther (2000). The second would be that the American raters who rated the TWE essays prior to Grant & Ginther's analysis, clearly were inclined to put more emphasis on rhetorical than on syntactic considerations. This touches on the point that we raised in the beginning, viz. that there is a need to strike a proper balance in the weight of the various competences in the assessment of L2 or FL writing.

With respect to the specific lexical features that we studied the situation is far more problematic. First of all, a direct comparison of our data to Grant & Ginther's is not possible, as they present raw figures while we have standardised ours. We feel that standardised scores are a more truthful reflection of specific lexical use, which makes for a fairer comparison among groups and between years. However, in most cases the standardised scores are not radically different from the raw scores, and reveal the same tendencies as the raw scores. So any differences between our scores and those of Grant & Ginther cannot be attributed solely to the different method of calculation.

Secondly, while Grant & Ginther's mean scores for the six lexical features show a "neat" increase from TWE level 3 to level 5, the standard deviation scores suggest not only that there is considerable overlap between the levels, but also that the essays of the various TWE levels constitute very heterogeneous groups. Honesty commands us to say that we did not test for statistic significance either, so that the best that can be said of either study is that they reveal tendencies, rather than hard and fast differences. However, the tendencies revealed in our study are quite different from those revealed in Grant & Ginther's.

Grant & Ginther conclude that writers increase their overall use of the specific lexical features studied as they become more competent, which shows their increased ability to state their desired messages in writing. When we look at our data we see this conclusion only partly confirmed. Clearly the poor students are the odd ones out with respect to the use of conjuncts (no increase, where the others show a clear increase), amplifiers (increase, where the others show a decrease), demonstratives (decrease, where the others show an increase) and downtoners (slight decrease, where the others show a dramatic decrease).

An interesting category is that of the hedges. Like Grant & Ginther's students, our students use very few hedges in general. However, contrary to what Grant & Ginther find, it is our poor students that use them most often. Moreover, the middle students are the odd ones out in this case as they show a decrease, where the others show a clear increase in their use.

The only way we can account for these differences is by assuming that, as we suggested above, the TWE essay writers are in a different stage in their English proficiency development, one in which the presence or absence of a certain lexical feature plays a far more crucial role than in the stage in which Dutch university students of English are.

4. Summary and conclusion

In this study we have looked into the relationship between the level of EFL writing competence and the occurrence and frequency of certain linguistic features. We have shown that it is certainly possible to relate a more advanced level of fluency unambiguously to a number of general features, such as essay length, sentence length, word length and type/token ratio. It is far more problematic, however, to do the same with the specific lexical features that we have studied.

Especially the differences between our data and the American TWE data presented in Grant & Ginther (2000) on the one hand, and the development figures for the Dutch data on the other, would seem to suggest that linguistic maturity and proficiency development are not unambiguous notions. The differences observed suggest that although relative levels of proficiency or development can be established on the basis of the frequency of certain of these features (such that more mature students are likely to write longer essays, for instance), these features cannot as yet be used to establish proficiency levels in absolute terms. In order to be able to do that we would not only have to study more features, including grammatical features and clause level features, but also, more importantly, study the complex interactions among them. As we go on collecting more student essays and gradually studying more of the lexical, grammatical and clause level features, and the way they interact, we will gain a better insight into the development of foreign language writing skills.

A last point we would like to mention here is that the comparison of the TWE data with our data suggest that the American raters who graded the TWE essays holistically probably placed a heavier emphasis on sociolinguistic and strategic competence than on grammatical competence. The raters who graded the Dutch students' essays probably put more emphasis on grammatical and discourse competence. This underlines the need, as we stated in our introduction, to weigh the various competences relative to each other, in order to arrive at a fair assessment of non-native writing skills.

Notes

1 Other measures that have been found to correspond to holistic and curriculum-based assessment (Wolfe-Quintero *et al.*, 1998), include Mean Length per T-unit (MLTU), Mean Length of Clause (MLC), Number of Clauses per T-Unit (C/TU) and the number of Dependent Clauses per Clause (DC/C).

2 We have based our discussion on the study of uncorrected output of Biber's tagger. It should be noted that Grant & Ginther (2000) apparently performed some post-editing of the tagged output files.

3 For Spanish, the corresponding figures, based on 22 essays, were as follows: mean essay length in 2002: 214 words (range: 153–306); in 2003: 320 words (range: 225–453).

4 We have at this stage not looked at the 2003 essays themselves. Though students are explicitly taught about the comma splice error, we suspect that the poor students have not quite overcome this problem.

5 Note that the term 'increase' in Grant & Ginther should not be interpreted in a temporal sense, since their data are not longitudinal. The term merely means a greater frequency of occurrence at level 5 than at level 3. In the discussion of our own data the terms 'decrease' and 'increase' do refer to development in time.

6 Grant & Ginther do not comment on the fact that level 4 students have a lower score than level 3 students. Level 4 students have better scores than level 3 students on all other lexical features.

7 De Haan (1992) has shown that a mere three prepositions, viz. *of*, *in* and *to*, account for over half of all the prepositional phrases in two different corpora of British English texts.

References

Biber, D. (1988), *Variation across speech and writing*. Cambridge: Cambridge University Press.

Biber, D. (1995), *Dimensions of register variation: A cross-linguistic comparison*. Cambridge: Cambridge University Press.

Canale, M. (1983), From communicative competence to communicative language pedagogy, in J.C. Richards & R. Schmidt (eds.), *Language and communication*. London: Longman. 2–27.

Canale, M. & Swaine, M. (1980), Theoretical bases of communicative approaches to second language teaching and testing, *Applied Linguistics*, 1: 1–47.

Chafe, W. (1985). Linguistic differences produced by differences between speaking and writing, in D. Olson, N. Torrance & A. Hildyard (eds.), *Literature, language and learning: The nature and consequences of reading and writing*. Cambridge: Cambridge University Press. 105–123.

Connor, U. (1990), Linguistic/rhetorical measures for international persuasive students writing, *Research in the Teaching of English*, 24: 67–87.

Connor, U. & Mbaye, A.. (2002), Discourse approaches to writing assessment, *Annual Review of Applied Linguistics*, 22: 263–278.

van Esch, K., de Haan, P., & Nas, M. (2004). El desarrollo de la escritura en inglés y español como lenguas extranjeras, *Estudios de Lingüística Aplicada*, 22: 53–79.

Ferris, D. (1993), The design of an automatic analysis program for L2 text research: Necessity and feasibility, *Journal of Second Language Writing*, 2: 119–129.

Ferris, D. (1994), Lexical and syntactic features of ESL writing by students at different levels of L2 proficiency, *TESOL Quarterly*, 28: 414–420.

Granger, S. (ed.) (1998), *Learner English on computer*. London & New York: Addison Wesley Longman.

Grant, L. & Ginther, A. (2000), Using computer-tagged linguistic features to describe L2 writing differences, *Journal of Second Language Writing*, 9: 123–145.

de Haan, P. (1987), Exploring the Linguistic DataBase: Noun phrase complexity and language variation, in W. Meijs (ed.), *Corpus linguistics and beyond.* Amsterdam: Rodopi. 151–166.

de Haan, P. (1992), The optimum corpus sample size?, in G. Leitner (ed.), *New directions in English language corpora: Methodology, results, software development*. Berlin – New York: Mouton de Gruyter. 3–19.

de Haan, P. & van Esch, K. (2004), Towards an instrument for the assessment of the development of writing skills, in U. Connor & Th. Upton (eds.), *Applied corpus linguistics: A multidimensional perspective.* Amsterdam – New York, NY: Rodopi. 267–279.

de Haan, P. & van Esch, K. (2005), The development of writing in English and Spanish as foreign languages, *Assessing Writing*, 10: 100–116.

Ortega, L. (2003). Syntactic complexity measures and their relationship to L2 proficiency: A research synthesis of college–level L2 writing, *Applied Linguistics*, 24: 492–518.

Polio, C. (2001), Research methodology in L2 writing assessment, in T. Silva & P. K. Matsuda (eds.), *On Second Language Writing*. Mahwah, NJ: Lawrence Erlbaum Associates. 91–115.

Reppen, R. (1994). Variation in elementary student language: A multi-dimensional perspective. Unpublished doctoral dissertation. Flagstaff: Northern Arizona University.

Roca de Larios, P., Murphy, L., & Marín, J. (2002). A critical examination of L2 writing process research, in S. Ransdel & M.L. Barbier (eds.), *New directions for research in L2 writing*. Dordrecht: Kluwer Academic Publishers. 11–47.

Shaw, P. & Liu, E. (1998), What develops in the development of second-language writing?, *Applied Linguistics*, 19: 225–254.

Silva, T. (1993). Toward an understanding of the distinct nature of L2 writing: The ESL research and its implication, *TESOL Quarterly*, 27: 657–677.

Wolfe-Quintero, K., Inagaki, S., & Kim, H.-Y. (1998). Second language development in writing: Measures of fluency, accuracy, and complexity. Technical Report No. 17. Honolulu, HI: University of Hawaii, Second Language Teaching and Curriculum Center.

A Contrastive Functional Analysis of Errors in Spanish EFL University Writers' Argumentative Texts: Corpus-based Study

JoAnne Neff, Francisco Ballesteros, Emma Dafouz, Francisco Martínez, Juan-Pedro Rica

Universidad Complutense de Madrid

Mercedes Díez

Universidad de Alcalá

Rosa Prieto

Escuela Oficial de Idiomas, Madrid

Abstract

This article reports on the initial results of the Spanish data from the ICLE Error Tagging Project (Louvain). The corpus consists of 50,000 words of texts (argumentative essays and literature examinations) written by English Philology students at two Madrid universities. The tag categories were: Form (F), Grammar (G), Lexico-grammatical aspects (X), Lexis (L), Word (W), Punctuation (Q), Register (R) and Style (S). All tags were triple checked by various native-speaker raters. The results show that grammar (35%) and lexis (28%) account for two-thirds of the errors, while punctuation accounts for 11%, form 9%, word 7%, lexico-grammatical factors 6% and register and style for 2% and 1%, respectively. The study proposes various areas of investigation which may be useful to others who are working with English-Spanish contrastive data: discourse/pragmatics; semantics; (lexis)/lexico-grammar; syntax; phonetics/writing systems; and non-structural factors (writing conventions).

1. Introduction

The concern of teachers and researchers with student errors has long been a controversial issue in different theoretical and pedagogical approaches to foreign and second language (L2) learning (Contrastive Analysis of the 1950s and 1960s; Error Analysis and Interlanguage Studies of the 1970s and 1980s; the return of Transfer[1] or Cross-linguistic studies of the 1990s). Even though some researchers (Schachter and Celce-Murcia, 1977; Wardhaugh, 1970) have had strong reservations concerning error analysis studies, most would not deny that there has recently been a revival of interest in cross-linguistic studies, both for verification of language universals and for pedagogical planning in L2 and translation training programs. With the increasing expansion of English as an international language, especially in what is known as the 'extended circle', calculated at some 375 million L2 speakers, and the 'expanding circle', calculated at some 750 million speakers of English as a Foreign Language (EFL) (Kachru and Nelson, 1996; Kachru, 1986), the need for more contrastive functional studies, including error analysis, seems evident. The difference between some previous attempts at carrying out a systematic analysis of errors or contrastive functional analysis is that the machine-readable corpora, along with software of various types (semi-automatic tagging, automatic parsing, etc.) of the present-day allow L2 researchers to call up a very large number of error types or contrastive structures as well as the text surrounding them.

Corpus-based studies on native texts (the British National Corpus, the Corpus de Referencia del Español Actual containing texts in Peninsular and varieties of Latin American Spanish, Davies' corpus of Spanish written texts from the 1200s to the 1900s, see Davies, this volume) have had a great influence on both synchronic and diachronic studies as far as lexico-grammatical findings. Learner corpora, however, and especially cross-linguistic learner corpora, are just beginning to present reliable information on syntactic, semantic and pragmatic features of learner texts as well as more quantitative data on error typology. In addition to the base-line data for each group of EFL learners, corpus-based learner projects, such as the ICLE (*International Corpus of Learner English)* Error Tagging Project, can provide valuable insights into more theoretical questions such as language universals or language typology (Comrie, 1984), as the usefulness of L2 data as valid for the search for language universals has long been acknowledged (Greenberg, 1991; Huebner and Ferguson, 1991; Hyltenstam, 1986). As well, base-line data from diverse EFL learners can help to explain the ways in which syntactic, semantic and pragmatic cues might influence EFL learner behavior (Gass, 1989; Thompson and Hopper, 2001). Data from EFL learners from different mother-tongue backgrounds can also shed light onto the relationship of lexis to syntax (Goldberg, 1995; Traugott, 1988), the processes of first language (L1) and second-language (L2) learning of lexis and grammatical properties (Bley-Vroman, 1989, 1990; James, 1989), the influence of transfer from the L1 to the L2, or cross-linguistic influence, (Johansson and Hasselgard, 1999; Odlin, 1989; Sharwood Smith and Kellerman, 1986), and the way in which transfer variables might interact with non-structural factors, such as differences in writing conventions between English and the mother-tongue (i.e., contrastive rhetoric). Among most grammarians, the correlation existing between grammatical structures and semantic/pragmatic functions is no longer a problematic claim. What still remains to be examined, however, is precisely which of these factors affecting grammatical-pragmatic relationships are those of real import[2].

This paper is an initial report on the SPICLE Error Tagging Project, the Spanish component of the ICLE Error Tagging Project, held at Louvain-le-Neuve[3]. The main objective of the international project is to categorize the most typical errors occurring in the corpora of writing produced by advanced learners of EFL from different mother-tongue backgrounds: Belgian (French), Bulgarian, Dutch, Italian, Japanese, Polish, Spanish, and Swedish. Once annotated for advanced learner errors, these data will provide a starting point for various types of cross-linguistic research (according to the research interests of each particular national team) and the elaboration of pedagogical tools (Tribble, 2000, 1997; Wichmann, et al., 1997).

2. The SPICLE Error Tagging Project

The early studies of the 1970s on Spanish-English contrastive linguistics (Taylor, 1975) struggled to come to terms with the then dominant theories of second language acquisition as "a creative process", in which it was thought that the learner uses strategies of overgeneralization and transfer of learning strategies (Taylor, 1975: 73-74) instead of relying on the transfer of native language structures. However, even then some researchers realized that the case of the "creative process" had been overestimated and that, at least in the early stages of acquiring a L2, "the first language acts as a filter through which the learner processes what he wishes to express" (Nash 1973:viii). Much of the severe criticism lodged against contrastive analysis (CA) may have been based on the mistaken idea that the purpose of CA was to predict learners' errors rather than to establish contrastive descriptions for pedagogical purposes. In addition, much of the early ESL research was based on translation of single sentences, or even parts of sentences, thus hindering the discovery of the functional/textual dimensions of ESL texts.

More recently, the field of contrastive rhetoric has contributed much to Spanish-English contrastive research in the work of Montaño-Harmon (1991) and Lux and Grabe (1991); however, some of these contrastive studies (Reid, 1990) have failed to distinguish carefully between novice writer features of academic essays and those characteristics which might truly be a result of the transfer of L1 lexico-grammatical patterns and discourse conventions. Furthermore, as has been pointed out by a number of researchers (Granger, 1998:9; Neff, *et al.*, 2004a), because the context of EFL learning is quite different from that of the ESL context, students learning in the former context may be far more subject to cross linguistic influence, which may affect both the number and the gravity of the resulting errors. In the development of process-oriented research, we seem to have forgotten what learners need and want (Corder, 1967/1985; Ferris, 2002; Hinkel, 2002): the correction of their errors.

Thus, the purpose of this paper is to provide quantitative data from Spanish EFL argumentative texts resulting from the initial analysis of errors in the SPICLE ERROR TAGGED CORPUS. As well, we discuss various methodological problems inherent in such a study. Finally, the study will propose various areas of investigation (Table 5) which may be useful to others who are working with English-Spanish contrastive data: discourse/pragmatics; semantics;

(lexis)/lexico-grammatical factors; syntax; phonetics/writing systems; and, non-structural factors (writing conventions).

2.1 Methodology

After the initial pilot tagging and consultation of all the teams participating in the international project, the SPICLE error tagging team contributed a small sub-corpus of 50,000 words, tagged for the following categories: *Form* (F) with the subcategories of (FM) form-morphology and (FS) form-spelling; *Grammar* (G), with the subcategories of (GA) grammar-article, (GADJCS) grammar-adjective comparative-superlative, (GADJO) grammar-adjective word order, (GADJN) grammar-adjective number, (GADVO) grammar-adverb word order, (GNC) grammar-noun case, (GNN) grammar-noun number, (GP) grammar-pronoun, (GVAUX) grammar-verb auxiliary, (GVM) grammar-verb morphology, (GVN) grammar-verb number, (GVNF) grammar-verb number finite-non-finite, (GVT) grammar-verb tense, (GVV) grammar-verb voice, (GWC) grammar-word class, and (GWCF) grammar-word class transfer; *Lexico-grammatical aspects* (X), with the subcategories of (XADJCO) lexico-grammar adjective complement, (XADJPR) lexico-grammar adjective dependent preposition, (XADJPRF) lexico-grammar adjective dependent preposition transfer, (XCONJCO) lexico-grammar conjunction complementation, (XNCO) lexico-grammar noun complementation, (XNPR) lexico-grammar noun dependent preposition, (XNPRF) lexico-grammar noun dependent preposition transfer, (XNUC) lexico-grammar noun count-noncount, (XPRCO) lexico-grammar preposition complement, (XVCO) lexico-grammar verb complement and (XVPR) lexico-grammar verb dependent preposition, and (XVPRF) lexico-grammar verb dependent preposition transfer; *Lexis* (L), with the subcategories of (LCC) lexis conjunction coordinating, (LCLC) lexis connector logical complex, (LCLS) lexis connector logical single, (LCS) lexis conjunction subordinating, (LS) lexis single, (LSF) lexis single transfer, (LP) lexical phrase and (LPF) lexical phrase transfer; *Word* (W), with the subcategories of (WRS/M) word redundant single/multiple, (WM) word missing and (WO) word order; *Punctuation* (Q), with the subcategories of (QM) punctuation missing, (QR) punctuation redundant, (Q C) punctuation confusing and (QL) punctuation instead of connector or vice-versa; *Register* (R); and, finally, *Style* (S), with the subcategories of (SI) style incomplete and (SU) style unclear.

In any project of this type, one of the major problems is inter-rater reliability. There will always be, between one category of linguistic phenomenon and another (say, for example, between what is categorized as a lexical phrase [LP] and what is deemed a lexico-grammatical aspect [X]), a continuum or cline, which can produce confusion about which error tag is to be applied. In the case of the SPICLE team, the raters carried out their work individually, using the tagger software provided by the Centre for English Corpus Linguistics of Louvain, and the tags were subsequently checked by another rater. As a further step to insure reliability, once all the tags had been double checked, they were all revised again by two native-speaker raters working together. As well, all the corrections, which are entered between dollar signs, were also checked. The count for each error was carried out by using Wordsmith Tools, version 3.1.

In the case of the Spanish team, still in the first stages of the project, the data from the Spanish EFL writers will be compared at a later date to the data from two native-speaker corpora, the LOCNESS corpus (American university writers, held at Louvain) and the MAD corpus (professional editorialists' texts and student texts in English and Spanish, held at the Universidad Complutense, English Philology, and created by the SPICLE team).[4]

3. The SPICLE Tagged Data

As seen in Table 1, the raw data for the SPICLE writers show the major categories for number of errors, G and L, which coincide partially with the totals for the international project. The percentages, based on the total number for G, 32%, is almost the same as in the international project, 35%, while the L error percentage is slightly higher, 30% in the Spanish data, as compared to 25% in the

Table 1. Categorization of errors for the Spanish EFL data

ERROR CATEGORY	RAW NUMBER OF ERRORS	% OF ERRORS PER CATEGORY
1. F	470	10%
2. G	1477	32%
3. X	276	6%
4. L	1408	30%
5. W	326	7%
6. Q	566	12%
7. R	88	2%
8. S	49	1%
TOTAL ERRORS	**4660**	**100%**

totals of the international data. As is true for the international data, in the Spanish data these two categories together, G and L, account for about two-thirds of all errors, and together with the lexico-grammatical governance category (X), at 6%, lexical or grammatical errors account for 69% of all errors. Punctuation, (Q), accounts for 12% of the Spanish EFL errors, while in the international data, Q totals are at 10%.

Figure 1 compares the types of errors in descending importance. These findings show that grammar, even for advanced Spanish EFL students, continues to pose serious problems and that lexis and punctuation are, most probably, grossly under-taught. However, these results seem to contradict what some researchers have found regarding lexical errors as the most prevalent error type. Meara (1984) has suggested that lexical errors are 75% to 80% more frequent than other error types. Of course, not all studies may be comparable, depending on what is counted as a "lexical error". In this study, if the F errors were added to the L errors, lexical errors would then outnumber the grammar and lexico-grammatical errors, but not by a very high percentage.

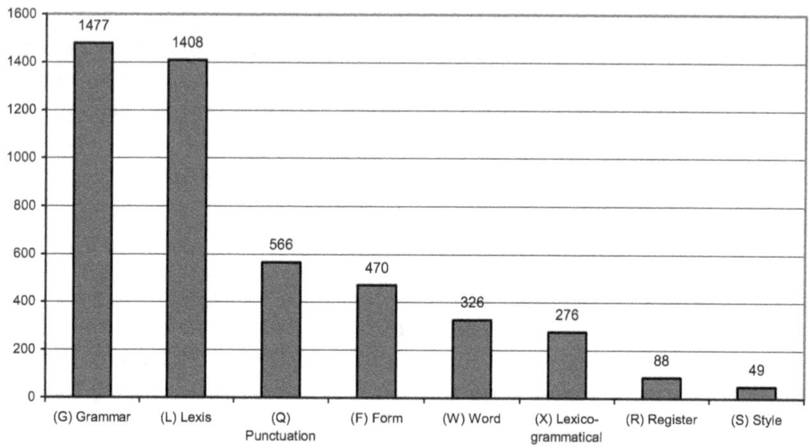

Figure 1. The results of the Spanish EFL error count for major categories

In the following sections, only the two major error categories (G and L) are dealt with, including possible causes for error types, and various pedagogical solutions are proposed.

3.1 Grammatical Errors (G) in the SPICLE Data

The G category groups together errors that violate general rules of English clause or phrase construction. As stated previously, it consists of seven major categories: (GA) articles; (GN) nouns (case and number); (GP) pronouns; (GADJ) adjectives; (GADV) adverb order; (GV) verb errors with six subcategories; and (GWC) word class. Figure 2 shows the comparison of the major categories or Grammar (G) errors, while Table 2 shows the raw figures for each of the major sub-types marked with an asterisk. In the discussion below, only those categories showing a high frequency of errors are dealt with, that is, GA, GN, and GV. The GP errors, although numerous, are not dealt with because of methodological problems. At the time this type of error was tagged, GP errors included all determiners, since a more specific tag was lacking in the main error types.

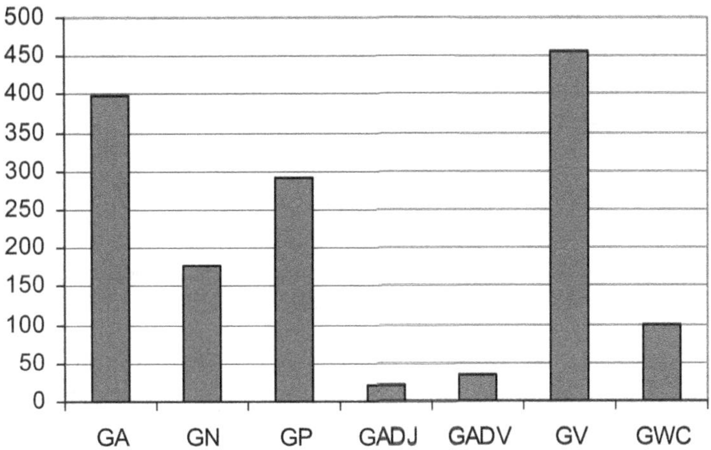

Figure 2. Comparison of number of Grammar (G) errors per category

Therefore, the data for this category will have to be called up and re-tagged. This revision of determiners will allow the SPICLE research team to make a much finer analysis concerning lexically rich quantifiers, denominal adjectives, etc. (Renouf and Sinclair, 1991).

Table 2. Raw figures for Grammar (G) errors

G	**1477**
GA*	398
GN*	178
GNC	76
GNN	102
GP*	291
GADJ*	21
GADJO	0
GADJN	11
GADJCS	10
GADV*	35
GADVO	35

GV*	456
GVN	108
GVM	21
GVNF	32
GVV	16
GVT	103
GVAUX	176
GWC*	98
GWC	91
GWCF	7

3.1.1 Grammar errors concerning article use

Although previous experience with Spanish EFL texts indicated that the high frequency of GA errors was to be expected, it would be very useful for the elaboration of teaching materials to understand which erroneous article uses remain in the texts of even advanced EFL Spanish learners.

Both in English and in Spanish, three types of articles can be used to signal generic reference, but the systems are not identical as can be observed in explanation (1).

(1) English: definite + SG N/ *zero* + Non-count N/Count PL/ indefinite + SG N/
Spanish: definite + SG N, PL N or Non-count N / indefinite + SG N

English uses the definite, the indefinite and zero article, while Spanish[5] uses the indefinite or definite article (SG or PL) with either SG or PL noun phrases (Leonetti, 1999: 871), as in the comparison of phrases in example (2a-c).

(2a) *A* cat is a domestic animal. *El* gato es un animal doméstico.
[A typical member of a class] (The cat as a domestic animal.)
(2b) *Cats* are domestic *animals*. *Los* gatos son animales domésticos.
[The class as an undifferentiated whole] (Cats as domestic animals)
(2c) *The* cat is a domestic animal. *El* gato es un animal doméstico.
[The class as represented by its typical specimen] (The cat as a domestic animal.)

In English, *the* (usually) and *a/an* (always) occur with singular count nouns (*The car*/*A car became a necessity of life*), while the zero article occurs with plural count nouns and with non-count nouns. The zero article is the only possibility with non-count nouns and it is also the most natural way of expressing generic reference, according to Quirk *et al.* (1985: 281) and to Biber *et al.* (1999: 265).

It is the zero-article use which causes the majority of problems in generic marking for Spanish EFL learners. In Figure 3, as can be observed, errors involving the use of the definite article are by far the most frequent (252 cases), as exemplified in (3a-d). The column marked "definite" shows the number of times a definite article was used, mostly instead of a zero article. Most of the misuses of the indefinite article reflect the use of a instead of an and the majority of those marked as zero reflect misuses of zero instead of the definite article.

Both (3a) and (3b) are examples of a definite article used with non-count nouns, probably due to transfer from the pattern in Spanish (corrections are placed between dollars signs). In (3c), the Spanish writer opts for the most common pattern in Spanish, a definite article + SG N, where zero article + PL N would be the preferred form in English; and, in (3d), the Spanish writer opts for a zero article when English (and Spanish) would have a definite article because this is a fixed expression, thus bringing our analysis back to a lexical perspective.

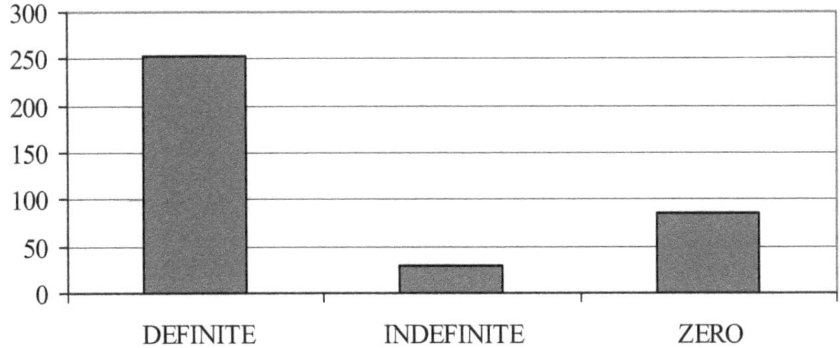

Figure 3. Comparison of Grammar-article (GA) error types

(3a) …we receive the mask of (GA) the 0 civilization
(3b) … frequency used (GA) the 0 irony and humour
(3c) … to be able to manage (GA) the 0 machine $machines$
(3d) … we will have to rehabilitate them, not punish them. (GA) 0 The death penalty and life (FSF) inprisonment $imprisonment $ will never…

In order to signal this type of reference, Spanish EFL students must have an understanding of both the ways in which generic reference can be signalled *and* the way in which this signalling works with count/non-count nouns in English. Unfortunately, offering the student rules and charts will not really increase student competency; that can only be done through use of readings, conversations and written exercises, including passages which specifically focus on these various aspects *together* -- generic marking and countability of nouns.

On the other hand, those nouns which use (or do not use) the article to signal the inner or outer relationship with institutions seem to have been properly acquired (*She is a regular churchgoer because she goes to church every...* [intrinsic relationship]; *The plumber went to the church in order to...* [extrinsic relationship]), most probably because these are learned as lexical expressions, i.e., as a whole. There were very few article errors involving lexical expressions such as *prison*, *university*, *church*, *hospital*, or *school*.

3.1.2 Grammar errors concerning noun number and case usage

The GN type of error consists of two categories: GNC, which has to do with errors in the use of the Saxon genitive, and GNN, those having to do with addition or omission of the plural morpheme. The total number of tokens for these types of errors is shown in Table 2. Errors in the Saxon genitive are frequent, both regarding the use of a genitive construction with an adnominal complement instead of a possessive determiner, as in example (4), and in the construction of a Saxon genitive when a denominal adjective is used in English, as in example (5).

(4) In (GNC) the poem of Donne $Donne's poem$ …
(5) … and what real feminists should try to do first is to change (GA) 0 the (GNC) female's $female$ mind, and then do the same …

The periphrastic possessive is particularly frequent and signals a transfer from Spanish possessive constructions with adnominal complements since, in Spanish, these complements cannot be pre-positioned (Picallo and Rigau, 1999: 980). The use of a possessive determiner instead of a denominal adjective is not frequent, but these circumstances are probably due to avoidance strategies. Neff *et al.* (2004a: 273) have noted elsewhere that, because of the constraints in their L1, Spanish EFL writers use more right-branching post-modification, which usually takes the form of prepositional phrases. The GNN errors are frequent but much less interesting from a typological point of view, as many of them involve simple errors in number (some of which could be due to carelessness). There are, however, some GNN errors which point to transfer from Spanish partitive constructions, as in examples (6), (7) and (8).

(6) … These (GNN) type $types$ of words are very difficult …
(7) … avoiding all (GNN) kind $kinds$ of Latin rhetorical formulae
(8) … a type of (GNN) games $game$ which I find …

Example (6) may be a simple spelling mistake, but it could also be the result of mispronunciation, causing confusion between the graphic forms of the words *this* and *these.* Transfer of partitive constructions in Spanish may also play a role, since a singular partitive can collocate with post-positioned prepositional phrases that have a singular *or* plural complement (*este tipo de palabras= lit.* "this type of words"). Examples (7) and (8) seem to suggest that misidentification of determiners (as to SG. or PL. markers) may also play a part; for example, the Spanish determiner *todo* ("all") does not indicate plurality and can, therefore, collocate with a following singular noun ("kind").

3.1.3 Grammar errors concerning verb use

As mentioned previously, the high percentage of GA errors was expected. However, what the SPICLE team did not expect was the high percentage of errors in the GV category: 26% of the total number of errors in G for the international data, and 31% for the Spanish data. These errors could not have been due to morphology, marked FM, for example, *forbaden* instead of *forbidden*, nor to spelling errors, marked F, for example, *she watchs* instead of *she watches*. Thus, a closer examination of the sub-types of verb errors, shown in Table 2, was in order.

In the Spanish data, for example, the three highest frequencies for GV are GVN (grammar-verb-number) with 108 errors (representing 23% of the verb errors), GVT (grammar-verb-tense) with 103 errors (representing 23% of the verb errors) and GVAUX grammar-verb-auxiliary) with 176 errors (representing 38% of the verb errors), the three together totaling 84% of the verb errors, as shown in Figure 4.

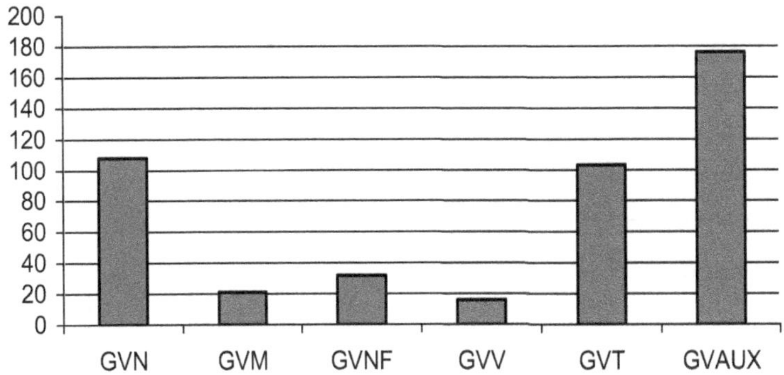

Figure 4. Verb error per category

An examination of the concordance lines for the Spanish data shows that many of the GVT errors (78%) are due to the lack of the *–s* morpheme of the third-person singular verb inflection. This result is not particularly surprising since many ESL studies (Dulay and Burt, 1973; Krashen, 1977; Lightbown, 1983) have found that the *–s* morpheme is one of the last ones to be learned. What is surprising is that 22% of the GVT errors show that Spanish EFL students affix the *–s* morpheme to concord with a plural noun. There were 28 occurrences of third person singular verb forms when a plural form is needed. In this group the error usually takes place in a relative clause. The antecedent is a plural noun which is located at a few words' distance in the sentence and the subject is the relative pronoun *who* or *which*. These interesting results call for further investigation, including the contrasting of the Spanish results with those of other teams.

The GVT errors totalled 102 tokens. In many cases the writer selected past or present perfect instead of a simple narrative present tense, and there is extensive shifting from one tense to another in contiguous sentences, with no apparent reason. The second most recurrent error is the use of present perfect instead of simple past, perhaps reflecting cross-linguistic influence.

The GVAUX category of auxiliaries includes primary auxiliaries (*have, be* and *do*) and modal auxiliaries. All erroneous uses of a primary or modal auxiliary are tagged as GVAUX, even if in some cases they are more of a question of tense

(6 occurrences in 175 tokens, which equals 3.4%). Most of the erroneous uses show two broad aspects: the selection of an incorrect modal verb, and an unnecessary use of the modal verb which is associated with transfer of writing conventions from L1. In the first case, the Spanish students' use of epistemic modals is extremely limited, which affects the learners' representation of evidentiality. The second case has to do with writer-reader interaction patterns, transferred from Spanish into English. Table 3 shows the error types found in this corpus. Only the first two, very numerous categories are examined here.

Table 3. Types of errors in the Grammar Verb Auxiliary use (GVAUX)

Type of error	**Tokens**
Selection of incorrect modal auxiliary	82
Unnecessary use of modal auxiliary	64
Necessary use of modal auxiliary	15
Wrong tense	8

The selection of an incorrect modal auxiliary accounts for 47% of this type of error, involving both epistemic, as in example (9) and deontic aspects, as in example (10).

(9) … reality (GVAUX) can $*may*$ also be noticed…
(10) We (GVAUX) do not have to $*should* not $ trust

Neff *et al.* (2003) found that, in comparison with native novice writers and native professional writers, Spanish EFL university students overuse the modal *can*, perhaps believing that this verb has the same epistemic range as the Spanish modal *poder* ("can"). In English, *can* has a dynamic meaning, signaling ability; only in the negative does it take on epistemic meaning. Example (10) shows that the Spanish EFL students not only have difficulty in distinguishing between formal (*should/needn't*) and informal registers (*have to*), but they also have problems in identifying the different meaning which some modals have in a negative clause as compared to an affirmative one.

The other, much more prevalent misuse of modal auxiliaries signals transfer from Spanish interactional patterns with readers, i.e., transfer of rhetorical patterns. As in examples (9) and (11), Spanish students frequently use a modal verb (almost always *can* or *could*) as a way of introducing either a new topic or additional information into the text.

(11) … we (GVAUX) can find $*we find*$ more of these examples…

This tendency was also found in the argumentative texts of Italian and French-Belgian EFL university students (but not the Dutch EFL students) (Neff, *et al.*, 2001). Since its use in individual sentences goes almost unnoticed, the overuse of this pattern can only be documented in corpus studies, such as this one, in which percentages for an entire body of writers' text can be calculated. These uses represent, strictly speaking, more of an *infelicity* (James, 1998) than an out-right error.

3.2 Lexical Errors (L) in the SPICLE Data

This general category deals with errors involving the semantic (conceptual or collocational) properties of words or phrases. It is divided into three large subcategories: Lexical Single (LS), Lexical Phrase (LP) and Connectives (LC). The raw figures, displayed in Table 4, show that single lexical items account for 60% of all lexical errors, lexical phrases for 27%, simple and complex logical connectors for 13%.

Table 4. Raw figures for Lexical errors (L)

L	**1408**	Percentage of total lexical errors
LS*	**839**	60%
LS	510	
LSF	329	
LP*	**381**	27%
LP	167	
LPF	214	
LC*	**188**	13%
LCL*	44	
LCLS	20	
LCLC	24	
LCC*	77	
LCS*	62	

Of the 510 tokens of LS errors, 23% comprise errors in prepositions or adverbs which are not dependent on nouns, adjectives or verbs, as in the following examples. Many preposition errors involve confusion of *in* or *on* (usually one of these instead of the other). This finding seems to point to cross-linguistic influence, as Spanish has only one preposition, *en*, which means both *in* and *on*. Other erroneous uses of prepositions also show transfer, as in example (14), an exact calque from preposition *desde* ("from").

(12) He cheats other people (LS) by in a special way…

(13) … becomes a nightmare (LS) at on the street.
(14) Hermione has been hiding away (LS) from for sixteen years, and after …

The next group of examples shows some errors that are not readily explicable, for instance, example (15). Perhaps, since *receive* and *achieve* are quite similar in sound, the student has simply written one lemma but actually meant to use the other. Other single lexical errors denote cross-linguistic interference as in the mixed uses of *say* and *tell.* This may be another case of the "split difficulty" (Stockwell, Bowen, and Martin, 1965), as in the mistaken uses of *in* and *on.* Supposedly, problems for L2 learners may appear when a form in their native language is equivalent to two forms in the target language, as in examples (16) and (17). English has two verbs, *say* (transitive) and *tell* (ditransitive), while Spanish has only one verb, *decir*, which can be transitive or ditransitive.

(15) … the reward that these kind of people should (LS) achieve $receive$ when they
(16) In the first two stanzas the poet (LS) says $tells$ the woman that she must …
(17) …she clearly (GVN) tell $says$ (LS) tell $says$ that she will pretend to h

Both of the following examples reflect problems in collocation and also may reflect the lack of reading in English, a major source of input for collocations. In general, the adjectival lexis seems especially limited in range. In both (18) and (19), the use of the word *big* reminds one of the basic vocabulary of L1 children.

(18) … (GA) the 0 television. I think it's a very (LS) big $important$ invention …
(19) … business in which you can get a (LS) big $large$ amount of money…

Another interesting question is that of collocation (examples 18 and 19). The term "collocation" was first used by Halliday and Hasan (1976: 287) as "…a cover term for the cohesion that results from the co-occurrence of lexical items that are in some way or other typically associated with one another, because they tend to occur in similar environments…". Until more recently, collocation was difficult to exemplify, but computer technology (Sinclair, 1991; Stubbs, 1996) and large corpora, such as the British National Corpus, have supported some of the rather intuitive statements originally made concerning collocation. Statistical methods have also been applied in order to measure "the degree of certainty that two words co-occur with greater than a chance probability" (Hunston and Francis, 2000: 231). As the *Oxford Collocations Dictionary for Students of English* (Oxford, 2002: vii) points out: "For the student, choosing the right collocation will make his speech and writing sound much more natural, more native-speaker-like, even when basic intelligibility does not seem to be at issue". In addition to being more "native-like", students' preciseness will increase with correct collocational choices. Again as this dictionary notes (Oxford, 2002: vii), in the two following grammatically-correct sentences, the second one obviously communicates more evaluative information than the first: *This is a good book and contains a lot of interesting details./ This is a fascinating book and contains a wealth of historical detail.*

For these same reasons, the category of lexical phrase (LP) will also be a major area of analysis for this research team. In focusing on two types of word combinations, collocations and lexical phrases (also called "formulae"), the team distinguishes between collocation, as referring to lexical items that are frequently found in the company of other lexical items rather than their synonyms (*average consumer*, *commit suicide*, *bitterly cold*, etc.[6], Van Roey, 1990), and lexical phrases (Nattinger and DeCarrico, 1992), referring to phrases which have a pragmatic rather than a syntactic function (Granger, 1998: 154) (*Come again?*, *it is said that …*, *we can say that…*, etc.). However, for the purposes of tagging, both collocations and lexical phrases are annotated as LP.

From the point of view of use, lexical phrases provide teachers and learners with a range of syntactic patterns, which can be graded for level of difficulty. Nattinger and DeCarrico (1992) present a number of diverse patterns such lexical phrases can take: from phrases that permit no modification (*How do you do*?) to those that allow modification of certain syntactic elements (*I wanna* + N Ph /Vb Ph). For written discourse, these researchers Nattinger and DeCarrico, 1992: 78-79) discuss the considerable differences between spoken and written discourse, including logical connection, temporal connections, exemplification and summary. This information, together with knowledge of discourse moves (Swales, 1990; Hyland, 2000) frequently found in academic discourse or argumentative texts will be of great help in aiding students to construct academically precise texts. The learning of these rather fixed syntactic patterns will make it easier for the students to concentrate on the lexical slot, and, thereby, provide for transitory stages in syntactic development (Alonso, *et al.*, 2000: 68). In addition, as Granger (1995: 145) has pointed out, "the formulaic nature of many pragmalinguistic rules has necessarily contributed to bringing the study of prefabs to the fore".

Of the 381 LP errors made by the Spanish EFL writers, 167 (45%) are LP and 214 (55%) are LPF, making the latter one of the areas that reflect major negative cross-linguistic influence. Some of the erroneous LP uses, such as examples (20) and (21), show that having a stock of logical connector phrases with which to initiate sentences would be of great use to advanced EFL student writers. Examples (22) and (23) appear to point to the great lack of reading in English on the part of Spanish EFL students.

(20) … (FS) british $British$ colonialism). <u>(LP) According to politics $In politics$</u> …

(21) <u>(LP) Connected with this point $regarding this point$</u> …

(22) …until studied at Eton, he (GVT) discover $discovered$ <u>(LP) difference of classes $class consciousness$</u>

(23) … turns into joy and all the problems <u>(LP) have an end $come to an end$</u>.

The various types of word-combination, collocations and formulae can be studied, as noted by Granger (1998: 155), in sub-areas comprising the collocational study of amplifiers and boosters (Quirk, *et al.*, 1985) and "sentence builders", with active and passive frames, some of which are commonly found in learner academic writing (*I think that...*, *we must not forget...*, etc.) but not in native academic writing. Granger's findings of more frequent writer visibility in non-native texts coincides with the findings of the SPICLE research group (Neff, *et al.*, 2004b: 152-153). In a study of the use of *I think* in the argumentative texts of professional editorialist, native university writers and non-native EFL writers (Dutch, French, Italian and Spanish), the SPICLE team found significantly greater use of *I think* in the non-native texts. In many of the cases, this lexical phrase was used to accompany metadiscourse markers ("As a conclusion, *I think* it is too extreme to affirm…") or as a way of introducing new topics ("Another subject that *I think* is important is the relationship…")

The LPF can usually be detected by re-phrasing in Spanish the exact phrase used by the student. In this way, loan translations become very apparent, as in example (24) in which "a punishment stroke" is based on the Spanish LP "un golpe de castigo", and in (25), in which "all the opposite" is based on the Spanish LP "todo lo opuesto".

(24) In Spain, <u>(LPF) a punishment stroke $strike against$</u> …
(25) … stop dreaming, but <u>(LPF) all the opposite $quite the opposite$</u>.

Again, as mentioned in other sections of this report, lexical exercises must be incorporated into the daily teaching of EFL teachers in Spain.

4. Contrastive error-analysis

This section of the research report briefly outlines some of the areas on which the SPICLE research team will focus in the coming year. Table 5 presents five major areas in which the SPICLE research team will carry out studies. In all the cases, the learner data will be contrasted among EFL writer groups, and the non-native writer data will be compared with native-speaker data, of novice writers (LOCNESS corpus) and with expert writers (ENGLISH-SPANISH CONTRASTIVE CORPUS, held at UCM, Marín and Neff, 2001).

Apart from the work on the Spanish data itself and on the typological, contrastive work on the international data, the SPICLE team wishes to advocate form-focused instruction. Since corpus linguistics methodologies have been applied to L2 data, and even before in small-scale studies, data-driven learning approaches have encouraged consciousness-raising activities for EFL learners through exercises in inductive reasoning (Granger and Tribble, 1998). The advanced- and less-advanced writer activities which will result from future work are meant as an initial contribution to forthcoming pedagogical work.

5. Conclusion

For both non-native and native students, learning the skills of written communication is a gradual and lengthy educational process which requires an increasing awareness of how language works. In another research paper (Neff *et al.*, 2004b), the SPICLE team has noted that American college students share

Table 5. Aspects for further SPICLE contrastive error-analysis research

- Discourse/pragmatic/stylistic
    - Construction of impersonal writer stance
    - Cleft and pseudo-cleft constructions
    - Subject-verb inversion (especially with those verbs which provoke inversion in Spanish, but not in English, e.g., *ocurrir*, *aparecer*, etc.)
    - Indirect questions
    - Theme/rheme patterns (using punctuation marks)
    - Other word order problems
- Semantics/lexico-grammatical
    - Complex lexical phrases (phraseology)
    - Multi-word verbs
    - Complementation of N, Vb, Adj
    - Strings of semantically related words
    - Lack of equivalencies in profiling (Cognitive Grammar, e.g., *rob/steal* and *rincón/esquina*)
- Syntax
    - Article use
    - Determiner use
    - Adverbial positions
    - Premodification and postmodification of N Ph (Particularly in head-initial constructions of possessive structures)
- Phonetics/phonology/writing systems
    - Cognate forms
    - Phonetic influence on written form (e.g., *is* for *it's*)
- Non-structural factors
    - Differences in writing conventions

some features of novice writing with their non-native counterparts, particularly in the establishing of impersonal stance. However, for EFL writers, the learning process is further complicated by the negative (and, sometimes, positive) transfer of lexis, syntactic constructions and rhetorical conventions from the mother tongue. For this reason, it is essential that writing teachers have at least some degree of knowledge of the EFL students' L1. Even if we focus on a relatively less complex area such as vocabulary, single lexical errors can be accounted for more systematically if we are aware of their syntactic, semantic, stylistic/pragmatic and collocational dimensions in the students' L1 (Carter, 1992).

As Odlin (1989) has noted, language transfer has been a central issue in applied linguistics, second language acquisition and language teaching for well over a century. Transfer, both positive and negative, is relevant to almost every aspect of linguistic studies because of the sizable interaction or interdependence among subsystems (discourse, morphosyntax, etc.) and between comprehension and production competencies. Accordingly, Odlin includes in his discussion areas such as: discourse, semantics, syntax, phonetics/phonology/writing systems, and non-structural factors, such as linguistic awareness and social context.

With Odlin's work as a basis, the participants in the *SPICLE Error Tagging Project* will carry out contrastive work with the various corpora on the aspects shown in Table 5. This constitutes the first step towards thinking about what type of pedagogical frameworks should be created for on-line work by students. Our research, covering grammatical as well as rhetorical aspects, will be of primary interest to teachers of Spanish-speaking EFL learners, but also to professionals in the fields of translation studies and second and foreign language acquisition.

Notes

1 Odlin (1989: 27) has defined transfer as "the influence resulting from similarities and differences between the target language and any other language that has been previously (and perhaps imperfectly) acquired".

2 Even within the systemic-functional Linguistics paradigm, there are those who view lexis as a "more delicate" level of grammatical description (Halliday, 1994), while considering that syntactic patterns constitute a more "core" element. Others (Francis, 1993; Sinclair, 1991) argue that explanations must take into account phraseology.

3 The ICLE project began in 1990 at Louvain. The SPICLE team (Spanish participants in the *ICLE*) joined the research group in 1993. See Granger, Dagneaux and Meunier (eds), 2002, for more details of the *ICLE* project.

4 The *MAD CORPUS* consists of 100 argumentative compositions in English and Spanish of 1st-yr and 4th-yr English Philology student writers (UCM and UAL), matched for author and topic; of 45 3rd-yr American

college students argumentative texts in English; and, of 20 professional editorial texts in English and Spanish (Neff, *et al.*, 2002).

5 Spanish can have nominals without articles, as in *Nos ofrecieron vino dulce*, but, according to Laca (1999: 902) these never refer to the totality of a class, but rather to part of the class (parti-generic).

6 Word combinations which count as "collocations" can be verified in the *Oxford Collocations Dictionary for Students of English*, 2002.

References

Alonso, C., J. Neff and J.P. Rica (2000), Cross-linguistic influence in language learning, *Estudios de Filología Moderna* 1: 65-84.

Biber, D., S. Johansson, G. Leech, S. Conrad and E. Finegan (1999), *Longman Grammar of Spoken and Written English*. Harlow: Longman.

Bley-Vroman, R. (1990), The logical problem of foreign language learning, *Linguistic Analysis* 20: 3-39.

Bley-Vroman, R. (1989), What is the logical problem of foreign language learning?, in: S. Gass and J. Schachter (eds), *Linguistic Perspectives on Second Language Acquisition*. Cambridge: Cambridge University Press, 41-68.

Carter, R. (1992), *Vocabulary: Applied Linguistic Perspectives*. London: Allen and Unwin.

Comrie, B. (1984), 'Why linguists need language acquirers', in: W. Rutherford (ed.) *Language Universals and Second Language Acquisition*. Amsterdam/Philadelphia: John Benjamins, 11-29.

Corder, S. P. (1967/1985), 'The significance of learners' errors' in: J. Richards (ed.) *Error Analysis: Perspectives in Second Language Acquisition*. London: Longman, 19-27.

Dulay, H. and M. Burt (1973), Should we teach children syntax? *Language Learning* 23: 234-252.

Ferris, D. (2002), *Treatment of Error in Second Language Student Writing*. Anna Arbor: University of Michigan.

Francis, G. (1993), A corpus-drive approach to grammar—principles, methods and examples in: M. Baker *et al.* (ed.), *Text and Technology: in Honour of John Sinclair*. Amsterdam: John Benjamins, 137-157.

Gass, S. (1989), How do learners resolve linguistic conflicts?, in: S. Gass and J. Schachter (eds), *Linguistic Perspectives on Second Language Acquisition*. Cambridge: Cambridge University Press, 183-199.

Goldberg, A. (1995), *A Construction Grammar Approach to Argument Structure*. Chicago/ London: University of Chicago Press.

Granger, S. (1995), Prefabricated patterns in advanced EFL writing: collocations and formulae, in : A. Cowie (ed.), *Phraseology: Theory, Analysis and Applications*. Oxford: Oxford University Press.

Granger, S. (1998), The computer learner corpus in: S. Granger (ed.) *Learner English on Computer*. London: Longman, 3-18.

Granger, S., E. Dagneaux and F. Meunier (eds) (2002), *International Corpus of Learner English*. Louvain: Université Catholique de Louvain Press.

Granger, S. and Tribble, C. (1998), 'Exploiting learner corpus data in the classroom: Form-focused instruction and data-driven learning', in: S. Granger (ed) *Working with Learner Language*. Harlow: Longman, 199-209.

Greenberg, J. (1991), 'Typology/universals and second language acquisition', in: T. Huebner and C. Ferguson (eds) *Cross-currents in Second Language Acquisition and Linguistic Theories*. Amsterdam: John Benjamins, 37- 43.

Halliday, M.A.K. (1994), *An Introduction to Functional Grammar*. (2nd edition). London: Arnold.

Halliday, M.A.K. and R. Hasan (1976), *Cohesion in English*. London: Longman.

Hinkel, E. (2002), *Second Language Writers' Text: Linguistic and Rhetorical Features*. Mahwah,
N.J.: Lawrence Erlbaum.

Huebner, T. and C. Ferguson (eds) (1991), *Crosscurrents in Second Language Acquisition and Linguistic Theories*. Amsterdam/Philadelphia: John Benjamins.

Hunston, S. and G. Francis (2000), *Pattern Grammar: A Corpus-driven Approach to the Lexical*
Grammar of English. Amsterdam/ Philadelphia: John Benjamins.

Hyland, K. (2000), *Disciplinary Discourses: Social Interactions in Academic Writing*. London/ New York: Longman-Pearson.

Hyltenstam, K. (1986), Markedness, language universals, language typology and language acquisition, in: C. Pfaff (ed.), *First and Second Language Acquisition Processes*. Cambridge, MA: Newbury House, 55-78.

James, C. (1989), Errors in Language Learning and Use: Exploring Error Analysis. London: Longman.

Johansson, S. and H. Hasselgård (1999), Corpora and cross-linguistic research in the Nordic countries, in: S. Granger, L. Beheydt, and J. P. Colson (eds), Contrastive Linguistics and Translation, a special issue of Le Language et L'Homme 34.1. Leuven: Peeters, 145-162.

Kachru, B.B. (1986), The Alchemy of English: The Spread, Functions and Models of Non-native Englishes. Oxford: Pergamon Institute of English.

Kachru, B.B. and C. L. Nelson (1996), 'World Englishes' in: S. L. McKay and N. H. Hornberber (eds) Sociolinguistics and Second Language Teaching. Cambridge: Cambridge University Press, 71-102.

Krashen, S. (1977), Some issues relating to the Monitor Model, in: H. Brown, C. Yorio and R. Crymes (eds), On TESOL '77. Washington, D.C.: TESOL, 144-158.

Laca, B. (1999), Presencia y ausencia de determinante, in: I. Bosque and V. Demonte (eds), Gramática descriptiva de la lengua española, Vol. I. Madrid: Espasa, 891- 928.

Leonetti, M. (1999), El artículo, in: I. Bosque and V. Demonte (eds), *Gramática descriptiva de la lengua española*, Vol. I. Madrid: Espasa, 787-890.

Lightbown, P. (1983), Exploring relationships between developmental and instructional sequences in L2 acquisition, in: H. Seliger and M. Long (eds), *Classroom Oriented Reseach in Second Language Acquisition*. Rowley, MA: Newbury House, 217-243.

Lux, P. and W. Grabe (1991), Multivariate approaches to contrastive rhetoric, *Lenguas Modernas*, 18: 133-160.

Marín, J. and J. Neff (2001), *The English-Spanish Contrastive Corpus*. Department of English Philology, Universidad Complutense de Madrid.

Meara, P. (1984), The study of lexis in interlanguage, in: A. Davies, C. Criper and A.P.R. Howatt (eds), *Interlanguage: Papers in Honour of S. Pit Corder*. Edinburgh: Edinburgh University Press, 225-235.

Montaño-Harmon, M. (1991), Discourse features of written Mexican Spanish. Current research in contrastive rhetoric and its implications, *Hispania,* 74: 417-425.

Nash, R. (1973), *Readings in Spanish-English Contrastive Linguistics*. Hato Rey, P.R.: Inter American University Press.

Nattinger, J. and J. DeCarrico (1992), *Lexical Phrases and Language Teaching*. Oxford: Oxford University Press.

Neff, J., E. Dafouz, M. Díez, R. Prieto and C. Chaudron (2004a), Contrastive discourse analysis: Argumentative text in English and Spanish, in: C. Moder and A. Martinov-Zic (eds) *Discourse across Languages and Cultures*. Philadelphia: John Benjamins, 261-275.

Neff, J., F. Ballesteros, E. Dafouz, M. Díez, F. Martínez, R. Prieto and J.P. Rica (2004b), The expression of writer stance in native and non-native argumentative texts, in: R. Facchinetti, and F. Palmer (eds), *English Modality in Perspective: Genre Analysis and Contrastive Studies*. Frankfurt am Main: Peter Lang, 141-161.

Neff, J., E. Dafouz, M. Díez, F. Martínez, R. Prieto and J.P. Rica (2003), Evidentiality and the construction of writer stance in native and non-native texts, in: J. Hladky (ed.), *Language and Function*. Amsterdam/Philadelphia: John Benjamins, 231-243.

Neff, J., M. Blanco, E. Dafouz, M. Díez, and R. Prieto (2002), *The Madrid Corpus (MAD)*. Department of English Philology, Universidad Complutense de Madrid.

Neff, J., F. Martínez and J. P. Rica (2001), A contrastive study of qualification devices in NS and NNS argumentative texts in English, in: *ERIC Clearing House on Language and Linguistics* (ERIC Document Reproduction Service, ED 465301). Washington, D.C: Educational Resource Information Center, U.S. Department of Education.

Odlin, T. (1989), *Language Transfer: Cross-Linguistic Influence in Language Learning*. Cambridge: Cambridge University Press.

Oxford University Press. (2002), *Oxford Collocations Dictionary for Students of English*. Oxford: Oxford University Press.

Picallo, M.C. and G. Rigau (1999), El posesivo y la relaciones posesivas, in: I. Bosque and V. Demonte (eds), *Gramática descriptiva de la lengua española*, Vol. I. Madrid: Espasa, 973-1025.

Quirk, R., S. Greenbaum, G. Leech and J. Svartvik (1985), *A Comprehensive Grammar of the English Language*. London: Longman.

Reid, J. (1990), Responding to different topic types: a quantitative analysis from a contrastive rhetoric perspective in: B. Kroll (ed.) *Second Language Writing: Research Insights for the Classroom*. Cambridge: Cambridge University Press, 191- 210.

Renouf, A. and J. Sinclair (1991), Collocational frameworks in English, in: K. Aijmer and B. Altenberg (eds), *English Corpus Linguistics*. London: Longman, 128-143.

Schachter, J. and M. Celce-Murcia (1977), 'Some reservations concerning error analysis', *TESOL Quarterly*, 11: 441-51.

Sharwood Smith, M. and E. Kellerman. (1986), Cross-linguistic influence in second language acquisition: An introduction, in: E. Kellerman and M. Sharwood Smith (eds), *Cross-linguistic Influence in Second Language Acquisition*. Oxford: Pergamon Press, 1-9.

Sinclair, J. (1991), *Corpus, Concordance and Collocation*. Oxford: Oxford University Press.

Stockwell, R., J. Bowen and J. Martin (1965), *The Grammatical Structures of English and Spanish*. Chicago: University of Chicago Press.

Stubbs, M. (1996), *Text and Corpus Analysis*. London: Blackwell.

Swales, J. (1990), *Genre Analysis*. Cambridge: Cambridge University Press.

Taylor, B. (1975), The use of overgeneralization and transfer learning strategies by elementary and intermediate students of ESL, *Language Learning*, 25 (1): 73-107.

Thompson, S. and P. Hopper (2001), Transitivity, clause structure, and argument structure: Evidence from conversation, in: J. L. Bybee and P. J. Hopper (eds), *Frequency and the Emergence of Linguistic Structure*. Amsterdam: John Benjamins, 27-60.

Traugott, E. C. (1988), Pragmatic strengthening and grammaticalization, *Berkeley Linguistics Society*, 14: 406-416.

Tribble, C. (2000), Genres, keywoods, teaching: Towards a pedagogic account of the language of Project Proposals, in L. Burnard and T. McEnery (eds), *Rethinking Language from a Corpus Perspective: Papers from the Third International Conference on Teaching and Language Corpora*. Hamburg: Peter Lang.

Tribble, C. and G. Jones (1997), *Concordances in the Classroom*. London: Longman.

Van Roey, J. (1990), *French-English Contrastive Lexicology: An Introduction.* Louvain-le-Neuve: Peeters.

Wardhaugh, R. (1970), 'The contrastive analysis hypothesis', *TESOL Quarterly*, 4: 123-30.

Wichmann, A., S. Fligelstone, T. McEnery, and G. Knowles (1997), *Teaching and Language Corpora*. London/New York: Longman.

How to End an Introduction in a Computer Science Article? A Corpus-based Approach

Wasima Shehzad (wasima@umich.edu)

National University of Sciences and Technology
Rawalpindi, Pakistan

Abstract

Where corpus linguistics has offered new perspectives on linguistic analyses, it has provided a myriad of opportunities to academic discourse analysts also. Much work has been done on the academic (MICASE) and scientific discourse (Atkinson, 1993; Cooper, 1985; Peng 1987; Swales and Najjar, 1987; Thompson, 1993). With the advent of the computer revolution, information technology continues to steamroll into our lives. In this information society a few linguists have paid scholarly attention to the discourse of computer science (CS) (Anthony 1999, 2000, 2001 and Pestiguillo 1999). This paper discusses the patterns of the ending of the introductions to research articles in CS based on the structures of introductions presented by Swales (forthcoming) and Lewin et.al. (2001) with a special focus on outlining the structure of the text of a CS research article A corpus of authentic academic texts of 56 research articles published during 2003 in five different journals of IEEE was analyzed using Wordsmith tools .The study reveals that the need for this metadiscourse of outlining the structure of the paper in the CS introductions arises because of the variable number of the sections, ranging from 4-11, and follows a variable order according to the technical needs of the paper. The use of the word SECTION, found throughout the corpus, is discussed with reference to the lack of structural variation in Computer Science research papers.

1. Introduction and Background

The Research Article (RA) in Computer Science (CS), has hardly sixty years of tradition and development since the first RA in CS, whereas many traditional disciplines such as medicine and physics have a long history of evolution. Atkinson (1993), for example, analyses the transformation of the medical RA from 1675 to 1975. Generally and widely accepted conventions for writing RAs have been presented by many authors for example: Ebel et.al. (1987), Gibaldi and Achter (1988), Oshima and Hoghe (1992), Booth (1993), Weissberg and Buker (1990) Swales and Feak (1994, 2004) and Lewin et.al. (2000). However, except for McRobb's (1990) instructions and suggestions for writing quality manuals for computer engineers, there is no specific handbook for writing RAs in Computer Science.

As compared to the linguistic investigation carried out in other sciences, the linguistic analysis of computer science discourse has been limited. For instance, the two main studies of the 1980's, Cooper (1985) and Hughes (1989) were limited to one part of the genre, Introductions, while Simpson (1989) focused on professional documentation and Mulcahy (1988) focused on computer instructions. Besides, Cooper's corpus included articles from electrical and electronics engineering only, which, despite having a great influence on the field of Computer Science, is not a "true" representation of the field.

It was not until the 1990s that comparative work on CS writing started. Corbett (1992) studied a corpus of RAs in three disciplines: history, biology and computing. This was perhaps the first attempt to distinguish comparatively the peculiarities of CS discourse.This line of investigation was further developed by Posteguillo (1995). Among his conclusions he maintained that 'scientific discourse in computing has a set of common distinct features which distinguishes it from the scientific discourse characteristics of other academic disciplines' (1995:26). Posteguillo (1999) reported that Swales' Create A Research Space (CARS) model, based on rhetorical moves and their component steps, was applicable to Introductions in Computer Science RAs but with some variations. For instance, computer RA Introductions use the claiming centrality and the making topic generalization steps on an optional basis but the review of previous research is not always used as Swales contends. A frequent application (70%) of the 'announcing principal findings move and indicating RA structure was also noted by him. However, Posteguillo's focus remained on the overall structure of the papers.

Another important figure in the study of CS RAs is Anthony (2000) who studied the structure and linguistic features of RA Titles in CS and structural differences and linguistic variations in RA Abstracts in CS. Using the 'Modified CARS Model' the structure of Abstracts was shown by Anthony to be largely similar in 408 articles from 6 journals, with small differences in the step usage. Earlier (1999), Anthony had applied the CARS model to the Introductions of 12 articles from a single journal, *IEEE Transactions on Software Engineering*. As an overall framework, he found the model successful except that the classification of definitions and examples into an appropriate step was missing.

The focus of the above mentioned studies has been on the overall structure of the articles, titles, abstracts and the beginning of the Introductions to CS articles. Relatively little attention has been paid to the last step of move three, the ending of the Introductions.

Swales (1990:159) emphasizes that a combination of 'brevity and linearity' contributes to the compositeness of engineering, as does Brown (1985). However, contrary to Swales' claim, as can be seen from Table 1, there is a definite trend of writing significantly longer Introductions in Computer Science as compared to other engineering disciplines such as electrical and electronics engineering (EEE). Average word length in both software engineering (SE; Anthony, 1999) and computer science, as represented in the present study, is double the length of Introductions in EEE, as Table 1 shows. One reason for longer Introductions in Computer Science RAs, as explained in the methodology section below, could be the overwhelming presence of the Outlining Structure step (discussed below).

Table.1 Comparative Introduction Lengths in Words

Discipline	No. of articles	Studies	Min.	Max.	Ave.
EEE	15	Cooper (1985)	195	924	491
SE	12	Anthony (1999)	591	1479	1000
CS	56	Present Study	347	2422	983

Nevertheless, there is a huge amount of difference between the minimum and maximum number of words in the present study. To validate the results between the minimum and maximum number of words, Introductions were further divided into five groups by word count, as Table 2 shows. Introductions were also looked at journal-wise to see if this trend is the characteristic of any particular journal or of Computer Science on the whole as a field.

Table. 2 Journal-wise Length (in words) of Introductions

No. of articles	Journals	Upto 500	500-1000	1000-1500	1500 - 2000	2000+
11	ToC	1	8	1	1	0
11	PAMI	0	6	4	0	1
11	SE	1	6	2	2	0
11	PADS	0	6	4	1	0
12	KDE	1	4	5	2	0
56		3	30	16	7	1
Percentage		**5%**	**54%**	**29%**	**11%**	**2%**

At this stage, an analysis of the words dedicated to this seemingly important step, Swales's Move Three Step e, or Outlining Structure, in terms of the total length of the Introductions would give us a fair idea of its significance. On comparing Table 2 with Table 3, it seems that on average 10% of the space in the Introductions is given to an explanation of the roadmap of the article. However, it cannot be concluded that the longer the Introduction, the larger the space for Move Three Step e, as the longest Introduction of 2422 words used only 104 words as compared to the Introduction of 951 words that used 266 words.

Thus, motivated by the pilot study the present paper is an attempt to provide a detailed account of ending Introductions in Computer Science with a focus on Outlining Structure.

Table.3 Length of the Outlining Structure Step in Words

No. of articles	Journals	Upto 50	50-100	100-150	150-200	200+	No outlining structure
11	ToC	1	5	3	0	1	1
11	PAMI	1	3	2	3	0	2
11	SE	1	6	0	2	0	2
11	PADS	1	5	3	0	0	2
12	KDE	1	5	3	1	0	2
56		5	24	11	6	1	9
Percentage		**11%**	**51%**	**23%**	**13%**	**2%**	

2. Methodology

2.1 The Corpus

The corpus for the present study, henceforth the Shehzad Computer Science Corpus (SCSC), is based on a collection of Introductions from 56 research articles published in five different journals from the IEEE Computer Society. The articles were taken from the issues of January to December 2003. The journals included: *IEEE Transactions on Computers* (ToC), *IEEE Transactions on Knowledge and Data Engineering* (KDE), *IEEE Transactions on Parallel and Distributed Systems* (PADS), *IEEE Transactions on Software Engineering* (SE) and *IEEE Transactions on Pattern Analysis and Machine Intelligence* (PAMI).

The articles were available in electronic form at the University of Michigan Library. As they were in PDF form, after downloading, they were saved in text-file format and cleaned of the page numbers, figures, tables, titles, headers etc. Then Wordsmith's (Scott, 2001) Wordlister and Concordancer Tools were used for the analysis.

2.2 The Reference Model

Theories of genre analysis and academic discourse have been tremendously influenced by Swales' Create A Research Space (CARS) model (1990) which has equally helped native and non-native speakers of English, both students and researchers, intending to publish their research works in reputable journals. Although the CARS model is well known, for the sake of comprehensiveness and reminder, Dudley-Evans' (2000:5) description of CARS is quoted here:

> The model captures the ways in which academic writers justify and highlight their own contribution to the ongoing research profile of the field by first establishing a topic for the research and summarizing the key features of the previous research, then establishing a gap or possible extension of that work that will form the basis of the writers' claims.

There are three moves in the model and each move has been further divided into obligatory and optional steps. Swales (1990) admits that all the steps may not be followed by all the disciplines but at the same time maintains that many of these steps will be widely distributed across different disciplinary areas. Interesting variations in the CARS pattern of moves and steps were found by Cooper (1985), Crooks (1986) and Anthony (1999). Since the corpora in these studies were somewhat small (15 articles in Cooper, 12 articles in Anthony), it is hard to establish that the particular disciplines in which these studies were carried out regularly and systematically use a variation on the general model.

Swales' (2004) revised CARS model as presented below, chosen for the analysis of the relatively larger Computer Science corpus of the present study, is more complex and elaborated than originally envisioned in his earlier studies.

Move One **Establishing a research territory**

a. by showing that the general research area is important, central, interesting, problematic, or relevant in some way (optional)

b. by introducing and reviewing items of previous research in the area (obligatory)

Move Two **Establishing a Niche**

a. by indicating a gap in the previous research, or by extending previous knowledge in some way (obligatory)

Move Three **Occupying the niche**

a. by outlining purposes or stating the nature of the present research (obligatory)

b. by listing research questions or hypotheses (PISF*)

c. by announcing principal findings (PISF*)

d. by stating the value of the present research (PISF*)

e. by indicating the structure of the RP (PISF*)

* Probable in some fields, but rare in others

3. Results and Discussion

3.1 Move Three Step e. Outlining the Structure of the Text

An important consideration for the writers of RAs who do not use the Introduction-Methods-Results-Discussion (IMRD) format widespread in the social and natural sciences (Swales, 1990) is whether they need to explain to their readers how the text is organized. Here the precursor is the announcement that a textual 'resolution' will follow (Labov and Waletzky, 1967). Swales (1994, 2004) suggests this step to be 'optional' for most RAs and 'obligatory' for dissertations. However, in CS RAs the structure-outlining option seems close to obligatory as 83.9% of the 56 RAs investigated in this study had it in their Introductions (cf. Anthony's (1999) 83.3% of the 12 articles of software engineering that he examined). Ninety two percent of ToC articles had this step and 82% of PAMI, SE, PADS and KDE (Table. 4). Although this figure does not show a great progression, the overall trend is in the same direction, i.e., of the inclusion of *outlining structure* in Introductions.

Table 4. Journal-wise Occurrence of Move Three Step e.

Journals	**ToC**	**PAMI**	**SE**	**PADS**	**KDE**
Percentage	**91%**	**82%**	**82%**	**82%**	**82%**

Similarly (although percentage is not given), Posteguillo (1999:144), briefly mentioning this step, reasons that in the absence of a 'well-defined macrostructure' -- what Swales (1990) calls, 'an established schema' -- for research articles in this new field, 'it is only natural that an indication of RA organization should be welcomed by readers, even if they are specialists in this field'. In 1985 Cooper suggested that such a step would be required in the absence of the IMRD format or when working in some new field. It has persisted today either because of earlier conventions or perhaps because CS articles still follow no fixed structure. Two complete examples of this part of the Introductions are given in the Appendix.

The purpose of having this step in the Introductions is to inform the audience about the rhetorical organization of the subsequent text, while also functioning to summarize the information to be provided in the rest of the paper. Thirty five of the 47 articles began Step e. with an 'organization' statement. 28 out of the 47 used some version of this formula:

$$\text{The} \left\{ \begin{array}{l} \text{rest} \\ \text{remainder} \end{array} \right\} \text{of} \left\{ \begin{array}{l} \text{the} \\ \text{this} \end{array} \right\} \begin{array}{c} \text{paper} \\ \text{is} \end{array} \left\{ \begin{array}{l} \text{organized} \\ \text{structured} \end{array} \right\} \begin{array}{l} \text{as} \\ \text{follows:} \end{array}$$

Examples of the primary signal of the onset of this step are given in Table 5.

Table 5. Patterns for Move Three Step e.

Pattern	**Occurrence**
The rest of this paper is organized as follows:	9
The rest of the paper is organized as follows:	7
The paper is organized as follows:	5
The paper is structured as follows:	3
The remainder of this paper is organized as follows:	2
The remainder of the paper is structured as follows:	1
The remainder of this paper is structured as follows:	1
The organization of the paper is as follows:	1
The organization of this paper is as follows:	1
The organization of the rest of the paper is as follows:	1
The outline of this paper is structured as follows:	1
The rest of this paper is structured as follows:	1
The rest of this document is organized as follows:	1
The work is organized as follows:	1
In the section that follows, ...	1
In the following section…	1
The next section….	2

In contrast, in the Hyland (2000) corpus of 240 research articles only six such examples were found, five out of 30 in cell biology articles and one in marketing. This could be an artifact of his sampling that included research papers primarily from the social sciences. Although this looks like a distinctive feature of Computer Science, some scholars and graduate students at the University of Michigan have indicated the presence of this pattern in the papers of Economics and Statistics, a fact that needs further investigation.

The extreme examples of this tendency were in three papers from the PAMI Journal and one from the KDE Journal, in which Move Three Step e had an independent sub-section within the Introductions with the headers;

a. 1.2 Goals and Outline of the Paper
b. 1.1 Organization
c. 1.4 Organization of the Paper
d. 1.2 Organization of the Paper

With respect to its position within Move Three, Move Three Step e is positioned as the last section of all the Introductions in Computer Science RAs except in one case where it appears early in the Introduction i.e; in the third paragraph of a three page introduction.

3.2 Recurring Lexical Items in Move Three Step e

The next obvious question is what follows the 'organization' statement. The word frequency list gave SECTION as the most prominent word of this part of the Introductions, which indicates it as a preferred lexical item, so the Wordsmith Concordance was used to get details. There were 292 concordance hits for the word SECTION in the Introductions of 56 RAs as compared to 890 hits in the complete texts of the RAs, which is 33% of the total occurrences. It is interesting to note that these hits were found in the last part/paragraph of the Introductions that was used for outlining the structure of the texts. This shows clearly that it is the main word used for describing the structure of the texts. Not surprisingly, the Hyland corpus of more than a million words has only 347 hits for the word SECTION with the present meaning. The word SECTION makes up 0.025 % of the Hyland corpus as compared to 0.181% of the present CSSC corpus.

The word SECTION is used as a noun with a numerical modifier (e.g., *section 2*) and also as a simple noun with adjectives (e.g., *next section*). The distribution of these nominal forms is shown in Table 6.

Table 6. Frequency of the major noun vs. number of articles

	No. of RAs	**Percentage**	**Subsections**
Noun +Numeral			
Section 2	47	84 %	3*
Section 3	51	91 %	5*
Section 4	46	82 %	2*
Section 5	43	77 %	
Section 6	38	68 %	
Section 7	22	39 %	
Section 8	7	12 %	
Section 9	6	11 %	
Section 10	3	5 %	
Section 11	1	2 %	
Modifier + Noun			
This Section	9	16 %	
Next Section	6	11 %	
Last Section	2	4 %	
Final Section	1	2 %	
Following Section	4	7 %	
The Section	2	4 %	

* Sections 2, 3 and 4 had 3, 5 and 2 subsections respectively and were numbered accordingly. 2.1, 2.2, 2.3; 3.1, 3.2, 3.3, 3.4, 3.5; 4.1, 4.2

So we see that up to a maximum of 11 sections in the articles have been mentioned in the RA Introductions. Section 2, 3 and 4 occur in more than 80% of the articles, whereas Section 5 occurs in 77%, Section 6 in 68% and rest of the sections occur in fewer than 50% of the articles. This demonstrates clearly that most of the Research Articles in Computer Science have four parts, a fairly large number have five to six while few have more than seven parts.

3.3 Structural Variation

With respect to variation, Hyland (2000:122) notes that 'Interpersonal metadiscourse concerns more explicitly interactional and evaluative aspects of authorial presence, expressing the writer's individually defined, but disciplinary circumscribed, persona.' (Hyland 2000:122). We have already seen individual variation in the use of the word SECTION. Some authors have used the discoursal adjectives such as *next, last, final, this, following* and *the*, to refer to the sections. *This* stands at the top of the list followed by *next.* Their number, however, as compared to the occurrence of Section as a noun with a numerical modifier, for example, *Section 2*, is quite low. The underlying reason may be that computer scientists think in terms of numbers, numbers seeming to them more logical than words.

Swales (1994:194) draws attention to the usage of a variety of sentence structures to report the structure of a paper. This is done to convey different attitudes to prepositional material, and the writers vary their tones, levels of intimacy and involvement with the reader. To look at the structural variation, it seems sensible to focus on the structures associated with SECTION since this is the most common theme. The linguistic attributes that collocate with the word SECTION have been divided into the following main categories:

Category	**Type**	**Example**
One	Section as subject	Section (2) *describes...*
Two	In section + we	In Section (2) *we present…*
Three	Section (passive)	. . . *is presented* in Section (2)
Four	Section as subject of *be*	Section (2) *is* the core of the…
Five	Other	(*see* Section 2)

The first category is heavily dependent on the use of verbs following the subject *Section*. The use of verbs continues in the second category but with the personal pronoun *we*. In the third category, passive is used with reference to *Section*. The fourth category is straightforward, with *Section* as the subject and active voice. The last category consists of the sentences that cannot be put in any of the above four e.g. (*see Section 6*), or are not clear with reference to the subject *Section.*

Table 7. Structural Variation in Sentences

	Section Nos	Entries	Cat. One	Cat. Two	Cat. Three	Cat. Four	Cat. Five
Noun+Numeral	Section 2	47	22	15	3	2	5
	Section 3	51	22	18	7	3	1
	Section 4	46	23	10	11	1	1
	Section 5	43	21	12	10	0	0
	Section 6	38	15	10	11	1	1
	Section 7	22	13	3	6	0	0
	Section 8-11	17	5	7	3	0	2
Total		**264**	**121**	**75**	**51**	**7**	**10**
Modifier+ Noun	next Section	6	1	4	1	0	0
	last/final Section	3	0	2	1	0	0
	This Section	9	3	3	2	1	0
	following Section	4	0	2	2	0	0
	The Section	2	1	0	1	0	0
Exception	A Section	1	0	0	0	0	1
Total		**25**	**5**	**11**	7	**1**	**1**
Grand Total		289	126	86	58	8	11
Averages			**7**	**5**	**3**	**0.44**	**0.61**

Table 7 and Table 8 reflect the higher use of Category One -- almost twice Category Two -- where the writers use *Section* in a Noun + Numeral construction. Category Two is the second most frequent structural variant and Category Three remains as the third most frequent. On the other hand, in the Modifier + Noun type, Category two is the most common variant followed by Category Three. Category One in the Modifier + Noun variant stands at number three in contrast to Noun +Numeral where it was the most frequent. There is a strong relationship between the Modifier + Noun structure and the use of inclusive *we*; the infrequent use of this variant shows the writers' tendency to distance themselves by using the Noun + Numeral structure.

Since the number of occurrences of Categories Four and Five is small as compared to the number of occurrences of the other categories, these categories require no further comment.

Table 8. Structural Variation Exemple Percentage

Category	Type	Example	Occurrence	Percentage
One	Section as subject	Section (2) *describes…*	126	44%
Two	In Section + *we*	In Section (2) *we present…*	86	30%
Three	Section (passive)	*… is presented* in Section (2)	58	20%

3.4 Changing Roles from Narrator to Actor

Lewin et.al. (2001:52) explain that 'the initiation of Move Three is always signaled by a reference to the authors as producers with the use of the pronoun *we,* which abruptly foregrounds the authors or their present work. Inclusive and second person pronouns providing a significant means to negotiate role relationships through relational markers have also been discussed by Hyland (2000). Contrary to their claim, in the last step of CS RA Introductions, the dominant role of the author is as narrator with a heavy usage of the word SECTION as compared to the inclusive *we* that is used to explain his role as actor.

Myers (1992:301) opines that deictic expressions are 'self-referential in the same way as performatives [and] work as *hereby* does in the tests for performative verbs' as they point to the text as an embodiment of claim. It appears here (see Table 9) that the choice of verbs is irrespective of whether the referent is personalized or not. The decision to choose between *we* and *section* seems to be based on necessity and reason whereas the choice of verbs is arbitrary.

3.5 The Conclusion of the Beginning

While the Outlining Structure step informs the reader about the various parts of the research article, including design implementation, algorithms and results etc, it also flags the last milestone of the journey, the conclusion. Some examples of the concluding sentence of the Computer Science Introductions are given here.

- A **conclusion** is given in the **last section.**
- **We** discuss… and, **in the final section conclude** with directions for future research.
- Section 9 **concludes** the paper **with final remarks.**
- **We conclude** with a discussion about future work **in the last section.**
- **Finally, we** draw the implications . . . and **conclude the paper.**

Table 9. Verbs (occurring more than once) associated with Narrator and Actor Roles

We + Verbs	No. of Occurrences		Section + Verbs	No. of Occurrences
discuss	18		presents	25
present	14		describes	20
explain	7		concludes	10
describe	6		discusses	11
conclude	4		provides	8
define	3		defines	5
give	3		introduces	5
introduce	3		gives	3
provide	2		reviews	2
			summarizes	2
			illustrate	2
			outlines	2
			includes	2
			proposes	2
			compares	2
			derives	2
			reports	2

4. Conclusion

Cooper's (1985) suggestion that computer scientists' use the Outlining Structure step because of the field's newness and thus absence of any well established format seems negated because, twenty years after her data, computer scientists are still doing the same thing. This implies that the reason lies somewhere else. One reason could be the lack of rhetorical choices available to the authors or it could be in the very nature of the field itself which compartmentalizes things, be it the tool bars of windows, programming subroutines, or system modules. Computer scientists like putting things into well-defined boxes and having something pop up every time you click a box, thus justifying the heavy use of road mapping through the Outlining Structure step in the Introductions of research articles. However, the structural variation used in this process is limited and highly amenable to pedagogical attention.

References

Anthony, L. (1999). 'Writing research article introductions in software engineering. How accurate is a standard model?' *IEEE Transactions on Professionnel Communication*. v. 42, pp. 38-4.

Anthony, L. (2001). 'Characteristic features of research article titles in computer science'. *IEEE Transactions on Professionnel Communication*. v. 44/3, pp. 187-194.

Anthony, L. (2000). Implementing genre analyssis in a foreign language classroom . TESOL Matters. V 10/3, PP. 18-24.

Atkinson, D. (1993). 'A historical discourse analysis of scientific research writing from 1675-1975: the case of the 'philosophical Transactions of the Royal Society of London''. *Unpublished PhD dissertation*, California: the University of Southern California.

Booth, V. (1993). *Communicating in Science: Writing a scientific paper and speaking at scientific meetings*. Cambridge: Cambridge University Press.

Brown, J.F. (1985). *Engineering Report Writing*. Solana Beach CA: United Western.

Cooper, C. (1985). 'Aspects of Article Introductions in IEEE Publications'. *Unpublished M.Sc. dissertation*. Birmingham: The University of Aston in Birmingham.

Corbett, J. B. (1992). Functional Grammar and Genre Analysis: a description of the language of learned and popular articles'. *Unpublished PhD dissertation,* Glasgow: The University of Glasgow.

Crooks, C. (1986). 'Towards a validated analysis of scientific text structure'. *Applied Linguistics* v. 7/ 1, pp. 57-70.

Dudley- Evans, T. (2000). 'Genre analysis: a key to a theory of ESP?' *Iberica* No. 2.

Ebel, H. F., Bliefert, C. and Russey, W. E. (1987). The Art of Scientific Writing. Weinheim/ New York: VCH.

Gibaldi , J. and Achter, W.S. (1988). *MLA Handbook for Writers of Research Papers* (3rd ed.). New York: The Modern Languages Association of America.

Hughes, G. (1989). 'Article introductions in computer journals'. *Unpublished MA dissertation*, Birmingham: University of Birmingham.

Hyland, K. (2000). *Disciplinary Discourses: Social interactions in academic writing*. Essex: Longman.

Labov,W. and Waletzky,J. (1967). 'Narrative analysis: oral versions of personal experience', In J. Helen (ed.) *Essays on the Verbal and Visual Arts*. Philadelphia: American Ethnological Society.

Lewin, A., Fine, J. and Young, L. (2001). *Expository discourse: a genre- based approach to social science research texts*. London/ New York: Continuum.

McRobb, M. (1990). *Writing Quality Manuals for ISO 9000 Series*. London: IFS Publications.

Mulcahy, P. I. (1988). 'Improving Comprehensibility of Computer Instructions: the effect of different text structures on success in performing procedures'. *Unpublished PhD dissertation*, University of Minnesota.

Myers, G. (1992). "In this paper we report…' Speech acts and scientific facts'. *Journal of Pragmatics*. v.17, pp. 295-313.

Oshima , A. and Hoge, A. (1992). *Writing Academic English*. Melano Park, CA: Addison- Wesley Publishing Company.

Posteguillo, S. (1995). 'Genre Analysis in English for Computer Science'. *Unpublished PhD dissertation*, Spain: Universitat De Valencia.

Posteguillo, S. (1999). 'The schematic structure of computer science research articles'. *ESP*, v. 18/ 2, pp. 139-160.

Simpson, M. D. (1989). 'Shaping Computer Documentation for Multiple Audience :An ethnographic study'. *Unpublished PhD dissertation*, Purdu University.

Swales, J.M. (1990). *Genre Analysis: English in Academic and Research Settings*. Cambridge: Cambridge University Press.

Swales, J. M. and Feak, C. (1994, 2004). *Academic Writing for Graduate Students*. Ann Arbor: University of Michigan Press.

Swales, J.M and Najjar (1987). The writing of research article introductions. Written Communication. v.4, PP 175-192.

Weissberg, R. and Buker, S. (1990). *Writing up Research: Experimental Research Report Writing for Students of English*. Englewood Cliffs, NJ: Prentice Hall Regents.

Appendix

a. The Shortest Example of Outlining Structure

The rest of the paper is organized as follows: The system settings appear in Section 2. Our algorithms for implementing a self-stabilizing group membership service appear in Section 3. Concluding remarks are in Section 4.

b. The Longest Example of Outlining Structure

The organization of the paper is as follows: In **Section 2**, we discuss related work. Next, we present the sweep strategy that is assumed throughout this paper in **Section 3** and, in **Section 4**, we discuss some additional details and assumptions regarding a hard disk. Notational conventions and a definition of the guaranteed throughput are given in **Section 5**. Next, we discuss, in **Section 6**, how the straightforward lower bound mentioned above can be determined. **Section 7** discusses the case where only one request has to be handled per batch, i.e., n ¼ 1. The case where n > 1 is handled next in **Section 8**. First, we consider the subproblem of determining a batch with maximum total seek time, assuming that the distribution of requests over the zones is given. For this subproblem, we propose an efficient algorithm and derive a structural property of batches with maximum batch time. This property will be used to efficiently construct batches with maximum total batch time. Next, we prove that the guaranteed throughput is given by the minimum throughput in two successive batches. This observation yields that the guaranteed throughput for n > 1 can be determined by using a similar algorithm as for constructing a single worst-case batch. This algorithm computes the maximum-weighted path in a directed a cyclic graph and runs in Oðz3 maxn2Þ time, where zmax is the number of zones of the disk. In **Section 9,** we discuss the consequences on the guaranteed throughput when using two alternative sweep strategies. Finally, we give some experimental results in **Section 10** and present conclusions in **Section 11**.

Does Albanian have a Third Person Personal Pronoun? Let's have a Look at the Corpus...

Alexander Murzaku

College of Saint Elizabeth

Abstract

The reference grammar of the Albanian language (Dhrimo et al. 1986) states that the personal pronoun paradigm includes a third person filled by the distal demonstrative pronoun ai *formed by the distal prefix* a- *and the pronominal root* -i*. Besides the deictic prefix* a- *which is used in the formation of all distals, the Albanian language makes use of the complementary prefix* k(ë)- *used in the formation of the proximals. Attached to pronouns and adverbs, they form a full deictic system. Separating a subset of the deictic system to fill a slot in a different paradigm appears strained at best. In addition to an etymological and descriptive overview, the paper offers a quantitative analysis of* ai *'that one' and* ky *'this one' which are part of this system. A corpus of Albanian language texts is defined and built. After verification in the nine million word corpus, discrimination tests offered by the reference grammar fail to establish any distinction between the demonstrative and personal pronoun uses. An analysis of the collocations generated by applying MI and T-scoring on data from the corpus provides a new view. The analyzed words, associating with their respective deictic paradigms and filling the same syntactic roles, are unified under only one monolithic category, that of demonstratives.*

1. Introduction

Roberto Busa, a pioneer in linguistic text analysis, often says that the computer allows and, at the same time, requires a new way of studying languages. In 1949, using "state of the art" computers, Busa started his search for new meaning in verbal records, in order to view a writer's work in its totality and establish a firmer base in reality for the ascent to universal truth (Raben 1987). Following the same asymptotic line towards clarity, this paper aims at better discerning the boundaries between grammatical categories through their usage in large amounts of texts.

The Albanian language, which preserves some archaic features of the Indo-European languages, has a long history of etymological and grammatical studies but the new capabilities offered by today's powerful computers have not yet exploited this history. This paper pioneers the effort to apply computational techniques to Albanian by focusing on determining the existence of Albanian third person personal pronouns in Albanian and their relationship to distal demonstrative pronouns via quantitative methods. By analyzing collocates and the structures in which these words appear in a newly built nine million word corpus, we will see that the distributions of what are called third person personal pronouns and demonstrative pronouns are equivalent and discriminating them as separate categories becomes a questionable task.

2. Personal and Demonstrative Pronouns

The reference grammar of the Albanian language (Dhrimo et al. 1986) describes the category of personal pronouns as a set of 1st, 2nd and 3rd person pronouns with their respective definitions of the person that speaks, the person spoken to, and what/who is spoken about. This follows a long tradition started in the second century B.C.E. with Dionysius Thrax' parts of speech in the Art of Grammar (Kemp, A. 1987). 1st and 2nd person pronouns refer to humans and hence the name of the feature "person." Because of its interchangeability with any noun and the distinctions between discourse and story, 3rd person could best be referred to as non-person (Benveniste, E. 1966) or, as Bhat (2004) prefers, proforms. Between proforms, though, there still remain deictic features better related to discourse. Even though the contrast between deixis and anaphora has been identified and analysed since Apollonious Dyscolus' second century C.E. work, there still seems to be confusion in the definitive labelling of these categories. According to Apollonius, anaphora concerns reference to some entity in language, while deixis to some entity outside language (Lehmann, W. 1982). The same categories have been described as endophoric and exophoric references (Halliday & Hasan, 1976). Claude Hagège (1992) includes both of them as the core of a larger and more exhaustive system called anthropophoric. While 1st and 2nd person pronouns are proper deictics or exophoric pronouns, third person suffers from its dual anaphoric and deictic nature making it hard to classify as one or the other.

The duality of third person – anaphoric and deictic – has become the subject of many studies focusing on one language or across languages. If the pronoun is purely anaphoric, it is classified as a 3rd person personal pronoun. If it is purely deictic, it gets relegated to a whole new set of demonstrative pronouns. This alignment between anaphoric and third person pronouns on the one hand and demonstratives on the other is counterintuitive. First, it ignores the anaphoric usage of proximal demonstratives. Second it unifies in the same paradigm 1st and 2nd person pronouns that refer to extra-linguistic actors of the speech act (such as *I* and *you* in English) with intra-linguistic references where the pronoun merely refers to another previously mentioned object (as in the overanalysed donkey sentences: *Pedro owns a donkey. He feeds it.* where *he* and *it* refer back to *Pedro* and *donkey* respectively). Demonstratives that are better related to the speech act are left in a separate paradigm. As always, confusion arises in the middle. From a sample of 225 languages, Bhat (2004) identifies 126 two-person languages with just 1st and 2nd person personal pronouns, and 99 three-person languages with a complete set of 1st, 2nd and 3rd person personal pronouns. Languages belonging to

two person systems either do not have a third person at all or what is considered as such has close ties to the demonstratives.
Following the above model, Albanian would have a two-person personal pronoun system. However, Albanian reference grammars refer to the deictic usage of pronouns as demonstratives and to their anaphoric usage as 3rd person personal pronouns. The anaphoric usage though is limited only to distal demonstratives.

3. Inventory of Personal/Demonstrative Pronouns in Albanian

Table 1. Inventory of Albanian personal/demonstrative pronouns

<table>
<tr><td rowspan="3"></td><td colspan="4">Distals</td><td colspan="4">Proximals</td></tr>
<tr><td colspan="2">Singular</td><td colspan="2">Plural</td><td colspan="2">Singular</td><td colspan="2">Plural</td></tr>
<tr><td>M</td><td>F</td><td>M</td><td>F</td><td>M</td><td>F</td><td>M</td><td>F</td></tr>
<tr><td>NOM</td><td>ai</td><td>ajo</td><td rowspan="2">ata</td><td rowspan="2">ato</td><td>ky</td><td>kjo</td><td rowspan="2">këta</td><td rowspan="2">këto</td></tr>
<tr><td>ACC</td><td colspan="2">atë</td><td colspan="2">këtë</td></tr>
<tr><td>DAT</td><td rowspan="2">atij</td><td rowspan="2">asaj</td><td rowspan="2" colspan="2">atyre</td><td rowspan="2">këtij</td><td rowspan="2">kësaj</td><td rowspan="2" colspan="2">këtyre</td></tr>
<tr><td>GEN
ABL</td></tr>
<tr><td>Old ABL</td><td>asi</td><td>aso</td><td>asish</td><td>asosh</td><td>kësi</td><td>këso</td><td>kësish</td><td>kësosh</td></tr>
</table>

<table>
<tr><td rowspan="3"></td><td colspan="4">Non-deictic</td></tr>
<tr><td colspan="2">Singular</td><td colspan="2">Plural</td></tr>
<tr><td>M</td><td>F</td><td>M</td><td>F</td></tr>
<tr><td>NOM</td><td colspan="2"></td><td rowspan="2">*ta</td><td rowspan="2">*to</td></tr>
<tr><td>ACC</td><td colspan="2">*të</td></tr>
<tr><td>DAT</td><td colspan="4"></td></tr>
<tr><td>GEN
ABL</td><td>tij</td><td>saj</td><td colspan="2">tyre</td></tr>
<tr><td rowspan="2">Old ABL</td><td rowspan="2" colspan="2"></td><td>sish</td><td>sosh</td></tr>
<tr><td colspan="2">syresh</td></tr>
</table>

Personal/demonstrative pronouns in Albanian inflect according to number, gender and case as shown in the table above. While nominative and accusative share only their plurals, genitive, dative and ablative share all the forms. The differences between genitive, dative and ablative are syntactic: genitive forms are always preceded by a pre-posed article also known as particles of concord: *i*, *e*, *të* and *së* 'of'; ablative forms are preceded by one of the many prepositions with adverbial origins such as *larg* 'far', *afër* 'near', *pranë* 'next to', *mes/ndërmjet* 'among', *midis* 'between', *para* 'before', *pas* 'after', *sipas* 'according to', *prej* 'from, of', *drejt* 'toward', *karshi/kundër* 'opposite', *krahas* 'alongside', *rreth* 'around', *brenda* 'inside', *përveç* 'aside', *gjatë* 'during', and *jashtë* 'outside'. There is a fourth row marked as "old ablative" - these pronouns are rarely used and mostly in dialectal or historical documents. By analogy with the noun inflection, where the plural indefinite of the ablative is marked by the ending "*-sh*," pronouns in this group take the same ending. The existence of this ending constitutes the reason for having a fourth case in Albanian (Friedman 2004).

Beside distals (starting in *a-*) and proximals (starting in *k(ë)-*), there is a third column labelled "non-deictic." The forms marked with an asterisk, even though nominative and accusative, can never appear in a sentence as subjects or objects respectively. They can only be found following prepositions such as nominative (*nga* 'from' and *tek/te* 'at, to') or accusative (*me* 'with', *mbi* 'on', *nën* 'under', *për* 'for', and *në* 'in'.). Nominative singular, old ablative singular and dative which fulfill the indirect object role do not have non-deictic forms.

It can be observed that distribution of gender over number and case is unbalanced. Nominative and old ablative have masculine and feminine for both singular and plural. Genitive, dative and ablative have both genders in singular but only one form for plural. Accusative has the opposite distribution with both genders in plural but only one in singular, conflicting with Greenberg's universal 45 which says that if there are any gender distinctions in the plural of the pronouns, there are some gender distinctions in the singular also (Greenberg 1966). Plank and Schellinger (1997) found out that there are a considerable number of languages that violate this universal – about 10% of their data set. By including case in their analysis and not just number and person, the Albanian demonstrative pronoun system shows that universal 45 exceptions could be even more.

4. The Origin of Albanian Demonstratives

Albanological studies were started in the early 19th century by linguists such as Von Hahn, Bopp, Camarda, Meyer, Pedersen and others. Most of these linguists were important Indo-European scholars and therefore many of their studies dealt with the place of Albanian in the Indo-European family tree. The Albanian language, preserving some archaic features of Indo-European, has been used as a source of information for deciphering phonetic and morphologic as well as syntactic reflections of Proto-Indo-European in today's languages. Albanian demonstratives reflect common developments with other Indo-European languages.

According to etymological analysis of the personal/demonstrative pronouns in Albanian, their roots are clearly derivations of the Indo-European demonstrative roots. According to Çabej (1976:31, 1977:109-110), these constructions in Albanian appear to be quite recent because they have not been subjected to the aphaeresis of the starting unaccented vowel. The common pattern in Albanian is from Latin *amicus* to Albanian *mik*; this has not happened in *atij* and *asaj*. By observing the two parallel paradigms, distal and proximal in Table 1, *a-* and *k(ë)-* can be identified as prefixes attached to the pronominal roots. The pronominal roots, or what is represented in Table 1 as non-deictic, are found unbound, without the prefixes *a-* or *kë-*, in 16th century writings. Today, these roots *tij*, *saj*, *tyre*, *të*, *ta*, *to* can be found unbound only when they are preceded by a preposition or article. This would mean that instead of the prefix, they are "bound" to a preposition or pre-posed article. The old ablatives *sish*, *sosh*, *syresh* are an exception.

There are a vast number of studies dealing with the etymology of the pronominal part of the demonstrative but very few are concerned with the deictic prefixes. Çabej sees the prefixes *a-* and *kë-* as hypercharacterization devices inferring that the pronominal part already had a demonstrative functionality. This hypercharacterization, apparently in analogy with the deictic adverbs of place, added granularity to an already existing system. Furthermore, *njito* or *njita* 'these' show how loosely attached the deictic prefixes are. The prefixes *a-* and *k(ë)-* are easily replaced when the deictic particle *nji*, equivalent of *ecco* in Italian or вот in Russian, is attached in front of the pronoun. The particle *nji* has nothing to do with distance reducing *ata/ato* 'those (m/f)' and *këta/këto* 'these (m/f)' to degree-less demonstratives. Çabej concludes that it is not the prefixes that transform them into demonstratives – they were demonstratives all along.

Demiraj (2002), analyzing the pronominal clitics in Albanian, concludes that they do derive from some disappeared set of personal pronouns. As for the demonstratives, he thinks that their different forms derive from a mix of different Indo-European demonstrative sets but that these words still do not have a clear origin. Bokshi (2004) instead concludes that there has been a unidirectional movement from demonstratives to personal pronouns. The first series of demonstratives deriving from the Indo-European demonstratives, with time, lost its deicticity and constituted the personal pronoun series. The two deictic prefixes were needed to reconstitute the demonstrative pronouns from these personal pronouns. Following the same pattern, he sees today a new move of distal demonstratives towards third person personal pronouns.

The conclusion that can be reached from these analyses is that old Indo-European demonstratives retained their demonstrative traits in Albanian and, in addition, reinforced their deicticity with the more visible deictic prefixes. As the language evolved, there has been a movement from personal pronouns to clitics, and from demonstratives to personal pronouns. The deictic prefixes, *a-* for distals and *k(ë)-* for proximals, are attached not only to old demonstratives but to other pronouns and adverbs as well: *atillë/këtillë* 'such as that/such as this', *aty/atje/këtu* 'there close to you/here close to me/there far from both', *andej/këndej* 'from there/from here', *aq/kaq* 'that much/this much' and *ashtu/kështu* 'that way/this way'. In *akëcili/akëkush* 'whoever' both prefixes are attached to achieve indefiniteness.

5. Third Person Personal Pronouns

From the synchronic point of view, by labeling the distal demonstratives (those that start in *a-*) as personal pronouns, Albanian grammarians need to establish a set of rules for distinguishing them from each other. The reference grammar of Albanian (Dhrimo, A. et al. 1986) provides two tests to achieve this distinction.

According to the reference grammar, these pronouns should be called personal when they replace a noun mentioned earlier, giving them a clear anaphoric function. But a quick corpus search will show that Albanian uses pronouns with both prefixes (*a-* and *k(ë)-*) in anaphoric functions. Furthermore, when needed to resolve antecedent ambiguity in text, Albanian does use the deictic features, as in "the former/the latter" in English. This logic could lead to the conclusion that the personal pronoun paradigm is in fact richer and contains both *a-* and *kë-* pronouns (Murzaku 1989).

> *...Koshtunica nuk preku ... për më tepër* ***ai*** *u përpoq ta mënjanojë Gjingjiçin, por* ***ky*** *arriti...* '...Kostunica didn't touch ... furthermore **he/that one/the former** tried to put aside Djindjic, but **he/this one/the latter** achieved...'

It is obvious that the second pronoun, having multiple possible antecedents, needs some other tool to differentiate it. By using the proximal demonstrative in opposition to the distal demonstrative, anaphora ambiguity is resolved with the calculation of distance inside the text.

The other test suggested by the grammar is that the use of the pronoun without the leading *a-* is an indicator that we have a personal pronoun rather than a demonstrative. This test seems to suggest that, if the non-deictic root of the pronoun is a personal pronoun, then anything it replaces is also a personal pronoun. Submitting a phrase search to any search engine, it can be seen that not only pronouns starting in *a-* can fill this slot. This search retrieved 5300 "*me ta*", 3000 "*me ata*" and 500 "*me këta*" in very similar syntactic structures.

> *...në suaza të Komisionit dhe i cili punon* ***me ta*** *çdo ditë...* '...in subgroups of the Commission and which works **with them**...'
> *...se ky më shumë rri ... e punon* ***me ata****...* '...because he/this one mostly stays ... and works **with them/those ones**...'
> *...më pas dërgon një koreograf, i cili punon* ***me këta****...* '...later sent a choreographer, who works **with them/these ones**...'

In the examples above, 'with them' is part of identical structures differing only in the use of the pronoun *me ta* a non-deictic, *me ata* a distal and *me këta* a proximal. It is obvious in this case that both distal and proximal demonstratives can be replaced by the corresponding non-deictic pronoun.

Both tests of pronoun status suggested by the reference grammar of Albanian, their anaphoric role and their substitutability, are rather ineffective in discerning personal from demonstrative pronouns.

6. Quantitative Analysis

Neither diachronic nor synchronic analyses until now have provided a good answer to our original question of whether there is a 3rd person personal pronoun in Albanian. Etymologically, there seems to be a constant move between these demonstrative and personal pronouns without a definitive answer on the origin of the deictic prefixes *a-* and *k(ë)-*. On the other hand, today's descriptive studies offer no clear division between personal and demonstrative pronouns. A part of speech is defined by the meaning and by the role that a word (or sometimes a phrase) plays in a sentence. While the introspective and diachronic analyses can provide good explanations and descriptions of the meaning as well as functionality and origin of these words, a quantitative analysis could complete it with a better view of how these forms are distributed in today's usage and what patterns they create in natural text. Following Firth's (1957) slogan "you shall know a word by the company it keeps," this new dimension, based on large scale data, brings additional arguments to the suggestion that today's Albanian is indeed a two person language and that the line of demarcation being sought between personal and demonstrative pronouns perhaps does not exist.

Analyzing the semantic content of the pronouns in question, the working hypothesis is that distal and proximal demonstratives are associated with words belonging to their respective deictic dimensions.

6.1 Corpus Building

Before starting any collocational analysis, the first step is the assembly of a suitable corpus and tools for exploring it. Quantitative corpus based analysis of Albanian is still in its initial phases. The efforts towards creating a balanced corpus have been unsuccessful and there are no accessible corpora for the research community. Another issue with the Albanian language is the relatively young age of the standardized language. The two main dialects, Toskë and Gheg, remain very much in use, confining the standard mostly to the written language. After the fall of communism in the early 1990's, new concepts, both technical and social, were introduced. The language has reacted with the introduction of newly created terms from internal resources or direct foreign word loans. So the lexicon of Albanian is now in a very "interesting" state.

Pronouns, which are the object of this study, are function words and the quality of collocations for such words should not be affected by the situation of the lexicon in general. However, the corpus needs to represent today's language in its entirety (Biber et al. 1998). Given many technical and time constraints, though, compromises were made in defining the sources for the material.

The corpus of Albanian language text used for this study was created by extracting content from several Internet sites and scanned material. The sites were selected following criteria of quality and content. The text contained in these sites had to be written in standard Albanian following the Albanian orthography rules and using the correct characters. These criteria eliminated most of the Albanian language Internet lists where Albanian is mixed with other languages and where writers almost never use the diacritics marks for *ë* and *ç*. As for the content, an effort was made to balance news items with literary prose and interviews. In addition to newspapers, literary, cultural and informational sites were included in the spider list and were regularly spidered for one year. To balance what might be labeled as just "Internet" text, works from the well known authors Ismail Kadare and Martin Camaj as well as some historical and philosophical books scanned or already in electronic form were included in the corpus.

Content acquired from the Internet required careful handling. Every downloaded page has been analyzed and cleaned by a page scraper, removing HTML tags and template elements. Obviously, the template text, repeated in every page from the same site, would distort the counts and diminish the statistical accuracy. The most salient example is the word *këtë* 'this' which has a count of 215,000 in Google. However, 19%, or 40,500 instances, are part of the phrase *këtë faqe* 'this page' or some other constructs like it that point to the page that contains it. These kinds of phrases usually appear in the template elements and eliminating them would prove beneficial to our collocational analysis. The remaining content after the clean-up is saved as text only and indexed for quick searching.

Having the data indexed provides a simple tool for eliminating duplicates. A few sentences from every new page are submitted as query terms to the search engine. If there is a 100% match, the new document is considered a duplicate and not stored. Obviously, there is the risk of eliminating texts that quote each other but in our data the quantity of eliminated text did not constitute a problem. The collection consists now of approximately 9 million tokens and 182,000 types.

6.2 Computational Tools

The tools for analyzing the corpus include a tokenizer, indexer, concordancer, collocator, set computation utilities, and a search engine allowing the use of regular expressions. All these tools are written in Java.

The tokenizer is configurable and uses rules specific to Albanian. There are also Albanian specific rules for collocation sorting where *a>b>c>ç>d>dh>e>ë>... >g>gj>... >l>ll>... >n>nj> ... >r>rr>s>sh>t>th>... >x>xh>y>z>zh.*

Manning and Schütze (1999) provide a list of criteria that define collocations, i.e. non-compositionality, non-substitutability and non-modifiability. Since the words being analyzed here are pronouns, the focus of the study is on the constellation of the strongly associated words surrounding the target that do not completely match the above definition of collocates. We will still refer to these words as collocates. They are computed by using Mutual Information (MI) as defined by Church and Hanks (1991) and T-score as defined by Barnbrook (1996) and implemented in Mason (2000). The MI-score is the ratio of the probability that two given words appear in each other's neighborhood with the product of the probabilities that each of them would appear separately. The MI-score indicates the strength of association between two words, whereas the T-score indicates the association's confidence level. While a positive MI-score shows that two words have more than a random chance of occurring close to each other, the T-score confirms that the high MI-score is not created by just two rare words that happen to appear close to each other or as Church et al. (1991) state: MI is better for highlighting similarity and T-scores are better for establishing differences among close synonyms. By combining the two, most false positives are eliminated.

6.3 Discussion of Results

The project aimed at two separate results. The first one was to create tools and datasets that would provide clean concordances and statistical data for our study. About 180,000 concordance lines (160 characters each) and the frequencies in the following table were generated for the eight *a-* pronouns and the corresponding *k(ë)-* pronouns of today's Albanian.

Table 2. Absolute frequencies of the *a-* and *kë-* forms

Distal		Proximal	
ai	22,556	ky	10,066
ajo	11,121	kjo	14,993
atë	11,228	këtë	35,610
atij	2,228	këtij	14,221
asaj	2,309	kësaj	11,694
ata	12,383	këta	2,439
ato	8,938	këto	12,395
atyre	2,957	këtyre	5,815
total	*73,720*	*total*	*107,233*

At a first glance, proximal demonstratives have an almost 30% higher frequency than the distal demonstratives. If distal demonstratives were personal pronouns as well, this double duty would imply that their frequency should be higher. By analyzing the data in more detail, we see that the distribution among the several forms is uneven with respect to case, gender and number. *Ai* (nom:sing:masc:dist) occurs twice as much compared to *ky* (nom:sing:masc:prox). But the corresponding feminine forms *ajo* and *kjo* are more evenly distributed with a slightly higher number for the proximal form. The same distribution can be seen for their corresponding feminine plural forms *ato* and *këto*. The distribution of masculine plural forms *ata* and *këta* is inversed with the distal form having five times more occurrences than the proximal. It should be noted that these forms are shared between nominative and accusative. Without getting into a detailed analysis of this irregularity, concordances of these words show that the proximal is in an adjectival role by a ratio of 3:1, while the distal is found by a ratio of 20:1 in pronominal roles. This unbalanced functional distribution of the masculine plural and the corresponding discrepancy in the number of occurrences need to be investigated further. Singular accusative and genitive/dative/ablative both singular and plural are heavily unbalanced in favor of the proximal forms.

The second goal was to find lexical-grammatical associations between the target words (personal and/or demonstrative pronouns) and words in their neighborhoods that would help define their similarities or differences. Word neighborhood (or span) is defined as the number of words on each side. By using a right and left span of 2 words and looking for links only with words that have frequencies bigger than 5, substantial lists of collocates for each of the pronouns were generated. Their frequencies varied between 150 and 2000.

Once the data was acquired, it was expected that some results would correspond to the initial hypothesis. But, as is always the case with statistics (which makes it interesting by the way), surprises were expected as well.

The following table exposes a few facts extracted from the collocations of *ai* and *ky*.

Table 3. Collocation table for *ai* and *ky*. Collocation is measured using MI-score and T-score.

KY				AI		
	MI	T	English		MI	T
atë	0.73	6.34	'him / that one'	atë	2.82	146.00
atje	2.11	5.39	'there close to him'	atje	3.76	53.79
aty	1.74	6.21	'there close to you'	aty	3.44	69.86
dje	1.48	25.66	'yesterday'	dje	2.78	179.03
është	4.09	1259.63	'is'	është	2.75	1105.09
këtë	1.39	68.20	'this one'	këtë	3.19	626.91
këtu	0.78	0.30	'here'	këtu	2.79	49.74
sot	2.57	31.01	'today'			
tani	2.92	43.38	'now'			
tashmë	3.32	33.60	'nowadays'			
			'far away'	tutje	3.35	6.89

One of the hypotheses was that pronouns from both paradigms can be found in the same functional slots. The verb *është* 'is' has the same very high collocation values (both MI and T-score) with *ai* and *ky*. Other verbs such as *ka* 'has' and *do* 'wants' have similarly high correlations thus implying that, at least in the subject role, *ai* and *ky* are equally distributed.

The other initial hypothesis was that the proximal pronoun *ky* 'this one' should have high collocation value with words distributed close to the axes I/HERE/NOW and the distal *ai* 'he/that one' with words far from the center of the speaking act such as THERE/THEN. *ky* does have exclusive high collocation values with *tani* 'now', *sot* 'today', *tashmë* 'nowadays'. The distal (*ai*) does have higher collocation values with *atje* 'there' and *dje* 'yesterday' as well as exclusive collocation with *tutje* 'far away'. But there was a surprise: *këtë* 'him/this one' and *këtu* 'here' have much higher values with *ai* than with *ky*. From a look at the concordances, a plausible explanation can be found based on the high frequency of narrative structures like:

> *...Shkodra pati fatin të ketë një artist të përmasave të tilla... Pikërisht **këtu** **ai** mësoi edhe ABC-në e parë në pikturë...* '...Shkodra was lucky to have an actor of such caliber... Right **here** **he/that one** learned his first ABC in painting...'
> ... *do të vijë një ditë që të tërhiqet nga këto vendime. **Këtë** **ai** e vërteton me faktin...* '...one day will come that he will regret these decisions. **He/that one** verifies **this** with the fact...'

In the first type of sentence, the writer refers to the place where he (the writer) is writing. The second type, as discussed in more length in Murzaku (1990), is a quite common endophoric deictic reference. *Këtë* refers to the latest text unit preceding the demonstrative and is always feminine referring to the complete phrase *këtë gjë* 'this thing'. Neither of these structures contradicts the collocate analysis.

7. Conclusions

As in many other languages, Albanian 1st and 2nd person pronouns are proper deictics. Third person has a dual anaphoric and deictic nature making it hard to be classified as one or the other. If the pronoun is purely anaphoric, it is classified as a 3rd person personal pronoun. If it is purely deictic, it gets relegated to a whole new set of demonstrative pronouns. While diachronic analysis provides a good explanation of how the demonstratives evolved in Albanian, synchronic analysis offers no clear division between personal and demonstrative pronouns. This new quantitative dimension moves us towards a better definition of personal and demonstrative pronouns. On the one hand, these pronouns do keep a high level of association with their corresponding deictic family. On the other hand, both groups find themselves associated with words such as verbs that agree with the analyzed pronoun and that would fit in the same syntactic role. The main conclusions reached by this analysis are:

i) Albanian demonstrative pronouns maintain their deictic functionality for both endophoric and exophoric references.
ii) Pronouns that contain *a-*, *kë-* or neither are syntactically interchangeable.
iii) Collocational analysis provides additional arguments for determining the syntactic unity of demonstratives while maintaining their deictic differences.

iv) Distals do not have a higher frequency of occurrence and therefore it is hard to make the argument that distals have been transformed into anaphoric pronouns.

Combining insights from diachronic studies with synchronic and quantitative studies, the implications that emerge include the primacy of deixis in the development of the pronominal systems in general. Albanian's lack of third person proper shows a path of language evolution that maintains its deictic elements both in referential and anaphoric functions. While both *a-* and *kë-* pronouns play the role of what is called third person they preserve their deicticity. The *ø-* pronouns, never appearing without a preposition, etymologically belong to the same demonstrative paradigm. Functionally, prepositions neutralize the need for deictic prefixes allowing them to disappear in some cases. The continuum between anaphoric and deictic functions does not include a cusp that divides the two. The lack of a 3rd person personal pronoun form classifies the Albanian language as a two-person language in Bhat's (2004) taxonomy.

Bibliography

Barnbrook, G. (1996). *Language and Computers.* Edinburgh: Edinburgh University Press.

Benveniste, E. (1966). *Problèmes de linguistique générale*. Paris: Gallimard.

Bhat, D. N. S. (2004). *Pronouns*. Oxford: University Press.

Biber, D., S. Conrad, R. Reppen. (1998). *Corpus Linguistics*. Cambridge: Cambridge University Press.

Bokshi, B. (2004). *Për Vetorët e Shqipes*. Prishtinë: Akademia e Shkencave dhe e Arteve e Kosovës.

Church, K. and P. Hanks. (1991). Word Association Norms, Mutual Information, and Lexicography, *Computational Linguistics*, 16(1), pp. 22-29.

Church, K., Gale, W., Hanks, P., Hindle D. (1991). Using Statistics in Lexical Analysis. In Zernik, U. (ed.), *Lexical Acquisition: Using On-line Resources to Build a Lexicon*. Hillsdale: Lawrence Erlbaum.

Çabej, E. (1976). *Studime Gjuhësore I, Studime Etimologjike në Fushë të Shqipes, A-O*. Prishtinë: Rilindja.

Çabej, E. (1977). *Studime Gjuhësore IV, Nga Historia e Gjuhës Shqipe*. Prishtinë: Rilindja.

Demiraj, S. (2002). *Gramatikë Historike e Gjuhës Shqipe*. Tiranë: Akademia e Shkencave.

Dhrimo, A., E. Angoni, E. Hysa, E. Lafe, E. Likaj, F. Agalliu, et al. (1986). *Fonetika dhe Gramatika e Gjuhës së Sotme Shqipe: Morfologjia*. Tiranë: Akademia e Shkencave.

Firth, J. (1957). A synopsis of linguistic theory 1930–1955. In the Philological Society's *Studies in Linguistic Analysis*. Blackwell, Oxford, pages 1–32.

Reprinted in *Selected Papers of J. R. Firth*, edited by F. Palmer. Longman, 1968.

Friedman, V. (2004). *Studies on Albanian and Other Balkan Languages*. Pejë: Dukagjini.

Greenberg, J. (1966). Some Universals of Grammar with Particular Reference to the Order of Meaningful Elements, pp. 73-113. In Greenberg, J. (ed.), *Universals of Language* (2nd ed.). Cambridge: MIT Press.

Hagège, C. (1992). Le système de l'anthropophore et ses aspects morphogénétiques. In Morel, M-A and L. Danon-Boileau (eds.), *La deixis: Colloque en Sorbonne (8-9 juin 1990)*. Paris: Presses Universitaires de France. pp.115-123.

Halliday, M. A. K. and R. Hasan (1976). *Cohesion in English*. London: Longman

Lehmann, W. (1982). Deixis in Proto-Indo-European. In Tischler, J. (ed.), *Serta Indogermanica: Festschrift für Günter Neumann zum 60. Geburtstag*. Innsbruck: Institut für Sprachwissenschaft, pp. 137-142.

Kemp, A. (1987). The Tekhne grammatike of Dionysius Thrax. In Taylor, D. (ed.), *The History of Linguistics in the Classical Period*, Amsterdam.

Manning, C. and H. Schütze. (1999). *Foundations of Statistical Natural Language Processing*. Cambridge: MIT Press.

Mason, O., (2000). *Programming for Corpus Linguistics*. Edinburgh: Edinburgh University Press.

Murzaku, A. (1989). Përemrat ai dhe ky në gjuhën shqipe, *Studime Filologjike*, 1.

Murzaku, A. (1990). Referenzialità dei pronomi deittici impuri dell'albanese. In *16th International Congress of Albanology*. Palermo.

Plank, F. and W. Schellinger (1997). The uneven distribution of genders over numbers: Greenberg Nos. 37 and 45. *Linguistic Typology*, 1, pp. 53-101.

Raben, J. (1987). Computers and the Humanities: some Historical Considerations. In Zampolli, A. (ed.), *Linguistica Computazionale, Volumi IV-V: Studies in Honor of Roberto Busa S.J.* Pisa: Giardini Editori, pp. 225-230.

The Use of Relativizers across Speaker Roles and Gender: Explorations in 19th-century Trials, Drama and Letters

Christine Johansson

Uppsala University

Abstract

In Present-day English, the development of the relativizers has been towards a more frequent use of that. *In 19th-century English, however, the* wh-*forms predominate. The present paper explores the distribution of* that *and the* wh-*forms* (who, whom, whose *and* which) *across speaker roles and gender in 19th-century Trials, Drama and Letters, and, in particular, describes the contexts in which* that *occurs. The data are drawn from CONCE, A Corpus of Nineteenth-Century English, consisting of 1 million words, covering genres representative of 19th-century English usage. The* wh-*forms are favoured by 19th-century letter writers, and speakers in Trials and Drama. A few female letter writers use* that *frequently, introducing a new, less formal, style in letter writing. In Trials,* that *is used most frequently by judges, lawyers and witnesses in typical environments: in cleft sentences;* that *is used with nonpersonal nouns and with pronouns such as* something, everything *and* all. *Playwrights may use* that *as a stylistic device to describe the speech of, primarily, waiters, maids, and other servants.*

1. Introduction

In Present-day English, the development of the relativizers has been towards a more frequent use of *that* (in certain cases this is now the norm, see Geisler and Johansson 2002). In 19th-century English, however, the *wh*-forms predominate. A previous study (see Johansson forthcoming) showed that *wh*-forms are used not only in formal scientific writing but also in letter writing and speech-related genres, such as Trials. The relativizer *which* is the most common of the *wh*-forms; it outnumbers *that* both with nonpersonal antecedents and in restrictive relative clauses.

The relativizer *that is* generally looked upon as less formal than the *wh*-forms (see e.g. Quirk et al. 1985: 1250,1255). The aim of the present paper is to explore whether *that* is an "informal" relativizer also in 19th-century English, if it is used by certain speakers in informal contexts, and if it is part of a less formal, male or female, writing style in letters. In other words, are these the contexts in which the relativizer *that* can compete with the predominant *wh*-forms? The data, which consist of 19th-century Trials, Drama and Letters, are drawn from CONCE, A Corpus of Nineteenth-Century English. This corpus consists of 1 million words covering genres representative of 19th-century English usage (see Kytö, Rudanko and Smitterberg 2000). Period 1 (1800-1830) and Period 3 (1870-

1900) were studied in order to detect any change in the use and frequency of, primarily, the relativizer *that*.[1]

In Trials and Drama, different *speaker roles*, that is, speakers of different social ranks and professional backgrounds are represented. It is possible to study the use of relativizers and relative clauses with reference to the speaker roles. In Trials, the speaker roles are 'Members of the legal profession' (mainly judges and lawyers) and 'Others' (e.g. doctors as expert witnesses, and other witnesses such as servants, neighbours, and relatives of the defendants). It has been found that 'Members of the legal profession' tend to use more educated and formal language whereas the speech of 'Others' may include colloquial features (see Johansson forthcoming). The speaker roles in Drama are 'Upper' (the gentry, people with high positions in society, or with money or property) and 'Others' (e.g. waiters, maids, cooks and country people). On the basis of the results of my previous study (Johansson forthcoming), it can be predicted that 'Upper' are likely to use a more formal style than 'Others'. In Drama, the speech situation will also be considered, i.e. who is addressing whom and the relative status between the participants. How the different speaker roles use relativizers and relative clauses in Trials and Drama is discussed in the two following sections. Section 4 then turns to the use of relativizers by men and women in 19th-century letter writing.

2. The Use of Relativizers across Speaker Roles in Trials

The Trials texts do not represent actual 19th-century spoken language but they approximate 19th-century speech since they consist of speech taken down as direct speech (see Kytö, Rudanko and Smitterberg 2000: 90-91,95). In the Trials texts, the scribe may have influenced the text to some extent. Explicit references, that is, the use of *wh*-forms, might have been considered important in correctly reporting a case. The use of *whom*, changing *which* with a person to *who/whom* or even changing *that* to a *wh*-form to make the text more formal might be examples of scribal alterations. Witnesses may also repeat a *wh*-form, e.g. pied piping or *whom* in reply to a question containing such a *wh*-form asked by a judge.

The speaker role 'Members of the legal profession' includes the Attorney General, Lord Chief Justice Bovill, Sir Charles Russel, Mr. Justice Park, Mr Serjeant Pell, Mr. Alderson and Mr Brougham. 'Others' includes doctors as expert witnesses; some representatives of whom are Dr. Wake, Dr. Hopper and Thomas Low Nichols (practising medicine but not a qualified doctor). Other witnesses are for example, Michael Maybrick (brother of one of the defendants), Elisabeth Nixon (housekeeper and governess) Alice Fulcher (servant), Ann Hopkins (cook), Maria Glenn (the victim of an abduction), Mr and Mrs. Stubbs (farmers at the Tichborne estate) and Reverend John Vause. The defendants, Charles Angus, Jonathan Martin, James Bowditch, Edwin Maybrick, Adelaide Bartlett and Sir Roger Tichborne are not interrogated in the text samples studied.

Members of the legal profession speak more than twice as much as 'Others'. In a representative sample of 5,000 words, the ratio is 7 to 3. On the other hand, members of the legal profession do not use more than twice as many relative clauses. As can be seen in Table 1a, they use 317 relative clauses in their speech, while other professions use 261. This is interesting to note, since it seems to indicate that the speech of members of the legal profession is not syntactically more elaborate. As is evident from Table 1a, the *wh*-forms predominate in the speech of both members of the legal profession (66%) and people with other professional backgrounds (68%).[2]

Table 1a. The Use of *Wh*-forms and *That* across Speaker Roles in *TRIALS* (Periods 1 and 3)

Relativizer	Members of the legal profession	Others	Total
Wh-	208 (66%)	178 (68%)	386 (67%)
That	109 (34%)	83 (32%)	192 (33%)
Total	317 (100%)	261 (100%)	578 (100%)

Doctors as expert witnesses, who are included in 'Others', use a fairly scientific or technical style in their speech, which includes the use of *wh*-forms, when they explain e.g. poisoning or diseases, as in example (1) (see also Johansson forthcoming). This fact may partly explain why the *wh*-forms predominate in 'Others' as well as in 'Members of the legal profession'.

(1) DR. BALDWIN WAKE, sworn: I have known many instances of monomania, I know that at certain times they have lucid intervals, and will be conscious of the error they have committed, and the delusion under which they labour; of this I know a striking case, if it were necessary on this occasion to state it. (Trials, Jonathan Martin, 1800–1830, p. 70)

Since *that* is regarded as a less formal relativizer than the *wh*-forms, it might seem somewhat surprising that judges and lawyers use *that* as frequently (34%) as 'Others' (32%). When 'Members of the legal profession' use *that*, they use it in its typical, i.e. most frequent, syntactic environments. These typical environments are listed in both early English grammars, such as Murray (1795) and in Present-day English grammars, e.g. Quirk et al (1985) and Huddleston and Pullum (2002). The typical syntactic environments of *that* studied in this paper are listed in Figure 1.

Typical syntactic environments of *that*
1. Restrictive relative clause
2. *All that*
3. Cleft sentence (*it is/was ...*)
4. Person(s), people, thing(s) as antecedents
5. Pronominal antecedent (personal and nonpersonal reference)
6. Other (any, no, same, only, superlative+N)

Figure 1: Typical syntactic environments of the relativizer *that*

As is obvious from Figure 1, the typical environments of *that* are with the general noun *person(s)* as antecedent, in cleft sentences, with nonpersonal nouns and with pronouns such as *something*, *everything*, and *all*. These environments are not only typical of *that* but also of the dialogue in the courtroom. *That* is used with *person(s)* in the special forms for questions and answers, and in cleft sentences with references both to people, time and place, in order to establish identities of people or the time and place for a crime. See examples (2) and (3).

(2) The ATTORNEY-GENERAL: Yes. In the Alresford circle you are a person that everybody knows?
(Trials, Sir Roger Tichborne, 1870–1900, p. 2153)

(3) Mr. Brougham: Was not the first thing you said to your wife when you heard the Minster was burnt, "surely it is not Jonathan Martin *that* has done it?" [p. 15] [...] Mr. Alderson: Was it in your presence *that* he read it? [p. 24] (Trials, Jonathan Martin, 1800–1830, p. 15, 24)

However, it is more interesting to look at examples of *that* where it occurs outside its typical environments. These examples, which are termed 'nontypical' in Table 1b, illustrate how the speaker roles may use *that* more 'freely'.[3]

Table 1b. The Use of *That* across Speaker Roles in *TRIALS* (Periods 1 and 3)

Relativizer	*That* (typical use)	*That* (nontypical use)	Total
Members of the legal profession	78 (72%)	31 (28%)	109 (100%)
Others	47 (57%)	36 (43%)	83 (100%)
Total	125 (65%)	67 (35%)	192 (100%)

Table 1b shows that generally, 'Members of the legal profession' use *that* more frequently 109/192 (or 57%) than 'Others' do 83/192 (or 43%) but they use it mainly in typical environments (72%). 'Others' use *that* more freely (43%), while they use 'typical *that*' in 57% of the examples. Still, the difference in frequency between 'typical *that*' and 'nontypical *that*' is not as great as with 'Members of the legal profession'.

'Members of the legal profession' might be expected to speak more formally than 'Others' if their educational and professional backgrounds are considered. In 19th-century English, as in Present-day English, the most formal relativizer is probably *whom* (see Schneider 1993: 492–493), but *whom* is not more frequent with 'Members of the legal profession' than with 'Others'. Seven examples of *whom* occur in each speaker role. Görlach (1999: 67) notes that *whom* is disappearing during the late Modern English period and increasingly replaced by *who*. More interesting to note are instances of the so-called hypercorrect *whom*, that is, *whom* used for *who* (see Quirk et al. 1985: 368,1050). The use of *whom* for *who* indicates that speakers were not certain how to use *whom* but suggests that they regarded it as formal and particularly suitable in certain contexts because it seemed 'more correct' than *who*. 'Others' would be expected to use *whom* instead of *who*, rather than the more educated 'Members of the legal profession'. However, the two examples of hypercorrect *whom* actually occur in the speech of judges, see examples (4) and (5).

(4) The ATTORNEY-GENERAL: Then you saw a man *whom* you were told was Sir Roger coming out of door?
(Trials, Sir Roger Tichborne, 1870–1900, p. 2447)

(5) Mr. Addison: No. For instance, this gentleman, *whom* you say looked like Mr Maybrick, he used to take it on the way down to the office, so that it could not do him any harm?
(Trials, Edwin Maybrick, 1870–1900, p. 226)

Whereas *whom* was and is regarded as a formal relativizer, the use of *which* with a personal antecedent might be assumed to have been as non-standard and informal in 19th-century English, as it is in Present-day English (but cf. Kjellmer, 2002). The use of *which* with a person as antecedent could be expected to be more frequent with 'Others' because they might be expected to use more non-standard features. There are, however, only two examples in Trials. One example is found in a question asked by a judge, the other in the evidence given by a friend or a neighbour of the defendant:

(6) Mr. Holroyd: Mrs. Jones, I believe, was the most intimate friend *which* the deceased, Miss Burns, had?
(Trials, Charles Angus, 1800–1830, p. 50)

(7) Mr. HENRY MILLS POWELL, sworn: There was a lady passing behind him, *which* I believe was his wife.
(Trials, Sir Roger Tichborne 1870–1900, p. 2155)

Pied piping (i.e. preposition+relativizer) in relative prepositional constructions is another feature that may indicate formal speech. *Stranding* of the preposition is usually looked upon as less formal where variation between the two constructions is possible (see Johansson and Geisler 1998).

Table 1c. Pied Piping and Stranding across Speaker Roles in *TRIALS* (Periods 1 and 3)

Speaker role	Pied piping	Stranding	Total
Members of the legal profession	29 (78%)	8 (22%)	37 (100%)
Others	13 (52%)	12 (48%)	25 (100%)
Total	42 (68%)	20 (32%)	62 (100%)

As Table 1c shows, stranding occurs in only 22% of the cases in the speech of 'Members of the legal profession', but 'Others' use pied piping and stranding to a fairly similar extent (52% and 48%, respectively).[4] Example (8) illustrates stranding with *that* in the speech of 'Others'.

(8) THOMAS LOW NICHOLS, sworn: Not at all. I always gave persons to understand what my position was. If they insisted upon my seeing a child or a patient *that* I thought I could be useful *to*, I ordinarily would go, but that was very rare. (Trials, Adelaide Bartlett, 1870–1900, p. 125)

Occasionally, a *wh*-form occurs with stranding, see example (9). As in example (8), a member of 'Others' is speaking.

(9) MARIA GLENN, sworn: They had a small poney *which* I was welcome *to* whenever I chose to ride. (Trials, James Bowditch, 1800–1830, p. 41)

Variation in preposition placement with one and the same prepositional construction is also possible. In example (10), *allude to* is used with both stranding and pied piping by 'Members of the legal profession' (Mr. Alderson and Mr Brougham):

(10) Mr. Alderson: These two documents, the tickets and the notes that have been alluded to in the evidence of the witness are in these words. [p. 39] [...] Mr. Brougham: Have you had any practice, in respect to insanity, except upon those accidental occasions to which you allude? [p. 42] (Trials, Jonathan Martin, 1800–1830, p. 39, 42)

In sum, the speech-related Trials genre contains speakers who might be expected to talk more informally, despite the context of the courtroom. The occurrence of *that*, associated with informal speech, however, cannot be attributed to such speakers. Instead *that* is frequent because it is used in its typical environments both by 'Members of the legal profession' and by people with other occupations in the rather formal dialogue of the courtroom.

Trials and Drama can be compared to some extent as both genres are speech-related, but Drama contains fictitious speech. How the use of the *wh*-forms and *that* can be exploited by an author to describe formal and informal speech situations or even certain characters will be discussed in the following section.

3. The Use of the Relativizers across Speaker Roles: Drama

In Drama, the speaker roles[5] are mainly distinguished according to information in the actual text, such as titles or references to status, e.g. Sir Richard Kato, Lady Susan, or the Dean. Mrs Mcfarlane is described by the playwright as "a Scottish country wife" and Angus Macallister is "a good-looking peasant lad". The characters may also describe themselves: Maggie Macfarlane refers to herself as "the puir Lowland lassie"; or they may be presented by other characters: Cheviot Hill is talked about as "a young man of large property" and "the gallant Englishman".[6]

The speaker/addressee relationship, i.e. the characters' relative status, is of great importance in the Drama texts. Some representatives of 'Upper' are Sir Richard Kato, Lady Susan Harabin, Admiral and Lady Darby, Belawney, Cheviot Hill, Miss Minnie Symperson, Miss Belinda Treherne (all four are wealthy young people), the Dean, Major Tarver and Mr Anson (a wealthy merchant). 'Others' are a more heterogeneous group, which includes Blore (a waiter), Parker (Miss Minnie Symperson's maid), Mrs. Macfarlane, Maggie Macfarlane, Angus Macallister (country people), Noah Topping (a constable), Hannah (former cook at the deanery, now Noah's wife) and Mr and Mrs. Ferment (owners of a pleasure ground).

When studying the Drama texts, it is immediately apparent that 'Upper' speak more than 'Others' and probably in a more elaborate way. The ratio is, as in Trials, 7 to 3, in a representative sample of 5,000 words. 'Upper' probably also speak in a more elaborate way since they use more than three times as many relative clauses as 'Others'. Table 2a shows that 'Upper' use 204 and 'Others' 63 relative clauses. Even if the plays are set among 'Others', such as Holcraft's play, *The Vindictive Man*, primarily representing the 19th-century 'middle class', 'Upper' still use more relative clauses than 'Others'. Gilbert's play *Engaged* includes both 'Upper' (Miss Treherne, Belawney, Cheviot) and 'Others' (peasants or country people: Angus, Maggie and Mrs. MacFarlane) but the relative clauses are mainly found in the speech of 'Upper'. In Gilbert's play, 'Others' are mostly Scottish, whereas 'Upper' are English. However, this geographical difference is not evident in the use of relativizers and relative clauses. The relativizer *that* is more frequent in Scottish English (see e.g. Romaine 1980) but in the play, *that* is not more common with the Scottish characters than with the English. Jones' play *The Case of the Rebellious Susan*, is set mainly among 'Upper' (Sir Richard, Lady Susan Harabin, Admiral and Lady Darby). 'Others' are represented by servants but they primarily answer orders given by 'Upper' and their speech contains no relative clauses.

Table 2a *Wh*-forms and *That* across Speaker roles in Drama (Periods 1 and 3)

Relativizer	'Upper'	'Others'	Total
Wh-	132 (65%)	36 (57%)	168 (63%)
That	72 (35%)	27 (43%)	99 (37%)
Total	204 (100%)	63 (100%)	267 (100%)

Table 2a shows that the *wh*-forms are more common than *that* both with 'Upper' and 'Others' but the difference is smaller between the use of a *wh*-form (57%) and the use of *that* (43%) with 'Others'.[7] Overall, in the Drama texts, the *wh*-forms are used in 63% of the cases and *that* occurs in 37% of the examples. By comparison, in Trials (see Table 1a) the distribution is 67% *wh*-forms and 33% *that*, i.e. *that* is slightly more common in Drama. In Drama, the use of the *wh*-forms and *that* can be exploited by the writer to describe formal (mainly *wh*-forms) and informal (*that*) speech situations or even certain characters, such as Sir Richard Kato, Cheviot Hill and Miss Treherne. All three characters are members of 'Upper' but *that* is frequent in their speech. Sir Richard, Cheviot and Miss Treherne are also the characters that speak most of the time in the respective plays, *The Case of the Rebellious Susan* (1873) and *Engaged* (1877). Sir Richard is addressing Jim and Lucien, two young well-to-do men, in example (11).

(11) Sir RICHARD: How do you account for it, Jim, (Suddenly brightening into great joviality and pride.) that the best Englishmen have always been such devils among the women? Always! I wouldn't give a damn for a soldier or sailor *that* wasn't, eh? How is it, Jim? [...] I think a good display of hearty genuine repentance in the present is all *that* can be reasonably demanded from any man. [...] Lucien, I 've got a case *that* is puzzling me a great deal.
(Drama, Henry Arthur Jones, *The Case of the Rebellious Susan*, 1894, pp. 50–51)

Example (12) is from one of Cheviot' s monologues and in (13) he is addressing his uncle Mr. Symperson. The language used is emotional and almost poetic (see Culpeper 2001:213) and for that reason *wh*-forms might be expected to occur. *Wh*-forms could have been expected also in Miss Treherne's utterances in examples (14) and (15), which exemplify the same kind of 'high-flown' language. It might be the case that when certain characters use *that* frequently, it is used also in situations where a *wh*-form would seem more appropriate. Compare, by contrast, example (22) below in which Cheviot describes his love for Minnie using *wh*-forms.

(12) CHEVIOT: It's a coarse and brutal nature *that* recognises no harm *that* don't [sic] involve loss of blood. [...]
(Drama, W. S. Gilbert, *Engaged*, 1877, p. 11)

(13) You know the strange, mysterious influence *that* his dreadful eyes exercise over me. [...] The light *that* lit up those eyes is extinct -- their fire has died out -- their soul has fled.
(Drama, W. S. Gilbert, *Engaged*, 1877, pp. 12–13)

Besides Cheviot, Miss Treherne speaks a great deal in *Engaged*. *That* occurs as frequently as in Cheviot's speech and 'nontypical *that*' is used. Miss Treherne is addressing Cheviot in both (14) and (15):

(14) MISS TREHERNE: Sir, that heart would indeed be cold *that* did not feel grateful for so much earnest, single-hearted devotion.[...]
(Drama, W. S. Gilbert, *Engaged*, 1877, p. 18)

(15) With a rapture *that* thrills every fibre of my heart -- with a devotion *that* enthralls my very soul!
(Drama, W. S. Gilbert, *Engaged*, 1877, p. 18)

In examples (11)-(15), *that* is used both in its typical environments (*all that*) and more freely (e.g. *a soldier or a sailor that*, *a course and brutal nature that* and *a rapture that*). The 'nontypical' use of *that* is more frequent in these examples, but in Table 2b, we see that the typical use of *that* is more common overall (76%) with both 'Upper' (74%) and 'Others' (81%). It seems that when characters use *that* often, as do those characters in examples (11)-(15), they also use it more freely. 'Upper' use *that* more often (72/99 or 73%) than 'Others' (27/99 or 27%) but this is of course a result of their speaking more and using more relative clauses.[8]

Table 2b. The Use of *That* in Drama (Periods 1 and 3)

Relativizer	That (typical use)	That (non- typical use)	Total
'Upper'	53 (74%)	19 (26%)	72 (100%)
'Others'	22 (81%)	5 (19%)	27 (100%)
Total	75 (76%)	24 (24%)	99 (100%)

People are very often the topic of conversation in the Drama texts; specific people are described as in Belawney's description of Cheviot and Sir Richard's description of *a dear good fellow*. People in general are described in Sir Richard's *the good folks who live in Clapham*, see examples (16)-(18). *Who* is the most common relativizer in Drama. In Letters, which are also about people to a very great extent, the relativizer *which* is the most frequent; see Section 4.

(16) BELAWNEY: You know my friend Cheviot Hill, *who* is travelling to London in the same train with us, but in the third class?
MISS TREHERNE: I believe I know the man you mean
BELAWNEY: Cheviot, *who* is a young man of large property, but extremely close-fisted [...]
(Drama, W. S: Gilbert, *Engaged*, 1877, p. 9)

(17) Lady SUSAN: Who's coming?
Sir RICHARD: Isn't there one very old friend, and a dear good fellow *whom* you would be pleased to meet again ?
Lady SUSAN: My husband! [...]
(Drama, Arthur Henry Jones, *The Case of the Rebellious Susan*, 1894, p. 39)

(18) Sir RICHARD: It is highly desirable that the good folks *who* live in Clapham should not be shocked. (Drama, Arthur Henry Jones, *The Case of the Rebellious Susan*, 1894, p. 44)

Whereas *who* and *whom* are frequent relativizers in Drama, *which* is the least common of the *wh*-forms. It occurs mainly in 'obligatory' environments, such as *sentential relative clauses* (see Quirk et al 1985: 1118–1120) and in non-restrictive relative clauses in general, as in example (19):

(19) MAGGIE: [...] Why, Angus, thou'rt tall, and fair, and brave. Thou'st a guide, honest face, and a gude, honest hairt, *which* is mair precious than a' the gold on earth! (Drama, W. S. Gilbert, *Engaged*, 1877, pp. 5–6)

In Trials, *which* is used at the expense of *that* in restrictive relative clauses. This is not the case in Drama, where w*hich* occurs in only 22% of the relative clauses, and *that* in 43%, which makes *that* the most common relativizer (compared to the individual *wh*-forms *who*, *whom*, *whose* and *which*). An example of how 'Others' use the relativizer *that* is illustrated in (20) below. When the characters Angus and Maggie, who are Scottish, talk to each other or about each other, *that* is used. When the English are discussed, *who* is used. The use of *that* is not depicted as a Scottish feature in Drama (see e.g. Romaine 1980) since the Scottish characters use *wh*-forms as frequently as *that.* However, the playwright represents the Scottish dialect by the spelling of certain words, as in examples (20)-(26) below (cf. also Culpeper 2001: 206, 212). Maggie and Angus are the characters classified as 'Others' who use the relativizer *that* most frequently, especially 'nontypical *that*'. Compare the discussion above of the 'Upper' characters, Sir Richard, Cheviot and Miss Treherne.

(20) ANGUS: Meg , my weel lo'ed Meg, my wee wifie *that* is to be, tell me what 's wrang wi' ee?
MAGGIE:Oh, mither, it's him; the noble gentleman I plighted my troth to three weary months agone! The gallant Englishman *who* gave Angus two golden pound to give me up!
ANGUS: It's the coward Sassenach *who* well nigh broke our Meg's heart! [...] MAGGIE: I 'm the puir Lowland lassie *that* he stole the hairt out of, three months ago, and promised to marry; [...]
(Drama, W. S: Gilbert, *Engaged*, 1877, p. 35)

In example (21), Angus uses *that* in the rather emotional description of his love for Maggie. When he talks about his rival, *who* is used instead. He is first addressing Cheviot, then Maggie:

(21) ANGUS: Nea, sir, it's useless, and we ken it weel, do we not, my brave lassie? Our hearts are one as our bodies will be some day; and the man is na' born, and the gold is na' coined, *that* can set us twain asunder! [...]CHEVIOT: (gives ANGUS money) Fare thee weel, my love -- my childhood's -- boyhood's -- manhood's love! Ye're ganging fra my hairt to anither, *who*'ll gie thee mairo' the gude things o' this world than I could ever gie 'ee, except love, an' o' that my hairt is full indeed!
(Drama, W. S. Gilbert, *Engaged*, 1877, p. 16)

Maggie's and Angus' (Others) descriptions of their love for each other can be compared with Cheviot's (Upper) description of his feelings of his beloved (Minnie), which is very formal and poetic (cf. Culpeper 2001:213). The phrase *The tree* ***upon which*** *the fruit of my heart* (in various versions) seems to be a quotation from a poem or an example of poetic diction in general. This phrase occurs nine times in the speech of different members of 'Upper'. Example (22) is from one of Cheviot's monologues:

(22) CHEVIOT: I love Minnie deeply, devotedly. She is the actual tree *upon which* the fruit of my heart is growing. [...] This is appalling! Simply appalling! The cup of happiness dashed from my lips as I was about to drink a life-long draught. The ladder kicked from under my feet just as I was about to pick the fruit of my heart from the tree *upon which* it has been growing so long.
(Drama, W. S. Gilbert, *Engaged*, 1877, pp. 31–32)

In Holcroft's play *The Vindictive Man*, a character appears called 'Cheshire John', who speaks in a dialect. John is described as "an absolute rustic" which might be a hint that his speech is not particularly elaborate. John uses only three relative clauses: the *that*-clause is in its typical environment (*the very thought that* in example (23)) and the two *which*-clauses are non-restrictive. Example (24) illustrates stranding, which is the only characteristic in John's use of relative clauses that could be looked upon as informal. John and his daughter, Rose, are described as "poor country people". In example (23), John is speaking to a member of 'Upper', Mr Anson, who is a wealthy merchant:

(23) John: Why, now, as I hope to live, thof I would no say a word, it's the very thought *that* has been running in my head aw day long.
(Drama, Thomas Holcroft, *The Vindictive Man*, 1806, p. 77)

In example (24), John is talking to Harriet, a friend of John's wealthy sister and in example (25) he is addressing Rose:

(24) John: (to Harriet) Madam (bows) Rose teakes it that you have a summit i' your noodle, *which* noather she nor I be suitable *to*;
(Drama, Thomas Holcroft, *The Vindictive Man*, 1806, p. 41)

(25) John: What then, after aw the din and uproar, *which* this inheritance ha' made, mun we pack home as poor as we went?
(Drama, Thomas Holcroft, *The Vindictive Man*, 1806, p. 63)

Rose has received a good education from her aunt, who has now passed away and whose money she and her father will inherit. Rose uses rather formal language, mainly *wh*-forms, as in example (26), in which she is speaking to her father.

(26) Rose: Hitherto I have lived blameless in that simple honesty *which* is the foundation of all lasting happiness, and *which* alone can smooth the adverse and rugged road of life.
(Drama, Thomas Holcroft, *The Vindictive Man*, 1806, p. 63)

Whom and pied piping are found in the speech of 'Upper'. Stranding is an alternative in example (27): ***whom** you have flown **with***. Major McGillicuddy is the man Miss Treherne is to marry but she has run away with Belawney:

(27) MCGILLICUDDY: Who is the unsightly scoundrel *with whom* you have flown -- the unpleasant looking scamp *whom* you have dared to prefer to me? (Drama, W. S. Gilbert, *The Engaged*, 1877, p. 20)

In the Drama texts, only two examples of stranding with *that* or a *wh*-form are found. They occur in Maggie's utterance (*I'm the puir Lowland lassie **that** he stole the hairt **out of***) and in Cheshire John's utterance (***which** noather she nor I be suitable **to***). Most examples of stranding in the Drama texts are with the zero relativizer. In Trials, many examples with stranding are with *that* and, occasionally, with a *wh*-form.

A more obvious example of a syntactic feature that describes the speech of 'Others' is the use of the relativizer *what*. In 19th-century English, as in Present-day English, it was looked upon as non-standard (see Görlach 1999: 86). In all, 11 examples of *what* occur in the Drama texts studied. In 10 of these examples, *what* is used in an environment which is typical of *that*: in cleft sentences, with pronouns such as *nothing*, *anything*, *something* and with superlative expressions. All examples of *what* are found in Pinero's play *The Dandy Dick*, in the speech of 'Others', and it seems as if *what* is used instead of *that* here. Only three examples of *that* occur with 'Others', to be compared with 11 examples of *what*. The two forms, *that* and *what* are similar in that they do not have personal/nonpersonal or case contrast and they cannot be preceded by a preposition, so stranding, in itself less formal, is the only possibility. Also, as stated earlier, *what* seems to be used in typical *that*-environments. Blore (a servant), Noah Topping (a constable) and Hannah (a former cook at the Deanery, now Noah's wife) are the characters that use *what* in *The Dandy Dick*. Blore and Hannah are speaking in example (28). Other features describing non-standard speech are Blore's '*h*-dropping' and the form *respectin'*.

(28) Blore: 'Annah, 'Annah, my dear, it's this very prisoner *what* I 'ave called on you respectin'
(Drama, Arthur Pinero, *The Dandy Dick*, 1893, p. 102)

Hannah is addressing members of 'Upper', the Dean and the Dean's sister, in examples (29) and (30):

(29) HANNAH: Ah, they all tell that tale *what* comes here. Why don't you send word, Dean dear?
(Drama, Arthur Pinero, *The Dandy Dick*, 1893, p. 111)

(30) HANNAH: Oh, lady, lady it's appearances *what* is against us.
(Drama, Arthur Pinero, *The Dandy Dick*, 1893, p. 131)

In Holcroft's play *The Vindictive Man* (1806), Mr Abrahams, who is a Jewish pawnbroker of probably German origin, almost exclusively uses *vat* as a relativizer. Mr Abrahams uses *vat* particularly in the combination *all vat* (possibly German *alles was*; cf. also *Parton*, *puy* and *und* in examples (31) and (32)). Possibly, *vat* could be the playwright's way of indicating Mr Abrahams' pronunciation of the relativizer *that* or possibly, *vat* could be the spelling of *what*. The form *vat* was included in the present study since it does occur in typical *that*-environments (with *all*, *something* and in cleft sentences) where *what* was also found (cf. the discussion of *what* above). Abrahams is doing business with Frederic, a well-to-do son of an officer in example (31) and with Emily, the daughter of a wealthy merchant, in (32).

(31) Abrahams: Parton me, Sair, you hafe someting *vat* I will puy.
Frederic: The devil is in Jews for buying!
(Drama, Thomas Holcroft, *The Vindictive Man*, 1806, p. 48)

(32) Abrahams: You shall see all *vat* I shall hear, und all *vat* he shall say.
Emily: Well!
(Drama, Thomas Holcroft, *The Vindictive Man,* 1806. p. 52)

The characters seem to be rather "stable" in their use of *that*, *wh*-forms and *what* in the different speech situations. 'Upper' use *wh*-forms when speaking to each other and to 'Others', with the exception of characters who frequently use *that* as a typical feature of their speech (Sir Richard, Cheviot and Miss Treherne). 'Others' also use *wh*-forms more frequently than *that* even if their speech is often less formal than that of 'Upper'. It is of no importance whom 'Others' address: servant to servant (Blore to Hatcham), master to servant (the constable Noah Topping to Blore), or members of 'Upper'. Hannah, who is a former cook at the Deanery, uses non-standard *what* when talking to the Dean and his sister. In Drama, it does not seem to be the case that the variation between the *wh*-forms and *that* is explored to any great extent in the description of 'Upper' and 'Others' or of dialects, e.g. Scottish versus English. A lower frequency of relative clauses and the use of non-standard *what* are probably features used by the playwright instead to describe the speech of 'Others' as compared with 'Upper'.

Gender-based differences in the use of *that* and the *wh*-forms are more obvious in 19th-century letter writing than in Trials and Drama. In Trials, women are seldom represented, and only as witnesses. In Drama, women speak more often than in Trials, and they are found both in 'Upper' and in 'Others'. However, their use of relativizers and relative clauses is influenced by the speaker role to a greater extent than their sex). In 19th-century letter writing, which is analysed in the next section, the writers, all famous authors of the time, are from similar social backgrounds.

4. The Use of the *wh*-forms and *that* across Gender: Letters

The *wh*-forms were looked upon as the norm in 19th-century letter writing (see, e.g., Murray 1795),[9] which for the most part was formal in style. In Letters, a *wh*-form occurs in 86% of all relative clauses. The use of *wh*-forms offers a more explicit method of referring to an antecedent since the forms have personal/nonpersonal and case contrast as opposed to *that* (see Quirk et al. 1985: 368). In Letters, non-restrictive relative clauses are common; thus a *wh*-form is favoured also for that reason. Sentential relative clauses, which are always non-restrictive, occur as comments on what has previously been written about in the letter; see example (33) below. People are common topics of the letters, referred to by personal names, which entail a non-restrictive relative clause, as in (34).

(33) He always speaks warmly & kindly of you, & when I asked him to come in to meet you at tea -- *which* he did -- he spoke very heartily --
(Letters, May Butler, 1870–1900, p. 223)

(34) I spent a long delightful afternoon with Mrs. Kemble, *who* sends you many messages. (Letters, Anne Thackeray Ritchie, 1870–1900, p. 193)

The letter writers are famous authors of the time, who could be expected to use educated language in their letters. The female letter writers in Period 1 (1800–1830) are Jane Austen, Sara Hutchinson, Mary Shelley and Mary Wordsworth. Period 3 (1870–1900) is represented by May Butler, Mary Sibylla Holland, Christina Rossetti and Anne Thackeray Ritchie. The male letter writers in Period 1 are William Blake, George Byron, Samuel Coleridge, John Keats and Robert Southey. The male letter writers who represent Period 3 are Matthew Arnold, Samuel Butler, Thomas Hardy and Thomas Huxley.

Three female letter writers, namely Mary Shelley, Mary Wordsworth (Period 1) and Mary Sibylla Holland (Period 3), use *that* frequently. In general, *that* is slightly more common in letters written by women (16%, see Table 3a) than in letters written by men (11%, see also Johansson forthcoming). The female letter writers might be looked upon as 'linguistic innovators' (see Romaine 1999: 175–177, Labov 2001: 292–293 and Geisler 2003) in that they introduce a more frequent use of *that*. An indication that female letter writing is less elaborate is that women use fewer relative clauses per 100,000 words (700) than men do (940/100,000 words) and that the relativizer *that* is used 116/100,000 words by female letter writers and 93/100,000 words by male letter writers.[10]

Table 3a *Wh*-forms and *That* in Women's and Men's Letters (Periods 1 and 3)

Relativizer	Female letter writer	Male letter writer	Total
Wh-	729 (84%)	780 (89%)	1509 (86%)
That	139 (16%)	100 (11%)	239 (14%)
Total	868 (100%)	880 (100%)	1748 (100%)

Women also use *that* more freely, with all types of antecedent (42%, see Table 3b), whereas men use *that* mostly in its typical syntactic environments (70%), e.g. in cleft sentences, as in example (35), with nonpersonal nouns and with pronouns such as *everything, all*, and *nothing*, as in example (36). Men use 'nontypical *that*' in only 30% of their usage of the relativizer *that*.

(35) [...] it is only at the seaside *that* I never wish for rain.
(Letters, Matthew Arnold, 1870-1900, p. 38)

(36) Nothing *that* gives you pain dwells long enough upon your mind [...]
(Letters, Samuel Coleridge, 1800-1830, p. 512)

In Table 3b, which presents the frequency of 'typical' and 'nontypical' *that* only, we see again that women use *that* more frequently with 139 examples (or 58%) than men with 100 instances (or 42%).[11]

Table 3b. The Use of *That* in Women's and Men's Letters (*LETTERS*, Periods 1 and 3)

Letter writer	That (typical use)	That (non-typical use)	Total
Female	80 (58%)	59 (42%)	139 (100%)
Male	70 (70%)	30 (30%)	100 (100%)
Total	150 (63%)	89 (37%)	239 (100%)

In Mary Wordsworth's letters (Period 1), the 'nontypical' use of *that* is best exemplified: 25 out of 45 examples of *that* are not in their typical environments. Wordsworth's letters also contain instances of *that* used with a personal antecedent, which is very rare in the letters. In example (37), *that* is used with a pronoun with personal reference (*those*).

(37) All I beg with much earnestness is that thou wilt take care of thyself -- but compare thyself with those *that* are well in things wherever you can agree & not with those *that* are ill –
(Letters, Mary Wordsworth, [1], 1800–1830, p. 166)

In Mary Shelley's letters, informal *that* is used more freely than by other letter writers. It is worth noting that Shelley's letters also have the highest frequency of *whom*, a formal feature, in Period 1. However, hypercorrect *whom* (see section 2), which could be a sign of the linguistic insecurity particularly typical of female language (cf. Coates and Cameron 1988: 17 and Romaine 1999: 155) does not occur.

Mary Wordsworth and Mary Shelley use *that* more freely than other female letter writers. Mary Sibylla Holland (Period 3), whose letter collections contain the most instances of *that* of all the letters in the study, uses *that* in its typical syntactic environments, such as cleft sentences, with indefinite determiners or *same* + noun and superlative + noun. Holland's use of *that* in typical environments is more regulated and could for that reason be regarded as more formal, particularly since other formal features occur in her letters, such as *whom* and the use of pied piping constructions. Table 3c shows that pied piping constructions, which are regarded as formal, are more frequent in letters written by men (85%) than in letters written by women (63%, see also Geisler 2003).[10]

Table 3c. Pied Piping and Stranding across Gender in *LETTERS* (Periods 1 and 3)

Letter writer	Pied piping	Stranding	Total
Female	40 (63%)	23 (37%)	63 (100%)
Male	82 (85%)	14 (15%)	96 (100%)
Total	122 (77%)	37 (23%)	159 (100%)

A good representative of a male letter writer who uses pied piping constructions is Lord Byron. In all 18 examples of his prepositional constructions, pied piping occurs. In 13 of these, there is a choice between pied piping and stranding.

(38) I have gotten a very pretty Cambrian girl there *of whom* I grew foolishly fond, [...] There is the whole history of circumstances *to which* you may have possibly heard some allusion [...]
(Letters, George Byron, 1800–1830, p.II, 155)

Stranding, on the other hand, is more frequently used by female letter writers (37%) than by male letter writers (15%). In example (39), which is from Jane Austen's letters, it is possible to see variation between pied piping and stranding.

(39) He was seized on saturday with a return of the feverish complaint, *which* he had been subject *to* for the three last years; [...] A Physician was called in yesterday morning, but he was at that time past all possibility of care --- & Dr. Gibbs and Mr. Bowen had scarcely left his room before he sunk into a Sleep *from which* he never woke. [p. 62] [...] Oh! dear Fanny, your mistake has been one *that* thousands of women fall *into*. [p. 173]
(Letters, Jane Austen, 1800–1830, p. 62, 173)

There is wide individual variation in the use of relativizers in the Letters. In Period 3 we find both the highest frequency (Mary Sibylla Holland, 30%) and the lowest (Christina Rossetti, 4%) of *that* in letters written by women. On the one hand, Holland can be compared to Mary Wordsworth (21% *that*) and to Mary Shelley (22% *that*) from Period 1 in her frequent use of *that*. However, Holland uses *that* in typical environments and Wordsworth and Shelley use *that* more freely. On the other hand, both Holland's and Rossetti's letter collections can be compared to those of Lord Byron. All three letter writers have examples of *whom* and of pied piping, which indicates a formal style. Rossetti's letter collection is similar to Lord Byron's letters also in another respect, i.e. the low frequency of *that*. This means that it is important to consider *individual* writing styles rather than compare female versus male use of the *wh*-forms and *that*. In Period 1, women seemed to be the 'linguistic innovators' since nearly 65% of the relative clauses with *that* are found in their letters. In Period 3, however, only Mary Sibylla Holland uses *that* frequently. The other female letter writers represented in Period 3 conform more to the norm: they use *wh*-forms in 92% of their relative clauses.

5. Conclusion

Two strategies are available for relative clause formation: a more explicit one with personal/nonpersonal and case contrast: the wh-forms (who, whose, whom and which) and the that or zero (see Quirk et al 1985: 366; the zero construction is not dealt with in this paper). Towards the end of the Early Modern English period (1500-1700), the *wh*-forms started being used more frequently and particularly in formal contexts. The relativizer *that*, which had been the most frequent relativizer in the Early Modern English period, was used, e.g. in Drama texts where Early Modern English speech was supposed to be represented (see Barber 1997: 214). Also in Present-day English, *that* is regarded as an informal relativizer compared to the *wh*-forms. It is frequent in informal speech situations and in speech generally. Using *that* in casual speech could even be regarded as the norm (cf. Biber et al 1999: 610-611, 616).

It is the 19th century that stands out as regards the use of *wh*-forms and *that* in relative clauses. In this period the *wh*-forms predominate but what is unexpected is that they are used to such a great extent even in speech-related genres such as Trials and Drama. When the relativizer *that* is used in these genres, it is not primarily as an informal relativizer or one representing a feature of speech. In Trials, where *that* occurs in 33% of the relative clauses, it is used in its typical environments e.g. in cleft sentences, with pronominal antecedents and with the antecedent *person(s)*, both by ‘Members of the legal profession’ and by people with other occupations. In other words, *that* is part of the rather formal language of trials since 'typical *that*' occurs in the dialogue of the courtroom (*you are a person* ***that*** *everybody knows*?; *are you sure it was shortly before six o'clock* ***that*** ...?).

In Drama, it is possible for the playwright to exploit the use of *that* and the *wh*-forms in describing informal or formal speech situations and even in the description of the speech of individual characters. The relativizer *that* is used slightly more frequently in Drama (37%) than in Trials, and it is the most common relativizer (43%) in Drama compared to the forms *who* (*whose*, *whom*) and *which*. In the plays included in the present study, certain characters from both 'Upper' and 'Others' do exhibit a frequent use of *that* but generally, the playwrights seem to be influenced to a very great extent by the norm that prevailed in writing at the time; i.e. the use of *wh*-forms. When a character is portrayed in a play, this is mostly done through spelling, which represents pronunciation features, or through vocabulary (cf. Culpeper 2001: 206, 209). An example of this kind of description is the way the playwright tries to show how Maggie and Angus speak (in W.S. Gilbert's play *Engaged*): *my wee wifie, . . .*

what 's wrang wi' ee? The relativizer *that* is more common in Scottish English but this was not exploited much by the playwright, i.e. *that* could have been more frequent in Maggie's and Angus' speech besides typical Scottish features of pronunciation and vocabulary.

It is only in Letters that the use of the relativizer *that* can be looked upon as a marker of an informal, less elaborate writing style, at least at the beginning of the 19th century. In 19th-century letter writing, the *wh*-forms are predominant in both letters written by women and in those written by men. *Wh*-forms are used according to the norm for good (formal) writing in the 19th century. At the beginning of the 19th century, a few female letter writers use *that* more frequently, thus introducing a new, less formal style, but female letter writers do not continue to use *that* frequently. At the end of the century they have conformed to the norm, i.e. using a *wh*-form in most of their relative clauses and using *that* only in its typical environments. If we turn to informal Present-day English writing, *that* is preferred to the *wh*-forms. At the end of the 19th-century, the female letter writers abandoned their "new" style of using *that* fairly frequently, and started using a more formal style with *wh*-forms. It might be the case that this usage has prevailed in Present-day English since women are often regarded as using more formal language (in writing and speech) than men.

Acknowledgements

I want to thank Christer Geisler, Merja Kytö and Terry Walker, Uppsala University, for valuable comments on my paper. I would also like to thank Christer Geisler and Erik Smitterberg, Stockholm University, for help with stastistical tests.

Notes

1 1 The zero relativizer is not included for the reason that it is diffcult to retrieve in a corpus-based study such as the present one. The full text of the Drama samples has been studied in order to investigate the speech situation and for this genre, some brief comments on the zero relativizer will be made.

2 The figures in Table 1a are not statistically significant; d.f.=1, chi-square:0.431 and p=0.512.

3 The figures in Table 1b are statistically significant; d.f.=1, chi-square:4.625 and p=0.032.

4 The figures in Table 1c are statistically significant; d.f.=1, chi-square:4.751 and p=0.030.

5 Culpeper (2001: 49-51) uses the terms *actant role* (e.g. villain, helper, hero) and the more sophisticated *dramatic role*, which establishes a link between character role and genre (e.g. in comedy).

6 On *self-presentation* and *other-presentation* (see Culpeper 2001: 167-169).

7 The figures in Table 2a are not statistically significant; d.f.=1, chi-square:0.878 and p=0.349.

8 The figures in Table 2b are not statistically significant; d.f.=1, chi-square:0.662 and p=0.416.

9 The use of *that* was restricted to the typical syntactic environments. Compare Murray (1795): "[A]fter an adjective in the superlative degree and after the pronominal adjective *same* it [that] is generally used in preference to *who* and *which*" (Murray 1795:149). According to Görlach (1999: 15), Lindley Murray's grammar (1795) was one of the most influential in the 19th century.

10 The figures in Table 3a are statistically significant; d.f.=1, chi-square:8.006 and p=0.005.

11 The figures in Table 3b are statistically significant; d.f.=1, chi-square:3.855 and p=0.05.

12 The figures in Table 3c are statistically significant; d.f.=1, chi-square:10.240 and p=0.001.

References

Barber. C. (1997) [1976], *Early Modern English*. 2nd edition. Edinburgh: Edinburgh University Press.

Biber, D., S. Johansson, G. Leech, S. Conrad and E. Finegan (1999), *Longman Grammar of Spoken and Written English*. London: Longman.

Coates, J. and D. Cameron (1988), 'Some Problems in the Sociolinguistic Explanation of Sex Differences', in: J. Coates and D. Cameron (eds.) *Women in Their Speech Communities: New Perspectives on Language and Sex*. London: Longman: 13–26.

Culpeper, J. (2001), *Language and Characterisation. People in Plays and Other Texts*. Edinburgh: Longman/Pearson Educational.

Geisler, C. (2002), 'Investigating Register Variation in Nineteenth-century English: A Multi-Dimensional Comparison', in: D. Biber, R. Reppen, and S. Fitzmaurice (eds.) *Using Corpora to Explore Linguistic Variation*. Amsterdam: Benjamins, 249–271.

Geisler, C. (2003), 'Gender-based Variation in Nineteenth-century English Letter-writing', in: P. Leistyna, and C. F. Meyer (eds.) *Corpus Analysis:*

Language Structure and Language Use. Amsterdam, New York: Rodopi, 86–106.

Geisler, C. and C. Johansson (2002), 'Relativization in Formal Spoken American English', in: M. Modiano (ed.) *Studies in Mid-Atlantic English*. Gävle: Gävle University Press, 87–109.

Görlach, M. (1999), *English in Nineteenth-century England*. Cambridge: Cambridge University Press.

Huddleston, R. and G. K. Pullum (2002), *The Cambridge Grammar of the English Language*. Cambridge: Cambridge University Press.

Johansson, C. and C. Geisler (1998), 'Pied Piping in Spoken English', in: A. Renouf (ed.) *Explorations in Corpus Linguistics*. Amsterdam: Rodopi., 82–91.

Johansson, C. (forthcoming), 'Relativizers in 19th-century English', in M. Kytö, E. Smitterberg and M. Rydén (eds.). *Nineteenth-century English: Stability and Change*.

Kjellmer, G. (2002), 'On Relative *Which* with Personal Reference', *Studia Anglistica Posnaniensia*, 37:17–38.

Kytö, M., J. Rudanko and E. Smitterberg (2000), 'Building a Bridge between the Present and the Past: A Corpus of 19th-Century English', *ICAME Journal*, 24:85-97.

Labov, W. (2001), *Principles of Linguistic Change, Volume 2: Social Factors*. Oxford: Blackwell.

Murray, L. (1795), *English Grammar*. York.

Quirk, R., S. Greenbaum, G. Leech and J. Svartvik (1985), *A Comprehensive Grammar of the English Language*. London: Longman.

Romaine, S. (1980), 'The Relative Clause Marker in Scots English: Diffusion, Complexity and Style as Dimensions of Syntactic Change', *Language in Society*, 9:227–241.

Romaine, S. (1999), *Communicating Gender*. Mahwah, New Jersey: Lawrence Erlbaum Associates.

Schneider, E. W. (1996), 'Constraints on the Loss of Case-marking in English *Wh*-Pronouns. Four Hundred Years of Real-time Evidence', in: J. Arnold, R. Blake, B. Davidston, S. Schwenter and J. Solomon, (eds.) *Sociolinguistic Variation. Data, Theory and Analysis*. Selected Papers from NWAV 23 at Stanford, 429–493.

www.ingramcontent.com/pod-product-compliance
Lightning Source LLC
LaVergne TN
LVHW020634300926
849161LV00004B/703
* 9 7 8 9 0 4 2 0 2 1 3 5 8 *